CABINETRY

The Woodworkers Guide to Building Professional-Looking Cabinets and Shelves

Edited by Robert A. Yoder

Reader's Digest

The Reader's Digest Association, Inc.
Pleasantville, New York/Montreal

The author and editors who compiled this book have tried to make all the contents as accurate and as correct as possible. Plans, illustrations, photographs, and text have all been carefully checked and cross-checked. However, due to the variability of local conditions, construction materials, personal skill, and so on, the publisher does not assume any responsibility for any injuries suffered, or for damages or other losses incurred that result from the material presented herein. All instructions and plans should be carefully studied and clearly understood before beginning construction.

**Library of Congress
Cataloging-In-Publication Data**
Cabinetry: the woodworkers guide to building
    professional-looking cabinets and shelves /
    edited by Robert A. Yoder
        p.   cm.
    ISBN 0-7621-0165-2 (hardcover)
    1. Cabinet-work. 2. Shelving (Furniture)
TT197.C215
684.1'6-dc20   91-23894
                               CIP

Printed in the United States of America

1 3 5 7 9 10 8 6 4 2 (hardcover)

Editor: Robert A. Yoder

Writers: Kenneth S. Burton, Jr., Michael
        Dunbar, Nick Engler, Ben Erickson, Nils
        Falk, William H. Hylton, David Page, David
        Schiff, Edward J. Schoen, Jim Tolpin,
        Robert A. Yoder

Cover and book design by Stan Green

Illustrations by Kathy Bray
Technical drafting by Frank Rohrbach
Illustration labeling by Bernie Siegle and
        Sally Onopa

Cover photography by Mitch Mandel

Black and white photography by Mitch Mandel,
except for the following:
    Deloye Burrel, pages 22 and 139; Karen
    Callahan, pages 2, 15, 160, 166, 167, 168,
    201, 207, 210, 211 and 214; John
    Christensen, page 121; Andrew Edgar,
    page 217, Jánis Miglavs/Image Source,
    page 114; Brent Nicastro, page 335; Anna
    Lisa Yoder, page 406; Richard Zies, page
    382

CONTENTS

Acknowledgments v

Introduction vi

Cabinets for the Living Room and Family Room

Corner China Cabinet *by Nick Engler* 2
Entertainment Center *by Ben Erickson* 22
Record Storage Cabinet *by Randy Pease* 40
Stereo Cabinet *by Glenn Bostock* 55
Display Case *by Tom Groller* 72
Archery Rack *by Tom Groller* 83

Cabinets for the Library and Den

Traditional Bookshelves *by Glenn Bostock* 100
Dovetailed Bookshelf *by William Storch* 114
Stickley Bookcase *by Jim Tolpin* 121
Kneehole Desk *by Ben Erickson* 139

Cabinets for the Dining Room

Huntboard *by David T. Smith* 160
Silver Chest *by Ben Erickson* 173
Cherry Buffet *by Glenn Bostock* 185
Pewter Cupboard *by David T. Smith* 201
Hanging Cupboard *by Michael Dunbar* 217
Dieters' Recipe Box *by Paul Good* 228
Hanging Corner Cabinet *by Tom Groller* 237
Cup Shelves *by Ron Day* 250

Cabinets for the Kitchen and Bath

Kitchen Cabinet Design *by William Draper and Robert Schultz* 258
Drawer Base and Sink Base Cabinets *by William Draper and Robert Schultz* . . . 267
Basic Kitchen Wall Cabinet *by William Draper and Robert Schultz* . . . 281
Installing Cabinets *by Bret Shaw and Ernie Kreider* 293
Bathroom Vanity *by Glenn Bostock* 299
Corner Vanity *by Glenn Bostock* 311

Cabinets for the Bedroom

Closet Organizer *by Kenneth S. Burton, Jr.* 326
Cedar-Lined Chest *by Glenn Bostock* 335
Chest of Drawers *by Edward J. Schoen* 346
Sarah's Lookout *by David Page* 362
Country Armoire *by Randy Pease* 382
Bedside Chest *by Milford Yoder* 406
Dressing Table *by Edward J. Schoen* 424

Special Techniques

Making Crown Molding 38
Planing Wood by Hand 52
Mitering a Beaded Frame 70
Cutting Through Dovetails 81
Cope-and-Stick Joinery 96
Mitering and Installing Crown Molding 110
Cutting Half-Blind Dovetails 155
Raising Panels on the Table Saw 200
Cove Cutting on the Table Saw 361
Tenoning Jig 375
Multiple Blind Splines 380
Chip Carving 402

◇ ◇ ── ◇ ◇

ACKNOWLEDGMENTS

I would like to extend special thanks to those people and organizations that helped make this book a success: Linda and William Deeter, for allowing us to photograph their kitchen; Dr. and Mrs. Burger for the use of their display case; John and Barbara Ball, for information on the life and work of Raymond Shoemaker; Prat and Company, of Glen Mills, Pennsylvania, for their fine pewter and redware; Dee Schlagel, for her photographic styling; Donald D. Buettner, for drawings of the Bedside Chest; Bret Shaw and Ernie Kreider, for their technical advice on cabinet installation; Marchell Goll, for her kitchen layout and design expertise; and Fred Matlack and Phil Gehret for their technical assistance.

I also want to applaud the designers, craftsmen, and contributors without whose help this book would never have been possible. They are:

Glenn Bostock, designer and maker of Cabinets and Millwork, Rushland, Pennsylvania

Kenneth S. Burton, Jr., Fine Woodworking and Design, Allentown, Pennsylvania

Ronald Day, Mount Clemens, Michigan

William Draper, Fine Custom Architectural Woodwork and Cabinetry, Perkasie, Pennsylvania

Michael Dunbar, author and Windsor chair maker, Portsmouth, New Hampshire

Nick Engler, Bookworks, Inc., West Milton, Ohio

Ben Erickson, Erickson Woodworks, Eutaw, Alabama

Nils Falk, Riverwood Studios, Frenchtown, New Jersey

Paul Good, Richlandtown, Pennsylvania

Thomas M. Groller, Palmerton, Pennsylvania

David Page, David Page Furniture and Design, Swarthmore, Pennsylvania

Randy Pease, East Greenville, Pennsylvania

Edward J. Schoen, Signature Gallery, Paoli, Pennsylvania

Robert Schultz, Living Quarters Designs, Inc., Buckingham, Pennsylvania

David T. Smith, The Workshops of David T. Smith, Morrow, Ohio

William Storch, Custom Woodworking, Corvallis, Oregon

Jim Tolpin, INTERWOOD, Carlotta, California

Milford and Susie Yoder, Fairview, North Carolina

Introduction

This book may not be what you think it is, and yet it *is* what you are looking for. It's titled *Cabinetry*, but it's about *woodworking*.

This is an important distinction, because today the term "cabinetry" evokes flake-board boxes with flake-board doors and plastic drawers. You might think of modular flake-board constructions in which one would store pots and pans, foodstuffs, electronic equipment, and household whatnots. Most cabinetmaking texts explain "the work triangle," which has to do with the siting of stove, sink, and refrigerator, not the table saw, band saw, and workbench, and such books detail the characteristics of plastic laminates and the various particleboards.

It's a paradox. Often we think of the cabinetmaker as being a skilled craftsman, someone who's invested years learning about wood and its characteristics, about woodworking tools, and about shaping wood with tools in the cabinetmaking shop. We think of hand-planed walnut or cherry surfaces, hand-cut dovetails, glistening hand-rubbed finishes. In our mind's eye, we see that sensitive, high-minded craftsman-artist working in his or her small shop, cutting panels on the table saw, plowing grooves with a router, chopping dovetails with chisels, or rubbing out an oil finish. Yet the first cabinet you think of, the single focus of more than a few cabinetry articles and books, the lone product of most cabinetmakers . . . is . . . the flake-board box.

Just look at the contemporary kitchen cabinet. While in this book you'll find cabinets with old-world style, hand-planed surfaces, dovetail construction, and natural finishes, the lion's share of kitchen cabinets are manufactured in factories—the same kinds of factories that produce automobiles, refrigerators, and televisions. The workers aren't skilled craftsmen, they're competent machine operators. The raw materials are not stacks of kiln-dried hardwood, but boxcar loads of medium-density fiberboard (MDF). The drawer bodies aren't maple or poplar, joined with hand-cut dovetails; they're literally punched from plastic-coated MDF, rolled into a box, and fastened with high-tech adhesive.

The point is: Don't look for contemporary flake-board cabinetry in this book. It's about *woodworking*.

As such, *Cabinetry* will pull you to the positive side of the paradox. It's your antidote to MDF, melamine, the 32-mm standard, and capital intensity. It's amateur woodworking in its highest form, that of people who do the work because they love it, not because they're paid to do it. Don't look here for tacky plywood boxes, for misproportioned pine cupboards stained chocolaty-brown. There's serious woodworking going on in this book, the work of those Old-World-style craftsmen. It's about the *higher* possibilities of cabinetmaking. Beyond the contemporary flake-board, built-in storage boxes, there's a whole other world. *Cabinetry* explores—in step-by-step detail—that other world.

This exploration should occupy the woodworking side of your brain for weeks. *Cabinetry* is a cache of woodworking know-how; you can flip through the pages and find, anywhere you stop, a nugget. This volume brims with tips on any aspect of woodworking—design, materials, joinery, tool operation, finishing—but particularly, of course, on true cabinetmaking.

The book works on several levels, none better than the ground floor—its project presentations. The project focus of *Cabinetry* sharply differentiates it from most of the other cabinetmaking books you've seen or heard of. It's an almost indispensable companion to those all-techniques books. It's one thing to page through Joyce's *Encyclopedia of Furnituremaking*, for example, and quite another to integrate the procedures and techniques he discusses one by one, in the making of a full piece. A silverware chest, for example, with tapered legs and several dovetailed drawers. Or a multi-doored buffet. A chest of drawers, or a frame-and-panel chest.

Applications are what *Cabinetry* is all about. Look at the projects. These are the best cabinet pieces we could find, all from exceptionally skilled individual cabinetmakers. They range from a small recipe box to a hanging corner cabinet, from a Stickley bookcase to a chest of drawers. All display sound engineering: materials that are aesthetically and economically appropriate, joinery that's right for the structure and use. The designs are reserved. And, of course, the prototypes are flawlessly executed.

Thirty specific cabinets are here for you to admire, study, learn from, and build. All the information you need is certainly here.

- A full range of drawings, extending from overall plan views chock-full with dimensions to cutaway sketches of isolated details. An experienced woodworker, brimming with confidence, anxious to make the chips fly, can probably work from the drawings alone.
- Detailed cutting lists. Every part and its dimensions are recorded. This catalog is invaluable, even to the professional.

- Step-by-step directions. The steps break the cabinets into logical subassemblies, both because that's the way you work and because it makes their construction easier to understand. The steps progress from a stack of rough-sawed lumber through the various machine operations to the joining of parts into subassemblies. Once you've made the subassemblies, the directions move step-by-step into making them into the final cabinet. Actual techniques do vary from person to person, so we present the builder's approach, often accompanied by an alternative.
- Special boxed features elaborate on how to perform basic cabinetmaking procedures—cutting dovetails, for example, raising panels on the table saw, or hand planing.
- Tips from the builders themselves explain how to resolve little dilemmas and problems that arise in the course of construction. These are, in the words of one woodworker, "the small things that only the one who's messed it up five times knows." If you follow the tips, you can avoid a lot of the aggravations.

These are great, methodical project presentations, giving the relative beginner all the details, but in such a way that the relative expert can get right to work. They even reward the browser, who can grab onto the dozens of practical tips while flipping through the pages.

The browsers often are working on a different level than the book's ground floor. They are able to pull back, and in the terms of the woody homily, see the forest created by all the trees. When you do pull back and look at this book as a whole, you see a great deal of woodworking know-how. Like a textbook on woodworking, *Cabinetry* tells how to make a joint—a rabbet-and-dado joint, for example, or a mortise-and-tenon joint. But unlike the textbook, it also demonstrates how to set up and make diverse joints, so you can efficiently finish what you've started. This book can be used as a practical applications manual.

The browsers among you may be the first to perceive that *Cabinetry* is working on an inspirational level as well. Paging through the book without pausing too long at any one perspective gives a great sense of the array. You're inspired to flip back through the pages and see how nice each project is and to pick out details you like (or don't like). You pause longer, and you admire the woodworking know-how that's gone into the individual pieces. These pieces were made with the finest materials and workmanship—hand-planed surfaces, hand-crafted joinery, hand-rubbed finishes. Yes, *Cabinetry* has flashes of excellence in its 30 projects.

As a practical matter, buying cabinets like the ones found in these pages isn't economically feasible for most of us. Face it, if you could afford these cabinets, you probably wouldn't be reading a book about how to make them. You'd be thumb-ing through your wallet for the wad of bills necessary to buy them. But as woodworkers, we need the inspiration these pieces provide, the aspirations they provoke.

Life is too full of economically feasible products. They usually are compromises, shortfalls, disappointments. And there's a positive psychology at work in that. To earn our daily bread, we get locked into piece-rate jobs—nail down n squares of shingles in an 8-hour day, process x forms an hour, tend to a client or patient every y minutes. Taking time to pay attention to a hobby is satisfying in a way that accumulating good production stats on the job never can be.

So browse and browse again. You'll be inspired to envision one of the cabinets in your own house. Or to mentally incorporate design or joinery elements into some project of your own. Or to revamp one of the projects presented to better suit your needs. Moreover, as you browse among the drawings or the tips, you'll hear the whisper, "You can make these cabinets." It is not only inspiration, it is something that urges you on.

You *can* make these cabinets.

CABINETS FOR THE LIVING ROOM AND FAMILY ROOM

CORNER CHINA CABINET
by Nick Engler

Since medieval times, when nobility kept their "plate" on open shelves, it has been the custom to display dinnerware in a case or on a stand. Each age has added its own twists to this practice, resulting in different pieces of display furniture.

During the eighteenth century, fine ceramic dinnerware, particularly oriental porcelain or "china," became the vogue among the upper class in colonial America. (They were following a fashion begun in England.) Cabinetmakers made china cabinets—large case pieces with shelves and glass doors—to display these pieces. The cabinets took the same basic form as a corner cupboard, a design that had evolved in England several centuries earlier. The fad for displaying one's "good china" spread to America's middle class. By the early nineteenth century, when this piece was built in southern

2

UPPER CASE EXPLODED VIEW

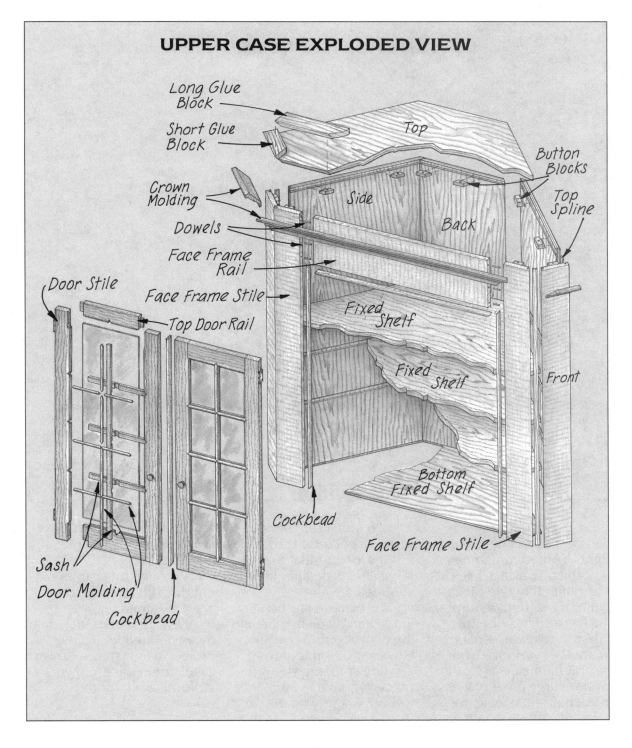

Long Glue Block

Short Glue Block

Top

Button Blocks

Crown Molding

Side

Back

Top Spline

Dowels

Face Frame Rail

Door Stile

Face Frame Stile

Top Door Rail

Fixed Shelf

Fixed Shelf

Front

Cockbead

Bottom Fixed Shelf

Sash

Door Molding

Cockbead

Face Frame Stile

3

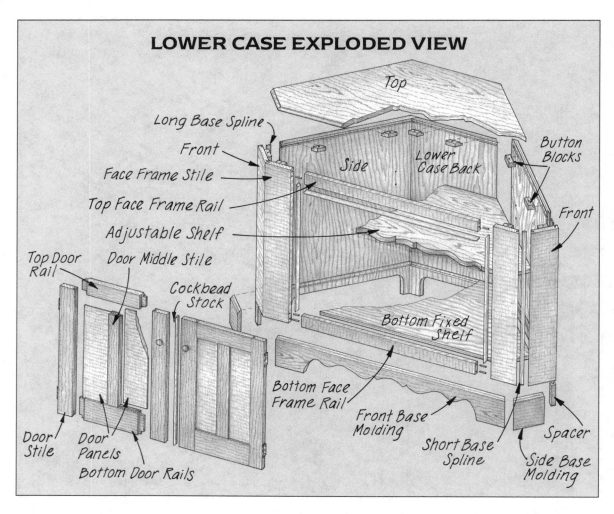

LOWER CASE EXPLODED VIEW

Top

Long Base Spline

Front

Face Frame Stile

Top Face Frame Rail

Adjustable Shelf

Side

Lower Case Back

Button Blocks

Front

Top Door Rail

Door Middle Stile

Cockbead Stock

Door Stile

Door Panels

Bottom Door Rails

Bottom Fixed Shelf

Bottom Face Frame Rail

Front Base Molding

Short Base Spline

Spacer

Side Base Molding

Ohio, the china cabinet had become a common sight in American homes.

Typically, a case like this was built all in one piece; but to make things simpler, the top and base of this cabinet are made separately. In another variance from tradition, this design calls for one large pane of glass in each door. An original colonial cabinet would have had 16 individual panes instead, because the technology for manufacturing large sheets of glass hadn't yet been developed.

You can use any cabinet-grade hardwood and matching plywood that you fancy. However, a nineteenth-century craftsman would probably have used cherry, walnut, or curly maple for a formal project such as this.

The cupboard shown is made from curly maple and walnut.

Although this cabinet is not difficult to build, there are a great many parts involved. To keep from being overwhelmed, make the project in four stages—lower case, upper case, crown molding, and doors.

FRONT VIEW

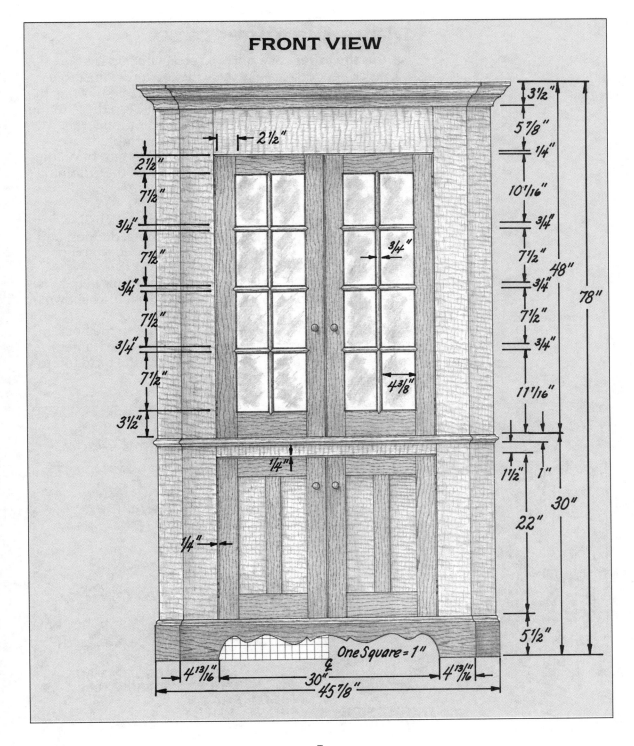

One Square = 1"

Make the lower case.

1 Cut the lower case parts to size. Glue up the stock needed to make the wide top and adjustable shelf. Cut and plane all the parts to the sizes shown in the Materials List, except the base moldings. Rip these to the proper width, but leave them 1 to 2 inches longer than called for. Later, you'll fit them to the assembled case.

Bevel both edges of the back at 45 degrees; bevel the back edges of the sides at 45 degrees, and the adjoining edges of the fronts and stiles at 22½ degrees.

2 Rabbet and dado the lower case parts. The lower case is assembled with simple rabbets, dadoes, and grooves. Cut the joints with a table-mounted router or dado cutter.

First cut ¾-inch-wide, ⅜-inch-deep dadoes in the back, sides, and fronts to hold the fixed shelf, as shown in the Lower Case Parts Layout.

Cut ⅜-inch-wide, ⅜-inch-deep dadoes in the back, sides, fronts, face frame stiles, and upper face frame rail to hold the button blocks that attach the base top to the base.

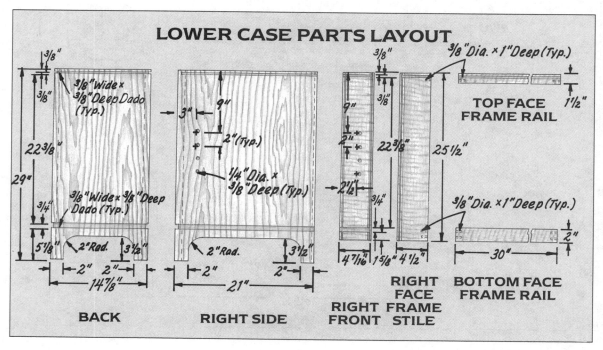

LOWER CASE PARTS LAYOUT

BACK RIGHT SIDE RIGHT FRONT RIGHT FACE FRAME STILE TOP FACE FRAME RAIL BOTTOM FACE FRAME RAIL

3 **Cut the spline grooves.** Cut ¹/₄-inch-wide, ³/₈-inch-deep spline grooves in the edge of the sides, fronts, spacers, and face frame stiles, as shown in Case/Cross Section and in the Lower Case Parts Layout.

When cutting the spline grooves, remember that the

MATERIALS LIST

Part	Dimension	Part	Dimension
Lower Case		**Lower Case Doors**	
Lower case back*	³/₄" × 14⁷/₈" × 29"	Top door rails (2)	³/₄" × 2¹/₂" × 11¹/₂"
Sides* (2)	³/₄" × 21" × 29"	Door stiles (4)	³/₄" × 2¹/₂" × 21⁵/₈"
Fronts (2)	³/₄" × 4⁷/₁₆" × 25¹/₂"	Door middle stiles (2)	³/₄" × 2" × 16³/₈"
Top face frame rail	³/₄" × 1¹/₂" × 30"	Door panels (4)	¹/₂" × 4³/₈" × 15¹/₂"
Bottom face frame rail	³/₄" × 2" × 30"	Bottom door rails (2)	³/₄" × 3¹/₂" × 11¹/₂"
Face frame stiles (2)	³/₄" × 4¹/₂" × 25¹/₂"	Cockbead stock (4)	¹/₄" × 1" × 31"
Top	1" × 18³/₄" × 46⁵/₁₆"	**Upper Case Doors**	
Bottom fixed shelf*	³/₄" × 16⁷/₈" × 45³/₄"	Top door rails (2)	³/₄" × 2¹/₂" × 11¹/₂"
Adjustable shelf	³/₄" × 16¹/₂" × 43¹/₈"	Door stiles (4)	³/₄" × 2¹/₂" × 38¹/₄"
Front base molding	³/₄" × 5¹/₂" × 39⁵/₈"	Bottom door rails (2)	³/₄" × 3¹/₂" × 11¹/₂"
Side base molding	³/₄" × 5¹/₂" × 4³/₄"	Sash stock (4)	¹/₄" × ³/₄" × 35"
Long base splines* (2)	¹/₄" × ³/₄" × 29"	Door moldings (20)	¹/₄" × ¹/₂" × 10"
Short base splines* (2)	¹/₄" × ³/₄" × 25¹/₂"	Cockbead stock (4)	¹/₄" × 1" × 40"
Spacers (2)	³/₄" × ³/₄" × 3¹/₂"		
Dowels (4)	³/₈" dia. × 2"		
Button blocks (10)	³/₄" × 1¹/₄" × 2"		
Upper Case			
Back*	³/₄" × 14⁷/₈" × 46¹/₄"		
Sides* (2)	³/₄" × 21" × 46¹/₄"		
Fronts (2)	³/₄" × 4⁷/₁₆" × 46¹/₄"		
Face frame stiles (2)	³/₄" × 4¹/₂" × 46¹/₄"		
Face frame rail	³/₄" × 7⁵/₈" × 30"		
Top*	³/₄" × 19³/₄" × 47³/₄"		
Fixed shelves (3)	³/₄" × 16⁷/₈" × 44¹/₈"		
Bottom fixed shelf	³/₈" × 16⁷/₈" × 44¹/₈"		
Dowels (6)	³/₈" dia. × 2"		
Button blocks (10)	³/₄" × 1¹/₄" × 2"		
Top splines* (4)	¹/₄" × ³/₄" × 46¹/₄"		
Crown Molding			
Long glue block	³/₄" × 2¹/₂" × 41¹/₈"		
Short glue blocks (2)	³/₄" × 2¹/₂" × 5¹/₂"		
Crown molding stock	³/₄" × 4¹⁵/₁₆" × 60"		

*Make these parts from plywood.

HARDWARE

2 glass panes, ¹/₈" × 10³/₈" × 33¹/₈"
As needed, #10 × 1¹/₄" flathead wood screws
4 flathead wood screws, #10 × 1"
8 butt hinges and mounting screws, 1¹/₂" × 2"
4 door pulls and mounting screws. Available from Cherry Tree Toys, P.O. Box 369, Belmont, OH 43718. Part #132. Specify oak, cherry, or walnut.
4 bullet catches. Available from Woodworker's Supply of New Mexico, 5604 Alameda Place, Albuquerque, NM 87113. Part #801-666.
16 glazing points
As needed, 6d finishing nails
As needed, 4d finishing nails
As needed, ³/₄" brads

grooves in the beveled edges must be perpendicular to the bevels. If you cut these grooves with a dado cutter, set the blade at 22½ degrees. If you use a router table, make a fence that tilts toward the bit at 22½ degrees to help guide the stock. These two setups are shown in the photographs.

4 Drill holes for the shelf supports. Drill a series of ¼-inch-diameter, ⅜-inch-deep holes in the sides and fronts for the shelf supports, as shown in the Lower Case Parts Layout.

5 Drill the face frame. The face frames are doweled together. Drill ⅜-inch-diameter, 1-inch-deep dowel holes in the ends of the face frame rails, as shown in the Lower Case Parts Layout. Drill holes in stiles to match those in the rails. Lay out the holes by putting dowel centers in the rail holes and pressing the rails and stiles together.

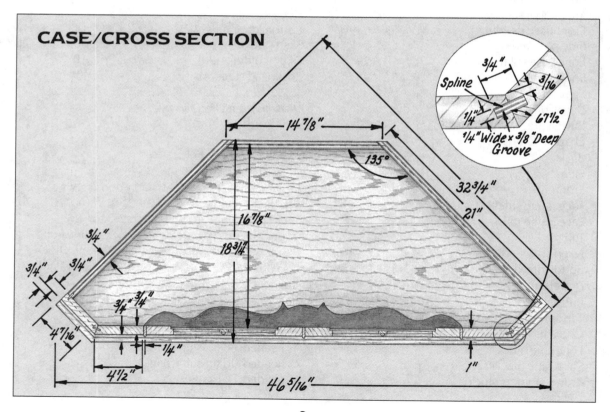

CASE/CROSS SECTION

6 Cut the shapes of the feet, lower case top, shelves, and molding. Lay out the shapes of the feet on the back and sides as shown in the Lower Case Parts Layout. Also lay out the shapes of the lower case top and adjustable shelf as shown in the Shelf and Top Layout, and the bottom edge of the front base molding as shown in the Front View. Cut the parts to shape with a band saw, coping saw, or saber saw. Sand the sawed edges.

7 Shape the lower case top and moldings. Shape the front edges of the lower case top and the top edges of the lower case moldings as shown in the Cabinet Joinery Detail and Shelf and Top Layouts. Cut the profile with a ¹/₂-inch piloted ogee bit in a hand-held router.

8 Make the button blocks. The top attaches to the case with button blocks, as shown in the Cabinet Joinery Detail. Make the blocks as shown. Be sure the protruding tongue fits in the dado you cut at the top of the lower case sides. Drill ³/₁₆-inch-diameter countersunk clearance holes in the blocks, as shown. Make 20 blocks—10 for the base unit, and 10 for the upper unit.

9 Assemble the base. Finish sand all the base parts. Glue the back and sides together, reinforcing the

Spline grooves must be cut perpendicular to the bevel. *Left:* When cutting them with a table-mounted router, run the bevel flat on the table. Use an angled fence to help guide the work past the cutter. *Right:* When using a table saw with a dado head to cut the groove, run the piece flat on the fence with the blade tilted perpendicular to the bevel.

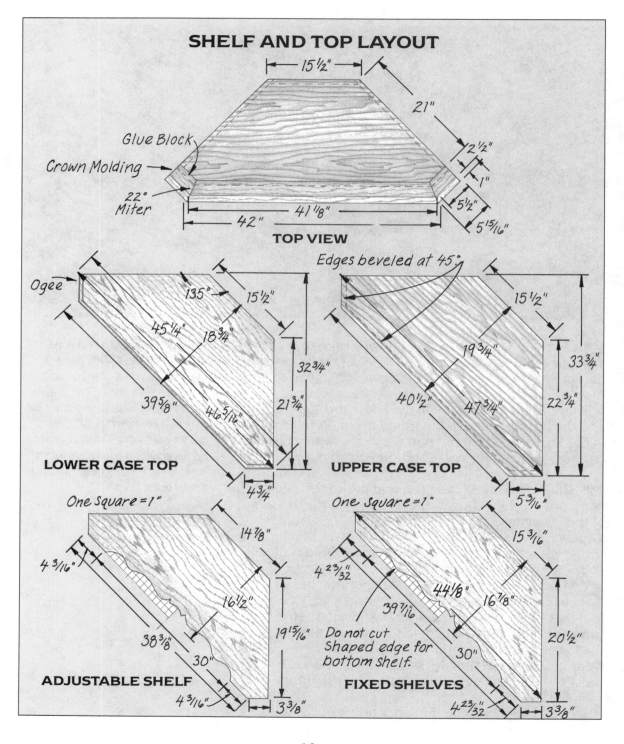

SHELF AND TOP LAYOUT

TOP VIEW

15 ½"
21"
2 ½"
1"
5 ½"
5 ¹⁵/₁₆"
Glue Block
Crown Molding
22° Miter
42"
41 ¹⁄₈"

LOWER CASE TOP

Ogee
135°
15 ½"
45 ¼"
18 ¾"
32 ¾"
39 ⁵⁄₈"
46 ⁵⁄₁₆"
21 ¾"
4 ¾"

UPPER CASE TOP

Edges beveled at 45°
15 ½"
19 ¾"
33 ¾"
40 ½"
47 ¾"
22 ¾"
5 ³⁄₁₆"

ADJUSTABLE SHELF

One Square = 1"
14 ⁷⁄₈"
4 ³⁄₁₆"
16 ½"
38 ³⁄₈"
19 ¹⁵⁄₁₆"
30"
4 ³⁄₁₆"
3 ³⁄₈"

FIXED SHELVES

One Square = 1"
15 ³⁄₁₆"
4 ²³⁄₃₂"
44 ¹⁄₈"
39 ⁷⁄₁₆"
16 ⁷⁄₈"
Do not cut Shaped edge for bottom shelf.
30"
20 ½"
4 ²³⁄₃₂"
3 ³⁄₈"

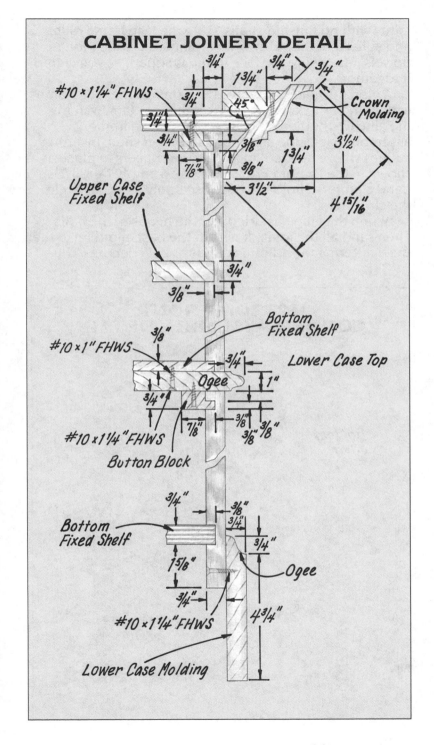

CABINET JOINERY DETAIL

Quick Tip: When doweling pieces together, plane a small flat on one side of each dowel before inserting it. This will allow any excess glue to escape when the joint is clamped tight. If you do not allow this excess glue to escape, it will be compressed in the bottom of the joint. This pressure could force the joint open.

joints with 6d finishing nails. Glue the face frame rails and stiles together with ⅜-inch-diameter, 2-inch-long dowels. Make sure the face frame is square as you clamp it together.

When the glue is dry, glue the fronts to the face frame with ¼-inch-thick, ¾-inch-wide splines. Again, wait for the glue to dry, then glue together the face frame assembly, back/side assembly, and fixed shelf, inserting splines where needed. Also glue the spacers in place as shown in the Bottom Front Corner Assembly Detail. Use band clamps to hold the base assembly together while the glue dries.

When the glue has dried, set the heads of the nails. Then sand all the joints flush. Fit the base molding to the case, mitering the adjoining ends at 22½ degrees. Glue

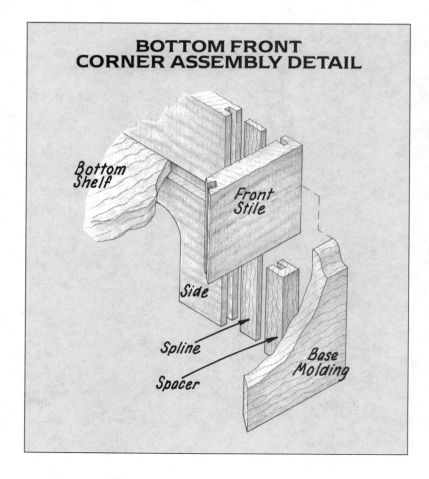

BOTTOM FRONT CORNER ASSEMBLY DETAIL

Bottom Shelf

Front Stile

Side

Spline

Spacer

Base Molding

the molding in place and reinforce it with #10 × 1¼-inch flathead wood screws. Drive the screws from inside the case, as shown in the Cabinet Joinery Detail.

Position the base top on the base assembly. Attach the top with the button blocks and #10 × 1¼-inch flathead wood screws. Do not glue the base top in place—the clips float in the dadoes, letting the top expand and contract with changes in humidity.

Make the upper case.

1 **Cut the upper case parts to size.** Glue up the stock needed to make the wide shelves. Cut the parts to the sizes shown in the Materials List.

2 **Cut the joinery in the upper case parts.** The upper case parts—back, sides, fronts, and face frame

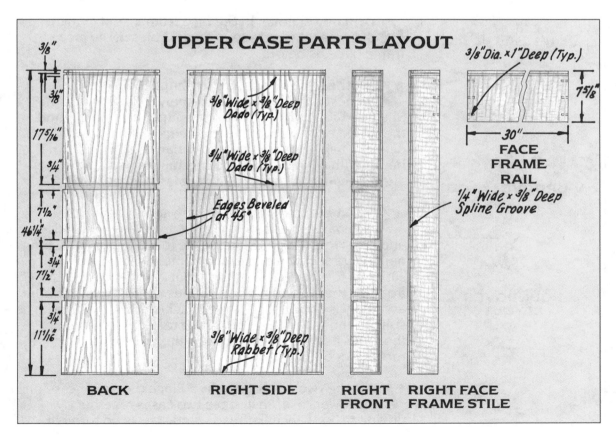

UPPER CASE PARTS LAYOUT

BACK　　　RIGHT SIDE　　　RIGHT FRONT　　RIGHT FACE FRAME STILE

members—are assembled in the same manner as the lower case parts.

As shown in the Upper Case Parts Layout:

Cut ³/₄-inch-wide, ³/₈-inch-deep dadoes in the back, sides, and fronts to hold the shelves.

Cut ³/₈-inch-wide, ³/₈-inch-deep dadoes in the back, sides, fronts, face frame stiles, and top face frame rail to hold the button blocks that attach the top to the case.

Cut ³/₈-inch-wide, ³/₈-inch-deep rabbets in the bottom ends of the back, sides, and front to hold the bottom shelf.

3 **Cut the spline grooves.** Cut ¹/₄-inch-wide, ³/₈-inch-deep spline grooves in the edge of the sides, fronts, spacers, and face frame stiles, as shown in the Case/Cross Section and the Upper Case Parts Layout.

Remember, the spline grooves in the beveled edges must be perpendicular to the bevels.

4 **Drill dowel holes in the face frame.** Drill ³/₈-inch-diameter × 1-inch-deep dowel holes in the face frame parts as before.

5 **Cut the top and shelves to shape.** Lay out the shapes of the top and fixed shelves as shown in the Shelf and Top Layout. Cut these shapes as before. Sand the sawed edges. Bevel the front edges of the top at 45 degrees, using a table saw or circular saw. Clean up the bevels with a hand plane. Be careful not to alter the angle because the crown molding is attached here.

6 **Assemble the top case.** Finish sand all the upper case parts, then assemble the unit. Glue the back and sides together, reinforcing the joints with 6d finishing nails. Glue and dowel the face frame together, making sure it is square and flat. When that glue is dry, glue the fronts to the face frame with splines. When the face frame assembly is dry, attach it to the back/side assembly with splines and glue. Use web clamps to keep pressure on the joints as the glue sets. Attach the top with the remainder of the button blocks.

7 **Put the two cases together.** Place the upper case on the lower case. Fasten the two cases together by driving #10 × 1-inch flathead wood screws up through

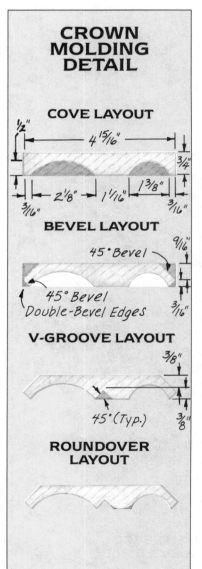

CROWN MOLDING DETAIL

COVE LAYOUT

½" 4¹⁵/₁₆" ³/₄" 2¹/₈" 1¹/₁₆" 1³/₈" ³/₁₆" ³/₁₆"

BEVEL LAYOUT

45° Bevel 9/16" 45° Bevel Double-Bevel Edges ³/₁₆"

V-GROOVE LAYOUT

³/₈" 45° (Typ.) ³/₈"

ROUNDOVER LAYOUT

Use a hand plane to round the flat. Make multiple passes with the plane until the rounded area blends with the upper (narrower) cove, making a graceful S-curve or ogee.

the lower case top and into the bottom shelf of the upper case, as shown in the Cabinet Joinery Detail.

Make the crown moldings.

To make the crown moldings, you must rough out the profiles on the table saw, then plane or scrape them to their final shape.

1 Cut the coves. Lay out the two coves on the ends of the molding stock as shown in the Crown Molding Detail/Cove Layout. Cut these coves by running the molding stock over the table saw at an angle. Both coves should be ½ inch deep, but they are two different widths. Because of this, you will have to make two different setups on the saw. For more on cutting coves, see "Cove Cutting on the Table Saw" on page 361.

2 Cut the bevels. Bevel the edges of the crown molding stock on a table saw. Set the saw blade at 45 degrees. Cut each edge twice, creating a narrow bevel and a wide one as shown in the Crown Molding Detail/Bevel Layout. While the saw blade is still set at 45 degrees, cut a ½-inch-wide V-groove near the center of the stock as shown.

Finally, use a hand plane to round-over the flat area

just above the V-groove, as shown in the Crown Molding Detail/Roundover Layout.

3 **Make and attach the glue blocks.** The crown molding is wrapped around the front of the cabinet with miters at the corners. It is reinforced with glue blocks glued to the upper case top. One long glue block is positioned behind the long section of molding and a short glue block is positioned behind each of the smaller sections of crown molding. Cut a 45-degree bevel on one side of the glue blocks as shown in the Cabinet Joinery Detail. Fit the glue blocks to the case as shown in the Shelf and Top Layout. Miter the glue blocks at the corners. Glue the blocks to the top, making sure the bevel on the glue blocks lines up with the bevel on the top.

4 **Attach the crown molding.** Miter adjoining corners of the crown molding, cutting the molding to length as you do so. The adjoining corners meet at 22½ degrees. Nail, but don't glue, the molding to the cabinet. Reinforce the crown molding with #10 × 1¼-inch flathead wood screws, driving the screws down through the blocks as

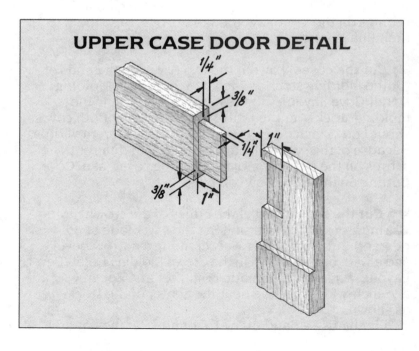

UPPER CASE DOOR DETAIL

shown in the Cabinet Joinery Detail. For more on this
technique, see "Mitering and Installing Crown Molding"
on page 110.

Make the doors.

Both upper and lower doors are joined with mortises and
tenons. The base door frame members, however, are
grooved to hold the base door panels, and the tenons are
haunched to fit these grooves. Consequently, the procedures for making the top joints and base joints vary slightly.

1 Cut the door parts to size. Measure the door open
ings in the case. If the dimensions have changed from
what is shown in the drawings, adjust the sizes of the
door parts accordingly. Cut the door parts to size, except
for the sash, moldings, and cockbead. Rip the sash stock
to the proper thickness and width, but don't cut it to
length yet. Don't cut the moldings and cockbead at all;
instead, just set aside stock for them.

2 Make the upper door joints. Lay out the mortises on
the door stiles as shown in the Upper Case Door

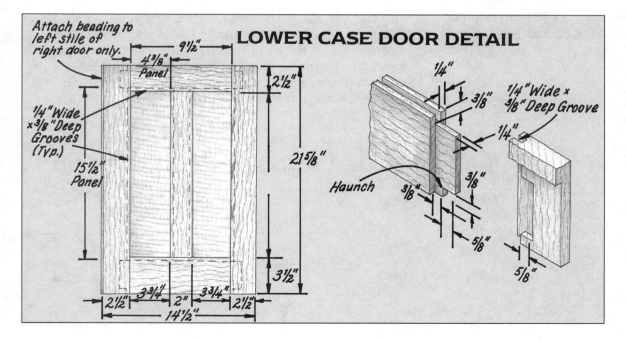

LOWER CASE DOOR DETAIL

Quick Tip: You can also use a plunge router to cut the mortises. Lay out the joint as shown. Chuck a ¼-inch bit in the router and position it over the layout lines. Use an edge guide as a fence to guide the router along the stock. Set the depth stop for the depth of mortise you want. Plunge-cut the ends of the mortise first. Rout out the waste in between with a series of cuts, each slightly deeper than the previous cut. Cutting the ends first ensures that the ends of the mortise will be straight up and down. If the router seems tippy, sandwich the stock between wider pieces to help balance the router.

Detail. Rough out these mortises by drilling a series of overlapping ¼-inch-diameter, 1-inch-deep holes. Clean up the sides and square the corners of each mortise with a chisel.

Make the tenons by cutting two 1-inch-wide, ¼-inch-deep rabbets in each end of the rails, one on each opposing face. The pairs of matching rabbets will form tenons. With a dovetail saw, remove ⅜ inch from the top and bottom of each tenon so that they fit their respective mortises.

3 Make the base cabinet door joints. Cut ¼-inch-wide, ⅜-inch-deep grooves in the inside edges of the base door rails and left and right stiles. Groove both edges of the middle stiles. Lay out the mortises on the stiles as shown in the Lower Case Door Detail. Cut mortises in the base cabinet doors as described previously for the upper cabinet doors. Make the tenons in the middle stiles by cutting two ⅜-inch-wide, ¼-inch-deep rabbets in each end. Make the tenons in the rails by cutting 1-inch-wide, ¼-inch-deep rabbets. Cut a ⅝-inch-wide, ⅜-inch-deep notch in the outside edge of each rail tenon to form a haunch, as shown in the Lower Case Door Detail.

4 Cut the raised panels. The panels in the lower doors are raised, as shown in the Panel and Stile/Cross Section. Bevel the door to the profile shown on a table saw with the blade set at 15 degrees. Use a hollow-ground planer blade, if you have one—it will leave a smoother cut. For more on cutting raised panels, see "Raising Panels on the Table Saw" on page 200.

PANEL AND STILE/CROSS SECTION

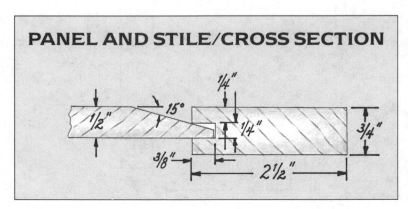

5 **Assemble the doors.** Finish sand the lower door parts and upper door frame members. Test fit the door frames. When you're satisfied that the members fit together properly, reassemble the door frames with glue. As you put the lower doors together, slide the panels into their grooves. Do not glue the panels in place—they must float in the grooves.

As you clamp the parts together, check that the frames are square and flat. After the glue dries, sand the joints clean and flush.

6 **Rout the upper doors.** When the glue dries, rout $1/2$-inch-wide, $1/4$-inch-deep rabbets to hold the glass in the back inside door edges, as shown in the Glazing Detail.

Rout a decorative $1/4$-inch-radius bead in the front inside edges of the door frames as shown in the Glazing Detail. Using a carving chisel, square the beads and rabbets where they turn a corner. From the front, the beads should look as if they were mitered together at the corners.

Install the window grid.

In an antique cabinet, each rectangle in a glazing grid holds a small pane of glass. In this updated design, however, the grid simply overlays a single large pane. The grid is made from two overlapping grids, as shown in the Glazing Detail. The rear grid, or sash, is half-lapped together. The front grid, or molding, is mitered together and glued to the sash.

1 **Cut the notches for the sash.** The sash fits into notches cut into the back of the door, as shown in the Glazing Detail. Lay out the notches according to the dimensions given in the Glazing Detail. Cut along the layout lines with a dovetail saw, and chisel out the waste. Be careful not to cut into the $1/4$-inch bead on the front of the door.

2 **Cut the V-notches.** Cut the V-notches for the door moldings in the $1/4$-inch bead on the front of the door. Refer to the dimensions given in the Glazing Detail. The cuts are made at 45 degrees with a dovetail saw.

3 **Make the sash.** Cut the sash stock to fit the door frames. With a dado cutter on the table saw, cut ³/₄-inch-wide, ¹/₈-inch-deep lap joints where the parts cross one another. Glue the sashes together. Finish sand them and glue them to the door.

4 **Make the door moldings.** Make the door moldings by routing a half-round bead in the edge of a

GLAZING DETAIL

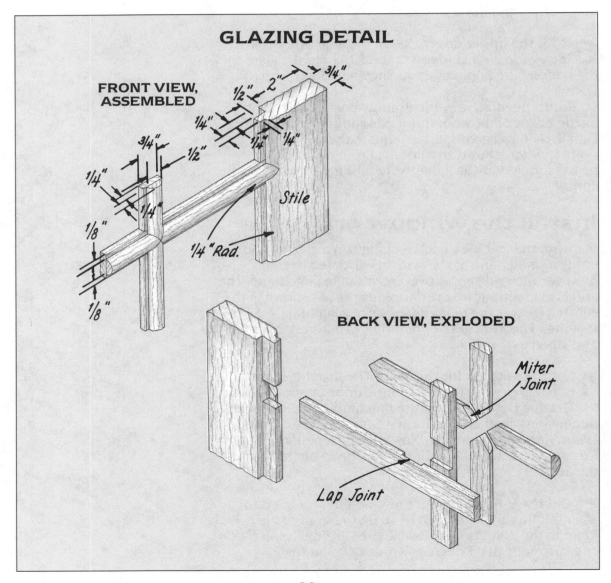

FRONT VIEW, ASSEMBLED

Stile

¹/₄" Rad.

BACK VIEW, EXPLODED

Miter Joint

Lap Joint

¹/₂-inch-thick, 3- to 5-inch-wide board. Then rip the half-round bead from the edge of the board.

Fit the moldings to the door frames, mitering the adjoining edges on the table saw. Finish sand the moldings and glue them to the sash.

Finish the cabinet.

1 **Install the cockbeads.** The upper and lower doors are surrounded by ³/₁₆-inch beads, often referred to as "cockbeading" by old-time cabinetmakers. Make the cockbeads using a method similar to that used for the door moldings. Rout a single ³/₁₆-inch bead into the face of a 1-inch-thick, 3- to 5-inch-wide board. Then rip a ¹/₄-inch-wide strip, including the bead, from the board.

Cut the cockbead to fit inside the door opening, mitering the adjoining ends. Attach the cockbead to the face frames with glue and ³/₄-inch brads. Cut a strip of cockbead to fit between both sets of doors. Attach the beads to each right-hand door with glue and ³/₄-inch brads.

2 **Hang the doors.** Mortise the door stiles and face frame stiles for the hinges. Hang the doors in the cases, leaving approximately a ¹/₁₆-inch gap between the stiles.

3 **Install the hardware.** Mount the door pulls as shown in the Front View. Drill holes for the bullet catches and install them.

4 **Apply finish.** Remove the doors from the cases and the hardware from the doors. Also detach the top case from the base case. Do any necessary touch-up sanding, then apply a finish to all wooden surfaces, inside and out. When the finish dries, replace the top on the base and hang the doors. Install glass in the doors, keeping the panes in place with glazing points and glazing compound. You may want to mix the glazing compound with stain or artist's oil paints so it matches the finished wood.

ENTERTAINMENT CENTER

by Ben Erickson

In this electronic age, hardly a year goes by without a new marvel of technology finding a place in our lives. Finding a place to keep these marvels is another story. This entertainment center takes that jumble of modern chrome and that rat's nest of wires, and organizes them in a cabinet of classic lines and beautiful wood.

At almost 6 feet high and 32 inches wide, this piece has plenty of room for a TV, VCR, and stereo equipment. It also has a pullout desk. The cabinet's pleasing proportions are reminiscent of traditional wardrobes, so that this cabinet blends with any decor.

I made my entertainment center from walnut. Cherry and mahogany would also be good choices. The cabinet is solid wood except the top, middle divider, and bottom, which are 3/4-inch plywood, and the back, which is 1/4-inch plywood. The doors that overlap the case are mounted with brass butt hinges, so that they can open 180 degrees.

Televisions come in a variety of sizes, so be sure to measure yours before starting this project. You can place the TV at the bottom or the top of the cabinet, depending on the viewing height you prefer. Proper ventilation to remove excess heat from electrical components is essential to avoid damaging them. To accomplish this, drill a row of holes or rout a slot in the back near the bottom and top of the area where the components will be located. Also, notch the shelves in the rear to allow space for wiring and unimpeded flow of heat.

The sides and doors of

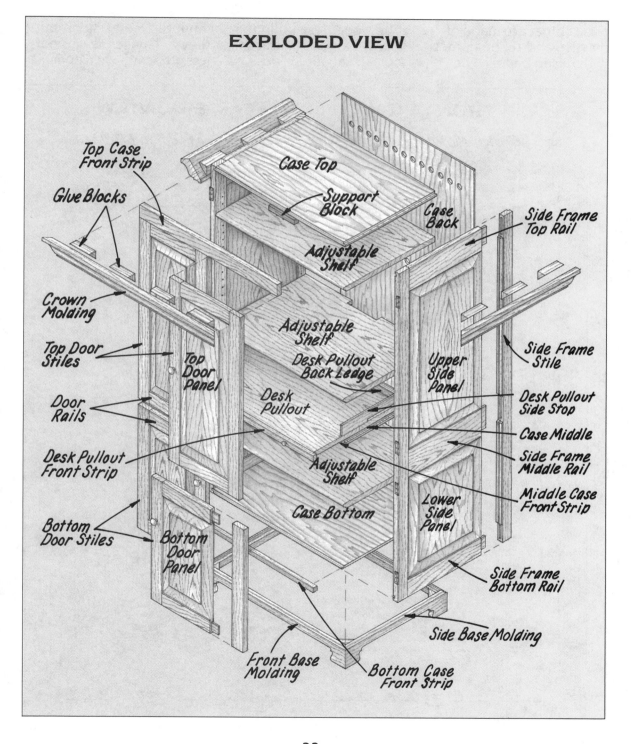

EXPLODED VIEW

Top Case Front Strip

Glue Blocks

Case Top

Support Block

Case Back

Side Frame Top Rail

Adjustable Shelf

Crown Molding

Top Door Stiles

Top Door Panel

Adjustable Shelf

Desk Pullout Back Ledge

Upper Side Panel

Side Frame Stile

Desk Pullout Side Stop

Door Rails

Desk Pullout

Case Middle

Desk Pullout Front Strip

Adjustable Shelf

Side Frame Middle Rail

Middle Case Front Strip

Bottom Door Stiles

Case Bottom

Lower Side Panel

Bottom Door Panel

Side Frame Bottom Rail

Side Base Molding

Front Base Molding

Bottom Case Front Strip

this cabinet are made of mortise-and-tenon frames with raised panels. The solid wood desk pullout slides in a wooden track. You can substitute side-mounted metal slides, but they will make the cabinet less attractive when opened.

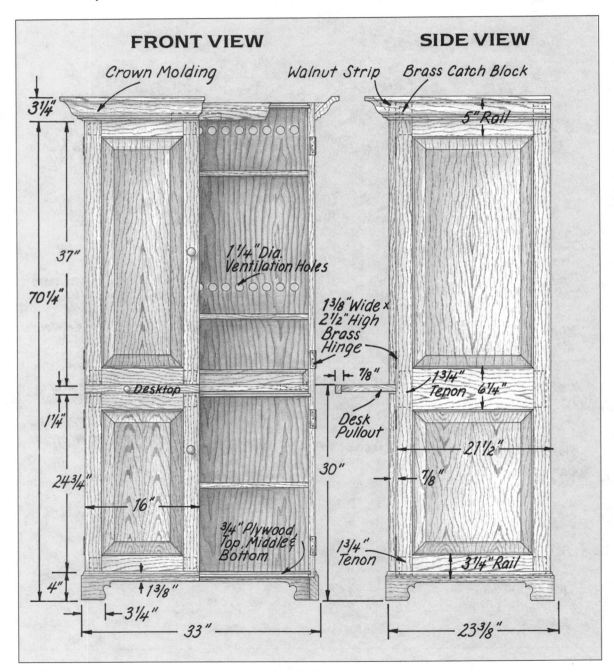

FRONT VIEW

SIDE VIEW

Crown Molding

Walnut Strip

Brass Catch Block

3¼"

5" Rail

37"

1¼" Dia. Ventilation Holes

70¼"

1⅜" Wide x 2½" High Brass Hinge

7/8"

1¾" Tenon

6¼"

Desktop

Desk Pullout

1¼"

21½"

24¾"

30"

7/8"

16"

¾" Plywood Top, Middle & Bottom

1¾" Tenon

3¼" Rail

4"

1⅜"

3¼"

33"

23⅜"

Make the frame, the panel sides, and the doors.

1 **Choose the stock and cut the parts to size.** All the parts of this cabinet are made from hardwood except for the case top, middle, bottom, and back, which are made from A-A grade plywood. Choose straight, flat hardwood stock, and joint, plane, cut, and rip all the parts to the sizes given in the Materials List, except for the base molding. Leave the base molding pieces about 2 inches longer than called for in the Materials List. I

MATERIALS LIST

Part	Dimension
Case	
Side frame stiles (4)	$7/8" \times 2\ 1/2" \times 66\ 1/4"$
Side frame bottom rails (2)	$7/8" \times 3\ 1/4" \times 20\ 3/4"$
Side frame middle rails (2)	$7/8" \times 6\ 1/4" \times 20\ 3/4"$
Side frame top rails (2)	$7/8" \times 5" \times 20\ 3/4"$
Upper side panels (2)	$9/16" \times 17\ 1/8" \times 32\ 5/8"$
Lower side panels (2)	$9/16" \times 17\ 1/8" \times 20\ 3/8"$
Case top	$3/4" \times 21\ 1/4" \times 31"$
Case middle	$3/4" \times 20\ 3/8" \times 31"$
Case bottom	$3/4" \times 21\ 1/4" \times 31"$
Top case front strip	$7/8" \times 2\ 1/2" \times 32"$
Middle case front strip	$7/8" \times 3/4" \times 30\ 1/4"$
Bottom case front strip	$7/8" \times 3/4" \times 32"$
Case back	$1/4" \times 31\ 1/4" \times 66\ 1/4"$
Base molding, front and rear (2)	$1\ 1/4" \times 4" \times 33"$
Base molding, sides (2)	$1\ 1/4" \times 4" \times 23\ 3/8"$
Crown molding stock	$1\ 1/8" \times 4\ 3/4" \times 10'$
Glue blocks for crown (10)	$1\ 5/8" \times 1\ 5/8" \times 4"$
Support block for catch	$1" \times 1" \times 6"$
Doors	
Door rails (8)	$7/8" \times 2\ 1/2" \times 15"$
Top door stiles (4)	$7/8" \times 2\ 1/2" \times 37"$
Top door panels (2)	$9/16" \times 11\ 5/8" \times 32\ 5/8"$
Bottom door stiles (4)	$7/8" \times 2\ 1/2" \times 24\ 3/4"$
Bottom door panels (2)	$9/16" \times 11\ 5/8" \times 20\ 3/8"$

Part	Dimension
Shelves	
Desk pullout (without front strip)	$1" \times 20\ 1/4" \times 30\ 3/16"$
Desk pullout front strip	$7/8" \times 1\ 1/4" \times 32"$
Desk pullout back ledge	$3/4" \times 3" \times 30"$
Desk pullout side stops (2)	$3/4" \times 2" \times 21"$
Adjustable shelves (as desired)	$1" \times 21" \times 30\ 1/8"$

HARDWARE

As needed, #8 × 1 3/4" drywall screws
As needed, #8 × 1 1/2" drywall screws
As needed, #8 × 1 1/4" drywall screws
8 brass hinges, 1 3/8" × 2 1/2". Available from Woodcraft Supply, P.O. Box 1686, Parkersburg, WV 26102. Part #16Q41.
4 brass ball catches. Available from The Woodworkers' Store, 21801 Industrial Blvd., Rogers, MN 55374. Part #28613.
12 adjustable shelf supports. Available from The Woodworkers' Store. Part #33894.
2 flat steel corner braces, 4"
4 brass knobs, 1 1/4" dia. Available from The Woodworkers' Store. Part #36475.
2 brass knobs, 3/4" dia. Available from The Woodworkers' Store. Part #36459.

chose straight-grained, plain wood for my frames, and saved my wider, highly figured boards for my panels. Try to glue up the panels from no more than two pieces, matching the grain carefully.

2 Mortise the stiles. Lay out ¼-inch-wide mortises in the door and side frame stiles where shown in the Side View and the Frame and Panel Detail. Make the mortises in the stiles by drilling a series of adjacent 2-inch-deep holes within the layout lines and cleaning out the waste with a chisel.

3 Cut the tenons on the rails. The rails on the doors and side frames have ¼-inch-thick × 1¾-inch-long tenons with ½-inch shoulders at the top and bottom, as shown in the Frame and Panel Detail. Cut the tenons with a dado cutter set up in a table saw. Guide the rails with the miter gauge as you cut the tenons. Test fit the tenons in their mortises and make any necessary adjustments.

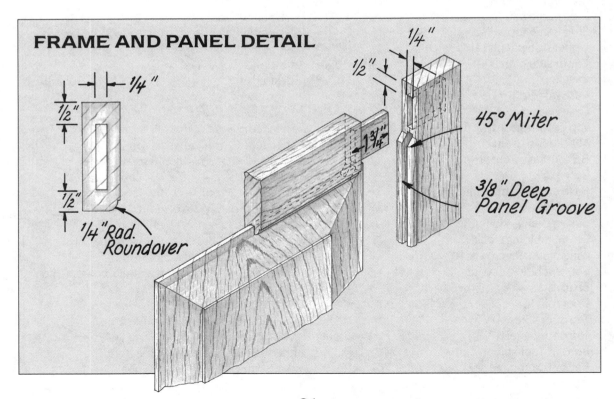

FRAME AND PANEL DETAIL

¼"

½"

¼"Rad. Roundover

½"

¼"

1¾"

45° Miter

3/8" Deep Panel Groove

4 **Rout a roundover on the rails and stiles.** Rout a ¼-inch-radius roundover in the front inside edge of the rails and stiles as shown in the Frame and Panel Detail. Notice that the middle rails of the side frames have a roundover on both face edges. Rout the bead with a table-mounted router and fence for a smooth bead.

5 **Cut a panel groove in the rails and stiles.** Rout a ¼-inch-wide × ⅜-inch-deep panel groove, centered in the edge of the frame stock.

6 **Miter the bead on the rails and stiles.** In order to assemble the stiles and rails, the beads must be mitered where the stiles and rails meet, as shown in the Frame and Panel Detail. Set the table saw blade at 45 degrees, and raise it until it just touches the reveal above the bead.

Miter the bead on the ends of the rails first. To cut the miter, guide the end of the rail's tenon along the table saw fence with a miter gauge set at 90 degrees.

Once you've cut the miters in the rails, lay out and miter the bead at the end of the stiles and at the end of the side frame middle rail. Guide the miter cut on the ends of the stiles with both the miter gauge and the rip fence. Position the rip fence so that placing the end of the stile against it will align the miter with the blade.

When making the cuts for the middle rails, guide the stock with the miter gauge and line up the layout lines with the blade. Cut away most of the waste between the miter and end of the stile with the table saw blade, and clean up the cut with a chisel.

For more on beaded-frame joinery, see "Mitering a Beaded Frame" on page 70.

7 **Raise the panels.** Raise the front of the panels on a router table with a panel raising bit or with a table saw, as explained in "Raising Panels on the Table Saw" on page 200.

8 **Assemble the frame and panel units.** Test fit the panels in their frames, and make any necessary adjustments. Assemble the stiles and rails around the panels by gluing the tenons into their mortises. Do not glue the panels in place; they must be able to move freely in their

Quick Tip: To see if a groove is truly centered in the edge of a frame, cut the groove down the length of a scrap piece that is the exact thickness as the rest of the frame. Then reverse the piece end for end and repeat the cut partway down the piece. The groove is centered if the second cut exactly fills the space occupied by the first groove.

Quick Tip: Raising panels is a heavy cut for the router and requires several passes. To cut down on router wear and tear and to speed up the process, remove most of the waste on the table saw and use the router to clean up the cut.

slots as they expand and contract with changes in humidity. Square the frame by measuring diagonally across the corners. If the measurements are equal, the frame is square. If not, make any necessary adjustments.

9 **Rabbet the sides for the back.** Cut $1/4 \times 1/2$-inch rabbets the length of the side stiles for the $1/4$-inch plywood back as shown in the Side Frame/Inside View.

Make the case.

1 **Cut the dadoes and rabbets.** The case top, middle, and bottom are rabbeted to form a tongue that fits

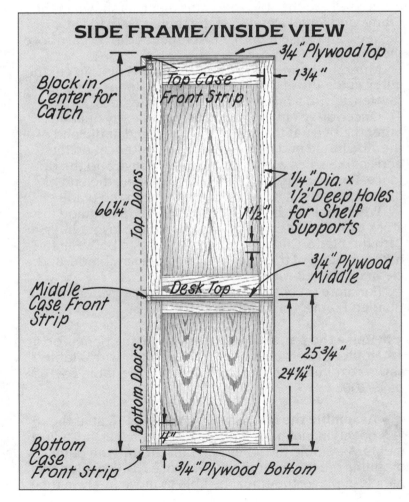

SIDE FRAME/INSIDE VIEW

into the side frames.

First, rout a dado to accept the tongue. A router guided against a straightedge is the best and safest method for making dadoes in big pieces such as the sides of this cabinet. Start by cutting dadoes in the rails with a ³⁄₈-inch-diameter straight bit in the router. Cut the top and bottom dadoes ³⁄₈ inch from the top and bottom of the sides as shown in the Rabbet and Dado Detail. Cut the top and bottom dadoes through, but stop the middle dadoes approximately ⁵⁄₈ inch from the front edges of the sides. (Don't bother to square off the edge of the dado. As drawn, it's long enough to hold the entire shelf, even with the rounded end. A solid strip you'll add later hides the dado from view.)

Put a ³⁄₈-inch rabbeting bit in the router and set it for a depth of ³⁄₈ inch. Make a test cut on a scrap piece of the plywood, and check that the resulting tongue fits into the dado. Adjust the depth of cut until you have a snug fit, then rabbet the ends of the three plywood pieces.

2 **Drill holes for the adjustable shelves.** Drill a series of ¹⁄₄-inch-diameter × ¹⁄₂-inch-deep holes for the adjustable shelf supports 1 ¹⁄₂ inches on center up each frame stile, as shown in the Side Frame/Inside View.

Drill holes for shelf pins with this jig to keep them properly aligned. Drill all the holes on one side first, and then reposition the jig to drill holes on the other side.

Quick Tip: Drill the adjustable shelf holes with the help of a template. Make the template from some scrap of plywood cut to the width of the side frame stiles. Lay out and drill the adjustable shelf holes, shown in the Side Frame/Inside View, on the template. Clamp the template to the side frame stiles, and drill through the holes in the template to locate the holes in the first side.

To make an identical set of holes on the second side, mark the front and top edges of the template, and make sure these marks line up with the top and front of the second side.

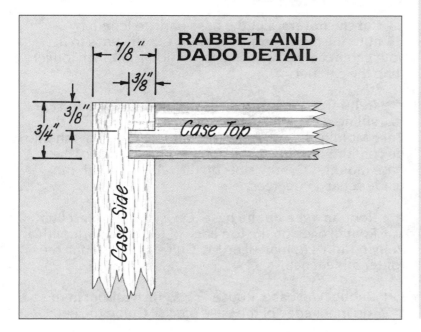

RABBET AND DADO DETAIL

⁷⁄₈″
³⁄₈″
³⁄₈″
³⁄₄″
Case Top
Case Side

3 Assemble the case. Glue and clamp the top, the shelf, and the bottom to the sides of the case. Make sure that the cabinet is square by measuring diagonally across the corners. If the measurements are equal, the case is square. Make sure the front edges of the top and bottom are flush with the front edges of the case side frames.

4 Attach the case front strips. Glue the case front strips onto the front edge of the case top, middle, and bottom as shown in the Side Frame/Inside View. The top and bottom case front strips are immediately above and below the door openings and create an opening for the door. The middle case front strip covers the front edge of the case middle, and is flush with the front edge of the side frames as shown.

5 Drill ventilation holes in the back. Drill two rows of 1 1/4-inch-diameter holes in the back as shown in the Front View. These holes are to dispel heat and allow wires to enter and exit. The exact location of the holes isn't critical.

Make the base.

1 Cut the miters. Cut the base parts to length by mitering the appropriate ends. Cut the base to fit your cabinet exactly. Each base molding is 1 inch longer than the cabinet.

2 Reinforce the miters with splines. Lay out and cut spline slots in the mitered corners as shown in the Base Molding Detail/Top View. Note that the slots should be contained within the rabbet in the top edge of the base molding. Cut the slots on the table saw with the blade set at 45 degrees.

3 Rout an ogee on the base. On a router table, cut a Roman ogee on the top edge of the base parts with a 1/4-inch-radius Roman ogee bit. Guide the cut along the router table fence.

4 Rabbet the base. Rout a 3/4 × 3/4-inch rabbet in the top inner edge of the base pieces. Guide the cut along the router table fence.

BASE MOLDING DETAIL

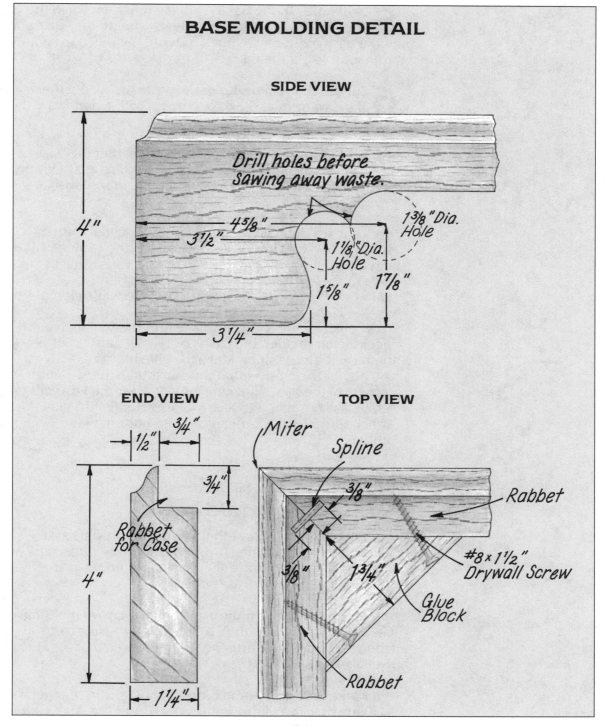

SIDE VIEW

Drill holes before sawing away waste.

4"

4⅝"

3½"

1⅜" Dia. Hole

1⅛" Dia. Hole

1⅝"

1⅞"

3¼"

END VIEW

½"

¾"

¾"

Rabbet for Case

4"

1¼"

TOP VIEW

Miter

Spline

⅜"

Rabbet

⅜"

1¾"

#8 x 1½" Drywall Screw

Glue Block

Rabbet

5 Drill holes in the base. Drill the holes shown in the Base Molding Detail/Side View to create the curves in the base molding. Clamp a block to the piece to keep from tearing out the back of the stock.

6 Cut out the remainder of the pattern. Cut out the rest of the pattern at the base corners with a band saw, scroll saw, or portable jigsaw.

7 Test assemble the base. Clamp together the base with a band clamp and test it to see if it fits snugly on the case bottom. If necessary, widen the rabbet with a rabbet plane.

8 Glue up the base. Before gluing up, cut a scrap of plywood that is as wide and long as the cabinet. Glue and clamp the base together with the scrap sitting in the base rabbets. The scrap will keep the bottom square as you work. Protect the corners of the base while clamping with an L-shaped wooden block.

While the glue is drying, make four triangular glue blocks to strengthen the base corners and also to attach the base to the cabinet. Make the glue blocks exactly as you did for the crown molding, and attach them to the corners of the base with glue and #8 × 1 1/2-inch drywall screws as shown in the Base Molding Detail/Top View. Attach the glue blocks flush with the bottom of the rabbet.

Make and install the crown molding.

1 Make the crown molding. Make the molding as explained in "Making Crown Molding" on page 38. You may be able to buy or have crown molding made in the same type of wood as the piece.

2 Miter the crown molding. Miter the crown molding, as shown in the photo, to fit around the front and sides of the cabinet. Trim the side pieces so that they are even with the back of the cabinet.

3 Make triangular glue blocks. Make seven triangular glue blocks to support the crown molding. Make the blocks from some $1\frac{5}{8} \times 1\frac{5}{8} \times 36$-inch scrap. Set your table saw blade at 45 degrees, and rip the scrap diagonally down the middle. Guide the stock against the fence with a push stick as you make the rip cut. When the rip is complete, set the table saw blade back to 90 degrees, and cut the glue block stock into 4-inch lengths.

Glue two blocks to each side crown molding and three to the front crown molding. The exact location is not important, but they must not interfere with the assembly of the miter joint.

4 **Attach the crown.** Glue the crown to the case. Attach it by screwing through the case and into the glue blocks and molding with #8 × 1¾-inch drywall screws as shown in the Molding and Glue Block Detail.

Make the desk pullout.

1 **Attach the front strip to the desk pullout.** Cut the desk pullout to size. Glue a $\frac{7}{8} \times 1\frac{1}{4} \times 32$-inch hardwood strip onto what will be the front edge of the pullout. Position the strip as shown in the Front and Side Views: It should be flush with the top of the pullout and centered left to right so that the overhang on each side covers the edges of the case sides.

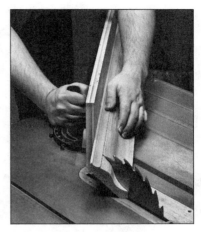

Place one inside edge of the molding on the saw table, and the other inside edge against a miter gauge fence. Cut the molding with the miter gauge set at 45 degrees and the blade at 90. If your saw blade doesn't cut all the way through the molding, finish the cut by hand.

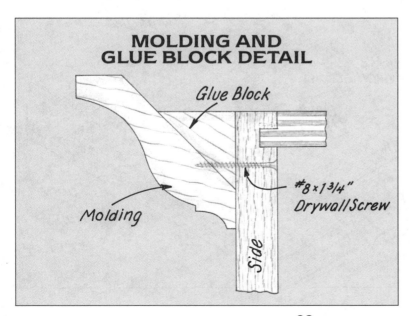

MOLDING AND GLUE BLOCK DETAIL

Glue Block

#8 × 1¾" Drywall Screw

Molding

Side

2 Make the desk supports. These supports are screwed to the inside of the cabinet, and the desk pullout slides underneath them, as shown in the Desk Pullout Installation Detail. I designed a homemade stop that made it impossible to accidentally pull the desk pullout all the way out. As you pull out the desk pullout, a metal tongue travels along a rabbet in the desk pullout supports, as shown in the Desk Pullout Installation Detail. The rabbet stops 7 inches from the front of the support. When the metal tongue reaches this point, the desk pullout stops in its tracks.

Cut a rabbet in the support, as shown in the Desk Pullout Installation Detail, stopping the rabbet 7 inches from the desk pullout front. Rout the top and front edges of the runners with the same Roman ogee you used for the top of the base.

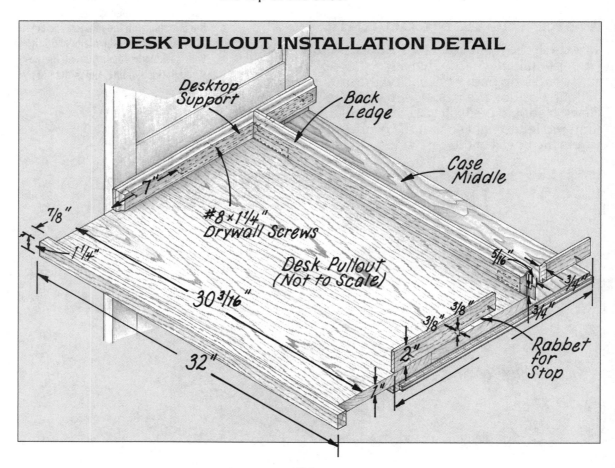

DESK PULLOUT INSTALLATION DETAIL

3 **Attach the support strips.** Put the desk pullout in place and use it as a guide in positioning the support strips on the inside of the case. Predrill and countersink the supports for #8 × 1 1/4-inch drywall screws. You want a snug fit but one that allows the desk pullout to come out without binding.

4 **Make the back ledge.** To keep objects from slipping behind the desk pullout, attach a ledge that extends 2 inches above the top, as shown in the Desk Pullout Installation Detail. As shown, the back ledge is shaped to fit against the profile of the desk support strips. Lay out the profile on the back ledge by holding it against the back edges of the support strips and scribing the profile on it. Cut the ends of the back ledge to shape with a coping saw. Sand the cut smooth.

Once you've cut the back ledge to shape, rout an ogee into the top edge of the back ledge that matches the ogee in the support strips. Attach the back ledge to the desk pullout with glue and #8 × 1 1/4-inch drywall screws.

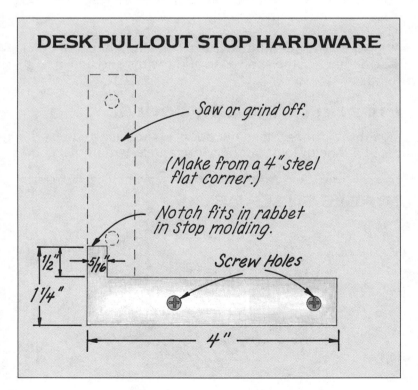

DESK PULLOUT STOP HARDWARE

Saw or grind off.

(Make from a 4" steel flat corner.)

Notch fits in rabbet in stop molding.

Screw Holes

1/2" 5/16"

1 1/4"

4"

5 **Make the desk pullout stop hardware.** Make desk pullout stops from 4-inch steel flat corner braces as shown in the Desk Pullout Stop Hardware. To make the stops, simply put the corner braces in a vice and cut them to the shape with a hacksaw. With the desk pullout in the case, screw the stop hardware to the back of the desk pullout ledge so that the metal tongue rides in the support strip rabbet, as shown in the Desk Pullout Installation Detail. Unscrew the stop to remove the desk pullout for finishing on both sides.

Make the shelves.

1 **Rout the edges.** This cabinet will accommodate up to four shelves. Make as many as you think you need. The front edges are spiced up with a routed profile. Rout the front edge as shown in the Adjustable Shelf Detail, using a classical bit and a ³/₈-inch roundover bit in a table-mounted router. A classical bit routs a cove and a roundover, separated by a small fillet. Rout the bottom edge of the shelf with the classical bit; then rout the top edge with the roundover bit.

2 **Notch the shelf back.** Cut a 1¹/₄ × 8-inch rectangle in the back of the shelves to allow wires and heat to pass.

Fit and hinge the doors.

1 **Fit the doors.** Place the doors in the case and test the fit. Plane or joint off the width and length until a good

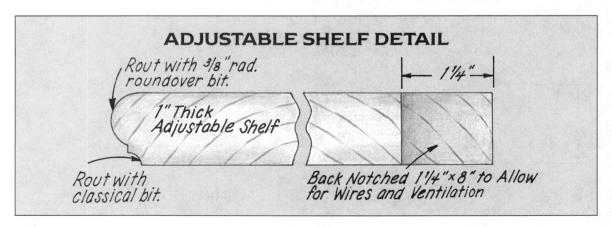

ADJUSTABLE SHELF DETAIL

Rout with ³/₈" rad. roundover bit.

1" Thick Adjustable Shelf

Rout with classical bit.

1¹/₄"

Back Notched 1¹/₄" x 8" to Allow for Wires and Ventilation

fit is achieved. Minor adjustments will need to be made after the doors are hinged, so take as little off as possible.

2 **Cut hinge mortises in the doors and cabinet.** Use thick, high-quality hinges for these large doors. To lay out the mortises, position the hinges on the cabinet, and trace around them with a marking knife. Rout a mortise half as deep as the hinge barrel in the cabinet. Clean up to the layout lines with a sharp chisel.

Position each door in its opening, and transfer the location of the hinge to it. Rout for the hinge as before.

3 **Attach the doors.** Hinge the doors and check their fit again, planing off any tight spots. Remove the hinges while finishing the doors and case.

Finish the cabinet.

1 **Sand the cabinet.** Sand all parts of the cabinet and doors. Round the sharp edges of the cabinet slightly as you sand.

2 **Apply finish.** Finish the inside and outside surfaces with your favorite finish. I used three coats of tung oil, sanding between coats with 220- or 320-grit paper, followed by steel wool and paste wax.

3 **Assemble the cabinet.** Attach the base to the case by driving #8 × 1 1/2-inch drywall screws through the glue blocks and into the case bottom. Stand the cabinet upright, slide the desk pullout into its opening, and screw the metal stops onto the back. Glue and nail the 1/4-inch plywood back on the case, checking to make sure the case is square as you work.

Insert the adjustable shelf supports in the holes and install the shelves.

4 **Attach hardware.** Mount the hinges on the doors and hang them. Screw the brass knobs onto the desk pullout and doors as shown in the Front View. Screw the catch support block in place behind the top case front top strip, and mount the brass ball bearing catches onto the catch support block, middle shelf, and doors.

Quick Tip: Save your soft brass screws for the final hanging, and use steel screws of the same size and length to test fit the doors.

MAKING CROWN MOLDING

Most lumberyards only sell crown molding in one species: pine. But you can make crown molding from the wood of your choice with nothing more than your table saw and router.

CROWN MOLDING PROFILE

Round-over with hand plane, finish with sandpaper.

Clean up cove with gooseneck scraper followed by sandpaper-covered convex block.

Final Shape (after Hand Cleanup)

1 Make a sample. Draw the pattern of the molding, as shown, on the end of a scrap piece the same width and thickness as the molding stock, and use this piece to test setups.

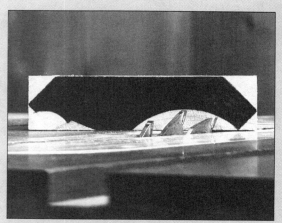

Lay out the molding on a sample.

2 Cut the large cove. Cut the large cove at the top of the molding on the table saw. Clamp a fence diagonally on the table saw, and pass the stock over the blade at an angle.

Cut a sample cove and adjust the angle as necessary. Begin cutting the cove with the blade very low, and make several passes until the proper height is reached. When you're satisfied with the shape of the cove, lower the blade and repeat the process on the actual molding.

Cut a cove against an angled fence.

3 Cut the fillet with a dado cutter. Set the dado cutter on the table saw at an angle of approximately 25 degrees. To set the proper height of the blade, raise it slowly up to the layout lines on the end of the scrap. Adjust the rip fence to position the fillet properly. Test it on your sample. Make any necessary adjustments, and cut the fillet on the actual stock.

Cut the fillet between the coves with a dado cutter.

Rip a bevel on the inside surfaces.

4 **Cut the small cove.** Rout the small cove with a 1-inch-diameter core box bit set up in a table-mounted router. Guide the cut against a fence.

6 **Hand shape and smooth the molding.** Clean up the saw marks and create the large roundover by hand. Clean up the round cove with a gooseneck scraper, followed by sandpaper wrapped around a rounded block. Use a block plane to create the large roundover. Sand the entire molding.

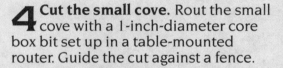

Rout the small cove.

5 **Make angled cuts at the edges.** Bevel the edges of crown molding on the table saw with the blade set at 45 degrees.

Finish shaping the molding by hand.

RECORD STORAGE CABINET

by Randy Pease

I originally designed this cabinet to store my record albums. My TV, VCR, and stereo all live in a corner cupboard entertainment center, but there was no room for my record collection. My wife was getting tired of tripping over old milk crates filled with records, so I decided I had

better come up with a solution, and fast. This may be the age of the compact disk, but I'm certainly not going to discard my LPs.

This design was inspired by a piece by William Draper. He operates a cabinetmaking shop in Perkasie, Pennsylvania, and I've worked with him and

learned from him for several years now. Draper's handcrafted country pieces feature raised panel doors set in traditional beaded frames.

I made my cabinet out of pine for two reasons: first, pine is very reasonably priced, and second, I hand plane it to remove

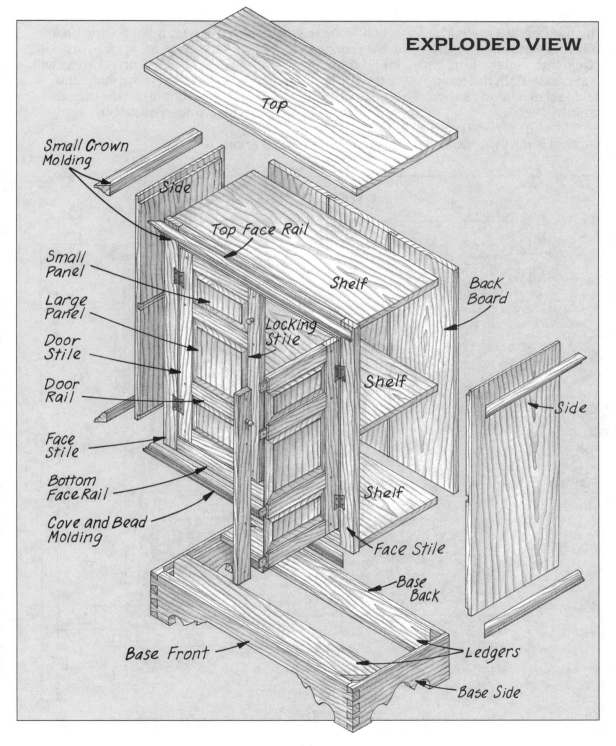

EXPLODED VIEW

Top

Small Crown Molding

Side

Top Face Rail

Shelf

Back Board

Small Panel

Large Panel

Locking Stile

Door Stile

Door Rail

Shelf

Side

Face Stile

Bottom Face Rail

Cove and Bead Molding

Shelf

Face Stile

Base Back

Base Front

Base Side

Ledgers

the lumberyard milling marks. By grinding a *slight* curve into a plane iron, you can create both the look and feel of a hand-planed country piece.

The chip carving on this cabinet is my own special touch. I began chip carving a few years ago and have found that it's a great way to turn an ordinary cabinet into something special.

I finished this piece with a spray-on stain. If you want the chip-carved areas to stand out, wipe on a penetrating stain instead; the chip-carved areas will accept more stain and become darker than the uncarved wood.

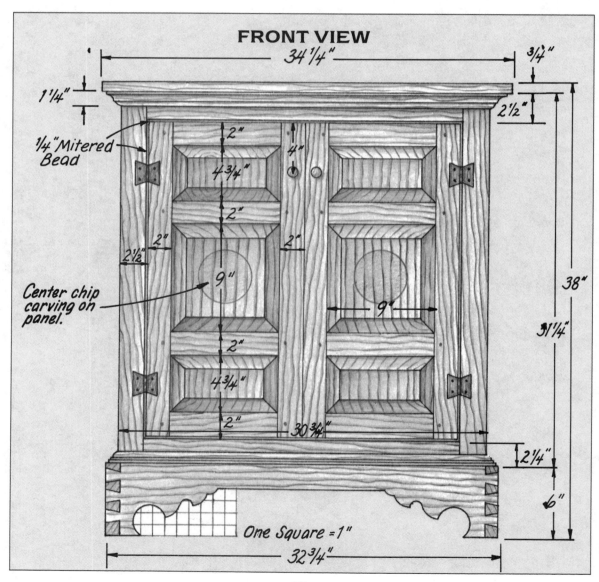

FRONT VIEW

1¼" ¼" Mitered Bead
2½" 2"
Center chip carving on panel.
9"
9"
2"
4¾"
2"
4"
2"
2"
4¾"
2"
34¼"
¾"
2½"
38"
31¼"
2¼"
6"
30¾"
One Square = 1"
32¾"

Make the case.

1 **Select the stock and cut the parts.** For this project, #2 common pine works well. Choose ¾- and 1¼-inch-thick stock that has small round knots (1-inch diameter or less), and avoid boards with knots on the edges. Glue together the wider parts, then joint, rip, and cut the parts to the sizes given in the Materials List.

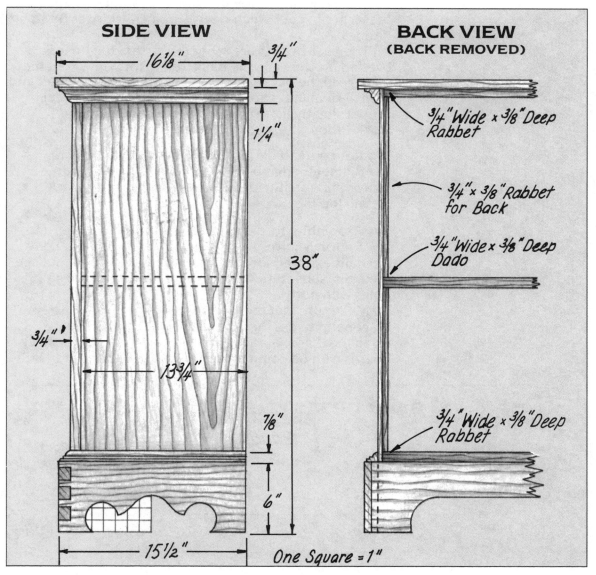

SIDE VIEW

16⅛"

¾"

1¼"

38"

¾"

13¾"

⅞"

6"

15½"

BACK VIEW
(BACK REMOVED)

¾" Wide x ⅜" Deep Rabbet

¾" x ⅜" Rabbet for Back

¾" Wide x ⅜" Deep Dado

¾" Wide x ⅜" Deep Rabbet

One Square = 1"

If you want to hand plane this piece, do so after gluing up the wider parts, but before assembling the cabinet. For complete step-by-step instructions, see "Planing Wood by Hand" on page 52.

2 Cut the rabbets and dadoes in the sides and back boards. Country pieces were often dadoed and nailed together. This cabinet is no exception. Lay out and cut the rabbets and dadoes in the sides as shown in the Back View, with a router and a ³/₄-inch straight bit. Adjust the router to cut ³/₈-inch-deep × ³/₄-inch-wide rabbets and dadoes.

The back boards are rabbeted so that the boards overlap, as shown in the Back Detail/Top View. Rout the rabbets in the back boards, as shown, with the router and ³/₄-inch-diameter straight bit. Set the bit depth to cut a rabbet slightly more than half the thickness of the stock—about ¹³/₃₂ inch in this case.

3 Rout a bead in the back boards. Put a ¹/₄-inch-diameter edge-beading bit in your table-mounted router, and rout the beads where shown in the Back Detail/Top View.

4 Assemble the case. Attach the upper, middle, and bottom shelves to the sides with 4d cut nails. Leave the nails exposed for a rustic look. If you'd rather not see the nails, substitute 4d finishing nails and fill the nail holes with putty.

Make sure that the case is square by measuring diagonally across the corners: The cabinet is square when the diagonals are equal in length. Attach the back boards with 6d common nails. Put two back boards side

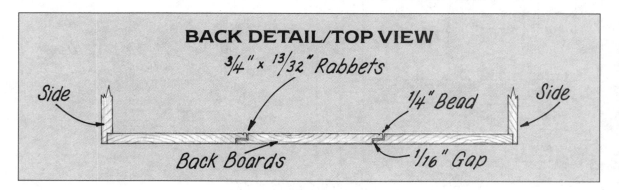

BACK DETAIL/TOP VIEW

³/₄" × ¹³/₃₂" Rabbets

Side

¹/₄" Bead

Side

Back Boards

¹/₁₆" Gap

by side, and then rip the third back board to fit into its opening. Leave about a ¹/₁₆-inch gap between the back boards, as shown in the Back Detail/Top View.

Next, put the top in place on the upper shelf as shown in the Front and Side Views, and secure it by driving #8 × 1¹/₄-inch drywall screws through the upper shelf and into the top.

Make the frame.

Once I've built the case, I build a face frame to hold the doors. I mortise and tenon the frame together, then glue and nail it in place. Like traditional country pieces, I run a small bead around the inside frame edge.

1 Rout a bead in the face rails and stiles. Put a ¹/₄-inch-diameter edge-beading bit in your table-mounted router. To support the stock as you rout, set up a fence on the router table. Rout the bead along the entire length of the face rails and the face stiles.

MATERIALS LIST

Part	Dimension	Part	Dimension
Case		Large panels (2)	³/₄" × 10" × 10"
Sides (2)	³/₄" × 13³/₄" × 31¹/₄"	Stiles (3)	³/₄" × 2" × 26¹/₂"
Back boards (3)	³/₄" × 11¹/₈" × 31¹/₄"	Locking stile	³/₄" × 2³/₈" × 26¹/₂"
Shelves (3)	³/₄" × 13" × 30¹/₄"	Rails (8)	³/₄" × 2" × 11¹/₂"
Top	³/₄" × 16¹/₈" × 34¹/₄"		
Face stiles (2)	³/₄" × 2¹/₂" × 31¹/₄"	**HARDWARE**	
Top face rail	³/₄" × 2¹/₂" × 28¹/₂"	As needed, #8 × 1¹/₄" drywall screws	
Bottom face rail	³/₄" × 2¹/₄" × 28¹/₂"	4 butterfly hinges, 2" × 2". Available from Horton	
Small crown molding stock	1¹/₈" × 1¹/₄" × 65"	Brasses, Nooks Hill Rd., P.O. Box 95,	
Cove and bead molding stock	³/₄" × ⁷/₈" × 65"	Cromwell, CT 06416. Part #HF-12.	
Base		As needed, 4d nails	
Front	1" × 6" × 32³/₄"	As needed, 6d finishing nails	
Sides (2)	1" × 6" × 15¹/₂"	As needed, 4d finishing nails	
Ledgers (2)	³/₄" × 4" × 31⁵/₈"	As needed, 4d cut nails	
Back	³/₄" × 6" × 31⁵/₈"		
Doors			
Small panels (4)	³/₄" × 10" × 5³/₄"		

Quick Tip: Lay out all your joints with a knife and a marking gauge. The razor-sharp lines they leave are easier to follow than the blunt lines left by a pencil.

2 Mortise the stiles. Lay out the mortises on the stiles and rails as shown in the Mortise and Tenon Layout. Drill a series of adjacent holes between the layout lines. Clean out the remaining waste with a chisel.

3 Tenon the rails. Cut the tenons on the ends of the rails with a dado cutter set up in a table saw. Adjust the blade height so that the resulting tenons will fit snugly in their mortises. All of the tenons should have 1/2-inch shoulders, as shown in the Mortise and Tenon Layout.

4 Miter the bead. As shown in the Mortise and Tenon Layout, the bead is mitered at the corner of the frame. When you cut the miter, you must cut away not only the bead, but also the quirk—the small groove left by the router bit between the bead and the rest of the wood.

Cut the rail and stile beads on the table saw with the blade set at 45 degrees. Adjust the blade so that it cuts through both the bead and the quirk. Miter the rails and stiles. For complete step-by-step instructions on beaded-frame joinery, see "Mitering a Beaded Frame" on page 70.

5 Assemble the frame. Put some glue into the mortises in the frame stiles, and insert the frame rail tenons into their appropriate mortises. Clamp the frame together, and make sure that the mitered beads are tight at the corners. Check the frame for squareness and make any necessary adjustments.

6 Peg the frame. Drill 1/4-inch peg holes through each corner of the frame, into the mortise and through the tenon, as shown in the Mortise and Tenon Layout. Contrary to popular belief, it is possible to drive a square peg into a round hole, especially when you are dealing with a soft wood like pine. Make several 1/4 × 1/4 × 1 1/4-inch pegs from some scraps of pine. Whittle the end of each peg to a bullet shape, and tap them into their holes with a hammer. When all of the pegs are in place, remove the clamps, and cut the pegs flush with the back of the frame.

7 Attach the frame to the case. Apply some glue to the front edge of the case, put the frame in place, and secure it to the case with 4d cut nails.

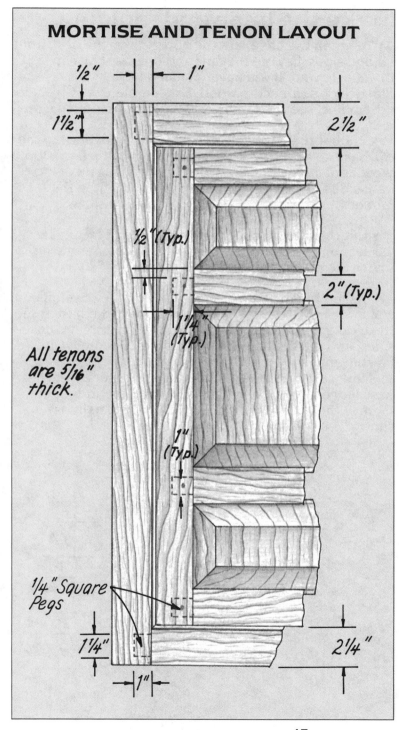

MORTISE AND TENON LAYOUT

½"

1"

1½"

2½"

½" (Typ.)

2" (Typ.)

1¼" (Typ.)

All tenons are ⁵⁄₁₆" thick.

1" (Typ.)

¼" Square Pegs

1¼"

1"

2¼"

Make the base and molding.

1 Dovetail the base. Cut the dovetails on the base front and sides. Lay out the tails and pins as shown in the Dovetail Layout. If you haven't cut many dovetails, practice on some scrap wood. For complete step-by-step dovetailing, see "Cutting Through Dovetails" on page 81.

2 Rabbet the base sides. I rabbet two ledgers into the base, to support the case, as shown in the Base/Top View. Rout $^7/_{16} \times ^3/_4$-inch rabbets along the inside of the base sides, as shown in the Base/Top View. Stop the rabbet 1 inch from the front of each side as shown.

3 Cut the base to shape. Lay out and cut the bracket feet on the front and sides with a band saw or a jig saw to the profile shown in the Front and Side Views.

4 Assemble the base. Spread glue on the dovetails and pins, and attach the base sides to the base front. Next, put glue in the rabbet at the back edge of the base sides, and put the base back into place. Secure it with 4d finishing nails.

Next, cut 45-degree notches in two corners of each base ledger as shown in the Base/Top View, and secure them to the base with glue and 6d finishing nails as shown.

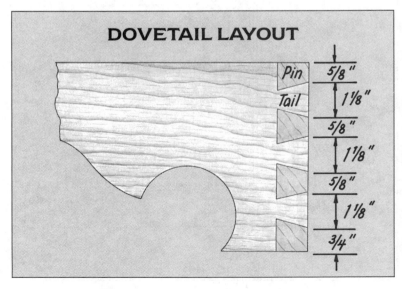

DOVETAIL LAYOUT

Pin — 5/8"
Tail — 1⅛"
5/8"
1⅛"
5/8"
1⅛"
3/4"

When the glue is dry, cut the base back with a jigsaw to the shape shown in the Back View.

5 **Attach the base to the case.** Lay the case on its back, and put the base in place against the case bottom. Screw through the ledgers and into the bottom shelf with #8 × 1 1/4-inch drywall screws to attach the base.

6 **Make and attach the molding.** You can make your moldings or buy similar moldings. Make the small crown molding on the router table with the combination of a 3/8-inch-radius roundover bit and a 1-inch-diameter core box bit. Cut the cove and bead molding with a 1 1/4-inch-diameter classical bit. Miter the moldings to fit.

Make the doors.

1 **Raise the panels.** Cut the bevels in the front surface of the panels as shown in "Raising Panels on the Table Saw" on page 200. You can also raise panels with a router, but you may not be able to get the exact profile that I've used on this cabinet.

Whenever you have a panel in a frame, you should leave some room for the panel to expand across the grain

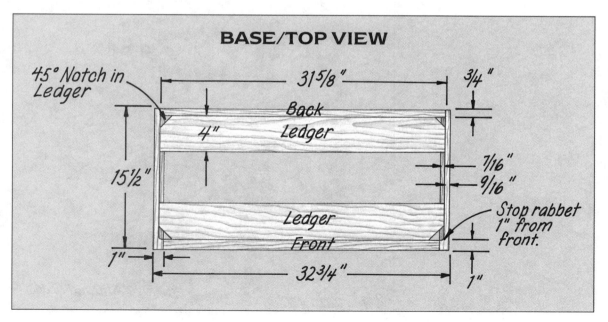

BASE/TOP VIEW

45° Notch in Ledger

31 5/8"

3/4"

Back Ledger

4"

15 1/2"

7/16"

9/16"

Ledger Front

Stop rabbet 1" from front.

1"

32 3/4"

1"

with changes in humidity. After you raise the panels, trim
$3/32$ inch from the panel edges parallel to the grain to
allow for this expansion.

2 **Chip carve the panels.** I love to chip carve because it
really makes a piece special. You can omit the
carving, of course, but you'll find it's easy to learn. The
only tools you need are two simple knives: one for
stabbing and one for cutting.

Enlarge the design shown in the Chip Carving Pattern,
and transfer it to the panel fronts. If you are new at chip
carving, practice carving on some scrap. For more
on this technique, see "Chip Carving" on page 402.

3 **Mortise the door stiles.** Lay out the mortises on all
of the door stiles as shown in the Mortise and Tenon
Layout. Drill a series of adjacent holes between the
layout lines. Clean out the rest of the waste with a chisel.

4 **Rabbet the locking stile and its mating stiles.** The
doors are rabbeted so that they overlap where they
meet, as shown in the Door Detail. Rout a rabbet in each
door stile as shown.

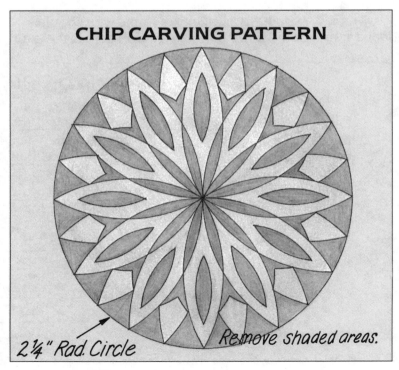

CHIP CARVING PATTERN

2 ¼" Rad. Circle

Remove shaded areas.

5 **Tenon the door rails.** Cut the tenons on the ends of the door rails with a dado cutter set up in a table saw. Adjust the blade height so that the resulting tenons will fit snugly in their mortises. Then cut 1/2-inch shoulders on the tenons, as shown in the Mortise and Tenon Layout.

6 **Cut the panel slot.** Put a 1/4-inch slotting cutter with a ball-bearing guide in your table-mounted router. Adjust the setup to cut a groove centered in the rails and stiles. Rout a slot along the entire length of the rails and from mortise to mortise in the stiles. Cut a groove on both sides of the middle rails.

7 **Assemble and hang the doors.** Test fit the doors. The panels should be snug in the panel slots, but not so tight that they might cause the rails and stiles to split. The tenons should also be snug but not overly tight. Make any necessary adjustments; then glue the tenons into the mortises and clamp each door together.

Make sure that the doors are square by measuring diagonally from corner to corner. If these measurements are equal, the assembly is square. If not, make any necessary adjustments. Make sure that you don't get any glue in the panel slots or on the panels. If the panels get glued into their slots, they are guaranteed to split.

While the doors are still in their clamps, drill 1/4-inch holes through the tenons and tap in 1/4-inch square pegs as shown in the Mortise and Tenon Layout.

When the glue is dry, fit the doors to the face frame. Because the door is the exact size of the opening, some stock will have to be trimmed from the doors' edges to produce a perfect fit. Trim the door edges to produce about 1/8-inch total free play, side to side and up and down. Hang the doors with butterfly hinges, as shown in the Front View.

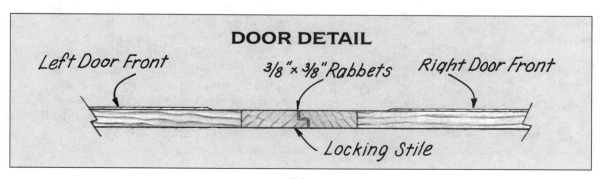

DOOR DETAIL

Left Door Front

3/8" x 3/8" Rabbets

Right Door Front

Locking Stile

PLANING WOOD BY HAND

Planing wood by hand was once the only way to get a flat piece of wood. Modern cabinetmakers reach for the plane for one of two reasons: to do some fine fitting, or as an alternative to sanding.

When hand-planing instead of sanding, try to recreate the gently undulating surface that a country craftsman's plane would have left. You can do the majority of your hand planing with a number-four metal bench plane. To get a coun-

GRINDING PROFILE

Grind bevel to form a curve.

1/32"

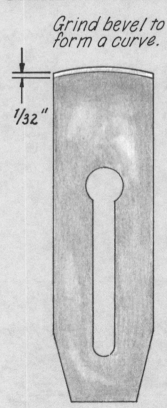

try look and feel, grind the plane blade so that the cutting edge has a gentle curve, as shown in the Grinding Profile.

The key to successful planing is a razor-sharp blade.

Sharpen the blade.

Before you grind the curve on the plane blade, flatten and smooth the back of the blade to a mirror-like surface. Do this by first sanding away the semicircular marks left on the blade by the manufacturing process. Tape a piece of 220-grit sandpaper to the surface of your table saw and carefully slide the back of the plane blade over it until you have completely removed the semicircular marks. Be sure to keep the blade perfectly flat as you remove these marks or you will round-over the blade edges.

Next, polish the back of your plane blade until it has a gray sheen with an 800- to 1200-grit polishing stone. Japanese water stones or ceramic stones are preferable to messy oil stones. When you've polished the back to a gray sheen, switch to a 6000- to 8000-grit stone and polish the back to a mirror shine. Without this mirror shine your blade can never be razor-sharp.

Next, grind the curve on the grinding wheel. The curve should follow the profile shown, and should have a 25-degree bevel. Don't worry too much about being exactly at 25 degrees. A sharp plane is a forgiving tool, even if the bevel is off by a good 5 degrees.

When you've ground the bevel to the profile shown, polish the edge first on the 800- to 1200-grit stone. Hold the bevel flat on the stone and push forward. Roll the blade slightly from side to side as you push, in order to sharpen the entire width of the blade. Repeat the process on the 6000- to 8000-grit stone to produce a razor-sharp edge. Flip the blade to its back occasionally and run it across the stone once to remove any burr that the sharpening created.

For a supersharp edge, create what is called a micro-bevel at the tip of the blade. Raise the back of the blade slightly—about 3 degrees—and drag the bevel along the length of the stone once (and only once!). The resulting edge is small, but it's sharp enough to shave with.

Attach the chip breaker. The leading edge of the breaker should be about $1/16$ inch from the cutting edge of the blade. Put both in the plane, and you are ready to make some curls.

Plane the wood.

1 Adjust the depth of the blade.
Sight down the bottom (or sole) of the plane and raise the blade until its curved profile just begins to appear.

While still sighting down the length of the plane bottom, center the curved profile of the blade on the width of the plane bottom by adjusting it with the lateral adjustment lever. This lever is between the plane handle and the plane blade on most planes.

2 Guide the plane with both hands.
A number-four bench plane is designed for two-hand control. Don't just push the plane from the back handle and let your other hand ride along on the knob. Exert pressure with both hands as you move the plane along the wood. Push the plane with your whole body, not just your arms.

Sight down the sole of the plane and adjust the blade.

Guide the plane by exerting equal pressure with both hands.

(continued)

PLANING WOOD BY HAND–Continued

3 Plane the wood. Plane in long, even strokes with the grain, and move systematically across the width of the stock, stroke by stroke. The plane should remove paper-thin curls from the surface of the wood. When you first start hand planing, it may be difficult to tell if your plane strokes have covered the complete width of the board. As a visual aid, draw a series of pencil lines across the stock. If all of the pencil lines have been removed by planing, then you can be sure you haven't missed any of the surface.

On longer boards, one long stroke may not be enough to cover the length of the board. Partial strokes with the plane can leave marks in the wood where the blade enters and leaves the wood. To minimize these marks, plane the front of the board first, then plane the middle of the board, and finally plane the bottom end of the board. As you move down along the length of the longer board, you will remove the marks where the blade entered the wood. Minimize the marks from the blade exiting the wood by pulling the blade out of the wood very gradually.

4 Slice across the knots. Knots tend to be much denser than the rest of the wood, and this can cause problems when hand planing. Planing straight and fast into a knot can cause the blade edge to shatter. When this happens, you must regrind and hone the edge. To keep the edge from shattering, plane slowly and hold the plane on an angle to the grain. In this way, you slice through the knot rather than plowing into it.

As a visual aid, draw a series of pencil lines across the stock, and plane the stock in long, systematic strokes.

Hold the plane at an angle to the grain and slice across the knots.

STEREO CABINET
by Glenn Bostock

Harmony is the hallmark of fine musical composition, and the same is true of good woodworking design.

The stereo cabinet shown here is a duet featuring two of North America's beautiful hardwoods —oak and walnut. The top and sides are oak, the base and door frame are walnut. An oak trim plays lightly along the inside of the door frame, culminating in a keystone inlay at the top. To save on the cost, make the cabinet back and drawer bottoms from plywood.

The cabinet has a full overlay glass door to keep dust from your valuable equipment without precluding the use of a remote control. Ventilation is provided through holes drilled in the cabinet back to keep your components cool.

I designed and built this cabinet back when we still spun 12-inch vinyl disks. Just a couple of modifications would bring the cabinet into the era of the compact disk. Make the drawer 2 inches taller and move each fixed shelf up 2 inches, and you'll create a handy CD drawer while retaining shelf space for those irreplaceable records. You could add dividers to keep the CDs organized. You might add another adjustable shelf for the CD player, or perhaps two if you need a place for a tape player or VCR.

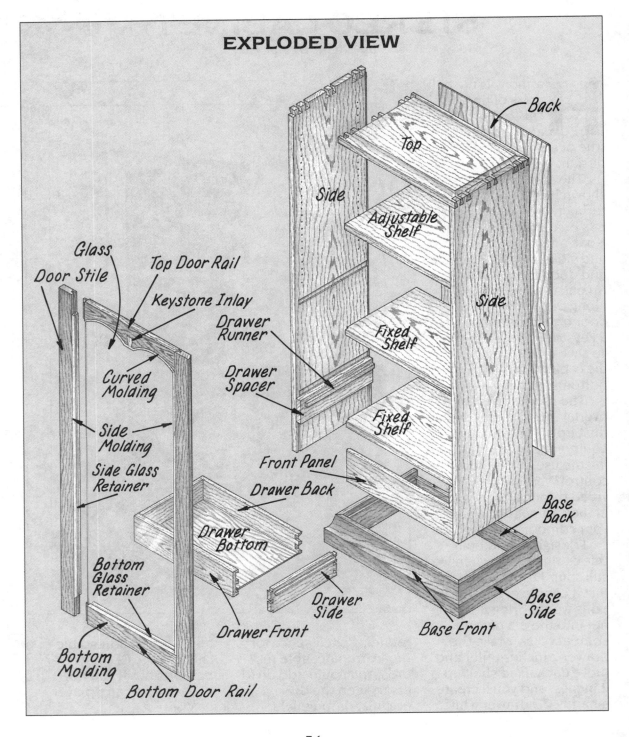

EXPLODED VIEW

Back

Top

Side

Adjustable Shelf

Side

Glass

Door Stile

Top Door Rail

Keystone Inlay

Drawer Runner

Curved Molding

Drawer Spacer

Fixed Shelf

Side Molding

Fixed Shelf

Side Glass Retainer

Front Panel

Drawer Back

Bottom Glass Retainer

Drawer Bottom

Base Back

Bottom Molding

Drawer Front

Drawer Side

Base Side

Bottom Door Rail

Base Front

Make the case.

1 **Cut the pieces to size.** Mill the wood for the top, sides, front, and rear panels to the sizes in the Materials List. If necessary, glue up boards for the wider pieces.

2 **Shape the top.** Cut the raised profile of the top, as shown in the Top Detail, with a 1 1/2-inch-cutting-width cove panel cutter in a shaper or table-mounted router. You also can make this profile on the table saw as described in "Cove Cutting on the Table Saw" on page 361. If you cut the profile on the table saw, offset the fence to cut a half cove in the edge of the panel.

Quick Tip: When removing a lot of wood with a router or shaper, make several shallow passes instead of one or two heavy ones. Removing wood a little at a time puts less strain on the tool and prevents chipping.

MATERIALS LIST

Part	Dimension	Part	Dimension
Case		Stiles (2)	$1'' \times 2^{1}/_{8}'' \times 49''$
Top	$1^{1}/_{2}'' \times 13^{1}/_{4}'' \times 20^{3}/_{8}''$	Curved molding blank	$1^{1}/_{4}'' \times 2^{1}/_{2}'' \times 18''$
Sides (2)	$3/_{4}'' \times 13^{1}/_{4}'' \times 52''$	Side molding stock	$3/_{8}'' \times 1/_{2}'' \times 96''$
Front panel	$3/_{4}'' \times 4^{1}/_{2}'' \times 19^{3}/_{8}''$	Bottom molding stock	$3/_{8}'' \times 1/_{2}'' \times 20''$
Rear panel	$3/_{4}'' \times 4^{1}/_{2}'' \times 19^{3}/_{8}''$	Side glass retainers (2)	$3/_{8}'' \times 3/_{8}'' \times 48''$
Fixed shelves (2)	$3/_{4}'' \times 12^{3}/_{4}'' \times 19^{3}/_{8}''$	Bottom glass retainer	$3/_{8}'' \times 3/_{8}'' \times 20''$
Back	$1/_{4}'' \times 19^{3}/_{8}'' \times 47^{1}/_{2}''$	Keystone inlay	$3/_{16}'' \times 1^{1}/_{4}'' \times 1^{1}/_{2}''$
Adjustable shelf	$3/_{4}'' \times 12^{3}/_{4}'' \times 18^{7}/_{8}''$		
Base		**HARDWARE**	
Front	$1^{3}/_{4}'' \times 4'' \times 23^{5}/_{8}''$	1 piece $1/_{8}''$-thick tempered glass, cut to fit	
Sides (2)	$1^{3}/_{4}'' \times 4'' \times 14^{7}/_{8}''$	As needed, #4 $\times$ 3/4" brass flathead wood screws	
Back	$3/_{4}'' \times 3^{1}/_{4}'' \times 21^{1}/_{8}''$	As needed, #8 $\times$ 1 1/2" drywall screws	
Glue blocks (2)	$3/_{4}'' \times 3/_{4}'' \times 3''$	As needed, #8 $\times$ 1 1/4" drywall screws	
Drawer		As needed, #8 $\times$ 1" drywall screws	
Front	$3/_{4}'' \times 3^{1}/_{2}'' \times 17^{5}/_{16}''$	As needed, #8 $\times$ 3/4" drywall screws	
Sides (2)	$5/_{8}'' \times 3^{1}/_{2}'' \times 13^{1}/_{4}''$	3 European-style cabinet hinges, 110° swing	
Back	$5/_{8}'' \times 3'' \times 17^{5}/_{16}''$	As needed, 4d finishing nails	
Bottom	$1/_{4}'' \times 11^{1}/_{2}'' \times 16^{9}/_{16}''$	4 adjustable shelf brackets	
Drawer spacers (2)	$3/_{4}'' \times 3^{1}/_{2}'' \times 12^{3}/_{4}''$		
Drawer runners (2)	$3/_{8}'' \times 1/_{2}'' \times 11^{5}/_{8}''$		
Door			
Top rail	$1'' \times 2^{3}/_{4}'' \times 17^{1}/_{8}''$		
Bottom rail	$1'' \times 2^{5}/_{8}'' \times 17^{1}/_{8}''$		

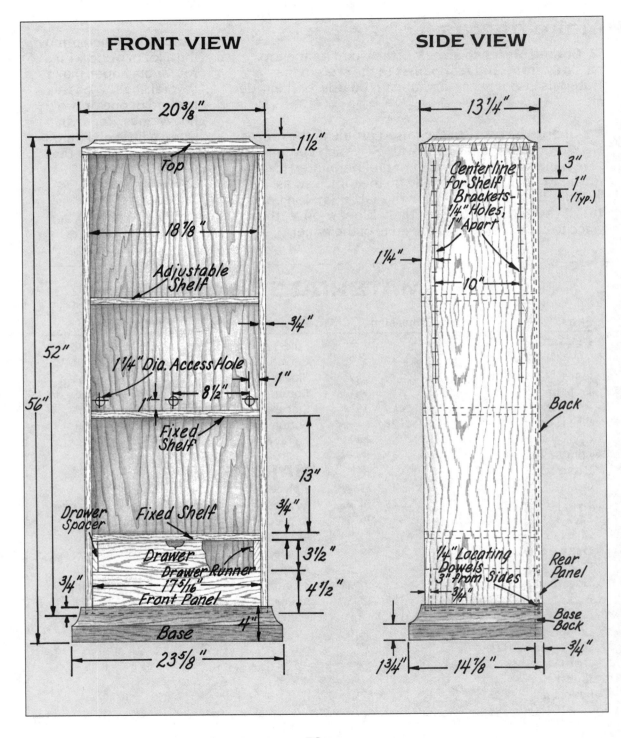

FRONT VIEW

SIDE VIEW

20³⁄₈"

13¹⁄₄"

1½"

Top

3"

1" (Typ.)

18⁷⁄₈"

Centerline for Shelf Brackets— ¼" Holes, 1" Apart

Adjustable Shelf

¾"

1¼"

10"

52"

1¼" Dia. Access Hole

56"

8½"

1"

1"

Fixed Shelf

13"

Back

¾"

Drawer Spacer

Fixed Shelf

3½"

Drawer

Drawer Runner

17⁵⁄₁₆"

¼" Locating Dowels 3" From Sides

Rear Panel

4½"

Front Panel

¾"

Base Back

¾"

Base

4"

23⁵⁄₈"

1¾"

14⁷⁄₈"

¾"

3 Cut the dovetails. Lay out the dovetails on the top as shown in the Top Detail. First cut the tails, which are on the cabinet sides. Trace around the tails to lay out the pins on the top. For more on dovetailing, see "Cutting Through Dovetails" on page 81.

4 Cut grooves for the front and rear panels. Two 4 1/2-inch-wide panels fit into the bottom of the cabinet as shown in the Front and Side Views. The inside front and back edges of each side panel are grooved to house tenons on the front and rear panels, as shown in the Back Detail. Start from the bottom of each side panel and rout the groove 1/4 inch wide × 1/4 inch deep. Make the groove 1/4 inch from the front edge and 4 1/2 inches long. Don't worry if the groove runs a little long; it will be covered by the drawer spacer.

5 Cut the shelf dadoes. Lay out the two fixed shelves according to the measurements given in the Front View. The shelves fit in dadoes 3/4 inch wide and 1/4 inch deep. Cut these dadoes with a router guided by a straightedge. Stop the dadoes 3/4 inch from the front edge. Square the front of each dado with a chisel.

6 Drill holes for the adjustable shelf pins. The adjustable shelves are supported by shelf pins. Lay out a series of holes for the pins. First lay out center lines for the holes as shown in the Side View. Start the holes 3

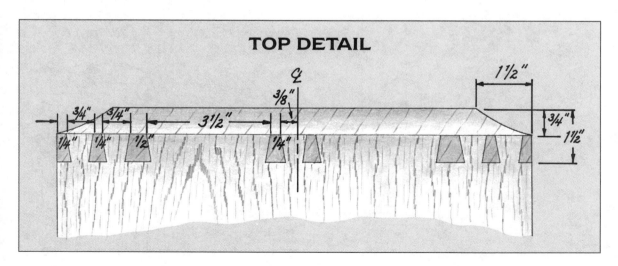

TOP DETAIL

inches down from the top of the cabinet and stop them approximately 3 1/2 inches from the upper dado. These holes can be spaced easily by using a piece of peg board as a drilling guide.

7 Make the shelves. Plane the shelf stock to fit in the shelf dadoes. The wood should slide into the dado easily without leaving gaps. When the wood is the proper thickness, cut fixed and adjustable shelves to the dimensions given in the Materials List.

The fixed shelves are wider than the stopped dado is long. Cut notches in the front corners of the two fixed shelves, so that you can slide the shelves into place. Cut

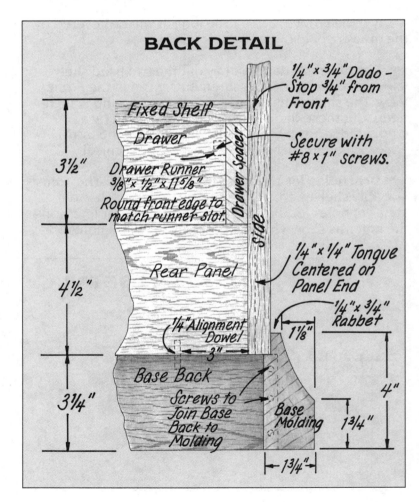

BACK DETAIL

1/4" x 3/4" Dado – Stop 3/4" from Front

Fixed Shelf

Drawer

Secure with #8 x 1" screws.

Drawer Runner 3/8" x 1/2" x 11 5/8"

Round front edge to match runner slot.

Drawer Spacer

Side

1/4" x 1/4" Tongue Centered on Panel End

Rear Panel

3 1/2"

4 1/2"

1/4" Alignment Dowel

3"

1/4" x 3/4" Rabbet

1 1/8"

Base Back

Screws to Join Base Back to Molding

Base Molding

4"

1 3/4"

3 1/4"

1 3/4"

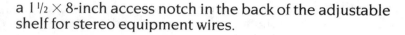

a 1 1/2 × 8-inch access notch in the back of the adjustable shelf for stereo equipment wires.

8 **Make the front and rear panels.** Cut the front and rear panels to the dimensions in the Materials List. Cut tenons on the panels with a dado cutter on the table saw. Check your setup beforehand by making a tongue on a piece of scrap and test fitting it into the groove.

9 **Finish sand the inside.** Finish sand the inside surfaces of the sides, top, and front and back panels. Finish sand both faces of the shelves.

10 **Assemble the case.** Test assemble the case and make any necessary adjustments. When everything fits perfectly, disassemble the case to prepare for gluing up. Put glue on the dovetails and in the dadoes and grooves. Assemble the case and clamp it. Make sure that the case is square, and make any necessary adjustments.

11 **Rabbet the back of the case.** Unclamp the case when the glue has dried. Put a 3/8-inch piloted rabbeting bit in the router and adjust depth to 1/2 inch. Rabbet the back inside edges of the case for the cabinet back. Square the corners of the rabbet with a chisel.

12 **Cut and install the back.** Cut the back to fit inside the rabbets, using the dimensions in the Materials List as a guide. Drill 1-inch access holes at the points indicated in the Front View.
   Test fit the back, then put glue into the rabbets and install the back with 4d finishing nails.

Make the base.

1 **Make the base molding.** Select a piece of 8/4 (eight-quarters) walnut long enough to make all three pieces of molding plus an extra side which you'll use to test setups. Mill the stock to the sizes in the Materials List, adding 2 inches of extra length to each piece. Cut the cove in the molding on the table saw as described in "Cove Cutting on the Table Saw" on page 361.

2 **Rabbet the base molding for the case.** The base sits on a rabbet in the top inside edges of the molding, as shown in the Back Detail. Cut it with a ³/₄-inch straight bit in a table-mounted router. Set bit height to ¹/₄ inch and set the fence so that it just touches the bit. If you prefer, cut the rabbet with a dado blade on the table saw.

3 **Miter and fit the molding.** Tilt the table saw blade to 45 degrees. Use the extra side and one end of the front base molding to test the setup. When you get a perfect 90-degree corner, miter the other end of the front base molding and the mating ends of the actual side pieces. Set the side pieces in place on the bottom of the case and scribe for 90-degree cuts flush with the back. Set the blade to 90 degrees and make the cuts.

4 **Rabbet the side molding pieces for the base back.** Rout ¹/₂-inch-wide × ³/₄-inch-deep rabbets along the end grain of the moldings, as shown in the Back Detail. Note the rabbets stop when they meet the rabbet you just routed. Rout the rabbets in a series of passes with a ¹/₂-inch-radius piloted rabbeting bit in the router as

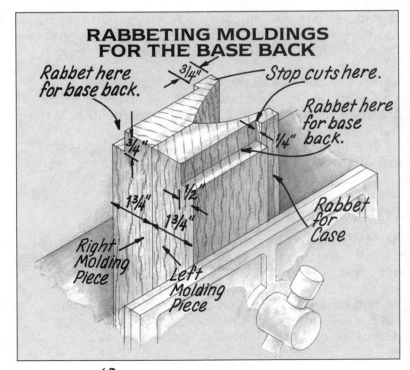

RABBETING MOLDINGS FOR THE BASE BACK

Rabbet here for base back.

³/₄"

Stop cuts here.

Rabbet here for base back.

³/₄"

¹/₄"

¹/₂"

1³/₄"

1³/₄"

Rabbet for Case

Right Molding Piece

Left Molding Piece

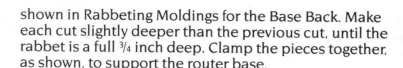

shown in Rabbeting Moldings for the Base Back. Make each cut slightly deeper than the previous cut, until the rabbet is a full ¾ inch deep. Clamp the pieces together, as shown, to support the router base.

5 **Make the base back.** Put the side moldings in place on the cabinet and measure across the back from rabbet to rabbet to get an exact length for the base back. Cut it to that length.

6 **Assemble the base.** Cut two blocks from scrap to reinforce the miter joints. Glue and clamp the blocks on the inside corners of the front piece, as shown in the Base Miter Joint Detail. Predrill and countersink each block for #8 × 1½-inch drywall screws. Insert the screws and remove the clamps.

Assemble the base one miter at a time. Apply glue to the joint, and glue and screw the support block in place, as shown. Glue and screw the base back in its rabbets.

Stand the cabinet in the base to make sure the base is square. Line adjoining surfaces of the base and cabinet with wax paper to avoid accidentally gluing the two together. Allow the glue to dry.

Make the drawer.

1 **Cut the drawer parts to size.** Mill wood for the drawer front, back, and sides to dimensions in the

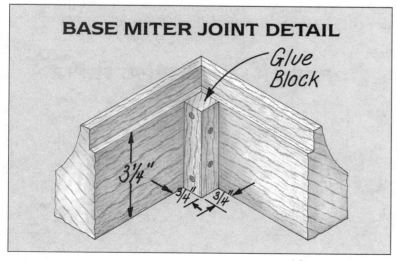

BASE MITER JOINT DETAIL

Glue Block

3¼"

¾" ¾"

Materials List. Notice that the back is ½ inch narrower than the sides. This allows the bottom to slide in from the rear.

2 **Cut the joints.** Lay out the dovetails on the ends of the drawer front and back as shown in the Drawer Detail. (See "Cutting Through Dovetails" on page 81 and "Cutting Half-Blind Dovetails" on page 155.)

3 **Rout the grooves for the bottom.** Cut these grooves with a ¼-inch straight bit in the router table. Set bit height to ¼ inch and set the fence ¼ inch from the bit.

Rout the groove on the front first. If necessary, adjust the location of the groove slightly, so that you don't rout through the dovetail pins. Rout the groove the entire length of the drawer front and sides.

4 **Rout the grooves for the drawer slides.** The drawers are side mounted: A runner on the cabinet side fits in a groove in the drawer side, as shown in the Drawer Detail. Rout the groove with a ½-inch straight bit. Guide the cut with the router's fence attachment.

5 **Cut the handle and sand the drawer parts.** Lay out the handle, as shown in the Drawer Handle Pattern, and cut it out with the band saw. Scrape and sand it to final shape. Finish sand all the inside surfaces.

6 **Cut the drawer bottom.** Test fit the drawer and cut a plywood bottom to fit in the grooves, using the dimensions in the Materials List as a guide.

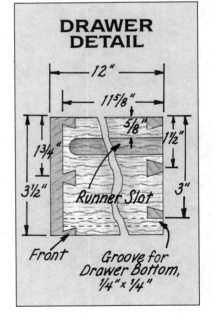

DRAWER DETAIL

12"

11⅝"

5⁄8"

1½"

1¾"

3½"

3"

Runner Slot

Front

Groove for Drawer Bottom, ¼" x ¼"

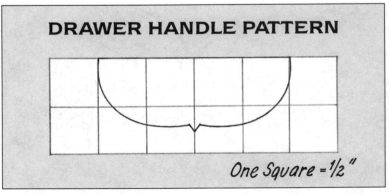

DRAWER HANDLE PATTERN

One Square = ½"

◇ ◇ ─────────────────────── ◇ ◇

7 **Assemble the drawer.** Apply glue to the mating surfaces of the dovetails, and assemble the drawer. Slip the bottom into place. Clamp the drawer, and make sure it's square. When the glue dries, drill a hole for a #4 × 3/4-inch wood screw and screw through the bottom into the drawer back.

8 **Make the drawer spacers.** Mill wood for the drawer spacers to the dimensions in the Materials List. Orient the grain so that it is perpendicular to the long dimension of the pieces. Cut the spacers to fit between the front panel and the lower fixed shelf, as shown in the Front View. Also make sure the drawer fits easily into the case with the spacers in place. If the fit is too snug, plane equally small increments from the thickness of both spacers. Sand the front edge of each spacer.

9 **Make the drawer runners.** Mill wood for the runners to the dimensions in the Materials List. Round the front end of each runner to fit the rounded end of the runner slots on the drawer. Sand the two runners, and make sure they slide easily in the runner slots.

10 **Mount the drawer runners.** Drill and countersink three 7/32-inch holes along the length of each runner. Position the runners 5/8 inch below the top of the spacer. Mount the runners on the spacers with #8 × 1-inch drywall screws. The holes are slightly oversized to allow for some adjustment when fine tuning the fit of the drawer.

11 **Install the spacers.** Screw the spacers to the inside of the cabinet with #8 × 1 1/4-inch drywall screws. Place the screws as shown in the Side View.

12 **Fit the drawer to the case.** Adjust the runners, if necessary, until the drawer front closes flush with the front of the case.

Make the door.

1 **Cut the parts to size.** Mill wood for the door frame to the dimensions in the Materials List. (See the Door Detail.)

2 Mortise the stiles. Lay out the mortises as shown in the Door Frame Detail. Rout them on the table-mounted router with a $5/16$-inch-diameter straight bit. Guide the stock against the router table fence, and make the cut in a series of passes.

3 Make tenons on the rails. Make these stub tenons with a dado cutter on the table saw. Test the fit of the tenon in the mortise. Make any necessary adjustments, and cut the actual tenons.

4 Make the keystone inlay. Cut the inlay to the dimensions shown in the Door Frame Detail. Carefully plane and sand off any saw marks.

5 Shape the top rail. Lay out the curves for the top rail as shown in the Door Frame Detail. Cut out the rail along these lines, then scrape and sand the rail to final shape. With a sharp knife, scribe the shape of the keystone inlay. Rout and chisel out this recess to a depth of $1/8$ inch. Put glue into the recess and tap the inlay into place. Plane it flush to the face and bottom edge of the rail.

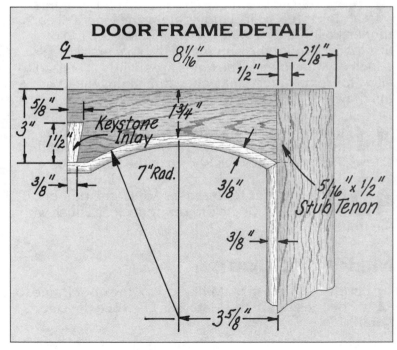

DOOR FRAME DETAIL

Make the curved molding.

1 **Mill the wood.** Mill wood for the curved molding to the dimensions in the Materials List. You'll make the molding in a series of steps. First you'll lay out and cut the top edge, which nestles against the door rail. Then you'll glue it into place. When the glue dries, you'll lay out and then cut the molding's bottom edge.

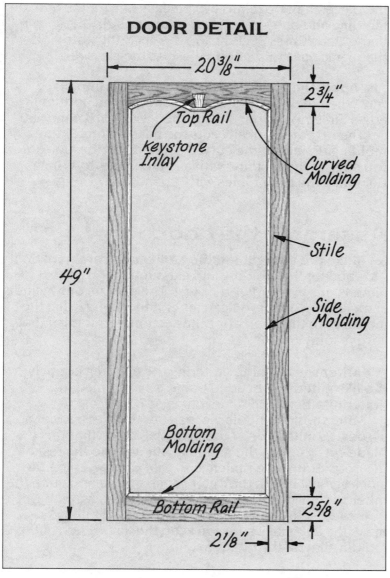

DOOR DETAIL

20 3/8"

2 3/4"

Top Rail

Keystone Inlay

Curved Molding

Stile

49"

Side Molding

Bottom Molding

Bottom Rail

2 5/8"

2 1/8"

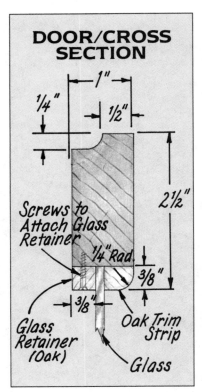

DOOR/CROSS SECTION

1"

1/4"

1/2"

2½"

Screws to Attach Glass Retainer

1/4" Rad.

3/8"

3/8"

Glass Retainer (Oak)

Oak Trim Strip

Glass

Quick Tip: If you do not have enough clamps to glue on a long strip of molding, use masking tape or duct tape to apply pressure to the joint. Simply stick the tape to one face of the door frame; then stretch it over the molding and stick it to the other face.

2 **Lay out the molding.** Put the molding blank behind the rail, and trace the curves in the rail onto the molding blank. Saw out the curved line, and carefully scrape and sand the blank to match the curve on the rail. When you have a perfect fit, mark one end of each piece so you can realign them.

3 **Rip the glass retainer.** The molding blank is thicker than the door frame members so that you can shape the piece, then rip it into two pieces—one for the outside molding and one for the glass retaining strip—as shown in the Door/Cross Section. Rip a ³/₈-inch-thick strip off the blank. Save this cutoff for use as the glass retainer.

4 **Apply the molding.** Glue the molding into place. When the glue dries, lay out and cut the bottom edge. First, rip the rail to a finished width of 3³/₈ inches.

The rip automatically cuts the flat sections of the molding. To lay out the curved sections, scribe along the top edge of the molding with a compass set to ³/₈ inch. Cut along the layout lines with a band saw.

Assemble the door.

1 **Make the straight molding and glass retainers.** Mill wood for the molding and glass retainers to the dimensions in the Materials List. The dimensions include extra length so that you can miter it to fit later. Glue the moldings to the door; apply no sections of molding that cover a joint.

2 **Miter the molding.** Mitering the molding is much like mitering a beaded frame, as explained in "Mitering a Beaded Frame" on page 70.

Miter the straight pieces first. Set the blade to cut a 45-degree miter. Adjust the blade height so that the blade cuts through the molding, but not into the rest of the door. Adjust the rip fence so that you can guide the stock against it with the miter gauge and can position the miter as shown in the Door Frame Detail.

Readjust the fence to set up the top rail miter. As you make the cut, make sure you keep the flat section of the molding flat on the table saw.

3 **Assemble the door.** Clamp the door together without glue. Make any necessary adjustments. Apply glue, and clamp the door together.

4 **Rout the door frame.** Round-over the inner front edges of the door frame with a 1/4-inch roundover bit. Rout a lip around the outside back surface of the frame, as shown in the Door/Cross Section, with a 1/2-inch cove bit. This will provide a recessed finger hold for opening the door.

Miter the top rail, keeping the center portion flat on the saw table.

5 **Fit the glass retaining strips.** Plane the curved cutoff from the molding blank to match the width of the straight glass retainers. Fit the glass retainers to the frame. Rather than miter the corners, you can cut each retainer square and slightly shorter than required. The gap that results will not be noticeable from outside the cabinet.

The retaining strips screw into place. Position the strips by cutting a narrow spacer from 1/8-inch Masonite. Sandwich the Masonite spacers between the molding and the retainer. The Masonite spacers fill in the space that will hold the glass. Drill through the retainer strip into the door for the screws. After the holes have been drilled, remove the Masonite spacers. Install the glass after the cabinet has been finished.

6 **Hang the door.** Hang the door with European-style cabinet hinges according to the manufacturer's instructions.

Quick Tip: Temporarily attach the molding with #4 × 3/4-inch steel screws. It will make driving softer brass screws easier when the time comes.

Finish the piece.

1 **Apply finish.** Finish sand the cabinet and apply finish. I find two or three coats of Watco Danish Oil, applied according to the directions on the can, give this cabinet an elegant look.

2 **Install the glass.** Make a pattern from 1/8-inch Masonite that fits into the glass rabbets. Have tempered glass cut for your door and install it. Attach the glass retainers with #4 × 3/4-inch brass flathead wood screws. Rehang the door.

MITERING A BEADED FRAME

Mitering the bead on a beaded frame isn't very difficult, but it does take precision. Whether your frames have mortises and tenons or are to be doweled together, all of the miters are cut on the table saw with the blade set at 45 degrees.

1 Miter the beads on the *ends* of the rails first. Guide the stock with a miter gauge set at 90 degrees. When mitering a tenoned rail, adjust the table saw fence so that when you slide the end of the tenon against it the blade miters the bead. The table saw blade should be just high enough to cut the miter; otherwise it may damage the tenon. If the rail isn't tenoned, clamp a wooden auxiliary fence to your table saw fence and adjust it so that the top of the blade just cuts into the auxiliary fence. To miter the bead, guide the end of the rail along the fence with a miter gauge set at 90 degrees.

2 Miter the beads on the edge of the rails. Lay out and miter the beads wherever necessary along the edges of the rails. Draw the layout marks on the back of the rails to reflect the width and position of any adjoining stiles. Line up the marks with the blade, and again guide the stock with the miter gauge as you cut the miters. Clean up the waste between the miters with a chisel.

3 Miter the bead at the ends of the stiles. When the miters have been cut into the rails, miter the bead at the end of each stile. Guide the cut with

Set the table saw blade at 45 degrees, and miter the beads on the ends of the rails.

Line up the layout lines with the blade, and miter the bead wherever necessary along the edges of the rails.

Miter the beads on the ends of the stiles.

both the miter gauge and the rip fence. Adjust the rip fence to position the miter properly: The distance between the outside of the miter and the end of the board should equal the width of the rail. Clean away the waste between the miter and end of the stile with a back-saw and chisel.

4 Miter the bead along the edges of the stiles. Finally, lay out and cut miters, if necessary, along the stiles' length to accept any adjoining rails. Draw layout lines on the back of the stiles, and line up the layout lines with the blade. Guide the stock through the blade with a miter gauge, and clean up the waste between the miters with a chisel.

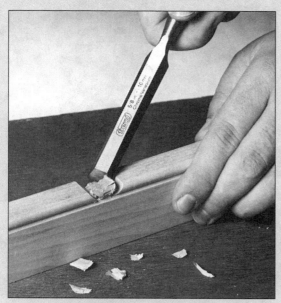

Lay out and cut miters wherever necessary along the edges of the stiles.

DISPLAY CASE
by Tom Groller

Here is a handsome case that can easily be adapted to display various kinds of collections. I designed it to be hung on the wall to keep the collection up and out of the way.

The glass door keeps the collection free of dust. You can customize the dimensions to fit the objects you have in mind.

If you collect light, small objects, you could cover the inside of the back with

cork and use it as you would a bulletin board. For larger, heavier objects, you could add a shelf or two. You might even add a small light inside the top of the case.

Make sure you know

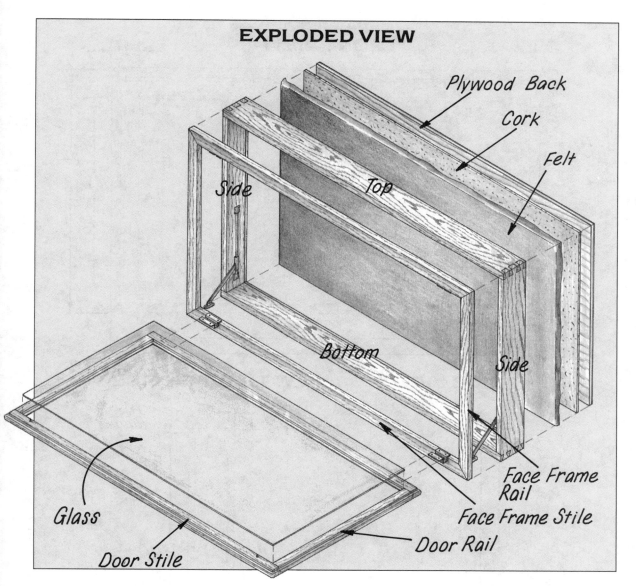

EXPLODED VIEW

Plywood Back

Cork

Felt

Side

Top

Bottom

Side

Face Frame Rail

Face Frame Stile

Door Rail

Glass

Door Stile

how you will hang your display case before you begin building it, since that can affect details of construction. I made this case of walnut; choose any hardwood you like.

You'll start this project by building the dovetailed box for the display case. Make and fit the door to the box. Add the cork and fabric-covered back to complete the piece.

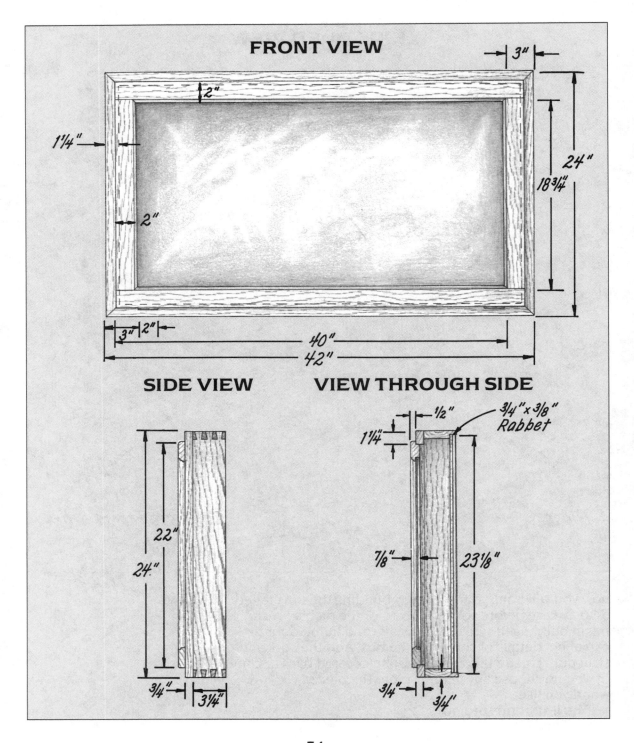

FRONT VIEW

3"

2"

1¼"

2"

24"

18¾"

3" 2"

40"

42"

SIDE VIEW

VIEW THROUGH SIDE

½"

1¾"

¾" x ⅜"
Rabbet

22"

24."

⅞"

23⅛"

¾"

3¼"

¾"

¾"

Build the case and face frame.

1 Prepare the stock. Plane, joint, rip, and cut wood for all of the parts to the dimensions given in the Materials List, except the face frame. Cut the face frame about 1 inch longer than called for in the Materials List.

2 Cut the dovetails. Scribe lines around the case pieces, marking the length of the dovetails. Lay out the tails on the case sides as shown in the Dovetail Detail. Saw out the tails down to the scribe lines, and chisel out the waste between the tails. Trace around the tails with a knife to lay out the pins. Cut out the pins and chisel out the waste between them. Check the fit, paring away any excess with a sharp chisel.

For complete step-by-step instructions for making dovetails, see "Cutting Through Dovetails" on page 81.

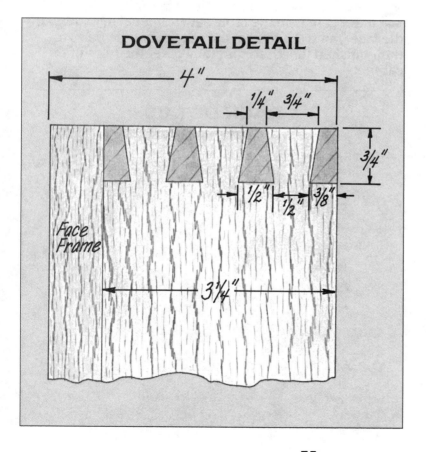

DOVETAIL DETAIL

Quick Tip: To get accurate miters, check your setup on some pieces of scrap. Set your table saw miter gauge at 45 degrees, and guide two pieces of scrap through the blade with it. Put the scrap miters together and make sure that the resulting angle equals 90 degrees. Adjust the miter gauge as necessary.

3 Rabbet the sides, top, and bottom to accept the back of the case. Cut a $3/8 \times 3/4$-inch stopped rabbet for the case back, as shown in the Back Detail, with a $3/4$-inch-diameter straight bit in a table-mounted router. Start and stop the cut $3/8$ inch from each end of the sides, top, and bottom. Guide the stock against the router table fence as you rout. Square the rounded ends of the rabbets with a chisel.

4 Sand the sides, top, and bottom, and glue the case together. Sand the inside surfaces of the sides, top, and bottom before you glue the case together. Be careful not to sand the dovetails and pins.

On a flat surface, glue and clamp the dovetails. Measure corner to corner to make sure the case is square. Clean up any excess glue.

5 Miter the frame parts. With a miter box, or with the miter gauge on the table saw, miter each member of the face frame. As you cut the miters, cut the parts to their finished length so that they cover the front of the cabinet.

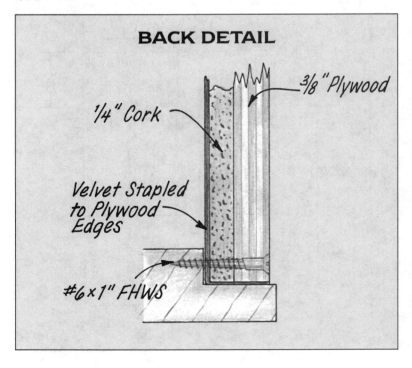

BACK DETAIL

3/8" Plywood

1/4" Cork

Velvet Stapled to Plywood Edges

#6 x 1" FHWS

When the parts have been mitered, glue and clamp them to the case.

Make the door.

1 **Cut the rail and stile joints.** The *cope-and-stick* joint is simple to make with a set of router bits. One bit cuts a profile on the edge of the parts. A second bit cuts a profile on the ends of the parts. The two profiles nestle together.

I cut the cope and stick as shown in the Door Detail with a Bosch Ogee Stile-and-Rail Set #85625M. The stile-and-rail set is made up of two router bit assemblies: one that cuts the cope, and one that cuts the stick. For complete step-by-step directions on cope-and-stick doors, see "Cope-and-Stick Joinery" on page 96.

As you follow the directions, note that I didn't build this door in quite the normal way. The horizontal door parts get the joinery normally associated with the stiles. The vertical parts receive the treatment normally associated with the rails. It may help to imagine that this door is lying on its side.

MATERIALS LIST

Part	Dimension
Case	
Sides (2)	$3/4'' \times 3\,1/4'' \times 24''$
Top/bottom (1 each)	$3/4'' \times 3\,1/4'' \times 42''$
Plywood back	$3/8'' \times 23\,1/8'' \times 41\,1/8''$
Cork	$1/4'' \times 23\,1/8'' \times 41\,1/4''$
Face Frame	
Rails (2)	$3/4'' \times 1\,1/4'' \times 42''$
Stiles (2)	$3/4'' \times 1\,1/4'' \times 24''$
Door	
Rails (2)	$7/8'' \times 2'' \times 40''$
Stiles (2)	$7/8'' \times 2'' \times 18\,3/4''$

HARDWARE

1 piece $1/8'' \times 18\,5/8'' \times 36\,5/8''$ glass (for door)
1 piece $27'' \times 45''$ velvet
As needed, #6 × 1" flathead wood screws

As needed, #12 × 2½" roundhead wood screws and matching washers
2 brass hangers (optional), $9/16'' \times 2\,1/16''$. Available from The Woodworkers' Store, 21801 Industrial Blvd., Rogers, MN 55374. Part #27557.
3 semi-concealed 2" brass hinges. Available from The Woodworkers' Store. Part #26997.
2 brass ball catches. Available from The Woodworkers' Store. Part #28613.
1 right-hand drop-front support. Available from the Woodworkers' Store. Part #30379.
1 left-hand drop-front support. Available from The Woodworkers' Store. Part #30395.
12' vinyl quarter-round molding

◇ ◇ ◇ ◇

2 **Assemble the door.** On a flat surface, glue and clamp the rails to the stiles. Make sure that the stiles are even with the ends of the rails, and measure corner to corner to make sure the door is square. The door is square when the diagonals are equal. Make any necessary adjustments, and allow the glue to dry.

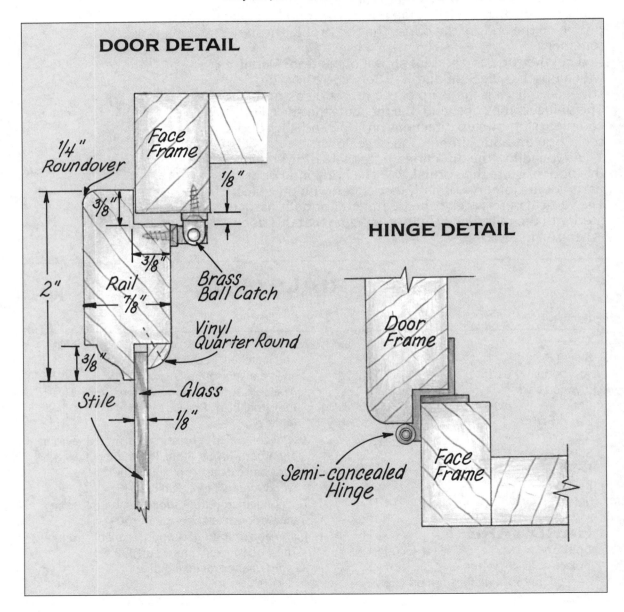

DOOR DETAIL

Face Frame

1/4" Roundover

3/8"

3/8"

1/8"

Rail

2"

7/8"

Brass Ball Catch

Vinyl Quarter Round

3/8"

Glass

Stile

1/8"

HINGE DETAIL

Door Frame

Face Frame

Semi-concealed Hinge

3 **Rout the rabbet for the glass.** As shown in the Door Detail, the glass fits into a $3/8 \times 3/8$-inch rabbet cut in the back of the door. The cope-and-stick cutters already cut a groove, which happens to be the bottom of the rabbet. All you have to do to form the rabbet is remove the tongue that was left over when the groove was cut. Remove this tongue with a $3/8$-inch rabbeting bit in a hand-held router. Secure the door, face down, on your work bench, and rout away the tongue. Square the corners with a chisel.

4 **Rout the outside rabbet.** This rabbet allows the back of the door to set into the frame, as shown in the Door Detail. With the $3/8$-inch rabbeting bit still in your router, cut the $3/8 \times 3/8$-inch rabbet in the back edge of the door.

5 **Round-over the front edge.** The front edge of the door is rounded-over as shown in the Door Detail. With a $1/4$-inch-radius roundover bit in your router, round-over the edge of the door as shown. Sand the door frame, including both rabbets.

6 **Mount the door hardware.** Position the semi-concealed hinges on the case bottom as shown in the Hinge Detail. Drill and screw the hinges to the case. Place the door on the case and mark the hinge positions. Drill and screw the hinges to the door.

Attach the ball catches to the top of the display cabinet and door. Screw the catch to the cabinet top first, then fit the strike to the door frame as shown in the Door Detail.

Mount drop-front supports on each side of the door. Follow the manufacturer's instructions for installation of this hardware.

Remove the door and hardware, and apply a finish to the door and the case. I rubbed an oil finish into my display cabinet and then buffed on a coat of wax.

7 **Insert the door glass.** Have the glass cut to fit at your local glass supplier. Hold the glass in place with a $1/4$-inch quarter-round molding, mitered to fit the frame. Carefully attach the molding with small brads.

Make the back and hang the cabinet.

1 Assemble the back. The back is made of a ¼-inch-thick layer of cork covered with velvet and backed with ⅜-inch plywood, as shown in the Back Detail.

Start by checking the fit of the plywood back in the rabbet at the back of the case. The listed dimensions allow ¹⁄₁₆-inch clearance all around to allow for the velvet. Adjust the size, if necessary, to fit your case.

At this point you need to decide how you will hang your cabinet on the wall. To mount mine I drilled two ⅜-inch-diameter holes through the plywood back, and secured the cabinet to the wall with #12 × 2½-inch roundhead wood screws and matching washers. I drilled the holes on 16-inch centers to match my wall studs. If you choose this method, it is best to drill the holes now.

As an alternative, you could mount your cabinet with the brass hangers listed in the Materials List.

Next, glue the cork to the plywood. (Quarter-inch cork is sold at office supply stores and craft stores.) Cut the cork slightly oversized and glue it to the case back with contact cement. With a utility knife, trim the extra cork flush with the plywood edge.

When the cork has been glued into place, cover it with fabric. Stretch the velvet around the cork and plywood back. Staple the fabric into one end. Work your way across the back, stretching and stapling the cloth to top and bottom edges as you do. Staple the fabric into the second end. Trim off the excess fabric so that it does not show from the back.

2 Screw the back to the case. Drill and countersink the back for #6 × 1-inch flathead wood screws, and screw the back to the display case as shown in the Back Detail.

3 Attach the case to the wall. Attach the cabinet to the wall studs with two #12 × 2½-inch roundhead brass screws and washers, or hang the cabinet with hangers screwed to the back of the cabinet.

CUTTING THROUGH DOVETAILS

Dovetails are easy to cut. Really, they are. For some reason, over the years some sort of mystique has been built up around this straightforward, commonly used joint. If you are worried about cutting this joint, spend time practicing on some scrap. With a little patience and careful layout, you'll quickly find that you can cut dovetails like a pro. One rule you should always remember when working with wood is that you can always take away stock but you can't add stock. So always cut to the waste side of your layout lines, and pare away stock little by little until everything fits just right.

1 **Lay out the length of the pins and tails.** Set a marking gauge to the thickness of the sides, and scribe a line around each side as shown. This scribe line is the base of the tails and pins. When cutting the joint, be careful not to cut beyond this line.

2 **Lay out the tails.** First, lay out the tails with a sliding T-bevel set at the appropriate angle—usually 14 degrees. Extend the layout lines across the end grain of the tail with a square. Using the T-bevel, transfer the angle of the tails from the end grain down to the scribe line.

3 **Cut out the tails.** Saw down to the scribe line, cutting on the waste side of the layout lines. A Japanese dozuki (dovetail saw), like the one shown here, is easy to control and cuts crisp lines. Watch your layout lines carefully:

Follow the angle of tails, and make sure you don't cut past either one of the scribe lines.

4 **Remove the waste between the tails.** Cut away most of the waste between the tails with a coping saw, and then clean up the cut with a chisel. First put your chisel on the face of the board and chop toward the middle.

Lay out the length of the tails and pins with a marking gauge.

Lay out the angled tails with a sliding T-bevel.

(continued)

CUTTING THROUGH DOVETAILS—*Continued*

Remove the waste by chopping from the end. When you're halfway through the board, flip it over and chisel from the other side. Undercut slightly as shown to ease assembly of the joint.

5 Lay out the pins. For best results, lay out the pins by tracing around the tails. Hold the tails against the end grain of what will be the pins, and trace around the tails with a marking knife. Carry your layout lines down to the scribe lines, and clearly mark the waste with a pencil.

6 Cut out the pins. Saw along the layout lines to the scribe lines, and chisel away the waste as before. Test fit the dovetails. Pare the pins to fit the tails using a chisel if necessary.

Cut out the tails with a dovetail saw.

Scribe the pins with the tails as your guide.

Cut away the waste between the tails with a coping saw and chisel.

Remove the waste between the pins with a dovetail saw and chisel.

ARCHERY RACK
by Tom Groller

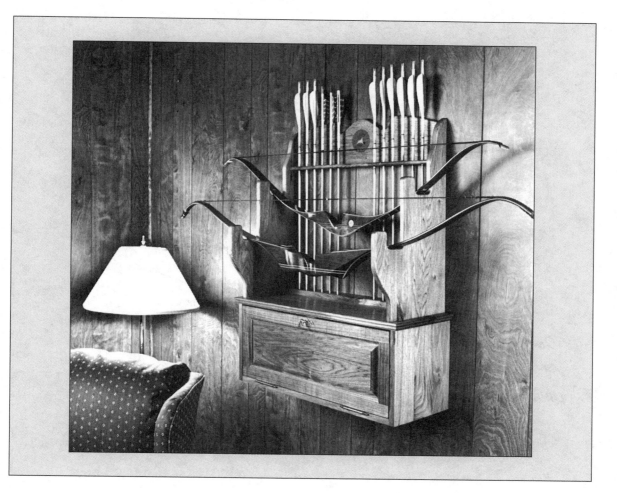

One of the great things about working in wood is that if you can't find something, you can build it. I designed this cabinet because I couldn't find an attractive way to display and store my archery equipment. The top has display racks, while the bottom door covers a storage cabinet subdivided for the odds and ends that seem to collect around any sport. Also included is a row of holes behind the bows that can hold a dozen arrows. You could easily adapt it for guns or other sports equipment.

The joinery is mortise and tenon throughout. A ready-made inlay in the crosspiece dresses up the design. The entire project is solid butternut, except the back, which is 1/2-inch plywood.

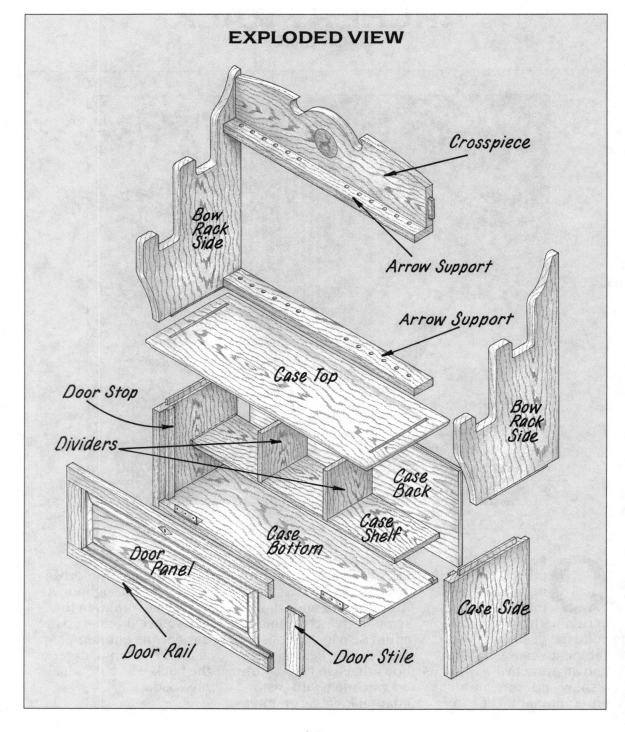

EXPLODED VIEW

Crosspiece

Bow Rack Side

Arrow Support

Arrow Support

Case Top

Door Stop

Dividers

Bow Rack Side

Case Back

Door Panel

Case Bottom

Case Shelf

Case Side

Door Rail

Door Stile

Make the bottom compartment.

1 **Prepare the stock.** Joint and plane the stock except the shelf dividers, which you will make later. If necessary, glue up narrower boards to make the wider parts. After the glue dries, rip and crosscut the stock for the case, the bow rack sides, and the crosspiece to the dimensions in the Materials List.

2 **Mortise the top, the case sides, and the bow rack sides.** The top's upper surface is mortised to accept the bow rack. The bottom surface is mortised for the case sides. Lay out both sets of mortises as shown in the Mortise Detail.

Rout the mortises with a plunge router and a 1/4-inch straight bit set to cut 9/16 inch deep. Guide the cut with either the router's fence attachment or a straight edge clamped to the stock. If you don't have a plunge router, drill a series of adjacent holes between the layout lines.

MATERIALS LIST

Part	Dimension
Case	
Sides (2)	3/4" × 10" × 11 1/8"
Top	7/8" × 10 1/2" × 28 1/2"
Bottom	3/4" × 10" × 27"
Back	1/2" × 10 5/8" × 26 3/4"
Shelf	1/2" × 5 3/4" × 26 1/2"
Dividers (2)	1/2" × 5 3/4" × 5 7/8"
Door stops (2)	3/8" × 3/4" × 9 7/8"
Door	
Door rails (2)	7/8" × 1 3/4" × 26"
Door stiles (2)	7/8" × 1 3/4" × 7"
Door panel	3/4" × 6 3/4" × 22 7/8"
Bow Rack	
Sides (2)	3/4" × 12 1/2" × 23 1/2"
Crosspiece	3/4" × 6" × 25 1/2"
Arrow supports (2)	3/4" × 2 1/4" × 24 1/2"

HARDWARE

As needed, #6 × 1 1/4" drywall screws

2 no-mortise hinges, 3" long. Available from Constantine's, 2050 Eastchester Rd., Bronx, NY 10461. Part #52D23.

1 lockset. Available from Constantine's. Part #75H20.

2 brass door supports. Available from Constantine's. Part #96J6.

1 escutcheon plate. Available from Constantine's. Part #KC6.

1 ready-made, 3"-dia. inlay. Available from Constantine's. Part #SV12.

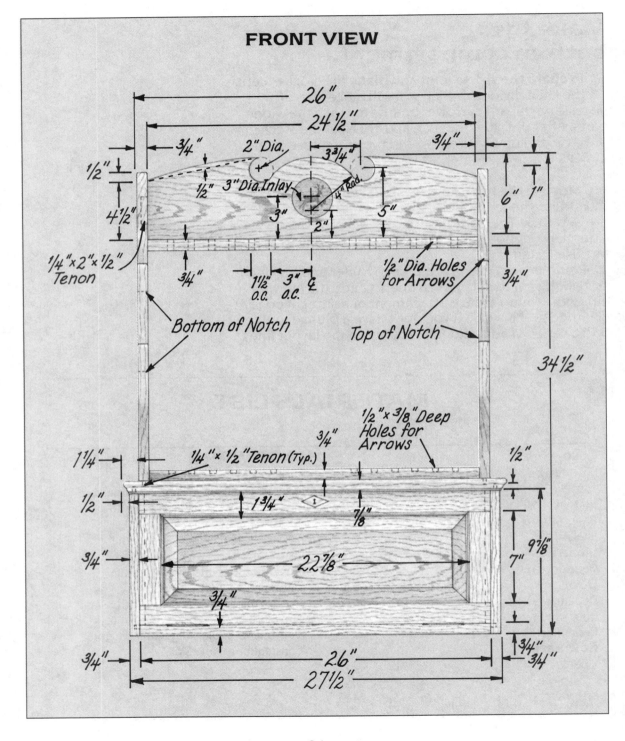

FRONT VIEW

SIDE VIEW

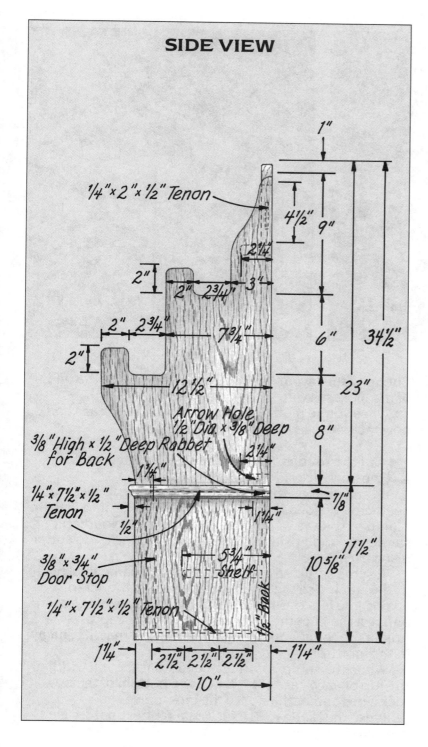

1"

¼" × 2" × ½" Tenon

4½"

9"

2¼"

2"

2" 2¾" 3"

2" 2¾"

7¾"

6"

2"

12½"

34½"

Arrow Hole
½" Dia. × ⅜" Deep

23"

⅜" High × ½" Deep Rabbet
for Back

2¼"

8"

1¾"

¼" × 7½" × ½"
Tenon

⅞"

1¼"

½"

11½"

⅜" × ¾"
Door Stop

5¾"
Shelf

10⅝"

½" Back

¼" × 7½" × ½" Tenon

1¼"

2½" 2½" 2½"

1¼"

10"

Left: Guide the plunge router against the fence to cut the mortises. Make the cut in a series of passes, each slightly deeper than the one before. *Right:* Guide the stock against the rip fence to cut the tenons.

Cut up to the layout lines with a chisel. Square the ends of the mortises with a 1/4-inch chisel.

Once you've mortised the top, mortise the case and bow rack sides as shown in the Side View.

3 Cut the tenons. Tenon the case sides and bottom, the bow rack sides, and the crosspiece.

Cut the tenons with a dado cutter on the table saw. Set the blade for a 1/2-inch-wide cut and raise it to 1/4 inch. Clamp or screw a wooden auxiliary fence to your table saw fence, and position the fence so that the dado cutter just grazes it.

Test the setup on a piece of scrap the same thickness as the stock. Use the miter gauge to guide the scrap against the fence. Cut a rabbet on both faces of the scrap, and test the fit of the resulting tenon in the mortise. Adjust the setup until you get a test tenon that fits snugly in the mortises.

When the setup is correct, cut tenons the full width of the top of each case side. Tenon the bottom of the bow rack sides and both ends of the crosspiece.

Raise the blade to 1/2 inch. Cut a rabbet on the case bottom to create a tongue that fits in the mortise.

4 **Cut the tenon shoulders.** Once you've cut the tenons, you'll have to stand the stock on edge to cut the tenon shoulders.

Leave the table saw fence where it is and raise the dado cutter height to 1¼ inches. Cut tenon shoulders on all the tenons, as shown in the photo. Hold the face of each piece against the miter gauge, and run the ends against the fence. Test fit the tenons in the mortises.

Cut the tenon shoulders with the board on edge.

5 **Rabbet the case sides, bottom, and top.** Put a ½-inch piloted rabbeting bit in the router, and set the depth for ⅜ inch. With outside faces down, rabbet the back edges of the sides to receive the ½-inch back. Rabbet the inside back edge of the case bottom, stopping at the tenon shoulders. Rabbet the inside back edge of the top, stopping 1¼ inches from each end. Square the ends of the stopped rabbet with a chisel.

6 **Dado the case sides.** The case shelf is housed in a stopped dado in the case sides. Lay out the dadoes as shown in the Side View. Put a ½-inch straight bit in the router and set it for a ¼-inch-deep cut. Guide the router against a straightedge clamped to the sides. You'll use

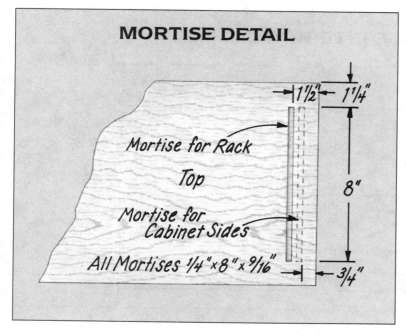

MORTISE DETAIL

Mortise for Rack

Top

Mortise for Cabinet Sides

All Mortises ¼" x 8" x 9/16"

1½" — 1¼"

8"

¾"

the same router bit and depth for Step 8, so leave the bit in place. Square the stopped edges of the dado with a chisel.

7 Make the shelf and dividers. Plane stock for the shelf and divider to fit into the dadoes. Make very light cuts in your last few passes through the planer, and check the fit after each one. When you get a snug fit, rip and crosscut the parts to the dimensions in the Materials List.

8 Dado the shelf and top. The shelf and top are dadoed to receive the vertical dividers shown in the Case Interior Detail. To cut these dadoes, lay the shelf and the top next to each other with their back edges touching. Align the center of the top with the center of the shelf. Clamp the pieces together and rout both sets of dadoes in one pass each, guiding the router with a straightedge clamped across the pieces.

9 Shape the top edges. Rout ¼-inch-radius roundovers on the front and sides of the upper edge of the case top. Rout the bottom of the same three edges with a 1½-inch-diameter Roman ogee bit to the profile shown in the Molding Detail.

MOLDING DETAIL

Rout with ¼" rad. router bit.

Top

Rout with Roman ogee router bit.

½"

Side

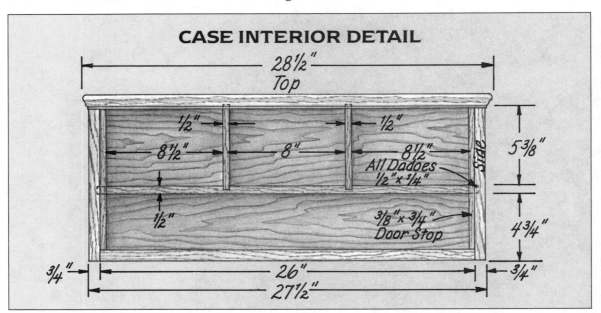

CASE INTERIOR DETAIL

28½"
Top

½"   ½"

8½"   8"   8½"
All Dadoes
½" x ¼"

Side

5⅜"

½"

3/8" x 3/4"
Door Stop

4¾"

3/4"   26"   3/4"
27½"

10 **Assemble the case.** Sand the inside of the case before assembling it. Glue the bottom to the sides, using pipe clamps or bar clamps to pull them together. Test fit the top to the sides during glue-up to keep the sides parallel when clamping. When the glue dries, remove the clamps from the sides and then glue and clamp the top onto the sides.

11 **Assemble the shelf and dividers.** Glue in the shelf and two dividers, sliding them in from the back.

Make the bow rack.

1 **Shape the sides.** Make a template of the sides, following the Rack Pattern. Trace the outline onto the stock. Before cutting out the sides, drill holes as shown for the inside corners. Complete the cuts with a scroll saw, jigsaw, or band saw with a narrow blade. Scrape or sand the edges until you have a smooth, fair shape; then round-over the edges with a 1/4-inch-radius roundover bit in the router.

2 **Shape the crosspiece.** Lay out the crosspiece as shown in the Front View. Using a compass, first lay out the 4 1/4-inch radius for the middle curve. Then lay out the 2-inch-radius circles at both sides. To lay out the gentle curves, make a mark on each end 4 1/2 inches from the bottom and draw a line between the marks and the tops of the circles. Mark the center of the line. Put a 1/4-inch-thick batten along the line and flex it up until there is 1/2 inch between the middle of the line and the batten.

Drill out the 2-inch-diameter top curves and complete the cuts with a scroll saw, jigsaw, or band saw. File and sand the cuts smooth. Round-over the top edge with a 1/4-inch-radius roundover bit.

3 **Install the inlay.** The inlay on this cabinet is ready made, and fits in a recess you rout in the crosspiece. Ready-made inlays are available in several diameters and patterns. Pick one you like, but remember, this cabinet is designed around a 3-inch-diameter inlay. A larger inlay may require redesigning the crosspiece.

Quick Tip: When duplicating a pattern on more than one piece, use a router with a flush trimming bit. Make the pattern from a 1/4-inch hardboard, like Masonite. Cut the edges and sand them smooth. Trace the pattern on the stock, and cut out the shape slightly oversized on the band saw or with a jigsaw.

To rout the precise shape of the pattern, attach it to the stock with double-sided carpet tape. Clamp the pieces together momentarily to ensure a good bond. As you guide the bearing of the bit against the pattern, the flush trimming bit routs the stock to shape. Pry off the pattern with a wide chisel when finished.

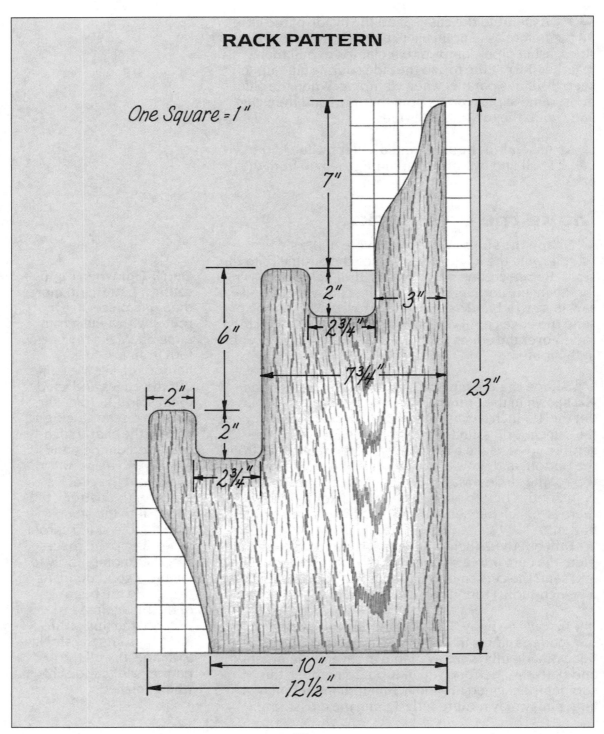

RACK PATTERN

One Square = 1"

Drill the outline of the inlay recess with a hole saw and rout away the waste.

Practice routing for the inlay on a piece of scrap. First, define the outside edge of the inlay with a 3-inch-diameter hole saw. Put the bit in the drill press and drill a $1/16$-inch-deep hole.

Rout out the waste within the circle with a $1/2$-inch-diameter straight bit in the router. Rout a recess as deep as the inlay is thick, being careful not to cut outside the circle. Test the fit of your inlay, and adjust the depth of cut as necessary.

Drill and rout the recess on the actual crosspiece. Glue the inlay in place with yellow glue. To clamp it in place, wrap a $3/4 \times 4 \times 4$-inch plywood scrap with wax paper. Clamp the plywood over the inlay. If the drill bit you used left a hole in the crosspiece back, fill it with sawdust mixed with epoxy.

4 Make the arrow supports. Rip stock to width for the arrow supports. Crosscut the bars to fit snugly between the shoulders of the crosspiece. Round-over the front edges on the top bar and the top front edge on the bottom bar with a $1/4$-inch-diameter roundover bit.

Lay out the position for the twelve holes on the top support as shown in the Front View. Clamp the two supports together, and on the drill press, drill $1/2$-inch-diameter holes through the top support and $3/8$ inch deep into the bottom support. Clamping the supports together prevents tearout and assures alignment of the holes.

5 **Assemble the bow rack.** Sand any places that will be hard to reach after assembly. Test assemble to be sure everything fits together well. Glue and clamp the crosspiece to the bow rack sides, and the bow rack sides into the case top. When the glue dries, glue the arrow supports between the sides.

6 **Attach the back.** Cut the back to fit, and attach it to the lower compartment with glue and screws or box nails.

Make the door.

Instead of mortise-and-tenon joints, this door relies on *cope-and-stick* construction. In cope-and-stick construction, a decorative detail on the edge of the stile nestles in a recess cut in the rail. The joint, shown in the Cope-and-Stick/Cross Section, is easily cut with a special router bit. I milled the stiles shown here with cope-and-stick bit #184-0105, available from Eagle America, P.O. Box 1099, Chardon, OH 44024. I raised the panel with the Eagle America panel raising bit #186-4015.

1 **Prepare the stock.** Joint, plane, and rip the stock for the door to dimensions in the Materials List. Cut the stiles to length. Leave the rails about 4 inches longer than listed dimensions.

2 **Cut the cope and tongue on the stiles.** Clamp the stiles between boards as shown in the photo. These boards, which are about 4 inches wide, prevent grain tearout during routing. Mill the cope and tongue on the end grain of the stiles in several passes. Position the cut so that the raised panel will protrude 1/16 inch above the surface of the frame.

3 **Cut the frame molding and groove on the frame.** Reverse the cutters on the bit to cut the molding and the 1/4-inch-wide × 3/8-inch-deep groove on the inside of the frame. Crosscut the rails to the lengths given in the Materials List.

4 **Raise the panel.** Test fit the frame, and cut the panel to fit into the groove, as shown in Door/Cross Section. Cut a panel 1/16 inch to 1/8 inch narrower than

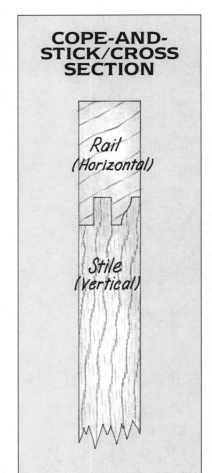

COPE-AND-STICK/CROSS SECTION

Rail (Horizontal)

Stile (Vertical)

measured, so that it has room to expand in humid weather. Raise the panel on the router table with an ogee-style horizontal raised panel cutter. Raise the panel in several passes, adjusting the fence to cut slightly deeper with each pass. On each pass, always cut the end grain first to prevent tearout.

5 **Sand the parts.** Before assembly, sand the molding on the inside of the frame, the raised part of the panel, and the back of the panel.

6 **Assemble the door.** Apply glue to the mating surfaces of the cope-and-stick joint, but not to the panel or its groove. Clamp with pipe clamps or bar clamps, and check to make sure the door is square.

7 **Install the door.** Fit the door to the opening, planing or jointing off any excess until there is a small, even gap between the door and the case. Hang the door using a pair of 3-inch-long, no-mortise hinges, or using traditional butt hinges. Install a lockset on the top of the door. With the door closed, reach through the back and mark the position for $3/8 \times 3/4$-inch door stops, which are shown as dotted lines in the Front View. Install the brass door supports listed in the Materials List, to keep the door from falling too far when opened. Remove all the hardware until after applying the finish.

8 **Apply finish.** Sand the cabinet and apply finish. I sanded the entire project with 120-grit paper, followed by 220-grit paper. I finished it with Watco Danish Oil. When the oil dried, I sanded it with 400-grit sandpaper followed by #0000 steel wool. Apply good paste wax to protect the finish.

Clamp pieces of scrap to the stiles to prevent tearout when routing end grain.

Quick Tip: Before assembly, rub a little paraffin on the corners of the raised panel to keep any excess glue from bonding the panel to the frame. Be careful not to get any wax on the visible parts of the panel, though, since it won't take finish.

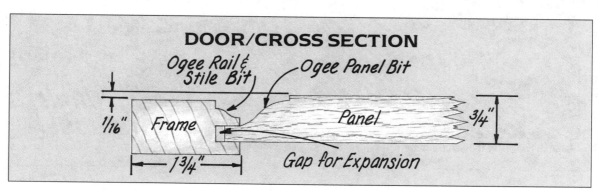

DOOR/CROSS SECTION

Ogee Rail & Stile Bit — Ogee Panel Bit

$1/16"$ Frame Panel $3/4"$

$13/4"$ Gap for Expansion

COPE-AND-STICK JOINERY

The cope-and-stick cutter set is made up of two router bit assemblies: one that cuts the cope and one that cuts the stick. The cope is a profile that is cut in the *ends* of the appropriate parts (usually the rails). The stick is a profile that is cut along the inside *edge* of the pieces.

1 Rout the stick on the edge of each stile and rail. Start by cutting the profile in the edge of each stile and rail.

First put the stile cutter into a table-mounted router. As you look at the bits, the stile cutter is the one that cuts the ogee profile and a ¼-inch groove. Adjust the bit's height to cut the desired profile. For a safe operation, set up a wooden fence so that the bit is mostly buried in the fence and the

guiding edge of the fence is even with the edge of the bit's bearing. Test the setup on some scrap and adjust it as necessary. When everything seems to be set up properly, cut the ogee profile and groove in the inside edges of the stiles *and* rails.

2 Rout the cope in the ends of the rails. Replace the stile cutter with the rail cutter, and position the fence as before. The rail cutter is designed to cut a profile in the *end* of each rail that locks into the profile cut by the stile cutter. Start by making the cut in some scrap, and keep adjusting the bit height until the stile and rail surfaces are flush when assembled. In order to stabilize the rails as you rout their ends, cut a 12 × 12-inch piece of ¾-inch-thick

Shape the edges of the stiles and rails.

Cope the ends of the rails.

The two profiles interlock, forming the cope-and-stick joint.

plywood, and back the rails up with it as you cut. The plywood will also help prevent the rails from chipping as the bit passes through them.

3 **Assemble the joints.** The cope-and-stick joints fit together as shown. To permanently assemble the joints, spread glue on the ends of the rails and clamp them between the stiles.

CABINETS FOR THE LIBRARY AND DEN

TRADITIONAL BOOKSHELVES

by Glenn Bostock

The beauty of this library, which I built for a local attorney's office, is that it looks elegant and is simple to build. What looks like an entire library is a series of individual bookshelves screwed together. The only joint in the whole library is the lowly butt joint.

While the butt joint is simple, it's nothing to laugh at: These bookshelves are strong and sturdy after five years. I expect they'll be strong and sturdy after 50 years. In Eastern Pennsylvania, where I work, I regularly see cabinets in 200-year-old farmhouses that were simply nailed together. It may have been the work of a carpenter or a lowly country cabinetmaker, but what they did made sense. When cabinets are attached to the wall, they become part of the wall, and derive much of their strength from it.

I designed these cabinets with two things in mind: the width of a sheet of plywood, and the width of the room. The sides are made from plywood 11¾ inches wide, so that you can cut four sides from one piece of plywood. The width of the cabinet was deter-

mined by the width of the wall they covered. If you change the widths to fit your wall, don't make the cases any wider than 36 inches. Longer shelves would bow under the weight of books.

Another consideration: Make your case sides 2 inches shorter than the ceiling of the room they'll be in. This will give you room to tip them into place. When you install the crown molding, it covers the gap.

EXPLODED VIEW

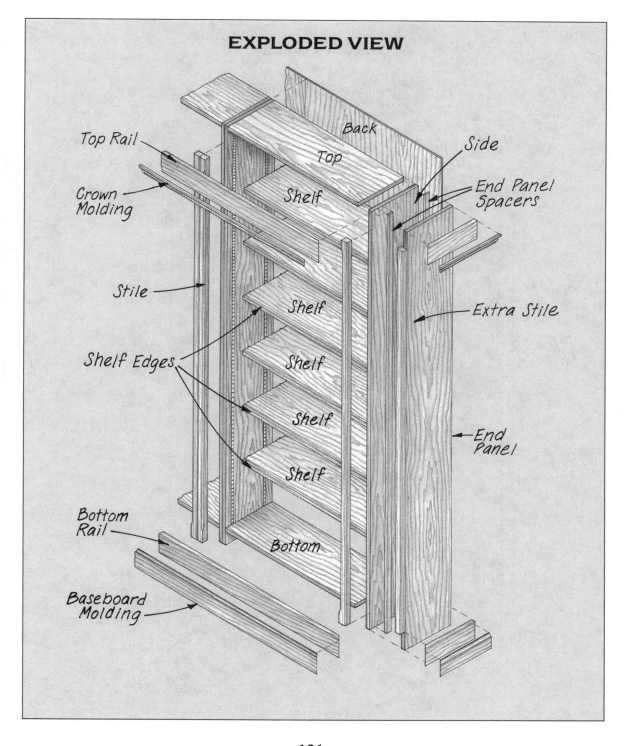

Top Rail

Crown
Molding

Stile

Shelf Edges

Bottom
Rail

Baseboard
Molding

Back

Top

Shelf

Shelf

Shelf

Shelf

Shelf

Bottom

Side

End Panel
Spacers

Extra Stile

End
Panel

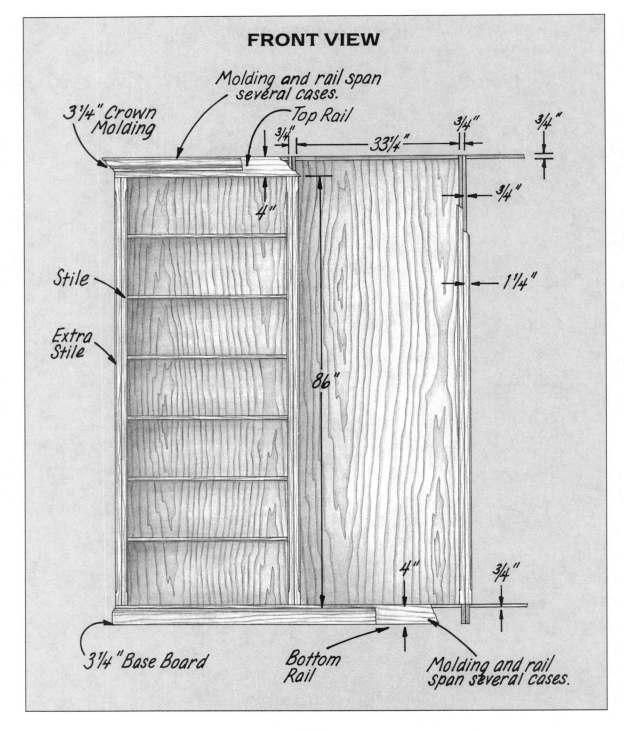

FRONT VIEW

Molding and rail span several cases.

3¼" Crown Molding

Top Rail

3¼"

33¼"

3¼"

3¼"

4"

3¼"

Stile

1¼"

Extra Stile

86"

4"

3¼"

3¼" Base Board

Bottom Rail

Molding and rail span several cases.

A pilaster is a ready-made shelf support. Rout a groove to recess it into the bookshelf side.

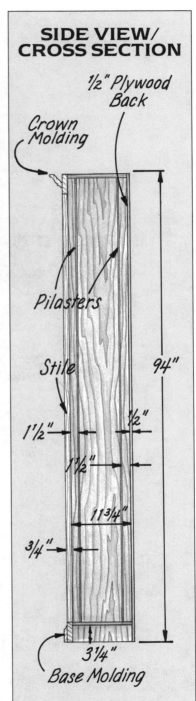

SIDE VIEW/ CROSS SECTION

Crown Molding

½" Plywood Back

Pilasters

Stile

94"

1½"

½"

1½"

11¾"

¾"

3¼"

Base Molding

Make the cases.

1 **Cut the plywood parts.** Rip all the plywood to width, and then crosscut it to length. If you don't have a radial arm saw or a table saw with large extension tables, crosscut the long pieces by guiding a circular saw against a straightedge.

2 **Cut a groove for the shelf standards.** The adjustable shelves are supported by commercially available shelf supports called pilaster standards. Despite the fancy name, these are nothing more than metal channels with slots in them for shelf supports. Although you can screw pilasters directly to a cabinet side, I prefer to recess them slightly in shallow grooves.

The grooves should be about ¼ inch deep, and wide enough to house the pilaster. Cut the grooves with the dado cutter on the table saw. Make a test cut in some scrap wood. Make sure the standards fit easily into the groove; you don't want to have to pound them in later.

Cut both grooves in each side with the same setup. Set the fence 1½ inches from the dado cutter. Cut a groove, guiding the plywood side against the fence. Rip the second groove by guiding the other edge against the fence.

3 **Assemble the cases.** You'll need a large flat work surface: The floor works great. Temporarily clamp the sides and top together. Predrill for #8 × 1½-inch drywall screws with a #8 combination bit, which drills a hole for the threads, the shank, and the head of the screw in one pass. The spacing of the holes isn't crucial: Try to get four screws in each joint. Slip the bottom into place, as shown in the Side View/Cross Section. Clamp and screw it into place.

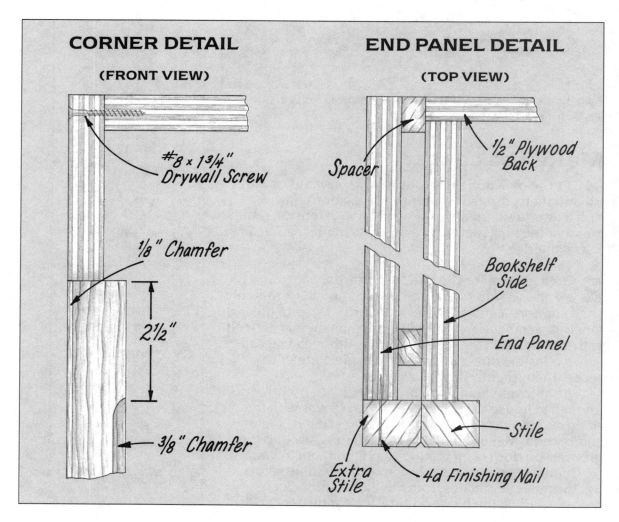

CORNER DETAIL

(FRONT VIEW)

#8 x 1¾"
Drywall Screw

⅛" Chamfer

2½"

⅜" Chamfer

END PANEL DETAIL

(TOP VIEW)

Spacer

½" Plywood
Back

Bookshelf
Side

End Panel

Stile

Extra
Stile

4d Finishing Nail

4 **Attach the back.** The back overlaps the entire back of the cabinet, as shown in the Side View/Cross Section. Cut the back to fit. Predrill holes as above, on 6-inch centers for #8 × 1 ½-inch drywall screws. Screw the back into place.

Make the face frames and install the stiles and shelf fronts.

1 **Prepare the stock.** Because I was building 12 cabinets, I saved money by purchasing rough-sawed poplar, which I planed and jointed myself. I used 5/4 (five-quarters) stock for the rails and 4/4 (four-quarters) stock for the stiles. If you are building only one or two units, you may save time by using dressed pine from the lumberyard.

Joint, plane, and cut the stock to the dimensions in

MATERIALS LIST

Part	Dimension	Part	Dimension
Bookshelf		Extra stile cleat (as needed)	³/₄" × 1 ½" × 94"
Sides (2)	³/₄" × 1 1¾" × 94"	Corner cleat (as needed)	³/₄" × ¾" × 94"
Top/bottom (1 each)	³/₄" × 1 1¾" × 33 ¼"		
Back	½" × 34¾" × 94"		
Shelves (7)	³/₄" × 1 1⅜" × 33 ⅛"	**HARDWARE**	
Shelf edges (7)	⅜" × ¾" × 33 ⅛"		
Stiles (2)	³/₄" × 1 ¼" × 86"	8 pilaster standards, 96" long, with 28 shelf clips per case	
Trim		As needed, #8 × 2" drywall screws	
Extra stiles (as needed)	³/₄" × 1 ¼" × 86"	As needed, #8 × 1¾" drywall screws	
Top and bottom rails	1" × 4" × as needed	As needed, #8 × 1 ¼" drywall screws	
Crown molding stock	¹¹/₁₆" × 3 ¼" × as needed	As needed, 6d finishing nails	
Baseboard molding stock	½" × 3 ¼" × as needed	As needed, 4d finishing nails	
End panel (as needed)	³/₄" × 12 ¼" × 94"		
End panel spacers (as needed)	½" × ¾" × 94"		

Stop routing the chamfer when the edge of the router first meets the end of the stile. Butt the stile against a stop block to make for consistent results.

the Materials List. Mill two stiles for each cabinet, and an extra stile for the cabinets at each end of a series of cabinets.

2 Chamfer the stiles. Chamfer the stiles as shown in the Corner Detail. Rout the 1/8-inch chamfer along the entire length of the stile with a hand-held router. Guide the cut with the router's fence attachment.

The 3/8-inch chamfer stops at both ends. Rout it with a hand-held router. Stop routing when the edge of the router base first meets the end of the stile. On my router, this means the chamfer ends 2 1/2 inches from the end of the stile. Don't worry about the dimension: Simply set up a stop block, like that shown in the photo, to automatically determine the length of the cut.

3 Attach the stiles. As shown in the Front View and the Side View/Cross Section, the stiles sit between the top and bottom rails; the rails, which cover several shelf units, abut the top and bottom of the stiles. I

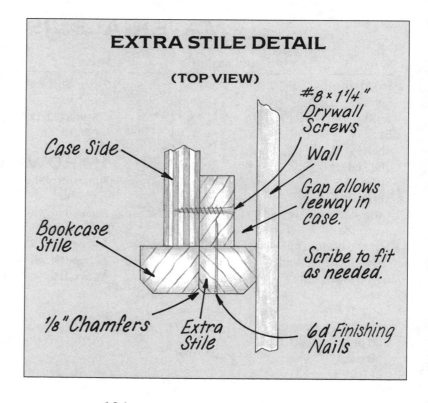

EXTRA STILE DETAIL

(TOP VIEW)

Case Side

Bookcase Stile

1/8" Chamfers

Extra Stile

#8 x 1 1/4" Drywall Screws

Wall

Gap allows leeway in case.

Scribe to fit as needed.

6d Finishing Nails

attached the stiles in the shop. Because the rails are 8 feet long and span several cabinets, I installed the rails on site. Install the rails with the 1/8-inch chamfer on the outside edge of the case as shown in the Corner Detail. Attach the stiles with glue and 6d finishing nails.

4 Prepare stock for shelf fronts. The front edges of the shelves are covered with 3/8 × 3/4-inch strips of wood. Joint, plane, and rip the stock to this width and thickness.

Crosscut the edge stock into pieces that are about 1 inch longer than the shelves. Put glue on the front edges of the shelves. Attach the edges with about 1/2-inch overhang on each end. Glue and nail the stock in place with 4d finishing nails. When the glue dries, use a backsaw to cut the edges flush with the sides. Sand the edges smooth and flush with the shelves.

Make panels, end stiles, and cleats.

When you place two bookshelves side by side, the adjacent stiles appear to form one wide stile. When a bookshelf is the last one in a series of bookshelves, attach an extra stile to create the same appearance. If the series of bookshelves end at a wall, simply nail an extra stile into place when installing the cabinet. If the end of the final bookshelf is visible, make an end panel and stile for it.

1 Make the end panel. You need this panel only if one end of the bookshelf is exposed. Cut the end panel to size. Attach the extra stile to the panel with 4d finishing nails and glue as shown in the End Panel Detail. Mill the spacers. Install the end panel and spacers when installing the bookshelves.

2 Cut the necessary cleats. If the bookshelf ends at a wall or goes around a corner, you'll need some cleats to attach the extra stile, as shown in the Extra Stile Detail and Corner Stile Detail. Mill the cleats to the sizes given in the Materials List.

Finish and install the bookshelves.

1 **Apply paint.** Fill all nail holes with wood putty. Finish sand all the solid wood parts of the cases. I painted mine with a coat of primer followed by two coats of semi-gloss latex paint. I prepainted the bookshelves and shelves but only primed the outside faces and edges of the stock for the rails and crown moldings. I cut these parts on-site to fit and finished them to match the paint in the rest of the room.

2 **Install standards.** The pilasters come in 8-foot lengths. Cut them to fit inside the cases. They are easy to cut with a hacksaw and a hand miter box. Make all the cuts at the top end of the standards. Then install the standards with the bottom end registered on the bottom of the case. This ensures that opposing support slots line up.

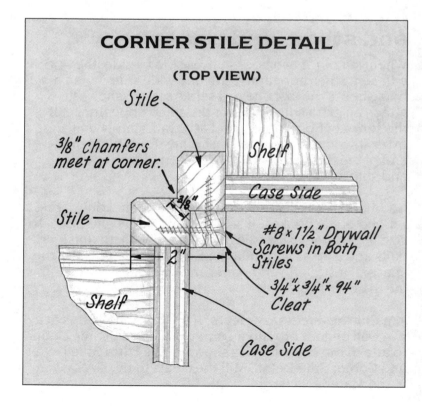

CORNER STILE DETAIL

(TOP VIEW)

Stile

3/8" chamfers meet at corner.

Shelf

Case Side

3/8"

Stile

#8 x 1½" Drywall Screws in Both Stiles

2"

3/4"x 3/4"x 94" Cleat

Shelf

Case Side

3 Install the cases. Installing these bookshelves is much the same as explained in the chapter Installing Cabinets on page 293. Begin installing in a corner of the room. If your cabinet will go around a corner, install both corner cabinets before installing any others. First, put both corner cabinets roughly in position. Screw them together with a cleat, as shown in the Corner Detail. Have someone help you slide the cabinets into position, and then shim them so that they are plumb and level.

If the cabinets only line one wall, then begin in a corner and work toward the other corner.

When you install the first cabinet, attach the extra stile as shown in the End Panel Detail. If necessary, scribe the stile to fit the wall.

Screw the first cabinet to the wall. Then install the neighboring cabinet, and screw the two together through the sides with #8 × 1 1/4-inch drywall screws. Run a minimum of eight screws through each side.

After you screw the cabinets together, attach the newly installed bookshelf to the wall with #8 × 2-inch drywall screws. Make sure each cabinet is screwed to at least two studs and that at least four screws go into each stud.

4 Install the end panel. If an end of the bookshelf is exposed to the room, install the end panel after installing the bookshelf. Scribe the panel to the wall if necessary. Nail the spacers to the bookshelf and nail the end panel to the spacers. Set the nails below the surface and fill the holes with putty.

5 Install the rails. Cut the rails to fit around the cases, attaching them with glue and 6d finishing nails. Use miter joints at outside corners and butt joints at inside corners.

6 Install baseboard molding and crown molding. The baseboard molding and crown molding are commercially available lumberyard moldings. Install the baseboard molding with 6d finishing nails. Tie the baseboard molding into the room's existing molding by coping it to fit over the profile of the existing molding. Install the crown molding as described in "Mitering and Installing Crown Molding" on page 110.

Quick Tip: If you have trouble nailing the crown molding to the ceiling, attach it with construction adhesive instead. This adhesive, which comes in a caulking gun tube, will work even if the ceiling has been painted. Put a bead of adhesive on the molding surface that will contact the ceiling, and press it into place. Then nail the molding into the bookshelf rails. Angle your nails slightly upward so they will push the molding into the ceiling. Use a putty knife to scrape off any adhesive that squeezes out. The adhesive will fill small gaps between the ceiling and the molding.

MITERING AND INSTALLING CROWN MOLDING

Crown molding is one of the many decorative elements in the cabinetmaker's design vocabulary. It wraps around the top of a cabinet, and is mitered at the corners. On floor-to-ceiling casework, crown molding serves as a transition between the cabinet and the ceiling. On shorter cabinets, it adds a bit of grandeur to the top of the piece.

While crown molding appears to be one solid, thick piece of wood, it is actually a relatively thin board attached to the cabinet at an angle, as shown. One short flat bevel is attached to the cabinet side with nails; a second bevel is attached to the ceiling or cabinet top with nails. Making crown molding this way saves wood, but requires a little extra care when mitering. When you cut the molding, set the blade at 90 degrees;

adjust the angle of the miter gauge, and hold the molding so that it leans against the miter gauge as shown.

Mitering Crown Molding.

1 Set up the table saw. Set the blade on the table saw perpendicular to the table. Set the miter gauge at one-half of the corner angle. If the molding wraps around a 90-degree corner, for example, set the miter gauge at 45 degrees.

Note that when you set the angle on

TABLE SAW MITER GAUGE SETUP

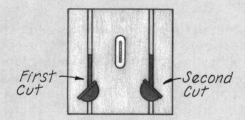

First Cut — Second Cut

MITER GAUGE POSITION FOR CUTTING OUTSIDE CORNERS

First Cut — Second Cut

MITER GAUGE POSITION FOR CUTTING INSIDE CORNERS

CROWN MOLDING PROFILE

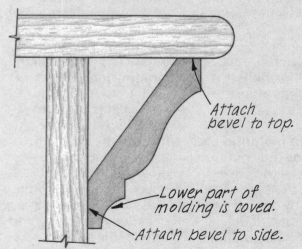

Attach bevel to top.

Lower part of molding is coved.

Attach bevel to side.

the miter gauge, you can set it to either the left or right of 90 degrees. Which you choose depends on whether you are cutting molding around an inside or an outside corner. Set the gauge as shown in the drawing.

2 **Miter the left molding.** Begin with the left side of the cabinet. The finished length of the molding equals the width of the side plus the width of the molding. Cut the molding about 2 inches longer than the finished length. You'll trim it to final length later.

Place the molding against the miter gauge so that the top of the molding is against the table saw, as shown. Put the bevel that goes against the cabinet side against the miter gauge. You are now holding the molding against the miter gauge at the angle at which it will be installed. Make sure the molding does not slip. Cut the first miter.

Cut the left side molding first. Lean the molding against the miter gauge with the molding's top edge against the saw table.

3 **Miter the front molding.** Your next cut finishes the corner that your first cut began. Put the miter gauge on the right side of the blade as shown. Start with a piece of molding about a foot longer than the front width of the cabinet. Hold the molding as before and miter it. Put the side and front moldings in place against the cabinet to check the fit of the joint. Make any necessary adjustments.

4 **Miter the second corner of the front molding.** Measure the width of the cabinet front, and mark the distance along the *bottom* of the front molding. Put the miter gauge on the left side of the blade and cut to the waste side of the line. Make repeated cuts,

Reset the miter gauge and put it to the right of the blade to cut the adjoining corner.

(continued)

MITERING AND INSTALLING CROWN MOLDING—
Continued

easing the stock over until your cut just touches the layout line.

To cut the right side molding, move and reset the miter gauge. Miter as before.

Reset and reposition the miter gauge to cut the second corner of the front molding. Make repeated cuts on the waste side of the line until your cut just touches the layout line.

Installing Crown Molding.

1 **Trim the left molding.** Install the crown molding in the same order you cut it in. Put the left molding into place on the cabinet. Align the lower

corner of the miter with the front edge of the cabinet. Mark the length of the molding on the end opposite the miter, and cut it square.

2 **Nail the molding into place.** Drive nails through the side molding and into the cabinet. Apply glue to the miter, and put the front molding against the side molding. Nail it into place.

3 **Trim and install the right molding.** Mark the length of the right molding as before. Nail it into place.

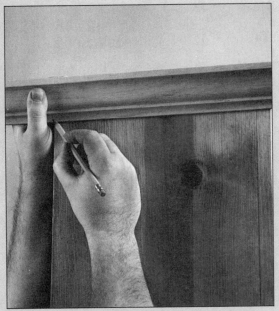

Cut the molding to length as you install it. Position the molding on the cabinet, and mark and cut the square end.

After marking the length of the right side molding, cut the back end square.

To install the molding, nail through the molding and into the cabinet.

DOVETAILED BOOKSHELF
by William Storch

Books are among my favorite things. They provide entertainment, information, companionship, and diversion. They fill me with wonder at others' thoughts and ideas. Simply being around books makes me feel good, while owning them makes me feel wealthy. Perhaps you feel the same way.

The only problem with books is storing them. Here's one solution: some simple yet elegant bookshelves. In building this project I received encouragement and design recommendations from an artist-friend, Diedrich Dasenbrock. As you can see from the photo, I built several units to make up a library. Each bookshelf looks fine, however, standing by itself. Make as many of these bookshelves as you like—even if it's only one. Feel free to modify the dimensions to suit your needs.

Construction of this bookshelf is very straightforward. It is simply a large, dovetailed box with shelves dadoed into the sides. The back is rabbeted into place. The whole unit rests on a short, black plinth which gives it a visual foundation.

I made the bookshelf's sides, top, bottom, and shelves from hard maple, though any hardwood could be used. The back and plinth are made from A-D grade plywood.

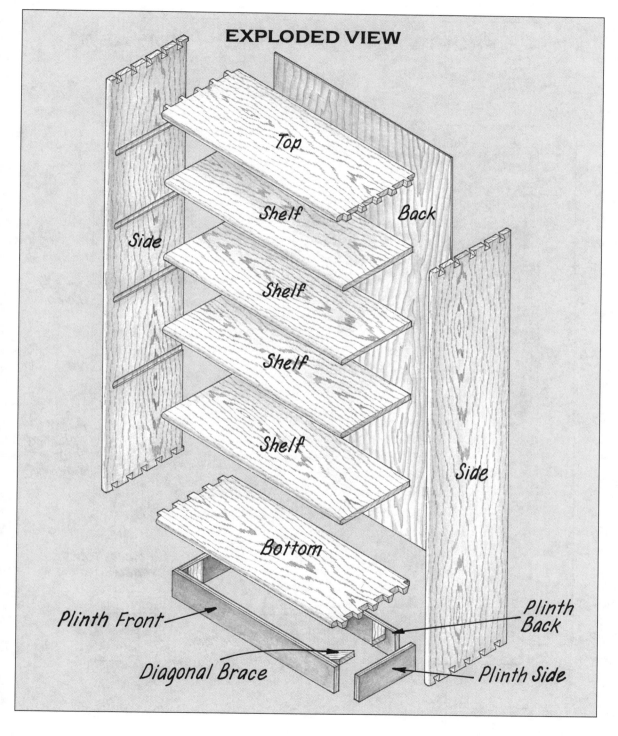

EXPLODED VIEW

Top

Shelf

Back

Side

Shelf

Shelf

Shelf

Side

Bottom

Plinth Front

Plinth Back

Diagonal Brace

Plinth Side

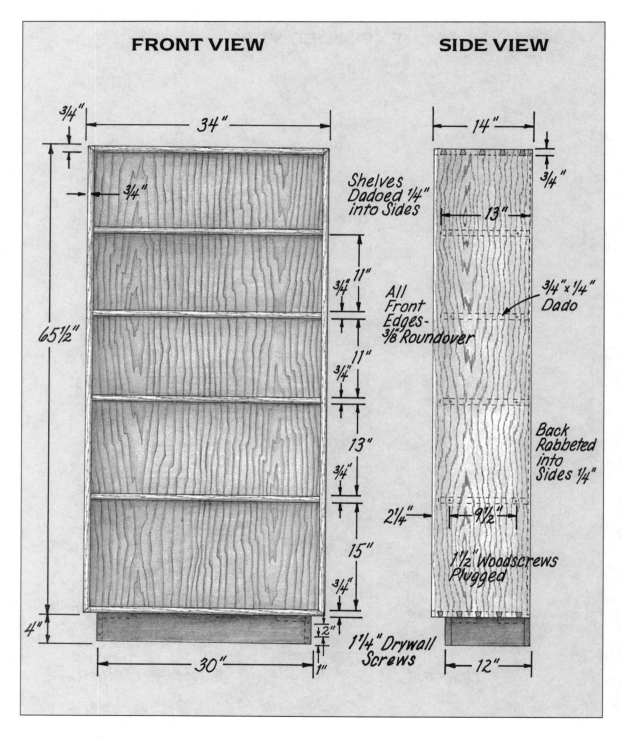

FRONT VIEW

SIDE VIEW

3/4"

34"

3/4"

65½"

3/4"

11"

3/4"

11"

3/4"

13"

3/4"

15"

3/4"

4"

½"

30"

1"

14"

3/4"

13"

Shelves
Dadoed ¼"
into Sides

All
Front
Edges-
⅜" Roundover

3/4" x ¼"
Dado

Back
Rabbeted
into
Sides ¼"

2¼"

9½"

1½" Woodscrews
Plugged

1¼" Drywall
Screws

12"

Make the case.

1 Cut the parts to size. Joint, plane, rip, and cut the pieces for the top, bottom, and sides of the case to the sizes listed in the Materials List. Edge-glue narrow boards to make up the wide pieces if necessary.

2 Cut the dovetails. Finish sand the four inside surfaces; then lay out the dovetails as shown in the Dovetail Spacing Layout. This dovetail layout is unique in that there are half-dovetails on the edges of the sides. Normally there would be half-pins on each edge of the top. Cut out the dovetails, and then lay out the pins by tracing around the tails onto the end grain of the top and bottom. For more information on dovetailing, see "Cutting Through Dovetails" on page 81.

3 Cut the dadoes. Lay out the 3/4-inch-wide × 1/4-inch-deep dadoes on the inside of the sides, as shown in the Front and Side Views. Note that these dadoes stop 3/4 inch from the front of the sides. Rout the dadoes, being careful not to mar the sanded surface.

Guide the router against a shop-made T-square to rout the dadoes.

Quick Tip: Make the dadoes in the sides by guiding your router against the jig shown in the Dado Jig Layout. Make the jig from 3/4-inch-thick plywood or hardwood scraps. Clamp the jig to the sides, and guide your router against it as you rout the dadoes as shown in the photo.

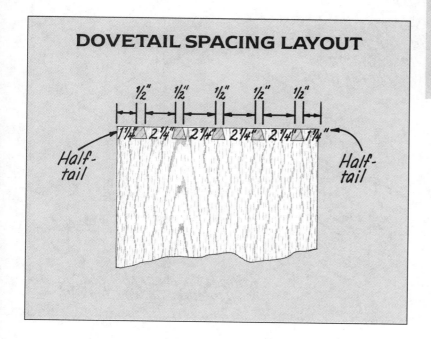

DOVETAIL SPACING LAYOUT

1/2"   1/2"   1/2"   1/2"   1/2"

1 1/4"   2 1/4"   2 1/4"   2 1/4"   2 1/4"   1 1/4"

Half-tail   *Half-tail*

Quick Tip: For snug-fitting shelves, plane the stock to fit the dado. After each pass through the planer, test fit a shelf in one of the dadoes. If you're working with pre-planed stock, you can still tailor the dado and shelf for a snug fit. Cut 1/2-inch instead of 3/4-inch dadoes into the book-shelf sides. After you've rounded-over the shelves, rout a tongue on each end of the shelf that fits snugly in the dado.

4 Cut the back rabbet. With a 3/8-inch rabbeting bit, rout a 1/4 × 3/8-inch rabbet for the case back on the back edge of the top, bottom, and sides. The cuts can be run off the ends of the top and bottom but must be stopped 3/8 inch from the ends of the sides so they do not show. Use a chisel to square the rounded corners of the rabbets.

Make the shelves and back.

1 Cut the parts to size. Joint, plane, and rip the stock for the shelves to the sizes listed in the Materials List. Make sure the thickness of each shelf matches the dado width. Before you cut the shelves to length, test fit the case for an exact measurement between the inside of the dadoes on both sides. While the case is assembled, measure and cut the plywood back to fit into its rabbets.

2 Round-over the front edges. Rout the front edge of each shelf with a 3/8-inch roundover bit set up in a table-mounted router. Round-over both edges on the

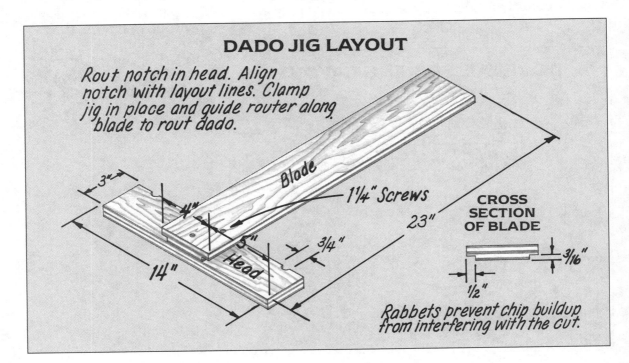

DADO JIG LAYOUT

Rout notch in head. Align notch with layout lines. Clamp jig in place and guide router along blade to rout dado.

Blade

3"

4"

1 1/4" Screws

Head

5"

3/4"

14"

23"

CROSS SECTION OF BLADE

3/16"

1/2"

Rabbets prevent chip buildup from interfering with the cut.

front of each shelf. Guide the stock against the router table fence as you rout.

3 **Fit the shelves to the dadoes.** Check how the front edge of the shelves fits into the rounded ends of the stopped dadoes. If necessary, carefully scrape and sand the shelf roundovers for a perfect fit. Make sure the shelves stop at the edge of the rabbet in back. If they don't, trim the back edge of the shelves until they are flush with the bottom of the rabbets.

Assemble the case.

1 **Test fit the case.** Assemble the case without glue and make sure all the parts fit well. Make any necessary adjustments.

2 **Drill pilot and plug holes in the sides.** With a $^3/_{16}$-inch drill bit, drill two clearance holes, slightly larger than the diameter of the screw shank, along each dado as shown in the Side View. Counterbore these holes to accept $^3/_8$-inch-diameter plugs. Make plugs from a length of $^3/_8$-inch dowel, or by plunging a plug cutter into the end grain of a maple block. The end grain of the plugs reflects the end grain showing in the dovetails.

3 **Glue up the case.** Apply glue to the dovetails and dadoes, and then assemble the case. Once the dovetails are clamped, drill pilot holes through the

---

MATERIALS LIST

Part	Dimension	Part	Dimension
Case		Plinth back	$^3/_4" \times 4" \times 30"$
Top	$^3/_4" \times 14" \times 34"$	Plinth sides (2)	$^3/_4" \times 4" \times 10^1/_2"$
Bottom	$^3/_4" \times 14" \times 34"$	Diagonal braces (4)	$^3/_4" \times 2" \times 5"$
Sides (2)	$^3/_4" \times 14" \times 65^1/_2"$		
Shelves (4)	$^3/_4" \times 13" \times 33"$	**HARDWARE**	
Back	$^1/_4" \times 33^1/_4" \times 64^3/_4"$	As needed, #8 × 1 $^1/_2"$ flathead wood screws	
Plinth		As needed, #6 × $^3/_4"$ flathead wood screws	
Plinth front	$^3/_4" \times 4" \times 30"$	As needed, #8 × 1 $^1/_4"$ drywall screws	

clearance holes in the sides and into the shelves for #8 × 1½-inch flathead wood screws. Drive the screws and plug the holes. Make sure the case is square, and then attach the back with #6 × ¾-inch flathead wood screws along each shelf and into the rabbet.

Finishing up.

1 Round-over the front edges of the case. Round-over the front edges of the sides, top, and bottom with a ⅜-inch roundover bit. Carefully hand shape the four inside corners with a chisel, file, and sandpaper to create the mitered appearance shown in the Front View.

2 Sand and apply the finish. Finish sand the case and apply a clear finish.

3 Make and attach the plinth. Cut the pieces to the sizes listed in the Materials List. Attach the front and back to the sides with #8 × 1¼-inch drywall screws, and plug the screw holes. Attach the diagonal braces at the top of the inside as shown in the Plinth Detail. When the plinth is assembled, sand and paint it with black semi-gloss enamel. When everything is dry, attach the plinth to the bottom of the bookshelf by screwing up through the diagonal braces and into the sides with #8 × 1¼-inch drywall screws.

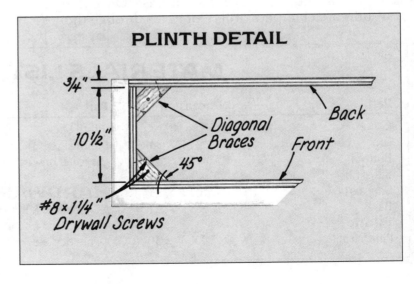

PLINTH DETAIL

¾"

10½"

Diagonal Braces

Back

Front

45°

#8 × 1¼" Drywall Screws

STICKLEY BOOKCASE
by Jim Tolpin

This piece is a close reproduction of the number 650 white oak bookcase listed in the L. and J. G. Stickley Furniture Company catalogs issued around the turn of the century. Unfortunately, no measurements were known to exist for this particular piece; all we had to go on was the illustration in an old catalog.

To develop a set of drawings and a construction plan, I embarked on a little detective work. Using a magnifying glass, I measured the height of the books shown sitting on the shelves. Assuming an average height of old books to be about 9½ inches, I used this as a scale to extrapolate the dimensions of the case.

The magnifying glass also uncovered some inter-

EXPLODED VIEW

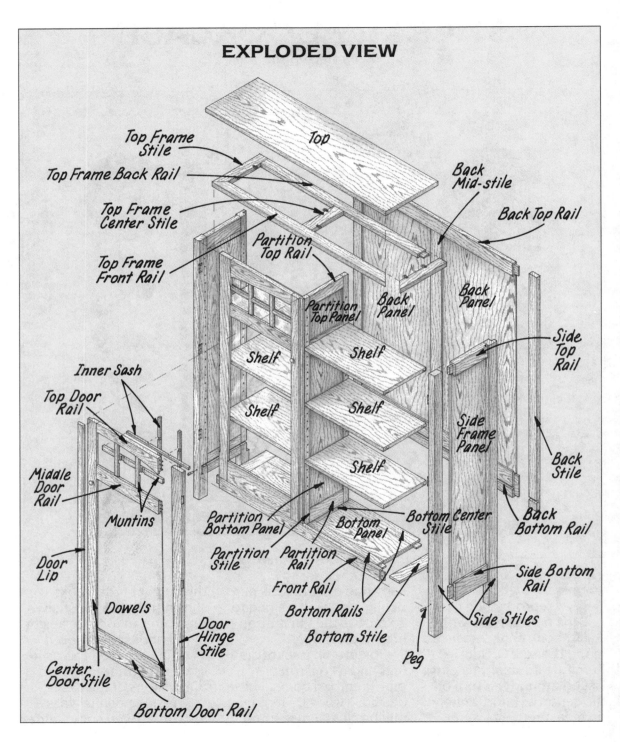

Top Frame Stile

Top Frame Back Rail

Top Frame Center Stile

Top Frame Front Rail

Top

Back Mid-stile

Back Top Rail

Partition Top Rail

Back Panel

Back Panel

Partition Top Panel

Inner Sash

Top Door Rail

Shelf

Shelf

Shelf

Shelf

Shelf

Shelf

Side Top Rail

Side Frame Panel

Back Stile

Middle Door Rail

Muntins

Door Lip

Partition Bottom Panel

Partition Stile

Partition Rail

Front Rail

Bottom Panel

Bottom Center Stile

Back Bottom Rail

Dowels

Bottom Rails

Bottom Stile

Center Door Stile

Door Hinge Stile

Bottom Door Rail

Peg

Side Bottom Rail

Side Stiles

esting aspects to this piece, reminding me once again how much there is to learn from the products of the designers and craftsmen of the old school. I noticed first that the hinge-side door stiles were tapered, from 3 inches at the top to 2 inches at the bottom. This subtle detail provides the piece with a certain elegance and gives it a definite sense of balance. Without the taper, the case would appear less substantial and might appear to tilt away from plumb when viewed from certain perspectives. Other nice touches that became evident were the nice curves in the upper door rails, the slight reveals created where side frame rails and the front rail met the corner stiles, and the diamond-shaped pin used to lock the tenons of the front rail. Additional detailing and the joinery were based on my familiarity with existing mission pieces.

MATERIALS LIST

Part	Dimension
Case	
Top frame front rail	$3/4'' \times 2 1/4'' \times 49 1/2''$
Top frame stiles (2)	$3/4'' \times 2 1/4'' \times 14''$
Top frame back rail	$3/4'' \times 2 1/4'' \times 47''$
Top frame center stile	$3/4'' \times 2 1/4'' \times 11 1/2''$
Back stiles (2)	$3/4'' \times 2 1/8'' \times 58 1/2''$
Back top rail	$3/4'' \times 3'' \times 45 3/4''$
Back bottom rail	$3/4'' \times 6 1/2'' \times 45 3/4''$
Back mid-stile	$3/4'' \times 2 3/4'' \times 51''$
Back panels (2)	$1/4'' \times 21 1/8'' \times 49 5/8''$
Bottom rails (2)	$3/4'' \times 2 3/4'' \times 42 7/8''$
Bottom stiles (2)	$3/4'' \times 2 3/4'' \times 12 3/4''$
Bottom center stile	$3/4'' \times 2 3/4'' \times 9 1/4''$
Bottom panels (2)	$3/4'' \times 7 7/8'' \times 19 11/16''$
Partition stiles (2)	$3/4'' \times 1 3/8'' \times 56 1/4''$
Partition rails (2)	$3/4'' \times 3'' \times 11 3/8''$
Partition top rail	$3/4'' \times 2 5/8'' \times 11 3/8''$
Partition top panel	$1/4'' \times 10 1/8'' \times 9 3/4''$
Partition bottom panel	$1/4'' \times 1/8'' \times 39 3/8''$
Side stiles (4)	$1 5/8'' \times 2 1/8'' \times 64 1/2''$
Side top rails (2)	$1 7/16'' \times 3'' \times 11 1/2''$
Side bottom rails (2)	$1 7/16'' \times 4'' \times 11 1/2''$
Side frame panel (2)	$3/4'' \times 10 1/4'' \times 52 1/8''$
Front rail	$3/4'' \times 2 3/4'' \times 47 3/4''$
Peg stock	$5/16'' \times 5/16'' \times 10''$
Top	$7/8'' \times 15'' \times 51 1/2''$

Part	Dimension
Shelves (6)	$3/4'' \times 12'' \times 22 7/16''$
Doors	
Door hinge stiles (2)	$3/4'' \times 3'' \times 55 3/4''$
Center door stiles (2)	$3/4'' \times 2'' \times 55 3/4''$
Top door rails (2)	$3/4'' \times 4'' \times 20''$
Middle door rails (2)	$3/4'' \times 2 3/4'' \times 20''$
Bottom door rails (2)	$3/4'' \times 5'' \times 20''$
Dowels (as needed)	$3/8''$ dia. $\times 2''$
Muntin stock	$5/16'' \times 11/16'' \times 10'$
Inner sash stock	$1/4'' \times 3/8'' \times 10'$
Door lip	$5/16'' \times 1'' \times 55 3/4''$

HARDWARE

As needed, $1/8''$-thick glass for doors, cut to fit
As needed, #8 $\times$ $1 3/4''$ flathead wood screws
As needed, #8 $\times$ $3/4''$ flathead wood screws
As needed, #8 $\times$ $1 1/4''$ drywall screws
8 desktop fasteners. Available from The Woodworkers' Store, 21801 Industrial Blvd., Rogers, MN 55374. Part #33597.
6 brass butt hinges, $1 3/8''$ wide $\times$ $2''$ long. Available from The Woodworkers' Store. Part #25817.
2 brass pulls, $1''$ dia.
1 brass hook-and-eye fastener
As needed, $7/8''$ brads

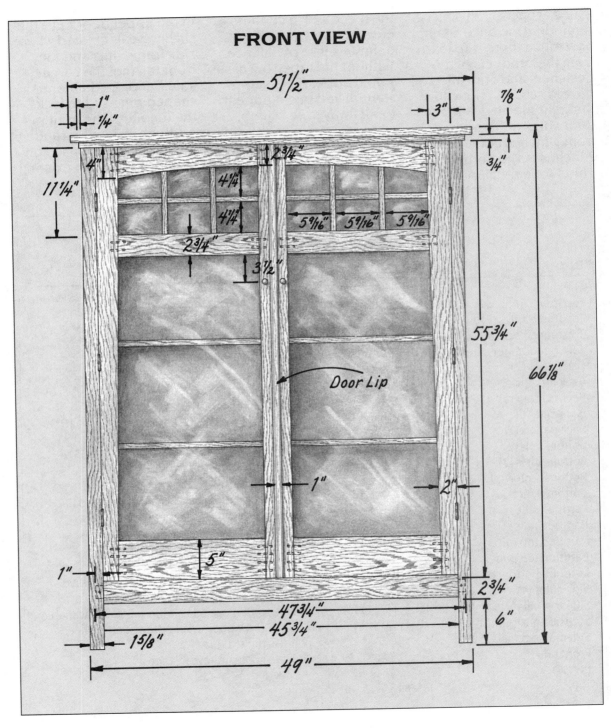

FRONT VIEW

51½"

1"

¼"

3"

⅞"

4"

11¼"

2¾"

4¼"

4¼"

5⁹⁄₁₆" 5⁹⁄₁₆" 5⁹⁄₁₆"

3¾"

2¾"

3½"

55¾"

66⅛"

Door Lip

1"

2"

5"

2¾"

1"

47¾"

6"

45¾"

1⅝"

49"

124

SIDE VIEW

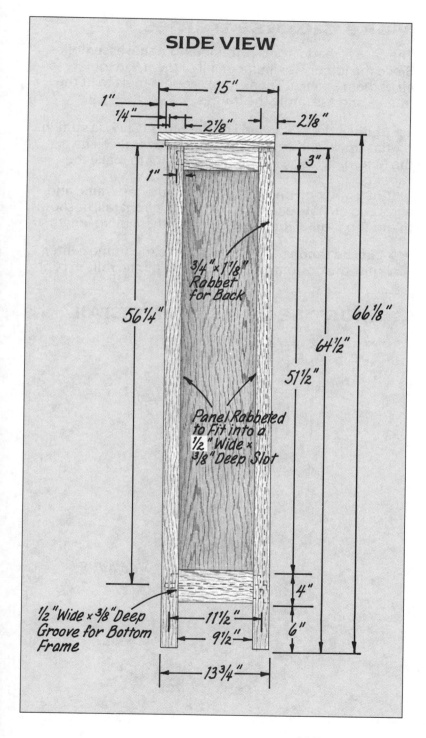

15"

1"

1/4"

2⅛"

2⅛"

3"

1"

3/4" × 1⅛"
Rabbet
for Back

56¼"

66⅛"

64½"

51½"

Panel Rabbeted
to Fit into a
½" Wide ×
⅜" Deep Slot

4"

½" Wide × ⅜" Deep
Groove for Bottom
Frame

11½"

9½"

6"

13¾"

Make the case frames.

The case is made from six frame-and-panel assemblies. Since the joinery is similar on all of them, cut joinery for all of them at once. Then cut plywood panels to fit the frames and assemble the frames.

1 **Choose the stock and cut the parts.** Choose straight, flat stock, and cut the parts to the sizes given in the Materials List. Glue boards together to make the wider parts.

Cut a miter on one end of each of the top frame and stiles and on both ends of the top frame front rail, as shown in the Top Frame/Top View. Then cut them all to length.

2 **Cut the tenons.** The tenons in the top frame center stile, the bottom center stile, and all the rails except

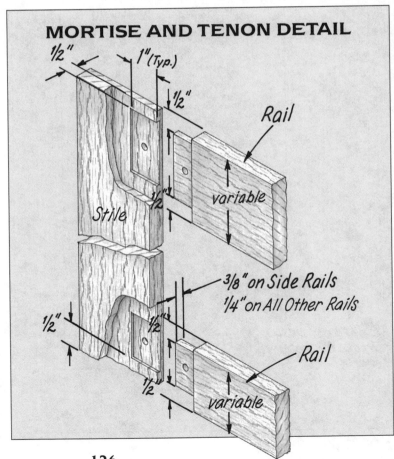

MORTISE AND TENON DETAIL

$\frac{1}{2}''$ $1''(Typ.)$ $\frac{1}{2}''$

Rail

Stile $\frac{1}{2}''$ variable

$\frac{3}{8}''$ on Side Rails
$\frac{1}{4}''$ on All Other Rails

$\frac{1}{2}''$ $\frac{1}{2}''$ Rail

$\frac{1}{2}$ variable

the side rails, are ¼ inch thick and 1 inch long, and have ½-inch shoulders, as shown in the Mortise and Tenon Detail. Cut all the tenon shoulders on the table saw with the miter gauge. Cut the cheeks on all but the side rails, with each rail or center stile upright in a tenoning jig. For more on cutting tenons, see "Tenoning Jig" on page 375.

Reset the tenoning jig and cut ³⁄₈-inch-thick tenons on the side rails.

3 **Mortise the stiles.** Mortise the stiles, except the tenoned center stiles, as shown in the Mortise and Tenon Detail. Rout the mortises in a series of passes with a plunge router. To provide extra support for the router, clamp a 4 × 4 to the back of the stock as you rout. Guide the cut with the router's fence attachment. To provide uniformity, always guide the router fence against the outside face of the stock.

If you do not have a plunge router, drill a series of adjacent holes between the layout lines, and chisel away the waste.

Cut ¼-inch-wide mortises for everything except the side rails. Rout ³⁄₈-inch-wide mortises for the side rails.

4 **Rout panel grooves.** Cut the panel grooves with a ¼-inch slotting cutter set up in a table-mounted router. Make a router table fence for this operation from a straight piece of scrap. Notch the fence so that it fits around the slotting cutter, and adjust it so that the cutter will only cut to a depth of ³⁄₈ inch. Clamp the fence in place. Adjust the height of the cutter so that it will cut a slot centered in the edge of the ¾-inch-thick stock.

Cut the slot in the ¾-inch-thick stiles and rails first. The slot should run all the way along the edge of the rails and center stiles, but only from mortise to mortise on the other stiles. Rout the slot along the entire length of both edges of the middle partition rail, bottom center stile, and middle back stile. (See the Partition Frame/Side View.)

5 **Rout panel grooves in the side stiles.** These parts are thicker and receive wider grooves, so you'll cut them in two passes.

Make the initial cuts without changing the settings on

Quick Tip: Cut a sample mortise before cutting the tenons, and check the thickness of the tenons by fitting them in the sample mortise.

Quick Tip: Lay out the mortises by tracing around the tenons. Arrange the parts of each frame on the bench as they will be when assembled. Scribe the top and bottom of the mortise on the edge of each stile by tracing along the tenons with a sharp knife. Lay out the sides of the mortise with a marking gauge.

the router table. Rout the parts faceup on the router table. Rout a slot along the entire length of the rails. On the stiles, rout a groove that ends 1 1/2 inches from the end of the rails.

Widen all the grooves with a second pass. Raise the bit 1/4 inch to create a 1/2-inch-wide slot. Rout the length of the rails as well as between the mortises on the stiles.

6 Cut the panels. Test fit the frames and measure for the panels that will go into them. Cut the partition top panel, partition bottom panel, and back panels from 1/4-inch plywood. Cut the side frame panels and bottom panels from 3/4-inch plywood or solid oak.

Rabbet the side and bottom panels with a 3/8-inch rabbeting bit to create a tongue that fits into the grooves you routed for them.

7 Assemble the frames. Test assemble the frames without glue and make any necessary adjustments. When satisfied with the fit, rub paraffin on the corners of the panels to keep them from sticking to the frames during glue-up. Apply glue to the joints and clamp the frames together.

Cut the case joints.

Once the frames are assembled, you must still cut a few joints in them so that you can put them together to form the bookcase.

1 Prepare the front rail. Cut a groove in the front rail to accept the bottom frame. Rout the groove on

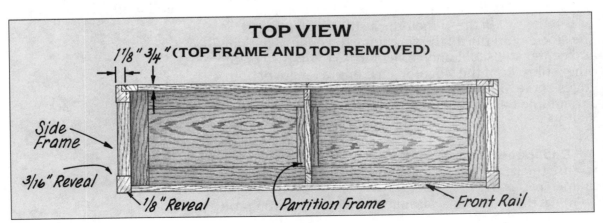

TOP VIEW

1 1/8" 3/4" (TOP FRAME AND TOP REMOVED)

Side Frame

3/16" Reveal

1/8" Reveal

Partition Frame

Front Rail

 Tilt the router base and then slowly drop the bit down into the stock.

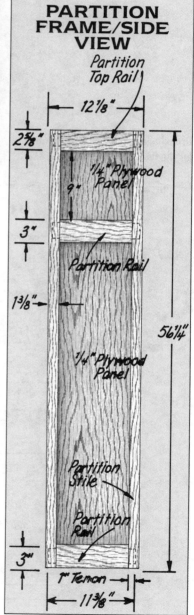

PARTITION FRAME/SIDE VIEW

Partition Top Rail

12⅛"

2⅝"

¼" Plywood Panel

9"

3"

Partition Rail

1⅜"

¼" Plywood Panel

56¼"

Partition Stile

Partition Rail

3"

1" Tenon

11⅜"

the router table with a ½-inch straight bit. Guide the stock against a fence as you rout.

2 Prepare the side frames. Lay out a groove for the bottom to match the location of the groove in the front rail. Note that this is a stopped groove at both ends. Rout the groove in several passes with a plunge router, guiding the router against a straightedge as you work. If you don't have a plunge router, begin the cut by tilting the router base and then lowering the bit into the wood, as shown in the photo.

Lay out and rout a rabbet for the back panel, as shown in the Top View. Make the cut with a ¾-inch-diameter straight bit, guiding the router against a straightedge clamped to the side.

3 Prepare the back frame. Rout a groove to house the bottom frame, as shown in the Back Frame/Front View. Locate the groove by putting the side and back frame panels together and transferring the location onto the back panel.

4 Prepare the bottom frame. Rout a rabbet to create a tongue around the edge of the frame, as shown in the Bottom Frame/Bottom View. Adjust the depth of cut so that the tongue fits into the groove for the bottom.

Drill shallow holes in the top frame for the figure-eight fasteners.

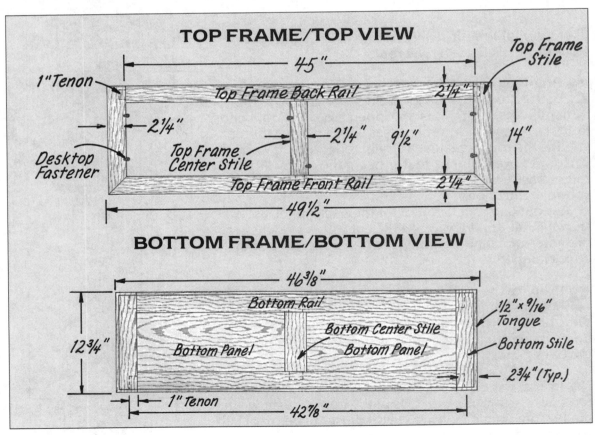

TOP FRAME/TOP VIEW

1"Tenon

Top Frame Stile

45"

Top Frame Back Rail

2¼"

2¼"

9½"

14"

Desktop Fastener

Top Frame Center Stile

2¼"

Top Frame Front Rail

2¼"

49½"

BOTTOM FRAME/BOTTOM VIEW

46³⁄₈"

Bottom Rail

½" x ⁹⁄₁₆" Tongue

12¾"

Bottom Panel

Bottom Center Stile

Bottom Panel

Bottom Stile

1" Tenon

2¾" (Typ.)

42⅞"

5 **Prepare the top frame.** The top is held to the top frame with commercially available desktop fasteners shaped like a figure eight. Drill mortises so that you can mount the fasteners flush with the surface of the frame, as shown in the photo.

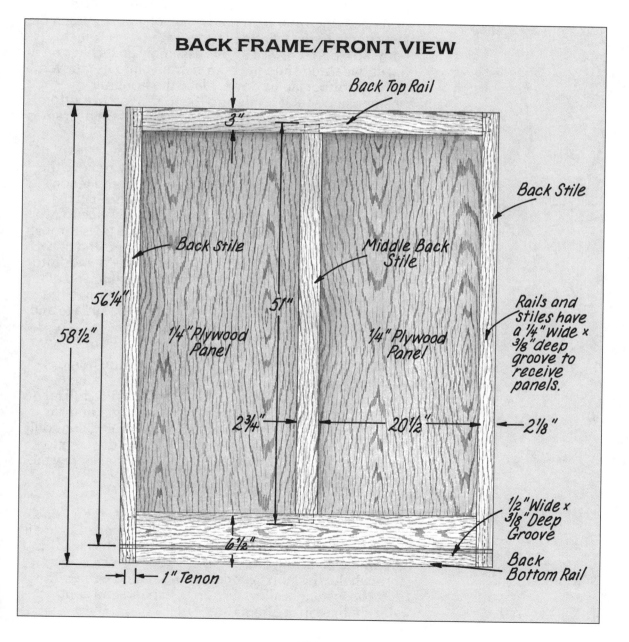

BACK FRAME/FRONT VIEW

Back Top Rail

Back Stile

Back Stile

Middle Back Stile

56¼"

58½"

51"

¼" Plywood Panel

¼" Plywood Panel

Rails and stiles have a ¼" wide x ⅜" deep groove to receive panels.

3"

2¾"

20½"

2⅛"

½" Wide x ⅜" Deep Groove

Back Bottom Rail

6½"

1" Tenon

Assemble the case.

1 Join the back frame, side frames, bottom frame, and front rail. Clamp the back frame in its rabbets. Drill holes through the back and into the sides with a #8 pilot bit. This bit cuts a recess for the screw head, and drills clearance and pilot holes all in one pass. Attach the back frame to the two side frames with #8 × 1¾-inch flathead wood screws. Lay this assembly on its back on a flat surface, and slide the bottom frame into its grooves with the rabbet facing down. Place the front rail in position and seat it firmly into the tongue of the bottom frame. Apply glue to the tenons and draw the side frames together with a pipe clamp.

2 Peg the front rail. When the glue is dry, remove the clamps and peg the front rail's mortise and tenon joints. First, drill a 5/16-inch-diameter hole through the face of the rail and through the tenon. Apply glue to two 5/16 × 5/16-inch square oak pegs and drive the pegs through the holes. Make the job easier by carving one end of each peg into a bullet shape. Tap the bullet-shaped ends into the peg holes, and as you do, orient the square end of the peg so that it forms a diamond shape in relation to the cabinet. Leave the pegs slightly proud of the surface and chamfer their edges to form low pyramids.

3 Install the partition frame. The partition frame is screwed into place. Center the partition frame between the sides, and clamp it into place. Predrill for #8 × 1¼-inch drywall screws through the top and bottom into the partition frame rail with a #8 pilot bit. Screw only into the rails of the partition frame. Screws driven into the end grain of the stiles will not hold as well. Screw the partition frame in place.

4 Install the top. Put the top in place, leaving a 1-inch overhang on the front and sides of the case. Secure it from below by driving #8 × 1¼-inch screws through the top frame back rail, and by driving #8 × ¾-inch screws through the desktop fasteners you installed earlier. The desktop fasteners allow the top to expand and contract with changes in the humidity.

Scribe a line along the edge of the stile and onto the rail to indicate both the rail length and the angle of the cut.

5 **Drill holes for the adjustable shelves.** Beginning 6 inches up from the bottom frame, drill a series of $1/4$-inch-diameter × $3/8$-inch-deep holes spaced 2 inches apart into the side and partition stiles. These holes will hold the shelf pins that support the shelves.

Make the doors.

The doors are also frame-and-panel construction. To simplify the joinery problems caused by the tapered rail, the door is doweled together. If you have a biscuit slot cutter, you can substitute biscuits for dowels.

1 **Cut the parts to size.** Cut the parts to the width and thickness given in the Materials List, but leave them about an inch longer than listed there.

2 **Taper the hinge stiles.** Note that only the inside edge of each hinge stile is tapered. Lay out the tapers on the hinge stiles as shown in the Front View. Cut the tapers on the band saw or with a jigsaw. As you cut,

Quick Tip: Cut a piece of pegboard to fit inside the cabinet. Drill through the holes in the pegboard to lay out shelf pin holes. You can slip a commercially available stop collar over the bit and lock it in place to prevent drilling holes that are too deep.

Locate matching dowel holes in the stiles and rails with dowel centers.

stay about $1/16$ inch to the waste side of the layout lines. Once the tapers have been cut, run the sawed edges over the jointer to remove the waste to the layout lines.

3 Lay out and cut the door rails. Spread the door parts out on a flat work surface. Butt the rails against the center door stiles, and lay the tapered hinge stiles *on top* of the rails. Position all of the parts as they will appear in the finished door. Move the pieces so that the overall width of the right door is 23 inches, and the overall width of the left door is 23 1/8 inches. Make sure the rails are 90 degrees to the center stiles. Transfer the angle of the taper onto the rails with a sharp pencil.

Crosscut the rails to length on the table saw. Cut the angle first. To set up the angled cut, adjust the miter gauge so that the angled layout lines on the ends of the rails are parallel with the saw blade. After you cut the angle, cut the rails to final length.

4 Cut the curve in the upper rail. Lay out the curve of the upper rail on a cardboard template. Flex a thin strip of wood to create the curve and have a helper trace along it with a pencil. The curve doesn't have to be exactly as shown in the Front View. I simply made an approximation of the curve that I found in the Stickley Catalog. When satisfied with the fairness of the curve, cut out the template and transfer the pattern to the top rails. Cut the curve and sand the edge smooth.

5 **Assemble the doors.** Assemble the door rails and stiles with ⅜-inch-diameter × 2-inch-long dowels. Drill two to four dowel holes on the ends of each rail on 1-inch centers. For example, the wide bottom rails should have four dowels on each end. Lay out and drill the 1-inch-deep dowel holes into the rails and stiles. Locate the exact position of matching dowel holes with commercially available dowel centers.

    Once you are satisfied with the fit of the dowels, glue and clamp the doors. Make sure that the doors are square, and wipe off any excess glue. When the glue dries, scrape off any remaining glue and continue to scrape until the joints are flush.

6 **Ship-lap the doors.** The center stiles overlap each other, as shown in the Door Lap Detail. Cut the rabbets with a dado cutter on the table saw. Screw a long

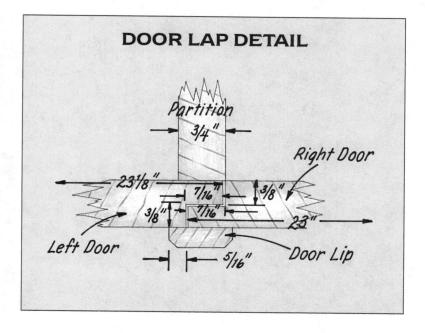

DOOR LAP DETAIL

auxiliary fence to the rip fence to prevent the frames from wobbling during the cuts.

7 **Rabbet for the glass.** Rabbet each door back where it will receive the glass. Use a ³/₈-inch rabbeting bit in a router. Adjust the router to cut a ³/₈ × ³/₈-inch rabbet. Chisel the rounded corners of the rabbet square.

Make the sash frames.

The upper section of the door has a sash frame that holds small panes of glass. The frame is really two simple

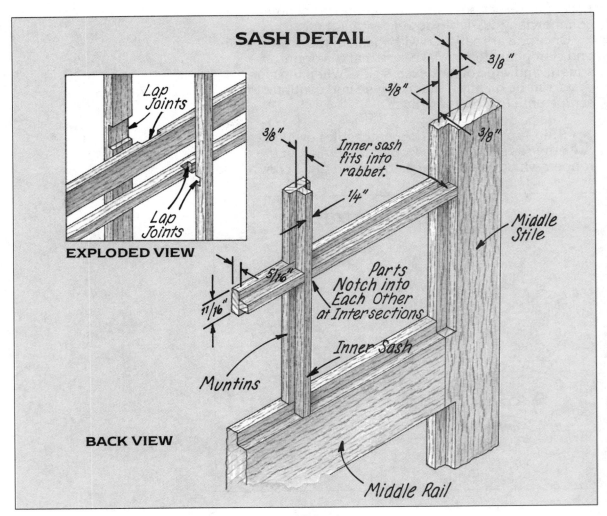

SASH DETAIL

Lap Joints

Lap Joints

EXPLODED VIEW

³/₈"

³/₈"

³/₈"

³/₈"

³/₈"

Inner sash fits into rabbet.

¹/₄"

Middle Stile

5/16"

11/16"

Parts Notch into Each Other at Intersections

Inner Sash

Muntins

BACK VIEW

Middle Rail

frames: an outer and an inner sash, as shown in the Sash Detail. Make the two separately, and then glue them together.

1 **Mill the sash muntins.** Joint and plane the muntins for the inner and outer sash to the thickness and width given in the Materials List, but leave them ½ inch longer than listed.

2 **Cut half-laps.** The muntins are half-lapped where they intersect. Lay out the half-lap joints, as shown in the Front View. The dimensions shown in the Front View are simply a guide. Because of variations in the taper, your actual dimensions may vary slightly. Cut the shoulders of the half-laps with a dovetail saw. Remove most of the waste in a series of crosscuts on the table saw. Chisel away the rest of the waste.

3 **Assemble the outer sash.** Glue the muntins together at the half-laps, and allow the glue to dry. When the glue is dry, hold the assembly in position against the front of the door. Carefully mark the muntins to fit within the opening, as shown. Cut the muntins to length with a dovetail saw.

4 **Make the inner sash.** The muntins are held in place by an inner sash. It, too, is a half-lapped grid. Cut the

Left: Cut half-laps with a dovetail saw and chisel where the muntins intersect.
Right: Glue the inner sash to the back of the muntins.

joints, as before, and glue the inner sash together. When the glue dries, glue the inner sash to the outer sash. Trim the ends of the inner sash to fit into the glass rabbet. Apply epoxy to the surfaces that meet the stile, and install the assembly into the back of the door frames.

5 Test fit the doors. With the case standing plumb and level, install the doors into their opening. Place $1/16$-inch-thick shims under the bottom edges of the doors. Each door should have about a $1/16$-inch gap around the entire perimeter. Adjust the gap, if necessary, by removing stock with a block plane.

6 Install the door lip and hinges. Use glue and $7/8$-inch brads to attach the door lip to the right side door, as shown in the Door Lap Detail.
Hang each door with three $1\,3/8 \times 2$-inch loose-pin brass butt hinges. Lay out the mortises for the hinges on the doors by tracing around the hinge leaves with a utility knife. Chisel or rout out the hinge mortises and screw the hinges into place on the doors. Set the doors in their openings and insert the $1/16$-inch shims under the doors. Mark the hinge location on the side frame and then chisel or rout the hinge mortises. Temporarily install the doors.

Apply finish.

1 Finish the doors and install the glass. Finish sand the doors and apply your choice of finish. Put the glass panes into their rabbets, holding them in place with glazing points. Putty the window in place.

2 Finish the case. Finish sand the exposed surfaces of the case and apply the finish. Be sure to apply equal amounts of finish to inside and outside surfaces to prevent unequal absorption of moisture and subsequent warping.
When the finish is dry, carefully mark and drill for the door pulls, and install them. Install a hook and eye to the inside of the left-hand door and the partition frame.

Quick Tip: Stain the glazing putty to match the wood you're using by mixing it with commercially available wood paint pigments.

KNEEHOLE DESK
by Ben Erickson

Whether you are a student studying for a test, a businessperson hard at work, or just looking for a place to balance the checkbook, a good solid desk lets the work flow smoothly. Organized storage is the key to good desk design. That's why this kneehole desk contains four 5¼-inch-deep drawers, two double-depth drawers for hanging file folders, and a divided pencil drawer. It also has two hidden storage compartments in the base, which you reach by removing the drawers.

If you're going to alter this design to suit your needs, there are several important dimensions to take into account. The most critical is the height of the top. Desktops for typing and computer applications should be between 26 and 28 inches high. Writing desks, like this one, are usually 30 inches high. In any event, the top should be at least 24 inches wide. The kneehole space should be no less than 25 inches and preferably 26 inches high, which you'll find eliminates the pencil drawer on typing desks. If your computer has a separate key-

board, the problem of height may be solved by making the desktop 30 inches high for writing and having the keyboard where the pencil drawer would be. The Woodworkers' Store (21801 Industrial Blvd., Rogers, MN 55374) carries drawer slides for this application. Make the kneehole at least 24 inches wide, larger if your chair requires it.

The sides of this desk are frame and panel, and the drawers are dovetailed together. It's made from solid Honduras mahogany,

though walnut, cherry, or the traditional oak are good choices. The desk requires about 32 board feet of 4/4 (four-quarters) lumber, and 25 board feet of 5/4 (five-quarters) lumber. The drawer sides and web frames require about 32 board feet of 4/4 secondary wood, such as poplar. As you'll see, I built the back from two layers of ¼-inch plywood and the drawer bottoms from a single layer of ¼-inch plywood. You'll be able to get all the plywood you need from one sheet.

139

EXPLODED VIEW

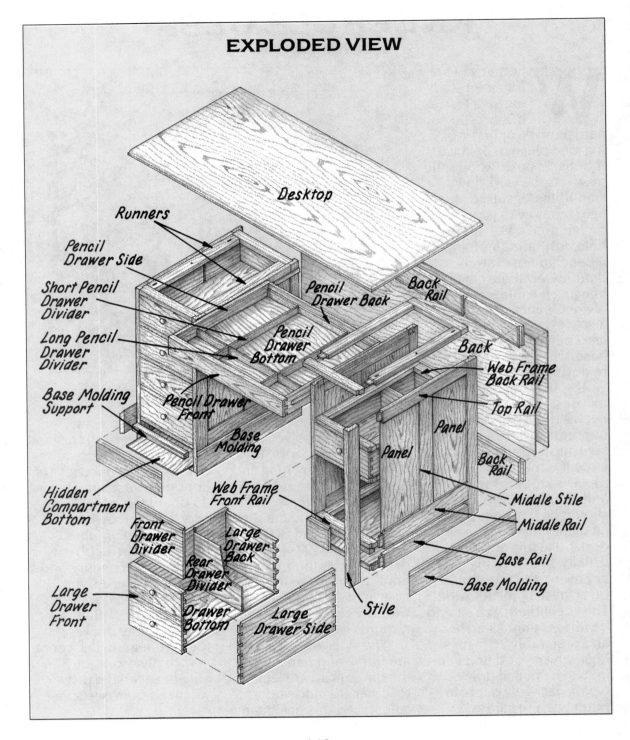

Desktop

Runners

Pencil Drawer Side

Short Pencil Drawer Divider

Long Pencil Drawer Divider

Pencil Drawer Back

Back Rail

Base Molding Support

Pencil Drawer Front

Pencil Drawer Bottom

Base Molding

Back

Web Frame Back Rail

Top Rail

Panel

Panel

Back Rail

Hidden Compartment Bottom

Web Frame Front Rail

Panel

Middle Stile

Middle Rail

Front Drawer Divider

Large Drawer Back

Rear Drawer Divider

Base Rail

Base Molding

Large Drawer Front

Drawer Bottom

Large Drawer Side

Stile

Make the frame and panel assemblies.

1 **Choose the stock and cut the parts.** Select straight, flat stock. Any of the parts that will not be seen from the exterior of the desk can be made from a secondary wood such as poplar. Joint, plane, rip, and cut all of the parts except for the drawer fronts and backs to the sizes given in the Materials List.

MATERIALS LIST

Part	Dimension	Part	Dimension
Frame-and-Panel Units		Large drawer backs (2)	$1/2" \times 10\,1/4" \times 11\,1/4"$
Top rails (4)	$3/4" \times 2\,1/4" \times 21\,1/4"$	Rear drawer dividers (2)	$1/4" \times 9\,1/2" \times 10\,3/4"$
Middle rails (4)	$3/4" \times 3\,1/4" \times 21\,1/4"$	Front drawer dividers (2)	$1/2" \times 9\,1/2" \times 10\,1/2"$
Base rails (4)	$3/4" \times 2\,1/4" \times 21\,1/4"$	Drawer bottoms (6)	$1/4" \times 11" \times 20\,3/4"$
Stiles (8)	$3/4" \times 2\,1/4" \times 29"$	Pencil drawer front	$1" \times 3" \times 24\,1/2"$
Middle stiles (4)	$3/4" \times 2\,1/2" \times 23\,3/8"$	Pencil drawer sides (2)	$1/2" \times 3" \times 21\,1/8"$
Panels (8)	$1/2" \times 8\,1/2" \times 20\,7/8"$	Pencil drawer back	$1/2" \times 2" \times 24\,1/2"$
Web Frames		Pencil drawer bottom	$1/4" \times 24" \times 20\,1/2"$
Front rails (10)	$3/4" \times 1\,1/2" \times 12"$	Short pencil drawer	
Back rails (10)	$3/4" \times 1\,1/2" \times 12"$	dividers (2)	$1/4" \times 1\,3/8" \times 19\,7/8"$
Runners (20)	$3/4" \times 1\,1/2" \times 20\,1/2"$	Long pencil drawer	
Base molding supports (2)	$1" \times 1" \times 11\,1/2"$	dividers (2)	$1/4" \times 1\,3/8" \times 23\,1/2"$
Hidden compartment		Pencil drawer slides (2)	$1/4" \times 7/8" \times 20"$
bottoms (2)	$1/4" \times 11\,1/2" \times 21\,5/8"$	Drawer stops (6)	$1/2" \times 1" \times 11\,1/2"$
Back			
Back rails (2)	$7/8" \times 4\,1/4" \times 50"$	**HARDWARE**	
Back (2)	$1/4" \times 21\,1/2" \times 50"$	As needed, #5 × 3/4" flathead wood screws	
Top and Molding		As needed, #5 × 1/2" flathead wood screws	
Desktop	$1" \times 24" \times 52"$	As needed, #10 × 1 1/4" roundhead wood screws	
Base molding stock	$3/8" \times 4\,1/4" \times 11'$	with washers	
Drawers		As needed, #8 × 1 1/4" drywall screws	
Small drawer fronts (4)	$1" \times 5\,1/4" \times 11\,1/2"$	As needed, #6 × 1 1/2" drywall screws	
Small drawer sides (8)	$1/2" \times 5\,1/4" \times 21\,1/8"$	As needed, #6 × 1" drywall screws	
Small drawer backs (4)	$1/2" \times 4\,1/4" \times 11\,1/2"$	8 brass knobs, 1" dia. Available from The	
Small drawer dividers (4)	$1/4" \times 4\,1/4" \times 10\,3/4"$	Woodworkers' Store, 21801 Industrial Blvd.,	
Large drawer fronts (2)	$1" \times 11\,1/4" \times 11\,1/2"$	Rogers, MN 55374. Part #36467.	
Large drawer sides (4)	$1/2" \times 11\,1/4" \times 21\,1/8"$	As needed, 3d nails	

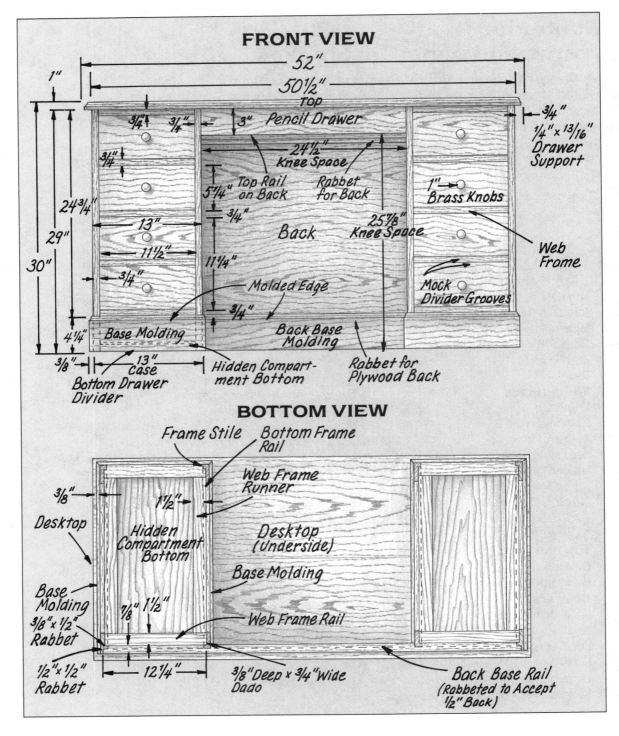

FRONT VIEW

52"
50½"
TOP
1"
3/4" 3/4" 3" Pencil Drawer
3/4"
1/4" x 13/16"
Drawer Support
24½" Knee Space
3/4"
Top Rail on Back
Rabbet for Back
5⅛"
3/4"
1" Brass Knobs
24¾"
13"
29"
25⅞" Knee Space
11½"
Back
Web Frame
30"
11¼"
3/4"
Molded Edge
Mock Divider Grooves
3/4"
Base Molding
Back Base Molding
4¼"
3/8"
13" Case
Hidden Compartment Bottom
Rabbet for Plywood Back
Bottom Drawer Divider

BOTTOM VIEW

Frame Stile
Bottom Frame Rail
3/8"
Web Frame Runner
1½"
Desktop
Hidden Compartment Bottom
Desktop (Underside)
Base Molding
Base Molding
3/8" x 1/2" Rabbet
7/8" 1½"
Web Frame Rail
1/2" x 1/2" Rabbet
12¼"
3/8" Deep x 3/4" Wide Dado
Back Base Rail (Rabbeted to Accept 1/2" Back)

142

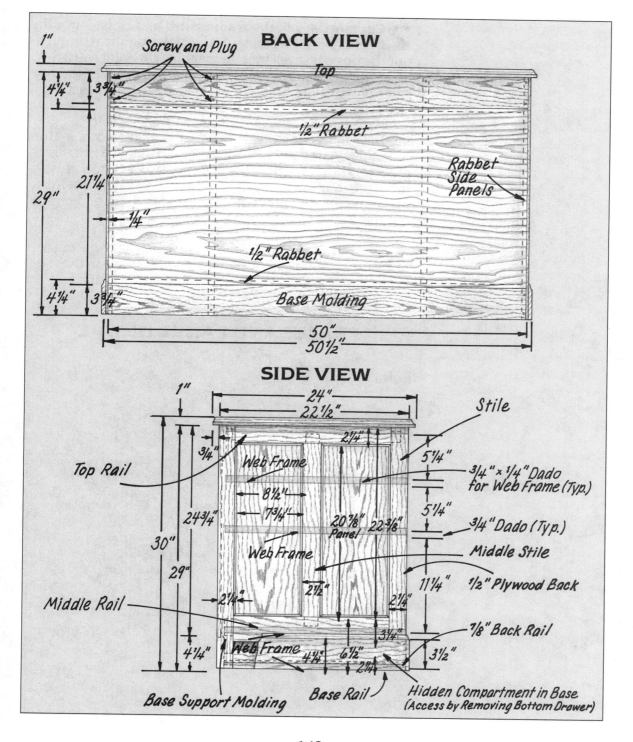

BACK VIEW

Screw and Plug

Top

1"

4¼"

3¾"

½" Rabbet

Rabbet Side Panels

21¼"

29"

¼"

½" Rabbet

4¼"

3¾"

Base Molding

50"

50½"

SIDE VIEW

1"

24"

22½"

Stile

¾"

2¼"

Top Rail

Web Frame

5¼"

¾" × ¼" Dado for Web Frame (Typ.)

8½"

7¾"

24¾"

5¼"

30"

20⅞" Panel

22⅜"

¾" Dado (Typ.)

Web Frame

Middle Stile

29"

2½"

11¼"

½" Plywood Back

Middle Rail

2¼"

2¼"

3¼"

⅞" Back Rail

4¼"

Web Frame

4¼"

6½"

3½"

2¼"

Base Support Molding

Base Rail

Hidden Compartment in Base
(Access by Removing Bottom Drawer)

2 **Cut mortises in the frame stiles and rails.** Since the frame-and-panel joinery is virtually identical throughout the desk, it saves time to machine the joints all at once. To further save time, make identical frames for the sides and the kneehole. Trim the kneehole frames to size later.

Lay out and cut ¼-inch-wide × 1½-inch-deep mortises in the frame stiles and rails where shown in the Side View. A hollow chisel mortiser on the drill press is great for this operation. If you don't have a hollow chisel mortiser, rout them with a plunge router or drill a series of 1½-inch-deep holes within the layout lines, and chisel out the waste.

3 **Cut tenons in the frame.** Cut tenons on the ends of the top rails, base rails, and middle stiles on the table saw with a dado cutter or tenoning jig. Cut a test

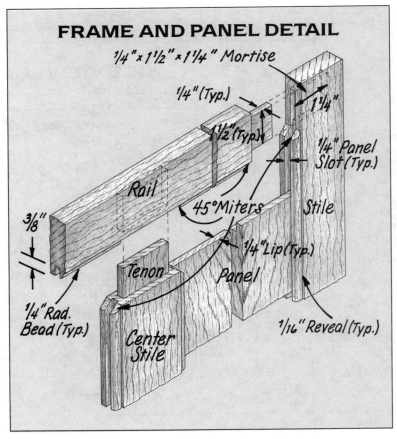

FRAME AND PANEL DETAIL

¼" × 1½" × 1¼" Mortise

¼" (Typ.)

1¼"

1½" (Typ.)

¼" Panel Slot (Typ.)

Rail

45° Miters

Stile

3/8"

¼" Lip (Typ.)

Tenon

Panel

¼" Rad. Bead (Typ.)

1/16" Reveal (Typ.)

Center Stile

tenon in a piece of scrap, and make sure that it fits snugly into the mortises. Make any necessary adjustments, and then cut the tenons in the actual rails and stiles.

All tenons are ¼ inch thick and 1¼ inches long, and have ½-inch shoulders.

4 **Cut the bead on the stiles and rails.** Rout a ¼-inch-radius roundover on the stiles and rails as shown in the Frame and Panel Detail. Rout the bead with a ¼-inch-radius roundover bit in a table-mounted router. Rout the profile to produce a ¹/₁₆-inch reveal above the bead.

5 **Cut panel slots in the stiles and rails.** Cut ¼-inch-wide × ³/₈-inch-deep panel slots in all frame parts except the base rails, as shown in the Frame and Panel Detail. Rout the panel slots with a ¼-inch slotting cutter set up in a table-mounted router. Cut panel slots along the entire length of the rails, along both edges of the center stiles, and between the mortises on the remaining stiles.

6 **Miter the bead on the rails and stiles.** Assembly of the frames and panels requires that the ends of the bead be mitered, as shown in the Frame and Panel Detail. Set the table saw blade at 45 degrees, and raise it until it just touches the reveal above the bead, as shown in the Mitered Bead Setup.

Miter the bead on the ends of the rails and center stiles first. After you miter the rails, miter the bead at the end of each stile. Clean away the waste between the

MITERED BEAD SETUP

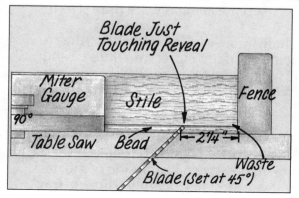

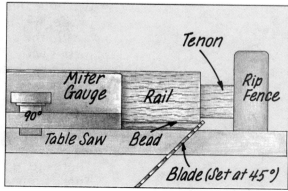

miter and the end of the stile with a backsaw and chisel.

You must also miter the beads at the end of the center stiles. Draw layout lines on the back of the rails to indicate where the miters should be. Align the layout lines with the saw blade, and guide the rails with the miter gauge to miter the bead.

7 **Rabbet the panels to fit into the panel slot.** The panels are $1/2$ inch thick, flat on the outside, and flush with the inside of the frames. This construction allows the drawers to slide easily against the sides.

Rabbet the back of the panels to create a $1/4$-inch-thick × $3/8$-inch-wide lip, which fits into the panel slots in the rails and stiles. Cut the rabbets on the table saw or with a router and rabbeting bit.

8 **Assemble the frames and panels.** Test fit the frame-and-panel assemblies, and make sure that each panel has about $3/32$ inch room to expand from side to side. If necessary, trim the width of the panel.

Disassemble the frame, and put glue in the mortises and on the tenons. Assemble the frames and panels, pulling them together with bar or pipe clamps. Make sure each frame is square by measuring diagonally across the corners. If the cross-corner measurements are equal, the assembly is square. Do not glue the panels in place: The panels must float free in the panel slots.

9 **Prepare the frames and panels to accept the back.** All four frame-and-panel assemblies must be modified slightly. The exact modification depends on the panel's position on the desk: The two units that make up the desk sides are rabbeted for the back, while the two units that make up the kneehole are ripped to the proper width.

Rip the kneehole frame-and-panel units so they're 22 inches wide. Then put a dado cutter into the saw and adjust the blade height and fence to cut a $1/2 × 1/2$-inch rabbet in the back stile of the side units as shown in the Back View.

Make the web frames.

There are ten web frames, five on each side of the desk. These frames tie the desk sides together. Three of the frames on each side provide ledges on which the drawers slide. The other two frames are at the top and bottom of the desk.

The sides of web frames are called runners, and the front and back are called rails.

1 Prepare the stock. The stock for the web frames is 1½ inches wide, but this is not critical and can be wider or narrower if desired. Everything but the front of the web frame can be made from a secondary wood such as poplar.

2 Cut and assemble the drawer frames. Cut ¼ × 1 × 1-inch tenons in the ends of the runners, and matching mortises at the ends of the rails, as shown in the Web Frame Detail. Glue and clamp the runners and rails together, and make certain the assembly is square.

When the glue has dried, cut a ¼ × ½-inch notch in the ends of the front web rails as shown in the Web Frame Detail.

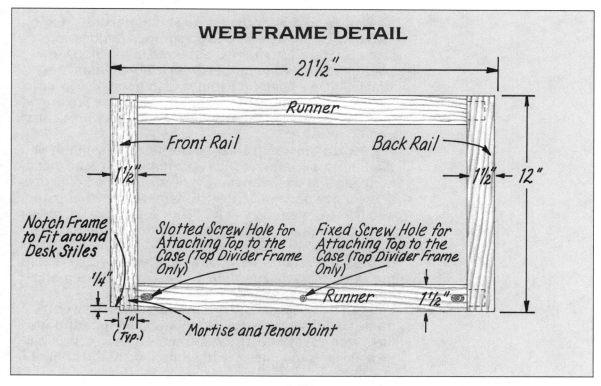

WEB FRAME DETAIL

21½"

Runner

Front Rail — Back Rail

1½" — 1½" ← 12"

Notch Frame to Fit around Desk Stiles

Slotted Screw Hole for Attaching Top to the Case (Top Divider Frame Only)

Fixed Screw Hole for Attaching Top to the Case (Top Divider Frame Only)

¼"

Runner — 1½"

1" (Typ.)

Mortise and Tenon Joint

3 **Drill screw holes into the top web frames.** The top of the desk is attached to the upper web frames with three #10 × 1¼-inch roundhead screws, which run through the outside web frame runner as shown in the Web Frame Detail. The center screw runs through a hole, as shown, and the other screws fit into slots. This allows the top to expand and contract with changes in humidity.

Drill the center holes first, and then make the slots. Rout the slots with a plunge router, guided by its fence attachment. First rout a ½-inch-wide × ¼-inch-deep groove for a washer and screwhead. Without changing the fence setting, put in a ³/₁₆-inch straight bit and rout the slot for the screw shank.

If you don't have a plunge router, drill starter holes and use a regular router and fence attachment. First drill a ⁵/₈-inch-diameter × ¼-inch-deep hole. Ease your router bit into the hole and rout the washer and head slots. Next drill a ⁵/₁₆-inch-diameter through hole, and ease your router bit into it to cut the shank slot.

Assemble the case.

1 **Dado and rabbet the frame and panel units.** Lay out ³/₄-inch-wide × ¼-inch-deep stopped dadoes and rabbets for the web frames, as shown in the Side View. Rout the dadoes and rabbets with a ³/₄-inch-diameter straight bit in a hand-held router. Clamp a straightedge to the frame and panel units to guide the router. Square off the end of the stopped dadoes and rabbets with a chisel.

2 **Attach the web frames to the sides.** Test fit the web frames in the frame and panel units. Make sure that the front edges of the web frame are flush with the front edges of the frame and panel units. Enlarge the notches in the web frames if necessary. Drive #8 × 1¼-inch drywall screws down through the top web frames and into the rabbets.

When the web frames fit correctly, glue them into the dadoes and rabbets. Apply glue to the stiles only. Clamp the assemblies together. Make sure that the assemblies are square, and allow the glue to dry.

Attach the base molding support under the web frame where shown in the Side View. Glue the supports flush with the front of the web frames. The supports will be used later to attach the base molding to the front of the case. Next, attach the hidden compartment bottom to the upper side of the bottom web frame with #5 × ³⁄₄-inch flathead wood screws.

Attach the back.

The back is rabbeted into two rails that run the length of the desk, as shown in the Back View. The rail ends are rabbeted to fit into the back stiles. I made the back from two layers of plywood. I nailed one layer into place, and then glued the second layer over it to hide the nails.

1 Make the back rails. Rabbet the rails for the back. Cut a ¹⁄₂ × ¹⁄₂-inch rabbet along one edge of the rails with a dado cutter on the table saw. Next, rout rabbets on the rail ends as shown in the Bottom View.

Dado the rails, as shown, to fit around the kneehole frames and panels. Double-check your rabbet and dado layouts by comparing the layout lines on the back rails with the actual cabinet parts.

2 Rout the profile in the back rails, the top, and the base molding. Put a ¹⁄₄-inch-radius Roman ogee bit in a table-mounted router, and adjust the setup to cut the profile shown in the Base Molding Detail. Guide the stock against the router table fence as you rout.

3 Attach the back. First, position the top and bottom rails as shown in the Back View. Drill, countersink, and counterbore through the rails into the stiles for #8 drywall screws. Screw and glue the rails into place with #8 × 1 ¹⁄₄-inch drywall screws.

The back is made up of two ¹⁄₄-inch-thick pieces of plywood: Install the first so that the better side faces the kneehole, and install the second so the better side is exposed. Glue and nail the first piece of plywood to the sides and rails with 3d common nails. Spread contact cement on the two back pieces, allow the glue to set up for a few minutes, and then press the two pieces together.

4 Attach the base molding. Miter the base molding to fit around the desk. Start with the kneehole molding. With a coping saw, cut the base molding to fit the ogee you routed on the back rail. Miter the molding to cut it to

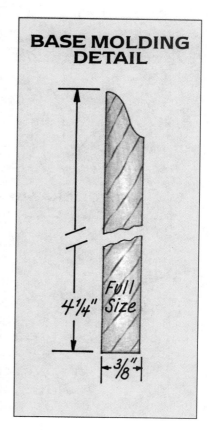

BASE MOLDING DETAIL

4¹⁄₄"

Full Size

³⁄₈"

length. Then miter the molding to fit the front and sides of the desk. Glue and clamp the molding into place.

Build the drawers.

1 **Size the drawer fronts and backs.** Whenever you are building drawers for a cabinet, it is a good idea to cut the parts to coincide with the actual openings. Measure each drawer opening, and cut a drawer front and back to fit in it with $1/16$-inch leeway, both up-and-down and sideways.

2 **Lay out and cut the dovetails.** Lay out tails on the drawer sides, as shown in the Large Drawer, Small Drawer, and Pencil Drawer Side Views. Notice that the

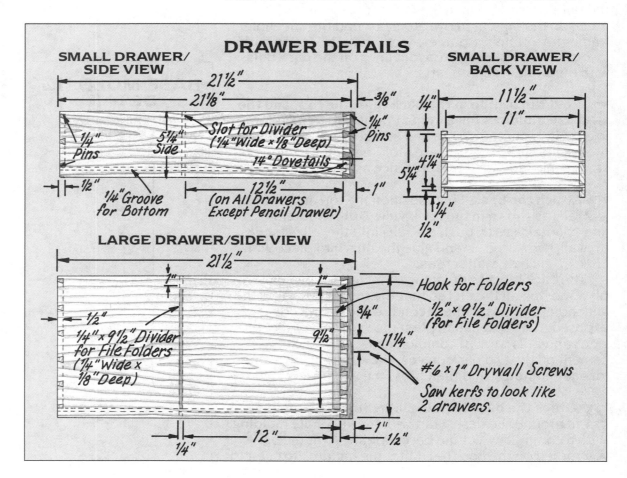

DRAWER DETAILS

SMALL DRAWER/ SIDE VIEW

21½"
21⅛"
3/8"
¼" Pins
5¼" Side
Slot for Divider (¼"Wide × ⅛"Deep)
¼" Pins
14° Dovetails
½"
¼"Groove for Bottom
12½" (on All Drawers Except Pencil Drawer)
1"

SMALL DRAWER/ BACK VIEW

¼"
11½"
11"
4¼"
5¼"
¼"
½"

LARGE DRAWER/SIDE VIEW

21½"
1"
1"
Hook for Folders
3/4"
½" × 9½" Divider (for File Folders)
¼" × 9½" Divider for File Folders (¼"Wide × ⅛"Deep)
½"
9½"
11¼"
#6 × 1" Drywall Screws
Saw kerfs to look like 2 drawers.
¼"
12"
1"
½"

dovetails in the front of the drawers are half-blind and the dovetails at the back of the drawers are through. Lay out and cut the tails first, and then lay out the pins directly from the tails. For more on dovetails, see "Cutting Half-Blind Dovetails" on page 155 and "Cutting Through Dovetails" on page 81.

3 **Cut the drawer bottom grooves.** Cut $1/4 \times 1/4$-inch grooves in the drawer fronts and sides for the ply-wood drawer bottoms with a dado cutter on the table saw.

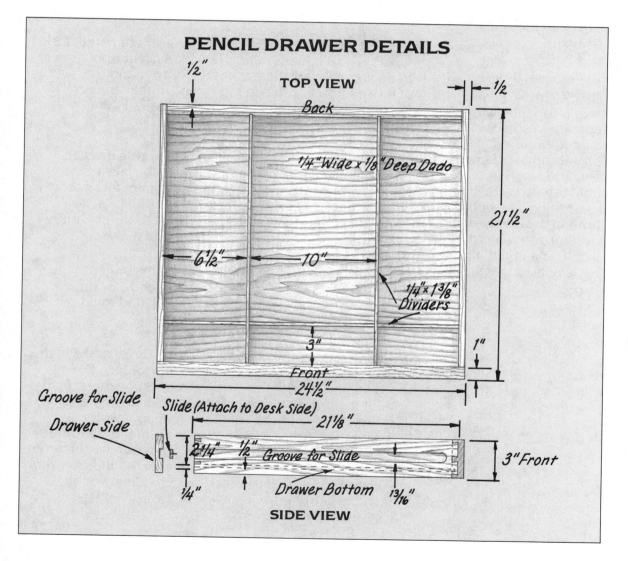

PENCIL DRAWER DETAILS

4 Cut slots for the drawer dividers. Cut 1/4-inch-wide × 1/8-inch-deep slots in the large and small drawer sides for the removable dividers. Position the slot as shown in the Small Drawer/Side View and Large Drawer/Side View.

5 Assemble the drawers. Glue and clamp the drawer sides into the front and back. Make sure that the drawers are square, and allow the glue to dry.

When the glue is dry, remove the clamps and slide the drawer bottoms in from the back.

6 Fit the drawers. Check each drawer's fit in the desk. There are always minor deviations in fit from drawer to drawer, so mark the back of the drawer and the inside of its web frame with corresponding Roman numerals. Fill any minor imperfections in the dovetail joints with wood filler.

7 Rout grooves in the face of the double drawer. Rout two 1/16-inch-wide grooves in the face of the double drawers to simulate the web frame rail as shown in the Front View. Rout the grooves with a 1/16-inch-diameter straight bit in a table-mounted router. Guide the drawer front against the fence to make the cut.

8 Round the drawer edges. Round the edges of the drawer sides and back with a 1/8-inch-radius round-over bit in a hand-held router. Lightly round the drawer faces with sandpaper.

9 Make the large drawer dividers. The dividers in the large drawers support hanging file folders. For a good fit, have a folder on hand when setting this up.

Cut the drawer dividers to the size in the Materials List. Round-over the top of the rear divider with a 1/8-inch-radius roundover bit in a table-mounted router.

To rout the front divider to the profile shown, first rout a 1/4-inch cove in one edge of the divider. Round-over the resulting tongue with a 1/8-inch-radius roundover bit. Attach the support to the inside of the drawer front with #6 × 1-inch drywall screws.

Slip the rear divider into its dado.

10 **Make the pencil drawer dividers.** To keep pencils from rolling around the pencil drawer, I divided it into six sections. The dividers simply slip in from the top of the drawer.

First, rout dadoes in the rear divider to accept the two long dividers. Cut lap joints at the intersections of the long and short dividers, as shown in the Drawer Divider Joint Detail. Cut the joints with a dado cutter on the table saw. Guide the stock with a miter gauge as you cut.

11 **Make the slots for the pencil drawer slides.** On the router table, cut a slot $^{13}/_{16}$ inch wide and $^1/_4$ inch deep on each side of the pencil drawer as shown in

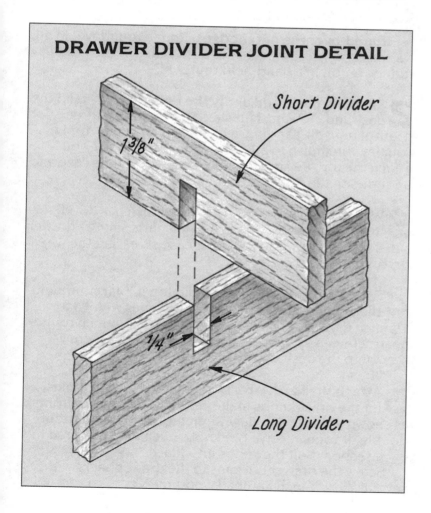

DRAWER DIVIDER JOINT DETAIL

Short Divider

$1^3/_8$"

$^1/_4$"

Long Divider

the Pencil Drawer/Side View. Stop the slot about 1 1/2 inches from the front of the drawer, as shown.

12 **Attach the pencil drawer slides.** Make 1/4 × 7/8 × 20-inch slides. Attach them to the case with #5 × 3/4-inch flathead wood screws so that the drawer will be suspended 1/16 inch below the desktop.

13 **Attach drawer stops.** Nail drawer stops, made from scrap wood, to the back of the drawer divider frames so that the drawers stop flush with the front of the desk.

Complete the desk.

1 **Round-over the outer edges.** Rout a roundover in all the exposed corners of the desk with a 1/8-inch-radius roundover bit in a hand-held router.

2 **Sand the parts and apply the finish.** Finish sand the desk and drawers. I finished this desk with three coats of tung oil, sanding lightly between coats. Apply your favorite finish to all parts of the desk before you attach the top. Be sure to finish the inside of the case and underneath the top to prevent warping.

3 **Wax the moving parts.** After the finish has dried, lightly sand and wax any moving parts such as drawer sides, web frames, and the inner case sides. Let the wax dry and buff off the excess.

4 **Attach the desktop.** Screw the top in place through the center holes in the top web frames with #6 × 1 1/2-inch drywall screws. Center the #10 × 1 1/4-inch round-head screws and washers in their grooves, and screw them into the desktop.

5 **Attach the hardware.** Drill 1/4-inch-diameter holes for the brass knobs in the center of the drawer fronts, as shown in the Front View. Remember that the bottom double drawers receive two knobs each, one centered in each section. Bolt the knobs into place.

Screw the drawer bottoms to the drawer backs with several #5 × 1/2-inch flathead wood screws.

CUTTING HALF-BLIND DOVETAILS

Half-blind dovetails are the preferred method for joining a drawer side to a drawer front, and are used almost exclusively for that purpose. The are called half-blind because they can be seen only from the side of the drawer. When the drawer is closed they are out of sight.

The only difference between a half-blind dovetail and a through dovetail is that the edges of the dovetail are completely contained within the pins. When you remove the waste between the pins, you actually cut an enclosed pocket for the dovetail.

1 Lay out the length of the tails and pins. Set a marking gauge to the length of the tails, and scribe a line around each drawer side as shown. This

scribe line is the base of the tails. When cutting the dovetails, be careful not to cut beyond this line.

With the marking gauge at the same setting, scribe one line along the end grain of the drawer front. This line indicates the length of the pins. You scribe the depth of the pins on the inside surface of the drawer fronts. Reset the marking gauge to the thickness of the drawer side and scribe the line.

Cut all the scribe lines $1/16$ inch deep by drawing a chisel or sharp knife along them. This creates a crisp shoulder for the joint.

2 Lay out the tails. Lay out the tails with a sliding T-bevel set at the appropriate angle—usually 14 degrees.

Scribe a line with a marking gauge to determine the lengths of the pins and tails.

Lay out the angle of the tails with a sliding T-bevel.

(continued)

CUTTING HALF-BLIND DOVETAILS—
Continued

Transfer the layout lines across the end grain with a square. Use the sliding T-bevel again to lay out the tails on the other side of the board.

3 **Cut out the tails.** Saw down to the scribe line, cutting just to the waste side of the layout lines. A Japanese dozuki saw, like the one shown here, is easy to control and cuts crisp lines. Watch your layout lines carefully: Follow the angle of the tails, and make sure you don't cut past either one of the scribe lines.

4 **Remove the waste between the tails.** Chisel out the waste between the tails. Put the chisel just on the waste side of the base line, and drive it with a mallet. Remove the waste by chopping

from the end of the board. Repeat the process. When you're halfway through the board, flip it over and chisel from the other side. After the first cut, angle the chisel slightly, as shown, to ease assembly of the joint.

5 **Lay out the pins.** For best results, lay out the pins by tracing around the tails. Hold the tails against the end grain of what will be the pins, and trace around the tails with a knife. The layout lines for the pins should go from the scribe line to the edge of the board. Transfer your layout lines down the face of the board, and clearly mark the waste with a pencil.

6 **Cut out the pins.** Saw along the layout lines to the scribe lines, and

Cut out the tails with a dozuki or dovetail saw.

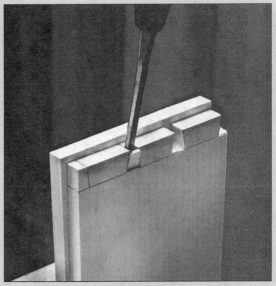

Chisel out the waste between the tails.

chisel away the waste to create pockets for the dovetails. Test fit the dovetails.

Pare the pins to fit the tails with a chisel if necessary.

Lay out the pins by tracing around the tails.

Chisel away the waste between the tails.

CABINETS
FOR THE
DINING ROOM

HUNTBOARD

by David T. Smith

During the Renaissance, the sporting gentry began to take the meal following a hunt standing up.

After spending hours in the saddle, it was more comfortable to stand up than to sit down. Furnituremakers built long, tall tables where the saddle-sore ladies and gents could stand as they ate. These became known as "huntboards."

When not needed for dining, a huntboard often became a sideboard. During an ordinary meal, it held the food that was being served on the main table.

It was used between meals to store serving bowls and to store cutlery and other utensils. The makers often added shelves above the tabletop and drawers beneath it to increase the storage space.

The popularity of the hunt gradually waned; but owing to its usefulness as a storage unit, the huntboard remained a common sight in kitchens and dining areas for many centuries. Folks continue to use them to this day. I adapted the hunt-

board shown from an early nineteenth-century design. A collection of my historically inspired pieces has been published in the book *American Country Furniture.*

EXPLODED VIEW

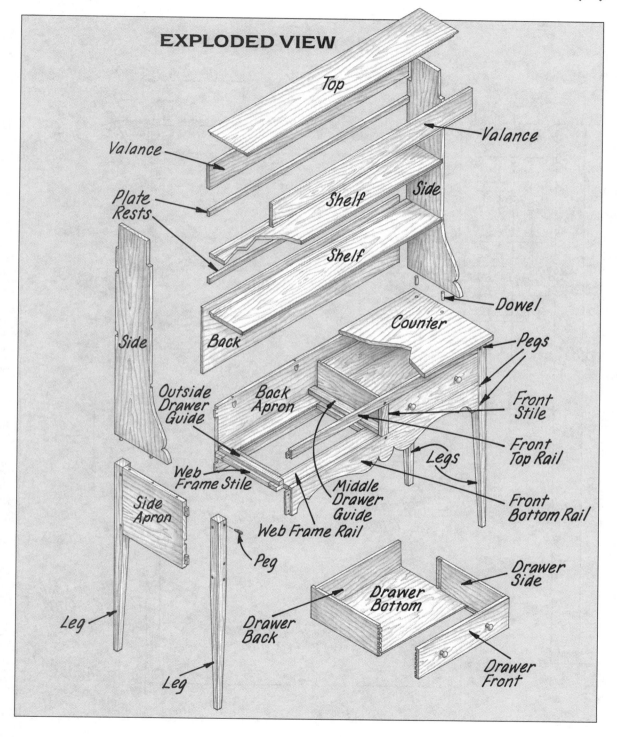

Top

Valance

Valance

Plate Rests

Shelf

Side

Shelf

Dowel

Side

Back

Counter

Pegs

Outside Drawer Guide

Back Apron

Front Stile

Front Top Rail

Web Frame Stile

Middle Drawer Guide

Legs

Front Bottom Rail

Side Apron

Web Frame Rail

Peg

Leg

Drawer Back

Drawer Bottom

Drawer Side

Drawer Front

Leg

FRONT VIEW

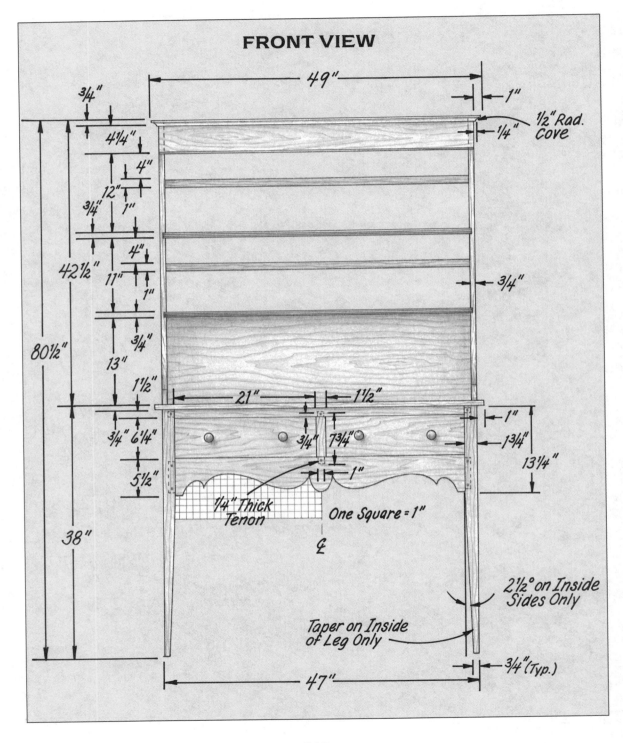

49"

1"

¾"

½" Rad. Cove

¼"

4¼"

4"

12"

¾" 1"

42½"

4"

11"

1"

¾"

13"

80½"

1½"

21"

1½"

¾"

¾" 3¾"

1"

38"

¼" Thick Tenon

One Square = 1"

₵

3" 6¼"

5½"

1"

13¼"

1¾"

2½° on Inside Sides Only

Taper on Inside of Leg Only

47"

¾" (Typ.)

SIDE VIEW

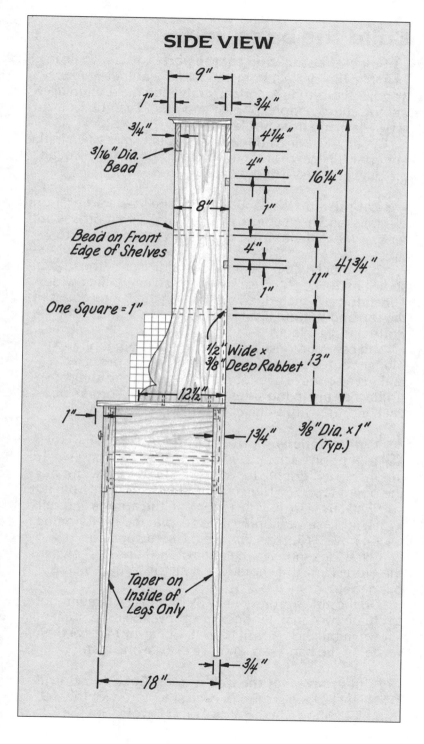

9"

1"

3/4"

3/4"

3/16" Dia. Bead

4 1/4"

4"

1"

16 1/4"

8"

Bead on Front Edge of Shelves

One Square = 1"

1/2" Wide x 3/8" Deep Rabbet

4"

1"

11"

41 3/4"

13"

12 1/2"

1"

1 3/4"

3/8" Dia. x 1" (Typ.)

Taper on Inside of Legs Only

3/4"

18"

Build the base unit.

1 Select the stock and cut the parts to size. You can make this project from almost any cabinet-grade wood, but old-time American craftsmen most often used walnut, cherry, maple, poplar, and pine. The huntboard shown is made from poplar.

Cut all the ³/₄-inch-thick pieces to the sizes given in the Materials List, except for the drawer fronts. You'll cut all the drawer parts to fit the cabinet later.

2 Cut the mortises and tenons. The legs, aprons, front rails, and front stile are assembled with mortises and tenons. Make the mortises first, then fit the tenons to them.

Cut ³/₈-inch-wide, ³/₄-inch-deep mortises in the legs, as shown in the Leg Mortise Layout. Also cut ¹/₄-inch-wide, 1-inch-long, ³/₄-inch-deep mortises in the facing edges of the top and bottom front rails, as shown in the Front Bottom Rail Layout.

You can rout these mortises with a straight bit in a plunge router, or rough them out on a drill press by making a series of overlapping holes. After routing or drilling, clean up the sides and square the corners of each mortise with a chisel.

3 Cut the tenons. Note that the side aprons have two tenons on each end, while the others all have single tenons. To cut double tenons, cut a tenon the width of the board first, and then cut the smaller tenons from it.

First, cut ³/₈-inch-wide tenons on the aprons and rails with a table saw tenoning jig, as explained in "Tenoning Jig" on page 375. Then change the setup and cut ¹/₄-inch-wide tenons in the ends of the stile, as shown in the Front View. Cut shoulders in all the tenons on the band saw.

On the side aprons, cut away part of the larger tenon to create two small tenons, one above the others, as shown in the Side Apron Layout. Cut away most of the waste on the band saw, and chisel away the rest.

4 Cut grooves for the web frames. Cut a ³/₄-inch-wide, ³/₈-inch-deep groove in each side apron for the web frames, as shown in the Side Apron Layout. Cut the

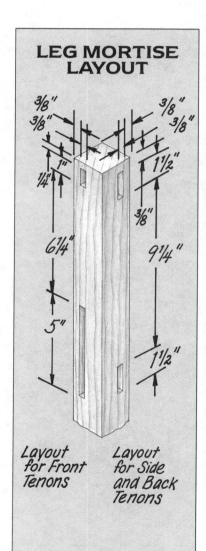

LEG MORTISE LAYOUT

³/₈″ ³/₈″
³/₈″ ³/₈″
1″ 1½″
¼″
6¼″ 9¼″
³/₈″
5″
1½″

Layout for Front Tenons   *Layout for Side and Back Tenons*

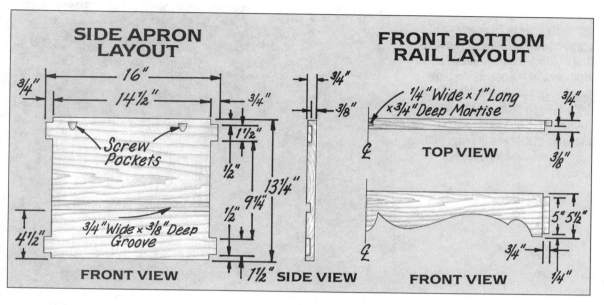

SIDE APRON LAYOUT

16"

14½"

¾"

¾"

Screw Pockets

1½"

½"

13¼"

9¼"

½"

4½"

3/4" Wide × 3/8" Deep Groove

FRONT VIEW

¾"

3/8"

1½" SIDE VIEW

FRONT BOTTOM RAIL LAYOUT

¼" Wide × 1" Long × ¾" Deep Mortise

TOP VIEW

¾"

3/8"

5" 5½"

¾"

FRONT VIEW

¼"

MATERIALS LIST

Part	Dimension
Base Unit	
Legs (4)	$1\frac{3}{4}" \times 1\frac{3}{4}" \times 37\frac{1}{4}"$
Side aprons (2)	$\frac{3}{4}" \times 13\frac{1}{4}" \times 16"$
Back apron	$\frac{3}{4}" \times 13\frac{1}{4}" \times 45"$
Front top rail	$\frac{3}{4}" \times 1\frac{1}{2}" \times 45"$
Front bottom rail	$\frac{3}{4}" \times 5\frac{1}{2}" \times 45"$
Front stile	$\frac{3}{4}" \times 1\frac{1}{2}" \times 7\frac{3}{4}"$
Counter	$\frac{3}{4}" \times 19" \times 49"$
Pegs (22)	$\frac{5}{16}" \times \frac{5}{16}" \times 1\frac{1}{4}"$
Dowels (4)	$\frac{3}{8}"$ dia. $\times 1\frac{1}{2}"$
Web Frames	
Web frame stiles (3)	$\frac{3}{4}" \times 3" \times 11"$
Web frame rails (2)	$\frac{3}{4}" \times 3" \times 46\frac{1}{4}"$
Outside drawer guides (2)	$\frac{3}{4}" \times 1" \times 14\frac{1}{2}"$
Middle drawer guide	$\frac{3}{4}" \times 1\frac{1}{2}" \times 16\frac{1}{2}"$
Upper Unit	
Sides (2)	$\frac{3}{4}" \times 12\frac{1}{2}" \times 41\frac{3}{4}"$
Shelves (2)	$\frac{3}{4}" \times 8" \times 46\frac{1}{4}"$
Top	$\frac{3}{4}" \times 9" \times 49"$

Part	Dimension
Valances (2)	$\frac{3}{4}" \times 4\frac{1}{4}" \times 47"$
Plate rests (2)	$\frac{3}{4}" \times 1" \times 47"$
Back	$\frac{1}{2}" \times 13\frac{5}{16}" \times 46\frac{1}{4}"$
Drawers	
Drawer fronts (2)	$\frac{3}{4}" \times 6\frac{3}{16}" \times 20\frac{7}{8}"$
Drawer sides (4)	$\frac{1}{2}" \times 6\frac{3}{16}" \times 16\frac{7}{8}"$
Drawer backs (2)	$\frac{1}{2}" \times 5\frac{11}{16}" \times 20\frac{3}{8}"$
Drawer bottoms (2)	$\frac{1}{4}" \times 16\frac{1}{4}" \times 20\frac{3}{8}"$

HARDWARE

As needed, #10 × 1¼" flathead wood screws

4 antique-finish brass knobs, 1¼" dia. Available from Paxton Hardware, Ltd., 7818 Bradshaw Rd., Upper Falls, MD 21156. Part #923.

As needed, 3d finishing nails

As needed, 6d square-cut nails. Available from Tremont Nail Company, P.O. Box 111, Wareham, MA 02571.

To make a screw pocket, first tilt the drill press table to 20 degrees and attach a fence to support the board. Drill a 3/4-inch-diameter pocket in the inside face of the board, stopping about 3/8 inch above the edge. Then drill a 3/16-inch-diameter pilot hole through the center of the pocket. The pilot hole should exit the edge of the board equidistant from the two faces.

grooves with a dado cutter on the table saw. Guide the stock against the fence as you cut.

5 Drill the screw pockets and dowel holes. The counter is attached to the base assembly with #8 × 1" drywall screws. These screws rest in screw pockets, bored into the inside faces of the aprons and the top front rail. Make these pockets on a drill press, drilling the pilot holes at a 20-degree angle, as shown in the photo. Each hole should enter the inside face and exit the top edge of the board. The location of these screw pockets is not critical, but they should be spaced evenly along the boards.

Also drill 3/8-inch-diameter, 1-inch-deep holes for locater dowels in the bottom ends of the sides, as shown in the Side View. Use a doweling jig to help guide the drill.

6 Taper the legs. As shown in the Front View, the legs taper from a 1 3/4-inch square to a 3/4-inch square. Cut these tapers in the inside faces of the legs, using a table saw and a tapering jig. Cut the jig from a scrap of 3/4-inch plywood to the profile shown in the Tapering Jig Detail. Put the leg in the jig, and guide it against the fence, as shown in the photo.

To taper a leg, place the leg stock in the jig with one of the inside faces toward the blade. Feed it into the table saw blade, guiding the jig against the fence. Turn the stock so that the other inside face is toward the blade and repeat.

Build the upper unit.

1 **Cut dadoes, grooves, and rabbets in the sides and shelves.** The upper unit shelves rest in ³/₄-inch-wide, ³/₈-inch-deep dadoes in the sides. The back rests in ¹/₂-inch-wide, ³/₈-inch-deep rabbets in the sides and bottom shelf, as shown in the Side View. In addition, the shelves are grooved to hold the edges of plates, as shown in the Shelf Profile. Rout these joints with a router and straight bit. Guide the router against a straightedge to make the cut.

2 **Cut the bottom front rail and sides to shape.** Lay out the shapes of the bottom front rail and sides as

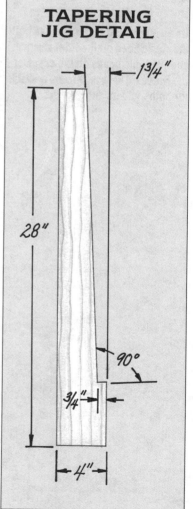

TAPERING JIG DETAIL

1³/₄"

28"

90°

³/₄"

4"

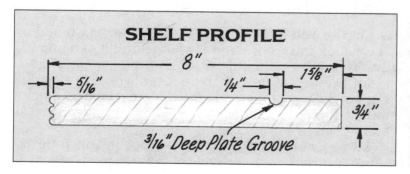

SHELF PROFILE

8"

5/16"   1/4"   1⁵/₈"

³/₄"

³/₁₆" Deep Plate Groove

167

Use a three-bead cutter to make both the single bead on the front valance and the triple beads on the edges of the shelves. These cutters are available for both molders and shapers.

shown in the Front View and Side View. Also lay out the notches in the sides as shown in the Side View. Cut the shapes and notches with a band saw or saber saw. Sand the sawed edges.

3 Shape the edges of the top, front valance, and shelves. Several parts of the top assembly are cut with decorative coves and beads. Using a table-mounted router, cut a 1/2-inch-radius cove in the ends and front edge of the top. Also cut 3/16-inch-diameter beads in the bottom edge of the front valance and the front edges of the shelves, as shown in the Shelf Profile.

Make the web frame.

1 Cut the web frame joints. The web frame is joined by tongues and grooves, and the assembled web frame rests in grooves in the side aprons.

Rout 1/4-inch-wide, 1/4-inch-deep grooves in the inside edges of the web frame rails. Make the cut with a 1/4-inch straight bit in a table-mounted router, and guide the stock against a fence.

With a tenoning jig on the table saw, cut 1/4-inch-thick, 1/4-inch-long tenons in the ends of the web frame stiles.

◇ ◇   ◇ ◇

2 **Assemble the web frame.** Lightly sand the web frame rails, stiles, and drawer guides. Glue the rails and stiles together as shown in the Web Frame Layout. Let the glue dry. Lay out the corner notches, cutting these with a hand saw or fret saw. Then attach the drawer guides with glue and #10 × 1¼-inch flathead wood screws.

Assemble the huntboard.

1 **Assemble the base.** Finish sand the legs, aprons, rails, stile, and counter. Test fit the base parts—including the web. When you're certain they all fit properly, glue them together. Check that the aprons and rails are square with one another as you tighten the clamps. When the glue dries, remove the clamps and sand all joints clean and flush.

Fasten the counter in place by driving #10 × 1¼-inch flathead wood screws up through the screw pockets. Do not glue the counter to the base assembly.

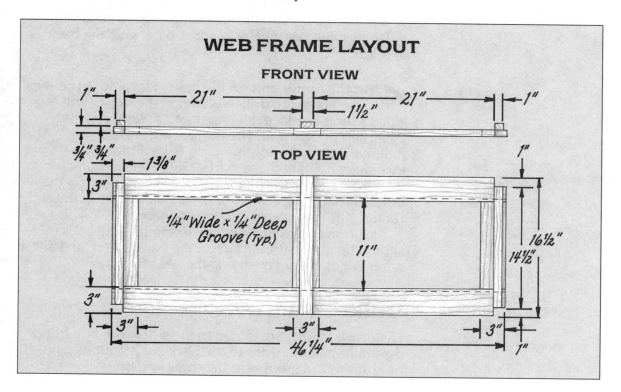

WEB FRAME LAYOUT

FRONT VIEW

1″ 21″ 1½″ 21″ 1″
¾″ ¾″

TOP VIEW

1⅜″
3″
¼″ Wide × ¼″ Deep Groove (Typ.)
11″
16½″
14½″
1″
3″
3″ 3″ 3″
46¼″
1″

2 **Peg the joints.** Colonial craftsmen often pegged their mortise-and-tenon joints for extra strength.

To peg your mortise-and-tenon joints, drill $5/16$-inch-diameter, $1\,1/4$-inch-deep holes in the outside faces of the legs. Drill the holes through all the mortises and tenons. Also drill holes through the mortise-and-tenon joints that hold the drawer stiles to the rails.

Whittle the pegs round on one end. Drive the pegs, round end first, into the holes until the square ends are flush with the outside surfaces. Cut off the round ends of the pegs that you've driven above and below the stiles—these will protrude slightly on the inside.

3 **Assemble the upper unit.** Finish sand the sides, top, shelves, valances, plate rests, and back. Test fit the parts, then glue together all the parts except the back. Check that the shelves are square with the sides as you tighten the clamps. When the glue dries, sand the joints clean and flush. Reinforce the glue joints with 6d square-cut nails and set the heads. These nails will reproduce the look of old-time hand-forged nails.

Fasten the back to the sides and bottom shelf with 3d finishing nails, setting the heads. Do not glue the back in place.

4 **Put the upper unit on the base.** Place dowel centers in the holes you drilled earlier in the upper unit sides. Carefully place the upper unit assembly on the base, and press down. The centers will leave small indentations in the counter. Drill $3/8$-inch-diameter, $1/2$-inch-deep holes at these marks. Glue $3/8$-inch-diameter, $1\,1/2$-inch-long dowels into the holes in the sides. Fit the other end of these dowels into the holes in the counter. Do not glue the dowels into the counter.

Position the top on the base assembly. The back edge should be flush with the face of the back apron, and all other edges should overhang the base by 1 inch.

Build the drawers.

The drawer fronts are joined to the sides with half-blind dovetails, and the sides to the backs with dadoes. The bottoms rest in grooves in the sides and fronts.

1 Cut the drawer parts. Because of construction
variations, the drawers may differ slightly from the
dimensions given in the Materials List. Use the Materials
List as a guide, but measure directly from the cabinet for
final dimensions. Cut the drawer parts to leave ¹/₁₆ inch

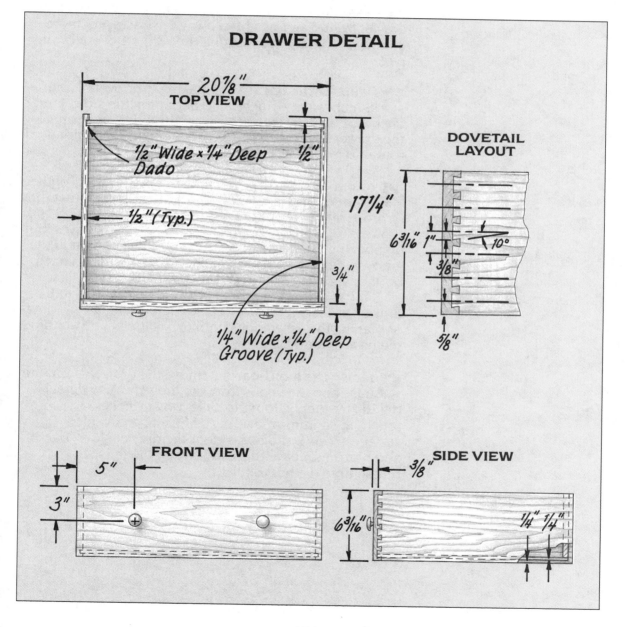

DRAWER DETAIL

20⅞"
TOP VIEW

½" Wide × ¼" Deep Dado

½"

½" (Typ.)

17¼"

¾"

¼" Wide × ¼" Deep Groove (Typ.)

DOVETAIL LAYOUT

6³/₁₆" 1"

10°

⅜"

⅝"

FRONT VIEW

5"

3"

SIDE VIEW

⅜"

6³/₁₆"

¼" ¼"

clearance above each drawer, and a total of $\frac{1}{8}$ inch side-to-side clearance.

2 Cut the dovetails. Lay out the dovetails on the side of the drawer, as shown in Drawer Detail/Dovetail Layout. Cut the tails with a dovetail saw, and chisel out the waste. Trace around the tails to lay out the pins in the drawer front. Saw and chisel away the waste. For more on drawer joinery, see "Cutting Half-Blind Dovetails" on page 155.

3 Dado for the back. After making the dovetails, cut $\frac{1}{2}$-inch-wide, $\frac{1}{4}$-inch-deep dadoes in the sides for the back. Cut $\frac{1}{4}$-inch-deep grooves in the sides and fronts for the drawer bottom. Use a dado cutter or a table-mounted router to make these joints.

4 Assemble the drawers. Finish sand the parts of the drawers, and test fit them. When you're sure that they fit properly, glue the fronts, sides, and backs of the drawers together. Slide the bottoms into the grooves, but do not glue them into place—let the bottoms float in the grooves. Drive a single 3d finishing nail up though each bottom and into the back to keep the bottom in place.

Sand the drawer joints clean and flush, and install drawer knobs. Fit the drawers to their openings, sanding or planing the assemblies until they slide in and out of the base smoothly.

5 Finish the huntboard. Remove the drawers from the base and the knobs from the drawers. Also detach the top assembly from the base. Do any necessary touch-up sanding and apply a finish to all wooden surfaces, inside and out, except the drawer sides, backs, and bottoms. Leave these raw. When the finish dries, reassemble the huntboard.

SILVER CHEST
by Ben Erickson

This traditional dove-tailed silver chest provides an elegant home for your finest tableware. It sits on a separate base, positioned by two dowels which allow for easy removal. A pull-out shelf in the base gives you a place to set silverware for sorting. The three drawers are lined with tarnish-resistant cloth. They provide ample storage space and may be divided into sections for various items.

You'll invest meticulous work in this compact piece, so it doesn't make sense to skimp on materials. I make chests like this one from solid walnut or cherry. Mahogany would also be a good choice. The drawer sides and backs may be made from a secondary wood, such as poplar, to save money and to dramatize the dovetails. As an alternative, I often make drawer sides from cherry or walnut sapwood that is unsuitable for face pieces.

The simple tapered legs are complemented by the brass Hepplewhite handles and brass knob. The nice thing about a small, complex piece such as this is that it lets you test your

skills without being a major drain on your pocketbook or taking up too much space in the shop. The silver chest and base require about 35 board feet of primary wood and 8 board feet of secondary wood.

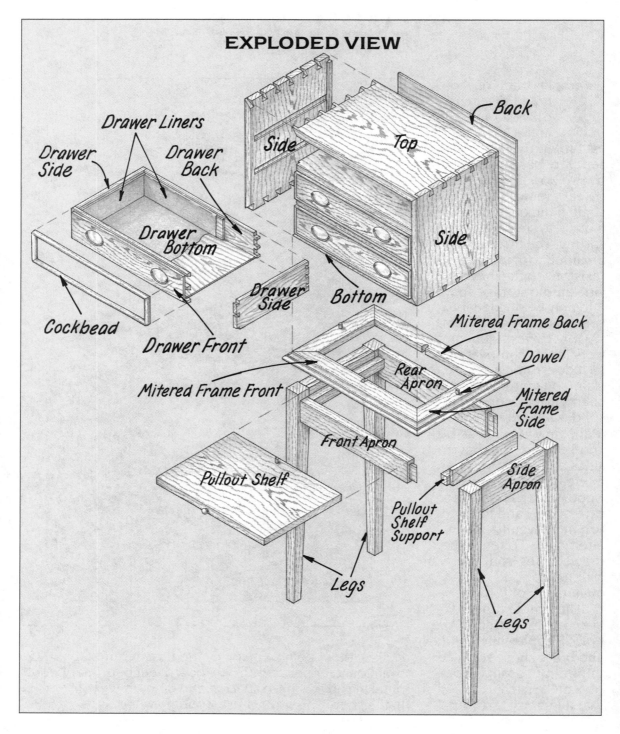

EXPLODED VIEW

Drawer Liners

Drawer Side

Drawer Back

Side

Top

Back

Drawer Side

Drawer Bottom

Side

Cockbead

Drawer Side

Bottom

Drawer Front

Mitered Frame Back

Mitered Frame Front

Rear Apron

Dowel

Mitered Frame Side

Front Apron

Pullout Shelf

Pullout Shelf Support

Side Apron

Legs

Legs

Build the base.

1 Choose the stock and cut the parts. Joint, plane, rip, and cut the parts to the sizes given in the Materials List, except for the drawer parts. You'll cut the drawer parts to fit later.

You will probably need to glue up several boards for the wider parts. The back can be made of plywood, but if you plan to make it of solid wood as I did, then glue up that panel, too.

For a striking effect, consider resawing and bookmatching a board for the case parts. To bookmatch, resaw an 8/4 (eight-quarters) rough-sawed board into two boards, each approximately 1 inch thick. Give the boards a few days to stabilize in your shop and then joint and plane them. Glue the boards edge-to-edge to make the sides, top, and back.

> **Quick Tip:** On the final pass, plane all pieces at the same planer setting. Record the position of the planer height handle in your cutting list in case you botch a piece and need to make another.

MATERIALS LIST

Part	Dimension	Part	Dimension
Base		Drawer backs (3)	$\frac{1}{2}'' \times 3'' \times 18\frac{1}{2}''$
Legs (4)	$1\frac{3}{4}'' \times 1\frac{3}{4}'' \times 29\frac{1}{4}''$	Drawer sides (6)	$\frac{1}{2}'' \times 4'' \times 11\frac{5}{8}''$
Front apron	$1'' \times 3'' \times 19\frac{3}{4}''$	Drawer bottoms (3)	$\frac{1}{4}'' \times 11\frac{3}{8}'' \times 18''$
Rear apron	$1'' \times 3\frac{3}{4}'' \times 19\frac{3}{4}''$	Drawer liners (6)	$\frac{1}{4}'' \times 3'' \times 10\frac{5}{8}''$
Side aprons (2)	$1'' \times 3\frac{3}{4}'' \times 12\frac{3}{4}''$	Drawer liners (6)	$\frac{1}{4}'' \times 3'' \times 17''$
Mitered frame sides (2)	$\frac{3}{4}'' \times 2\frac{3}{4}'' \times 14\frac{1}{2}''$		
Mitered frame front/ back (2)	$\frac{3}{4}'' \times 2\frac{3}{4}'' \times 21\frac{1}{2}''$	**HARDWARE**	
Dowels (8)	$\frac{1}{4}''$ dia. $\times 1''$	As needed, #5 $\times \frac{3}{4}''$ flathead wood screws	
Dowels (3)	$\frac{3}{8}''$ dia. $\times 1\frac{1}{4}''$	As needed, #8 $\times 2''$ drywall screws	
Pullout shelf supports (2)	$1\frac{1}{4}'' \times 2'' \times 11\frac{1}{2}''$	As needed, #8 $\times 1\frac{1}{2}''$ drywall screws	
Pullout shelf	$\frac{3}{4}'' \times 12\frac{1}{2}'' \times 17\frac{7}{16}''$	6 bright brass Hepplewhite handles, $2\frac{1}{2}''$ wide	
Case		(2" boring). Available from The Woodworkers'	
Sides (2)	$\frac{3}{4}'' \times 13'' \times 15''$	Store, 21801 Industrial Blvd., Rogers, MN	
Top	$\frac{3}{4}'' \times 13'' \times 20''$	55374. Part #E1126.	
Bottom	$\frac{3}{4}'' \times 13'' \times 20''$	1 bright brass knob, $\frac{3}{4}''$ dia.	
Drawer shelves (2)	$\frac{3}{4}'' \times 12\frac{1}{4}'' \times 19''$	As needed, $\frac{3}{4}''$ brads	
Back	$\frac{1}{4}'' \times 14'' \times 19''$		
Drawers			
Drawer fronts (3)	$1'' \times 4'' \times 18\frac{1}{2}''$		

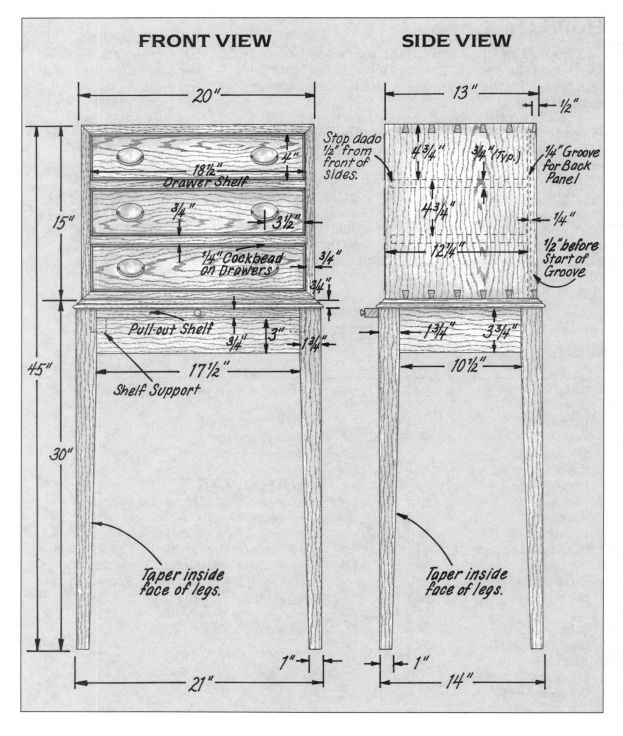

FRONT VIEW

SIDE VIEW

20"

13"

½"

4"

18½"
Drawer Shelf

15"

Stop dado
½" from
front of
sides.

4¾"

¾" (Typ.)

¼" Groove
for Back
Panel

¾"

3½"

4¾"

¼"

½" before
Start of
Groove

¼" Cockbead
on Drawers

¾"

12¼"

¾"

Pull-out Shelf

3"

¾"

3"

1¾"

1¾"

3¾"

45"

17½"

10½"

Shelf Support

30"

Taper inside
face of legs.

Taper inside
face of legs.

1"

1"

21"

1"

14"

2 **Cut mortises on legs.** Examine each leg for the two best adjoining faces and make these the outsides of the leg. Then pick your two best faces and make these the front of the front legs. Place all four legs together and mark the tops to indicate positioning. Also, mark the top with an arrow to indicate which faces receive mortises.

Lay out and cut the ³⁄₈-inch-wide × 1 ¹⁄₈-inch-deep mortises on the legs as shown in the Mortise and Tenon Detail. I cut the mortises with a hollow chisel mortiser on the drill press. If you don't have a hollow chisel mortiser, you have two choices: either cut the mortises with a plunge router, or drill a series of ³⁄₈-inch-diameter holes within the layout lines and clean to the layout lines with a chisel.

Note in the Mortise and Tenon Detail that the mortises for the front skirt are different from all the others.

Quick Tip: Cut the mortises ¹⁄₁₆ inch deeper than the length of the tenon. The gap ensures that the tenon shoulders fit tightly and provides a place for excess glue.

3 **Cut tenons on aprons.** Make the 1 ¹⁄₈-inch-long tenons, as shown in the Mortise and Tenon Detail, with a dado cutter in the table saw. Adjust the blade

MORTISE AND TENON DETAIL

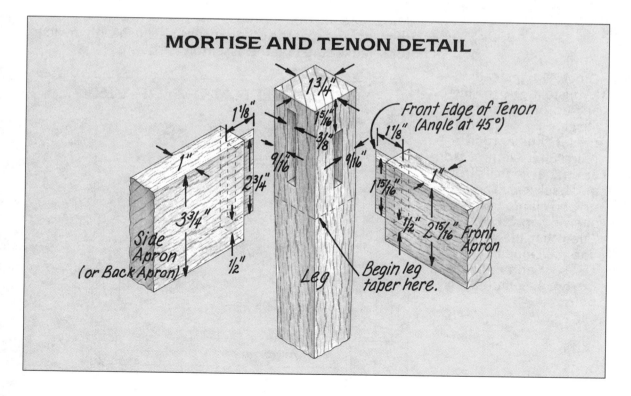

height so that the resulting tenons fit snugly in their mortises. All tenons have ½-inch shoulders, as shown in the Mortise and Tenon Detail.

Cut a 45-degree miter on the ends of the tenons as shown in the Mortise and Tenon Detail.

4 Taper the legs. Each leg is tapered on its two inside faces so that the legs are 1 inch square at the bottom. These tapers begin 4 inches from the top. Lay out the tapers and cut them on the band saw or with a tapering jig on the table saw. Joint or plane off the kerf marks.

5 Round-over the legs and aprons. Use a router and a ⅛-inch-radius roundover bit to round-over the corners of the legs and the bottom edges of the aprons before assembly. Slightly round the bottom edges of the legs with sandpaper to keep them from catching and splintering on rough surfaces.

6 Assemble the legs and aprons. Spread glue on the tenons, and clamp the legs and aprons together. Make sure the front apron is ¹³/₁₆ inch below the top of the legs, and that the other aprons are flush with the leg tops. Make sure that the assembly is square.

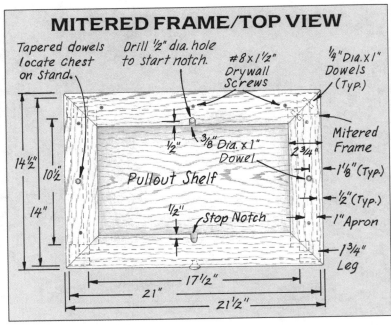

MITERED FRAME/TOP VIEW

Tapered dowels locate chest on stand.

Drill ½" dia. hole to start notch.

#8 x 1½" Drywall Screws

¼" Dia. x 1" Dowels (Typ.)

Mitered Frame

⅜" Dia. x 1" Dowel

½"

Pullout Shelf

2¾"

1⅛" (Typ.)

½" (Typ.)

Stop Notch

1" Apron

1¾" Leg

14½"

10½"

14"

17½"

21"

21½"

7 Make the mitered frame for the base.

A mitered frame sits on top of the legs to support the drawer unit. Miter the stock for the frame, cutting the pieces to length as you do. Reinforce the mitered corners with dowels as shown in the Mitered Frame/Top View. Glue and clamp the mitered frame together.

After the glue is dry, rout the mitered frame to the profile shown in the Routing Detail in three steps. First, rout the bead with a 3/8-inch-radius roundover bit. Then rout the cove with a 3/4-inch-diameter core box bit. Finally, rout a 1/8-inch roundover with a 1/8-inch-radius roundover bit.

After routing, attach the frame to the base aprons with #8 × 1 1/2-inch drywall screws as shown in the Mitered Frame/Top View.

With the mitered frame in place, drill and cut the stop notches shown in the Mitered Frame/Top View. A dowel in the shelf catches in these notches to prevent the shelf from sliding out or in too far. First, drill 1/2-inch-diameter holes where shown, and then open the holes to the edge with a backsaw to create the notch.

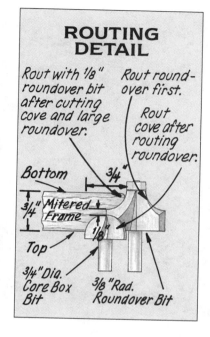

ROUTING DETAIL

Rout with 1/8" roundover bit after cutting cove and large roundover.

Rout roundover first.

Rout cove after routing roundover.

Bottom

3/4"

3/4" Mitered Frame

1/8"

Top

3/4" Dia. Core Box Bit

3/8" Rad. Roundover Bit

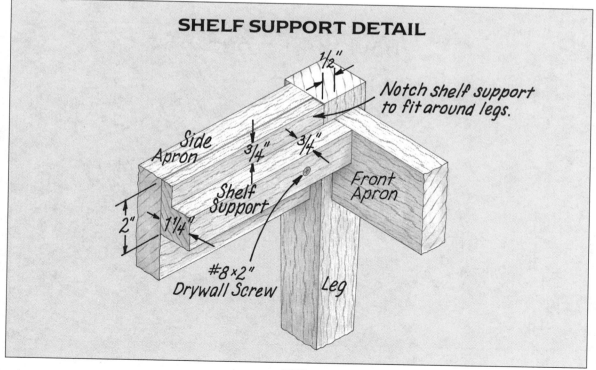

SHELF SUPPORT DETAIL

1/2"

Notch shelf support to fit around legs.

Side Apron

3/4"   3/4"

Shelf Support

Front Apron

2"   1 1/4"

#8 × 2" Drywall Screw

Leg

8 **Cut and attach the shelf supports.** Rabbet the shelf supports as shown in the Shelf Support Detail, and notch their ends to fit around the legs. Cut the rabbet with a dado cutter or on the router table. Notch the ends with a backsaw or dovetail saw.

Glue and screw the supports to the side aprons, as shown, so that the bottom of the rabbet is even with the top of the front apron.

Make the case.

1 **Cut the dovetail joints.** The case is dovetailed together. The tails are cut in the sides, and the pins are cut in the top and bottom, as shown in the Dovetail Layout. I like to miter the front corner pins, although it's optional. If you choose not to cut the miters, lay out and cut the tails on the side. Lay out the pins from the tails, and cut and chisel away the waste. For more on dovetailing, see "Cutting Through Dovetails" on page 81.

If you choose to miter the front corner pins, start by laying out and cutting the pins in the top and bottom. Cut and chop the pins in the normal way, but after they are

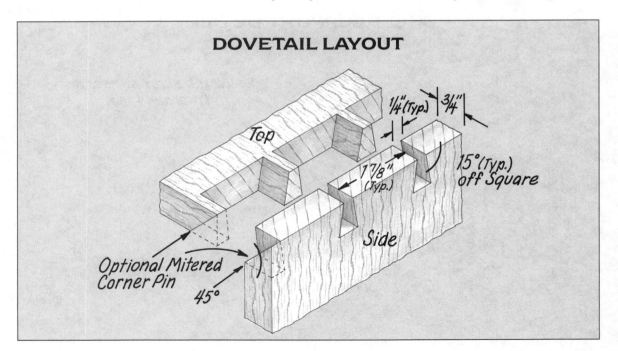

DOVETAIL LAYOUT

Top

1/4" (Typ.)

3/4"

1 7/8" (Typ.)

15° (Typ.) off Square

Side

Optional Mitered Corner Pin

45°

cut, miter the front corner pins as shown in the Dovetail Layout. Next, lay out and cut the dovetails to fit the pins, but don't remove the waste in the front socket. Instead, miter the waste to fit with the mitered corner pins. Carefully cut the miters, shown in the Dovetail Layout, with a dovetail saw and chisel.

Check the fit of the tails and pins, and make any adjustments by paring with a sharp chisel.

2 Rout a groove for the case back. After cutting the dovetail joints, cut a ¼-inch-wide × ⅜-inch-deep groove for the back as shown in the Side View. Rout the groove with a ¼-inch-diameter straight bit in a router. Guide the cut with a router fence attachment. The grooves run the entire length of the top and bottom, but stop ⅜ inch from the ends of the sides.

If you have a plunge router, simply raise and lower the bit at the start and end of the cut. If you have a standard router, start by tilting the router so that only the edge of the base rests on the stock. Slowly tilt the base down so that the bit cuts into the stock. Make the cut, and then tilt the router on its base until the bit is free of the stock. Square the corners of the groove with a chisel.

3 Rout the drawer shelf dadoes. The two solid wood drawer shelves are dadoed into the case sides. The drawer shelves are positioned as shown in the Front View to allow 4 inches of space for each drawer. The dadoes begin at the back panel, and stop ½ inch from the front, as shown in the Side View.

Lay out and rout ¼-inch-deep dadoes with a ¾-inch-diameter straight bit in a hand-held router. Clamp a straight edge to the side to guide the router as you make the cut.

Cut a ¼ × ½-inch notch in the front corners of each shelf to fit around the stopped dado.

4 Assemble the case. Gluing up the case is the most demanding part of making this chest, so have someone help you. First, test fit the case and make any necessary adjustments. Then put glue in the dadoes and on the pins and tails. As you clamp the case together, fit the back into its groove. Make sure the case is square, and allow the glue to dry.

Slowly tilt the base down so that the bit cuts into the stock. Make the cut, and then tilt the router on its base until the bit pulls completely out of the stock.

5 **Lay out and drill the positioning dowel holes.** The case is positioned on the base by two dowels. To perfectly align the holes, drill the holes in the base first and insert dowel centers in the holes to lay out the matching holes on the case. Push the case down on the dowel centers. Drill the matching dowel holes where the dowel centers leave their marks.

Glue the positioning dowels into the holes in the mitered frame. When the glue is dry, taper the exposed part of the dowels with files and sandpaper so that they slide easily into the matching holes in the case.

Make the drawers.

1 **Measure the drawer openings.** In order for the drawers to slide properly, there should be 1/16-inch leeway from side to side and from top to bottom. Because actual dimensions may vary, use the measurements in the Materials List only as a guide. Measure the drawer openings, and cut each drawer to fit its opening.

2 **Cut drawer dovetails and bottom grooves.** The drawer sides are joined to the drawer front with half-blind dovetails, and to the drawer back with through dovetails. Lay out the tails as shown in the Drawer/Side View. For complete directions on cutting dovetails, see "Cutting Through Dovetails" on page 81 and "Cutting Half-Blind Dovetails" on page 155.

Quick Tip: No matter how carefully they've been made, drawers will fit separate openings in the same cabinet differently. Custom fit the drawers to their openings, and then mark them by chiseling corresponding Roman numerals on the backs of the drawers and their openings.

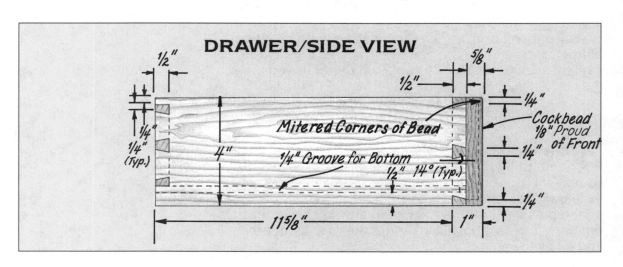

DRAWER/SIDE VIEW

1/2" 5/8" 1/2" 1/4" Cockbead 1/8" Proud of Front 1/4" 1/4" (Typ.) 1/4" *Mitered Corners of Bead* 4" *1/4" Groove for Bottom* 1/2" 14° (Typ.) 1/4" 11 5/8" 1"

Lay out the groove as shown, so that it is just above the drawer front bottom pin. Rout it on the router table, guiding the cut against a fence.

3 **Assemble the drawer.** Spread glue between the tails and pins, and clamp the drawers together. Make sure that the drawers are square, and then slip the drawer bottom in from the back. When the glue dries, fasten the drawer bottom by drilling for and driving #5 × 3/4-inch flathead wood screws through the bottom and into the back.

4 **Fit the drawers.** When the glue is dry, fit the drawers into their openings. Sand or hand plane the drawer if necessary so the drawer operates smoothly and doesn't bind. Glue drawer stops to the back of the case, as shown in the Drawer/Side View. Position the stops so that when the drawer is pushed all the way in, the drawer front is flush with the front of the cabinet.

5 **Cut rabbets for the cockbead.** The cockbead, as shown in the Front View, serves to frame and enhance the drawer fronts. Rout a 3/16 × 1/2-inch rabbet around the edge of the drawer front to hold the cockbead, as shown in the Cockbead Detail. Rout the rabbet on a router table, guiding the cut with a fence.

6 **Make and apply the cockbead.** You'll need about 12 linear feet of cockbead, but make plenty extra. You'll be glad you have it if you miscut any of the miters. To make the cockbead, start by routing a 3/16-inch-diameter bead in the face of several pieces of 3/4-inch-thick scrap. The 3/16-inch-diameter edge-beading bits are available from Eagle America, P.O. Box 1099, Chardon, OH 44024 (part #160-0302).

Once you have routed the beads, rip them away from the stock on the table saw. Next rip the cockbead into 5/8-inch strips. Sand or hand plane the edges smooth. Guide the rounded edge of the cockbead against the fence as you rip it to width.

Next, finish sand the drawer fronts in preparation for the cockbead. Miter the cockbead to fit in the rabbets around the drawer fronts. Glue and clamp the cockbead

Quick Tip: Although the drawer back is narrower than the side, begin with a back the same width as the side. Cut the joinery as shown. When you rout the grooves for the drawer bottom, rout one in the back, too. Use the groove in the back as a guide for cutting the back to width.

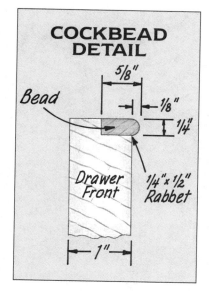

COCKBEAD DETAIL

Bead

5/8"

1/8"

1/4"

Drawer Front

1/4" x 1/2" Rabbet

1"

to the top and bottom rabbets first. Make sure that the pieces do not move during clamping.

After the glue is dry, dab a little glue in the rabbets at the sides of the drawer fronts and put the cockbead into place. Tack the cockbead to the sides with ³/₄-inch brads.

7 Drill for the hardware. Lay out and drill holes for the hardware as shown in the Front and Side Views.

Complete the silver chest.

1 Apply the finish. Finish sand the chest and base, and apply a clear oil and a varnish. Wax the sliding parts after finishing so that they will glide easily. Attach the handles when the finish is dry.

2 Install the pullout shelf. Put the pullout shelf into its slot and align its front edge with the front edge of the front apron. Drill a hole for the stop pin, using the rear notch as a guide. Put the bit in the back of the notch, and drill a ³/₈-inch diameter × ³/₈-inch-deep hole. Glue the dowel into the hole.

3 Install silver cloth. Silver cloth keeps silver from tarnishing. The best way to install it is to wrap it around plywood liners that fit into the drawer.

Cut the liners to fit around the inside of the drawer. Cut silver cloth to wrap around the liners. Attach the cloth to the liners with spray adhesive.

If you choose, you may also make drawer dividers. Cut the dividers from ¹/₄-inch plywood, and wrap them with silver cloth as above. Screw through the drawer bottom to attach the dividers. Attach an extra piece of cloth to the rear of the drawer to spread over the silverware.

CHERRY BUFFET
by Glenn Bostock

As a professional cabinetmaker, I like to design the pieces I build. But I'm a businessman, too. If a customer designs a piece and wants it built, you'd better believe I'll build it.

This buffet is a happy result of one such collaboration. It was designed by a customer, Raymond Shoe-

maker. Mr. Shoemaker knew his stuff: He learned carpentry from his father, a German immigrant, and went on to run one of the largest construction companies in the Middle Atlantic States. Cabinetmaking was his hobby. However, his health was failing, so he asked me to build this piece for his daughter.

When they see photos of this buffet, customers are always impressed by its elegance. Part of the beauty of this cabinet is its simplicity. At the heart of the construction is a simple plywood box. Although the trim is quite elegant, it's simple to make. The left-hand doors open to adjustable shelves; the right-

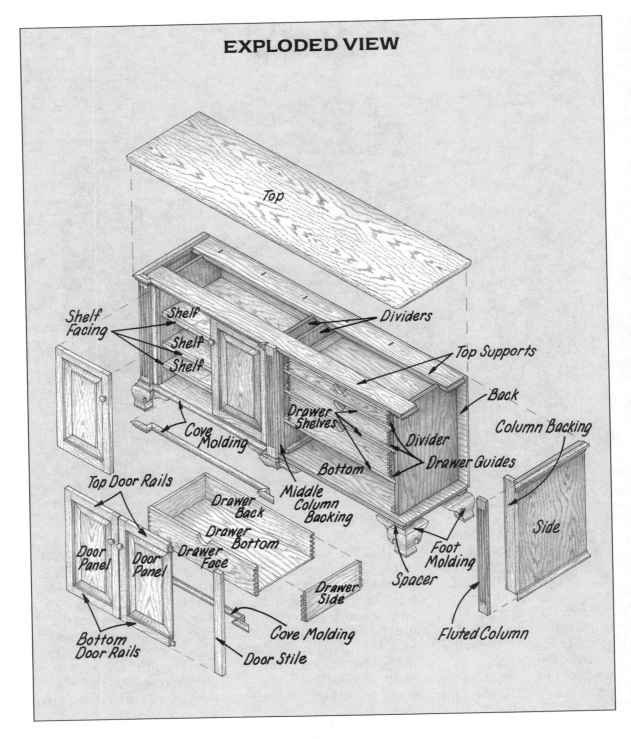

EXPLODED VIEW

Top

Shelf Facing

Shelf

Shelf

Shelf

Dividers

Top Supports

Back

Column Backing

Drawer Shelves

Divider

Drawer Guides

Cove Molding

Bottom

Middle Column Backing

Side

Top Door Rails

Drawer Back

Drawer Bottom

Drawer Face

Foot Molding

Spacer

Door Panel

Door Panel

Drawer Side

Bottom Door Rails

Cove Molding

Door Stile

Fluted Column

186

hand doors open to drawers. You can simplify construction even more by putting shelves behind both sets of doors.

I built the cabinet case from cherry-veneer plywood. This eliminates the need to edge-glue boards. Except for the sides, the case could be inexpensive birch plywood, stained cherry-colored. The rest of the cabinet, including the top, facings, moldings, feet, drawer faces, and doors, is solid cherry. Build the case of the cabinet first, including the dividers for the two compartments and the drawer shelves. Glue and clamp the face pieces to the cabinet, including the columns, moldings, and column backing pieces. Add the feet, then make and add the top. Make and fit the drawers on the drawer shelves. Finally, make and fit the doors.

MATERIALS LIST

Part	Dimension
Case	
Sides (2)	$3/4'' \times 19^{3}/8'' \times 27^{3}/4''$
Top supports (2)	$3/4'' \times 5'' \times 73''$
Bottom	$3/4'' \times 19^{3}/8'' \times 73''$
Dividers (4)	$3/4'' \times 18^{1}/4'' \times 26^{3}/4''$
Back	$3/8'' \times 27^{5}/16'' \times 73^{1}/8''$
Fluted columns (3)	$5/8'' \times 2^{1}/2'' \times 28''$
Column backing (2)	$3/4'' \times 2^{3}/4'' \times 26^{1}/4''$
Middle column backing	$3/4'' \times 4^{1}/2'' \times 26^{1}/4''$
Cove molding stock	$3/4'' \times 1'' \times 22'$
Foot molding stock	$1^{3}/8'' \times 5'' \times 12'$
Support blocks (5)	$1^{3}/4'' \times 1^{3}/4'' \times 5''$
Spacers (4)	$1/4'' \times 2'' \times 2''$
Top	$15/16'' \times 21^{1}/2'' \times 77''$
Drawer shelves (3)	$3/4'' \times 17^{1}/2'' \times 31^{3}/4''$
Drawer shelf edge banding	$3/4'' \times 3/4'' \times 31^{3}/4''$
Drawer guides (8)	$7/8'' \times 1^{1}/8'' \times 18''$
Shelves (3)	$3/4'' \times 17^{1}/2'' \times 31^{1}/8''$
Shelf facing	$3/4'' \times 3/4'' \times 96''$
Drawers	
First drawer face	$5/8'' \times 3^{5}/16'' \times 29''$
First drawer sides (2)	$3/8'' \times 3^{5}/16'' \times 17''$
First drawer back	$3/8'' \times 2^{9}/16'' \times 29''$
Second drawer face	$5/8'' \times 4^{7}/8'' \times 29''$
Second drawer sides (2)	$3/8'' \times 4^{7}/8'' \times 17''$
Second drawer back	$3/8'' \times 4^{1}/8'' \times 29''$

Part	Dimension
Third drawer face	$5/8'' \times 6^{5}/8'' \times 29''$
Third drawer sides (2)	$3/8'' \times 6^{5}/8'' \times 17''$
Third drawer back	$3/8'' \times 5^{7}/8'' \times 29''$
Fourth drawer face	$5/8'' \times 8^{1}/2'' \times 29''$
Fourth drawer sides (2)	$3/8'' \times 8^{1}/2'' \times 17''$
Fourth drawer back	$3/8'' \times 7^{3}/4'' \times 29''$
Drawer bottoms (4)	$1/4'' \times 16^{3}/4'' \times 28^{5}/8''$
Doors	
Top door rails (4)	$3/4'' \times 1^{3}/4'' \times 14^{5}/8''$
Bottom door rails (4)	$3/4'' \times 2^{1}/4'' \times 14^{5}/8''$
Door stiles (8)	$3/4'' \times 1^{3}/4'' \times 25^{7}/8''$
Door panels (4)	$3/4'' \times 12^{5}/8'' \times 22^{1}/2''$

HARDWARE

As needed, #10 × 2" flathead wood screws
As needed, #10 × 1 1/4" flathead wood screws
As needed, #6 × 1" flathead wood screws
As needed, #6 × 3/4" flathead wood screws
As needed, #8 × 1 1/4" drywall screws
As needed, #8 × 1" drywall screws
8 Soss invisible hinges, 1/2 × 1 3/4". Available from The Woodworkers' Store, 21801 Industrial Blvd., Rogers, MN 55374. Part #26526.
4 magnetic catches. Available from The Woodworkers' Store. Part #28944.
4 brass pulls, 3/4" dia. Available from The Woodworkers' Store. Part #36459.

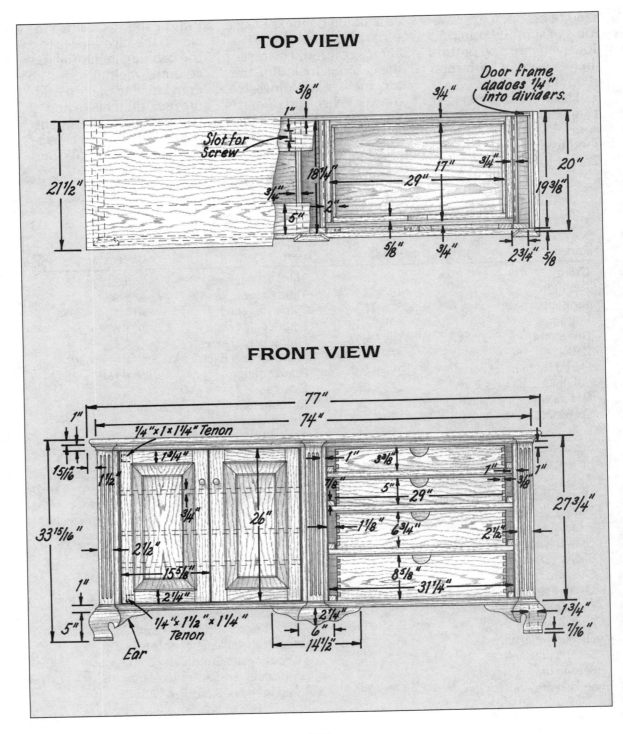

TOP VIEW

FRONT VIEW

Build the cabinet.

1 Cut and mill the wood. Because some of the plywood
pieces are large and it is important to have clean
edges, have someone help you cut the plywood. On the
table saw cut ¾-inch cherry plywood for the sides, top
supports, bottom, drawer shelves and dividers to the
dimensions given. Although the sides must be cherry-
veneer plywood, the other parts can be another hardwood plywood, such as birch. Cut the back from ⅜-inch
plywood to the dimensions given.

2 Rout the side joints. The two 5-inch-wide top
supports and the cabinet bottom join to the buffet
sides with ¼ × ¼-inch tongue-and-groove joints. Rout the
grooves in the sides with a ¼-inch straight bit and a fence
attached to your router. Position the grooves as shown in
the Case Joinery Detail.

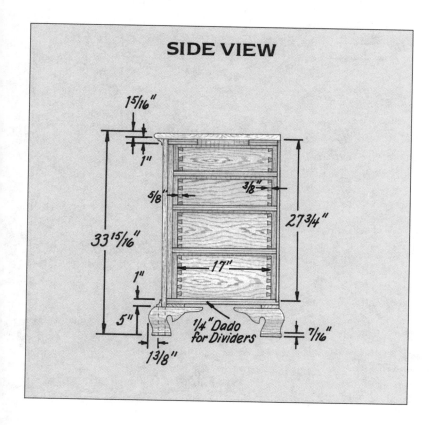

SIDE VIEW

Adjust the router's fence attachment and rout odd-sized rabbets with a straight bit.

3 **Rout the top and bottom tongues.** Rout rabbets to create the $1/4 \times 1/4$-inch tongues in the bottom and top supports with a $1/2$-inch or larger straight bit and fence on your router.

4 **Cut the dadoes for the divider.** The center and end-panel dividers sit in $1/4$-inch-deep dadoes cut in the top supports and bottom. Lay out and rout these dadoes with a $3/4$-inch straight bit. Guide the router against a straightedge clamped across the case members. The dividers should slip easily into the dadoes.

5 **Rout the back rabbet.** Rout a $3/8 \times 5/16$-inch rabbet in the back edges of the sides and bottom for the

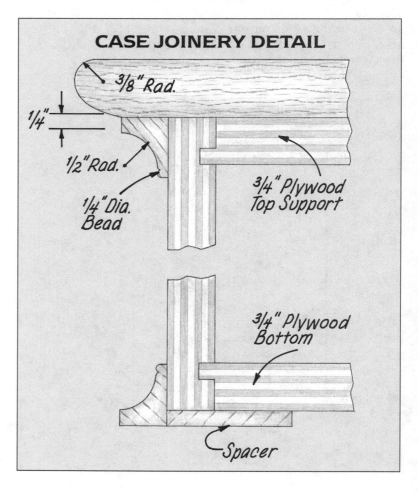

CASE JOINERY DETAIL

3/8" Rad.

1/4"

1/2" Rad.

1/4" Dia. Bead

3/4" Plywood Top Support

3/4" Plywood Bottom

Spacer

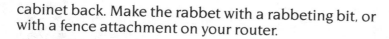

cabinet back. Make the rabbet with a rabbeting bit, or with a fence attachment on your router.

6 **Drill holes for the shelves.** On the drill press, drill holes for the adjustable shelves in two dividers.

7 **Dado the dividers for the drawer shelves.** The top three drawers ride on ¾-inch drawer shelves. Lay out and cut the dadoes ¼ inch deep with a ¾-inch straight bit in the router. Guide the router against a straightedge to make the cut. Stop the dadoes ¾ inch from the front edge of the divider. Square the ends of the dadoes with a chisel.

8 **Glue together the cabinet.** Assemble the cabinet on the floor. Glue and clamp the sides to the bottom. Glue the four dividers into the bottom dadoes. Glue the top supports in place, clamping the tongues into the side grooves, and clamping the dividers in their dadoes. Measure across diagonal corners to make sure the cabinet is square. Equal measurements mean the cabinet is square. Sight along the front and back edges to make sure the cabinet is flat.

Glue the edge banding onto the drawer shelves. When the glue has dried, apply glue to the shelf dadoes, and slide the drawer shelves into place.

Quick Tip: To align your holes perfectly, make a drilling guide. In a ¾ × 2 × 30-inch piece of wood, lay out and drill a line of ¼-inch holes spaced 2 inches apart. Mark the bottom edge of the guide. Clamp the guide to the dividers one at time. Set the depth stop on the drill press and drill out the holes, drilling down through the guide holes into the divider. Drill a set of holes in the front and back of each divider.

Attach the columns and moldings.

1 **Mill the wood.** Mill wood for the fluted columns, column backings, and moldings to the dimensions given in the Materials List.

2 **Bead and attach the column backing boards.** Rout a ¼-inch-diameter bead on the edges of the column backing boards. Cut the bead with a beading bit in a table-mounted router, or with a scratch stock. Glue and clamp the cherry backing boards to the cabinet dividers and sides.

3 **Flute and attach the columns.** Lay out the flutes as shown in the Column and Trim/Cross Section. The

For safety's sake, rout narrow moldings on a wider board. When you rip the molding to width, position the *scrap* between the fence and the blade.

flutes stop 1 inch from the top and bottom of the column, as shown in the Front View.

Rout the flutes with a fence attachment and a ³/₈-inch round nose or core box bit in your router. Glue and clamp the columns to the column backing boards.

4 Make the molding. You can cut the cove and bead molding with a shaper, as I did, or with a combina-

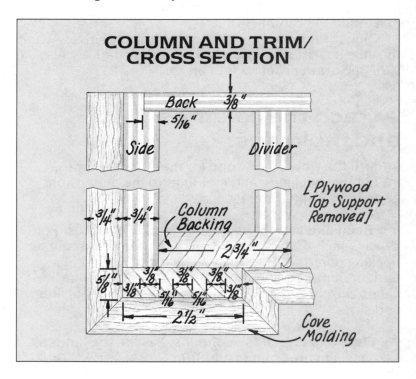

COLUMN AND TRIM/ CROSS SECTION

tion of router bits. If you rout the molding, cut the cove with a ½-inch radius cove or core box bit. Rout the bead with a ¼-inch beading bit. For safety, cut the molding on wider stock, then rip the molding to final width.

5 **Attach the moldings.** Glue and clamp the moldings to the top and bottom edges of the front and sides of the cabinet. Miter the moldings around each of the fluted columns as shown in the Column and Trim/Cross Section.

Make the feet.

1 **Mill the wood.** Mill enough wood to make the feet on the buffet. About 10 feet should be plenty. Mill wood for the support blocks.

2 **Make the foot molding.** Each foot is a large ogee-type molding made on the table saw and mitered together. A support block behind each foot strengthens and helps attach the foot to the cabinet.
  Draw the profile of the foot on the end grain of the molding blank. Cut the cove section by running the molding diagonally across the table saw blade against a fence. The angle of the fence determines the angle of the

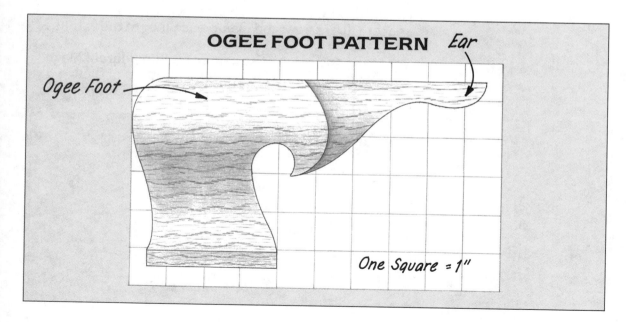

OGEE FOOT PATTERN *Ear*

Ogee Foot

One Square = 1"

profile; test your setup on a piece of scrap to make sure it is correct.

For more on cove cutting, see "Making Crown Molding" on page 38.

When the cove section of the ogee is cut, cut the convex section. Using a standard rip fence, rip a series of bevels along the upper section of the molding to rough out the top of the foot. Hand plane and sand the molding to the final shape shown in the Ogee Foot Pattern.

3 Make the feet. Each foot is made of three sections that wrap around the corner of the cabinet. A fourth section, called the ear, fits against the foot, as shown in the Front View. Miter the foot molding and ear to fit.

Glue and tape together the feet and ears. When the glue dries, transfer the Ogee Foot Pattern to the molding stock. Cut the feet to shape on the band saw. Clean up the band saw cuts with files and sandpaper.

Glue and clamp a $1^{3}/_{4} \times 1^{3}/_{4} \times 5$-inch support block behind each foot.

4 Attach the feet. Drill and countersink for #$10 \times$ 2-inch flathead wood screws from the inside of the cabinet into each foot support block. Fill the $^{1}/_{4}$-inch space between the 1-inch cove molding and the $^{3}/_{4}$-inch plywood cabinet bottom above each foot with a $^{1}/_{4} \times 2 \times 2$-inch spacer. Glue, screw, and clamp each foot to the cabinet.

5 Make and attach the center molding detail. Make the molded detail in the center bottom of the cabinet from the foot molding. Miter pieces to wrap

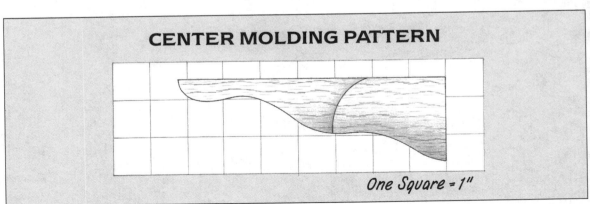

CENTER MOLDING PATTERN

One Square = 1"

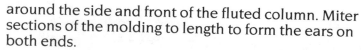
around the side and front of the fluted column. Miter sections of the molding to length to form the ears on both ends.

Assemble the parts that wrap around the column, and cut them to shape on the band saw as shown in the Center Molding Pattern. Cut the ears to shape. Attach the center molding to the cabinet with glue and #8 × 1-inch drywall screws.

Make the cabinet top.

1 Mill the wood. Mill, to the thickness given in the Materials List, enough cherry boards to make the top, leaving them all about 1 or 2 inches longer than specified in the Materials List. Joint and edge-glue the boards. Rip and crosscut the top to final dimensions.

2 Shape the top edge. Rout a ½-inch chamfer on the bottom edge with a chamfering bit in your router. Round-over the top edge with a ⅜-inch radius roundover bit in the router. Hand plane and sand the edges to final shape.

3 Attach the top. Screw the top to the cabinet from below. Drill and countersink the front plywood support from below for six #10 × 1¼-inch flathead wood screws. Rout or drill 1-inch-long slots in the back plywood support for six #10 × 1¼-inch flathead wood screws. This allows the top to expand and contract with seasonal humidity changes.

Build the drawers.

The drawers have through dovetails front and back, so the end grain of the drawer sides shows on the drawer faces. The sides can be cherry, or you may choose a contrasting wood for the sides. If you prefer, make half-blind dovetails that hide the end grain on the sides.

1 Mill the wood. Mill wood for the drawer faces, sides, backs, and drawer guides to the dimensions given in the Materials List. Cut ¼-inch hardwood plywood for the drawer bottoms to the dimensions given.

2 Make the dovetails. Scribe a stop line around both ends of each drawer side equal to the length of the tails. Lay out the tails on the side, as shown in the Drawer Detail. Saw and chisel out the waste between the tails. Do not cut beyond the stop line.

Lay out the pins in the drawer faces and backs directly from the tails with a marking knife. Carry the layout lines down to a stop line marking the length of the pins. Saw and chisel out the waste between the pins, undercutting the waste slightly. Check the fit with the tails, paring away any excess with a sharp chisel. For more on dovetails, see "Cutting Through Dovetails" on page 81.

3 Cut the bottom groove. Rout a $1/4 \times 1/4$-inch groove in the drawer faces and a $1/4 \times 3/16$-inch groove in the sides for the drawer bottoms. If you position the bottom as shown, it is not necessary to stop cuts on the face, since the dovetails hide the groove when the drawer is assembled. If you make through dovetails, stop the grooves on the sides $1/4$ inch from the front edge.

4 Cut the drawer handles. Lay out and cut the handles in each drawer face on the band saw. Clean

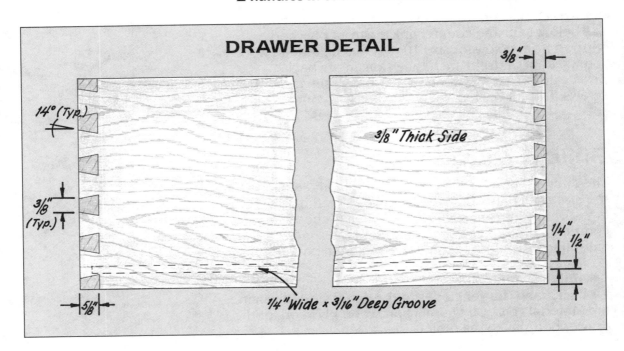

DRAWER DETAIL

14° (Typ.)

3/8" (Typ.)

5/8"

3/8" Thick Side

3/8"

1/4" 1/2"

1/4" Wide × 3/16" Deep Groove

up the sawed edge with a sanding sleeve chucked in the drill press.

5 Assemble the drawers. Sand the inside of the drawers. Glue and clamp the drawers together on a flat surface. Make certain the drawers are square by measuring diagonally across the corners. The drawers are square when the measurements are equal.

Sand the bottoms. When the glue is dry, slide the bottoms in from the back. Drill and countersink through the bottoms into the drawer backs for three #6 × 3/4-inch flathead wood screws.

6 Attach the drawer guides. The drawer guides glue and screw to the drawer shelves. Position them so that the drawers, when pulled out, will clear the doors. Drill and countersink the guides for #8 × 1 1/4-inch drywall screws.

Apply a small bead of glue to the guides and clamp them into place. Test fit the drawer to the opening. Make any adjustments necessary before screwing the guides to the drawer shelves.

7 Attach the cabinet back. Put the back in its rabbets and attach it with glue and #6 × 1-inch flathead wood screws.

Make the raised panel doors.

These raised panel doors have a unique profile, which I cut with a special shaper-cutter. Feel free to make a standard raised panel: It will be virtually indistinguishable from the one I made.

1 Mill the wood. Mill wood for the door rails and stiles to the dimensions given. Mill wood for the panels to thickness, leaving it 1 inch longer than called for. Edge-glue the pieces to get sufficient width. When the glue is dry, cut the panels to final dimensions.

2 Rout the mortises. Lay out and rout the mortises in the stiles. Clamp a 1 1/2 × 1 1/2-inch spacer between two stiles to give the router some bearing surface. Rout the mortises with a 1/4-inch straight bit in the plunge

To position tenon shoulders automatically, clamp a stop block to a fence on the miter gauge. Put the rail against the block for perfectly aligned shoulders.

router with a fence attachment. Square the ends of the mortises with a chisel.

If you do not have a plunge router, make the mortises by drilling overlapping holes on the drill press. Clean up and square the drilled mortises with a chisel.

3 Cut the rail tenons. Cut the matching tenons in the rails on the table saw. Crosscut the tenon shoulders with a miter gauge. Screw an extension fence to the miter gauge, and clamp a stop block to it to position the shoulders. Cut the cheeks of the tenons with a tenoning jig on the table saw.

4 Rout the inside edge detail. Rout the 1/4-inch-radius half-round edge detail on the inside of the rails and stiles with the router in the router table. Set the depth of cut to cut a 1/16-inch step, or fillet, as shown in the Door/Cross Section.

Rout the bead along the entire length of the rails and stiles. Miter the roundover as explained in "Mitering a Beaded Frame" on page 70.

5 Cut the panel groove. Rout a 1/4 × 5/16-inch groove in the rails and stiles to accept the raised panel. Set up the cut on the router table, and guide it with a fence. Cut stopped grooves in the stiles. Begin the cut by lowering the stile over the bit, as shown in the photo. End the cut by lifting the end off the bit. Square off the ends of the stopped grooves with a 1/4-inch chisel.

6 Cut the raised panel. Make the raised panels on the table saw, or with a raised panel cutter on the shaper

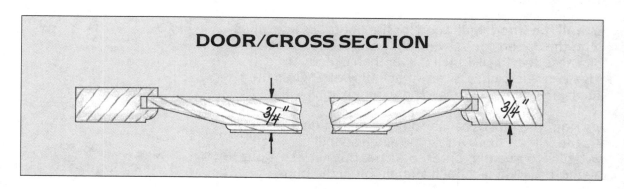

DOOR/CROSS SECTION

To rout a groove between mortises, hold the stile against the router fence. Lower the stile over the cutter and rout a groove, guided by the fence. Lift the back end of the stile from the table to complete the cut.

or router. For more information on raising panels, see "Raising Panels on the Table Saw" on page 200.

7 **Glue together the doors.** Sand the doors. The panels must expand and contract with changes in humidity: Prefinish them so that they do not get glued in place. On a flat surface, glue and clamp the tenons into the mortises.

As you pull the joints together, set the panels in place in the grooves. Measure diagonally across the corners to ensure that the doors are square. Sight across the doors to make sure they are not twisted.

8 **Hang the doors.** The doors are mounted on invisible hinges. Rout or drill the mortises for these hinges, according to the size and shape of the hinges you buy.

Drill small holes in each door for the brass door pulls. Attach magnetic catches to the cabinet after the finish is dry to hold the doors closed. The Materials List mentions a source for all these parts.

9 **Make the shelves.** Cut the shelves from cherry plywood. Glue solid cherry strips onto the shelf face edges to hide the plywood.

RAISING PANELS ON THE TABLE SAW

Raising panels on the saw requires running stock through the saw on edge. To keep the panel from wobbling, screw or clamp a tall auxiliary fence to your table saw fence as shown. Hold the panel against the auxiliary fence as you cut.

1 Cut the bevels. To set up the cut, put the table saw fence with the attached auxiliary fence to the left of the blade, and set the saw blade at 15 degrees. The saw blade should tilt away from the fence. Adjust the rip fence to cut a bevel that at its narrowest is as wide as the groove for the panel—1/4 inch in this case. Raise the blade so that it will just cut through the panel as shown. Cut a bevel on all four edges of the panel.

2 Cut the tongue. Set the blade at 90 degrees. Adjust the blade height and fences to cut a tongue that snugly fits into the door groove.

When the bevel and tongue have been cut, sand and scrape the sawed edges smooth.

Guide the panel against the tall auxiliary fence as you cut the bevel.

Cut a tongue that fits snugly into the panel groove.

PEWTER CUPBOARD
by David T. Smith

During the eighteenth and nineteenth centuries, the pewter cupboard or "hutch" was an especially popular form of kitchen storage. The shelves on the bottom half of the piece were enclosed, making a cupboard, while those on the top half were open. Often, the open shelves were not as deep as the cupboard, and they were therefore said to "step back."

The form remains popular even today, especially among decorators who appreciate country-style furniture. I adapted this particular pewter cupboard from a late-eighteenth-century American design.

You can make the pewter cupboard from almost any cabinet-grade wood; however, old-time American cabinetmakers would most likely have used walnut, cherry, maple, poplar, or pine. They also used a very hard wood, like maple or hickory, for the pegs that hold the tenons in the mortises. The cupboard shown is poplar with maple pegs.

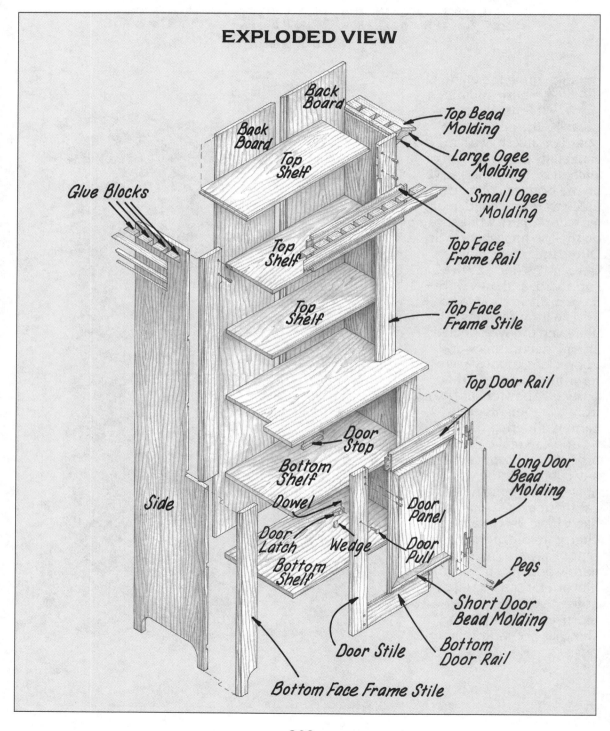

EXPLODED VIEW

Back Board

Back Board

Top Shelf

Glue Blocks

Top Shelf

Top Shelf

Side

Door Stop

Bottom Shelf

Dowel

Door Latch

Wedge

Bottom Shelf

Door Stile

Bottom Face Frame Stile

Top Bead Molding

Large Ogee Molding

Small Ogee Molding

Top Face Frame Rail

Top Face Frame Stile

Top Door Rail

Long Door Bead Molding

Door Panel

Door Pull

Pegs

Short Door Bead Molding

Bottom Door Rail

202

Build the case.

1 **Select the stock and cut the parts to size.** Glue together pieces to make the sides in two steps. First, glue up a panel 12¼ × 84 inches. When the glue dries, glue a 5 × 37¼-inch piece to the panel's lower edge, creating the profile shown in the Side View.

Cut the stock for the large ogee molding about ½ inch wider and 1 to 2 inches longer than specified in the Materials List. Set aside some 3- to 4-inch-wide stock to make the small ogee molding, door bead molding, and top bead molding, but don't cut them to size yet.

Cut the parts for the door about ½ inch longer and wider than specified. Cut the rest of the parts to the sizes given in the Materials List.

2 **Cut the joinery in the sides and back boards.** The sides, shelves, counter, and back boards are all joined with simple rabbets and dadoes. With a router or a dado cutter, cut ¾-inch-wide, ⅜-inch-deep dadoes in the sides to hold the shelves and counter, as shown in the Side View.

Cut ½-inch-wide × ⅜-inch-deep rabbets along the

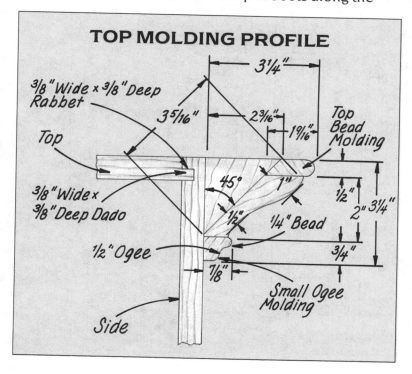

TOP MOLDING PROFILE

⅜" Wide × ⅜" Deep Rabbet

Top

⅜" Wide × ⅜" Deep Dado

½" Ogee

Side

3⅝"

3 5/16"

2¾"

1 9/16"

45°

1"

½"

¼" Bead

⅛"

Top Bead Molding

½"

2" 3¼"

¾"

Small Ogee Molding

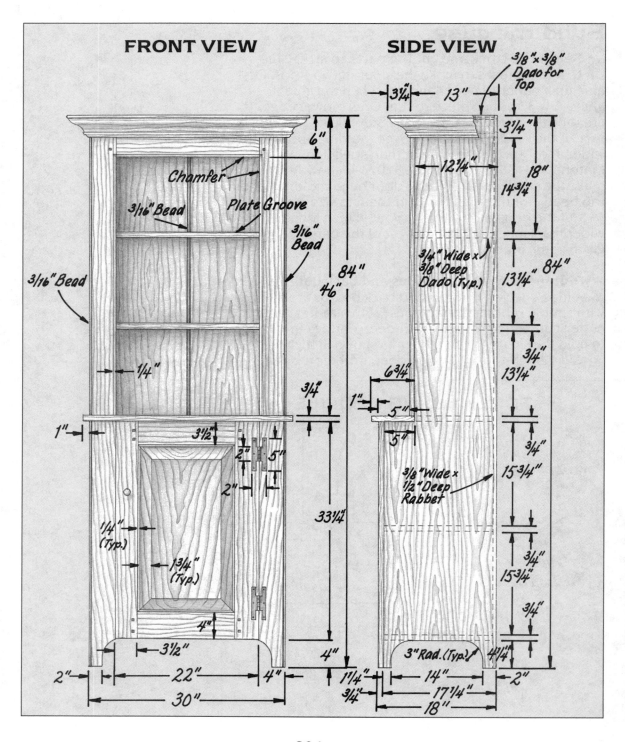

FRONT VIEW

SIDE VIEW

Chamfer

3/16" Bead

Plate Groove

3/16" Bead

3/16" Bead

6"

84"

4-6"

1/4"

3/4"

1"

3 1/2"

2"

5"

2"

1/4"
(Typ.)

1 3/4"
(Typ.)

33 1/4"

4"

3 1/2"

2"

22"

4"

4"

30"

3/8" x 3/8"
Dado for
Top

3 1/4"

13"

3 1/4"

12 1/4"

18"

14 3/4"

3/4" Wide x
3/8" Deep
Dado (Typ.)

13 1/4"

84"

13 1/4"

3/4"

6 3/4"

1"

5"

5"

3/4"

3/8" Wide x
1/2" Deep
Rabbet

15 3/4"

3/4"

15 3/4"

3/4"

3" Rad. (Typ.)

4 1/4"

1 1/4"

3/4"

14"

2"

17 1/4"

18"

back edges of the sides to hold the back boards.

Cut ³/₈-inch-wide × ³/₈-inch-deep dadoes near the top edges of the sides to hold the top shelf, as shown in the Side View and the Top Molding Profile.

3 **Rabbet the top shelf and back boards.** Put a ³/₈-inch-diameter rabbeting bit in the router. Cut a ³/₈-inch-deep rabbet on a piece of scrap to create a tongue. Check the fit of the tongue in the top shelf dado, and make any necessary adjustments. Rabbet both ends of the top shelf, as shown in the Top Molding Profile.

Rout rabbets in the adjoining edges of the back boards, as shown in the Back Board Joinery Detail.

4 **Cut the shapes of the sides and counter.** Lay out the shape of the feet on the sides as shown in the Side View. Lay out the counter as shown in the Counter Layout. Cut the shapes with a saber saw or a coping saw, and sand the sawed edges.

5 **Cut the beads and moldings.** The outside corners of both the top and bottom face frame stiles have a decorative ³/₁₆-inch bead, shown in the Front View. The chamfer on the top stiles will be cut later.

One of the back boards is also beaded, as shown in the Back Board Joinery Detail. Cut these beads with a shaper, router, or molding head on the table saw.

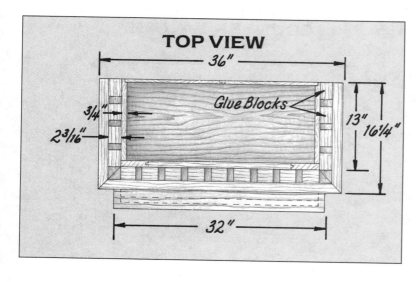

TOP VIEW

36"

Glue Blocks

³/₄"

2³/₁₆"

13"

16¹/₄"

32"

◇ ◇ ━━━ ◇ ◇

6 **Assemble the case.** Test fit the sides, shelves, counter, back boards, and bottom face frame members. Finish sand these parts, then assemble them with glue. Reinforce the glue joints with 6d square-cut nails, and set the heads of the nails. The cut nails will duplicate the look of old hand-forged nails.

Make the top face frame.

The top face frame consists of a top rail and two side stiles. The rail has twin tenons on each end. Mortise the stiles first. Then cut a single wide tenon on the rail. On the bandsaw, cut the tenon into smaller tenons that fit the mortises.

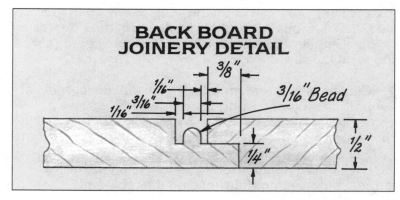

BACK BOARD JOINERY DETAIL

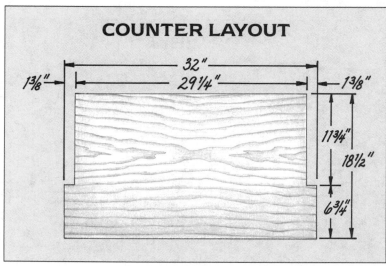

COUNTER LAYOUT

Cut decorative beads with a molder and beading knives. Similar cutters are also available for routers and shapers.

MATERIALS LIST

Part	Dimension
Case	
Sides (2)	$3/4'' \times 17\,1/4'' \times 84''$
Top shelves (3)	$3/4'' \times 11\,3/4'' \times 29\,1/4''$
Bottom shelves (2)	$3/4'' \times 16\,3/4'' \times 29\,1/4''$
Back boards (2)	$1/2'' \times 14\,13/16'' \times 84''$
Bottom face frame stiles (2)	$3/4'' \times 4'' \times 37\,1/4''$
Counter	$3/4'' \times 18\,1/2'' \times 32''$
Top face frame stiles (2)	$3/4'' \times 4'' \times 46''$
Top face frame rail	$3/4'' \times 6'' \times 24''$
Doors	
Top door rail	$3/4'' \times 3\,1/2'' \times 17''$
Door stiles (2)	$3/4'' \times 3\,1/2'' \times 33\,1/4''$
Door panel	$1/2'' \times 15\,5/8'' \times 26\,1/2''$
Bottom door rail	$3/4'' \times 4'' \times 17''$
Long door bead moldings (2)	$1/4'' \times 1/4'' \times 25\,1/2''$
Short door bead moldings (2)	$1/4'' \times 1/4'' \times 15''$
Door pull	$1\,1/4''$ dia. $\times 2\,5/8''$

Part	Dimension
Door latch	$5/8'' \times 1'' \times 2\,5/8''$
Wedge	$1/4'' \times 1'' \times 1\,1/2''$
Dowel	$1/4''$ dia. $\times 7/8''$
Door stop	$3/4'' \times 3/4'' \times 6''$
Pegs (12)	$5/16'' \times 5/16'' \times 1\,1/4''$
Crown Molding	
Large ogee molding stock (2)	$1'' \times 3\,5/16'' \times 40''$
Top bead molding stock (2)	$1/2'' \times 1\,9/16'' \times 40''$
Small ogee molding stock (2)	$3/4'' \times 7/8'' \times 36''$
Glue blocks (17)	$2\,3/16'' \times 2\,3/16'' \times 2\,1/2''$

HARDWARE

#6 × 1" roundhead wood screws
2 H-hinges, 5"
As needed, 6d finishing nails
As needed, 4d finishing nails
As needed, 6d square-cut nails. Available from Tremont Nail Company, P.O. Box 111, Wareham, MA 02571.

1 Mortise the face frame stiles. Lay out the mortises as shown in the Top Face Frame Joinery Detail. Rough out each mortise by drilling a line of overlapping $1/4$-inch-diameter × 1-inch-deep holes between the layout lines. Clean up the sides, and square the corners of each mortise with a chisel.

2 Cut tenons on the face frame rail. Cut the tenons with a table-mounted router or a dado cutter on the table saw. Check your setup on a piece of scrap the same width and thickness as the rail. Start by making a 1-inch-wide × $1/4$-inch-deep rabbet across one end of the test piece. Rotate the board 90 degrees and cut another rabbet. Continue until you have cut all four surfaces of the rail to form a $1/4$-inch-thick × 1-inch-long tenon.

Test the tenon in the mortise. Adjust the cutter height so that the tenon fits snugly. When the setup is correct, cut a tenon on each end of the rail.

On the bandsaw, cut each tenon into two smaller tenons which fit into the mortises. Chisel away the waste between the tenons.

3 Assemble the face frame. Finish sand the face frame rail and stiles. Glue the top stiles and the rail

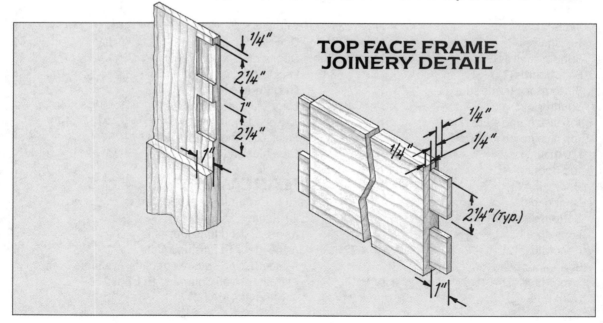

TOP FACE FRAME JOINERY DETAIL

$1/4$"
$2 1/4$"
1"
$2 1/4$"
1"
$1/4$"
$1/4$"
$1/4$"
$2 1/4$" (Typ.)
1"

together, making sure the parts are perpendicular.

The joints are reinforced with wooden pegs; this technique was common on eighteenth-century furniture. Whittle the pegs so that the bottom ends are round. Drill $5/16$-inch-diameter holes through the mortises and tenons; then drive the pegs, round end first, through the holes from the outside. Keep driving them until the square ends are flush with the outside surface. Cut the round peg ends flush with the inside surface.

4 **Chamfer the face frame.** Using a router and a piloted chamfering bit, cut a chamfer along the inside edges of the frame, as shown in the Front View. With a carving chisel, square the chamfers where they meet at a corner so that they appear to be joined by a miter.

5 **Install the face frame.** Glue the face frame to the assembled case. Again, reinforce the glue joints with cut nails and set the heads. Use a hand plane, if necessary, to make the face frame flush with the cabinet sides.

Make the door.

The door has a haunched mortise-and-tenon joint, which allows the groove for the panel to run the entire length of both rails and stiles. When making a haunched mortise and tenon, the same rule of thumb applies—cut the mortises first, then fit the tenons to them, as shown in the photos on the following pages.

1 **Trim the door parts.** Measure the size of the door opening. If it varies from the opening as drawn, adjust the dimensions of the door accordingly. Cut the parts to size.

2 **Cut the door joinery.** Rout $1/4$-inch-wide $\times$ $3/8$-inch-deep grooves for the door panel along the entire inside edge of the rails and stiles. Lay out the mortises as shown in the Door Joinery Detail. Cut the mortises as you did with the top face frame.

Using a router or a dado cutter, make $1/4$-inch-thick $\times$ 1-inch-long tenons on both ends of each rail, as described

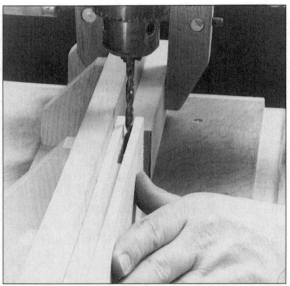

To make haunched mortise-and-tenon joints, first cut grooves in the inside edges of both the rails and the stiles. These grooves will hold the panel in the assembled frame.

Using a drill press, rough out the mortises in the stiles. For each mortise, drill a series of overlapping holes in the bottom of the groove. These holes should be the same diameter as the width of the groove.

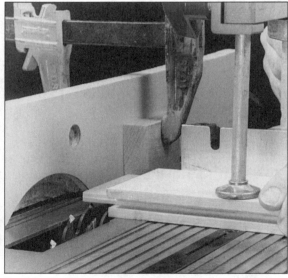

Clean up the sides and square the ends of each mortise with a chisel. If you have one, use a mortising chisel, which works best for this task.

To make the tenons, cut a wide rabbet in each end of each rail. Turn the rail over and cut another. The two rabbets will form a tenon.

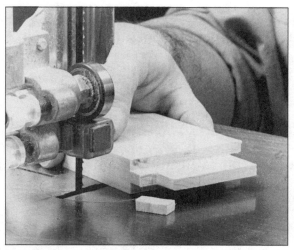

Cut a notch in the outside edge of each tenon to create a haunch.

When you fit the rails to the stiles, the haunches will fill the grooves in the stiles. The outside edges of the rails should be flush with the ends of the stiles.

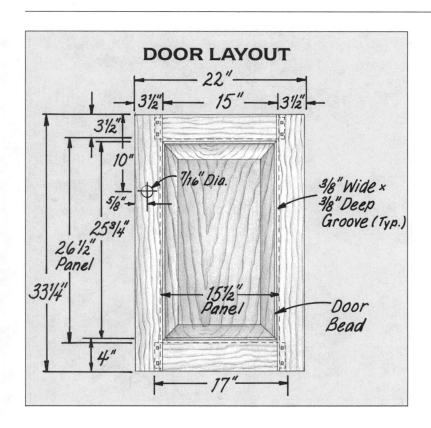

DOOR LAYOUT

22"
3½" — 15" — 3½"
3½"
10"
⁷⁄₁₆" Dia.
⅝"
25¾"
26½" Panel
33¼"
4"
17"
15½" Panel
³⁄₈" Wide × ³⁄₈" Deep Groove (Typ.)
Door Bead

previously. This time, however, cut just the two faces of these boards—do not rabbet the edges. With a dovetail saw or a band saw, cut a notch in the outside edge of each tenon to create the "haunch," as shown in the Door Joinery Detail. When you fit the parts together, the haunches will fill the grooves in the stiles.

3 **Cut the raised panel.** The outside surface of the door panel is beveled to fit into the grooves in the door frame. Using a table saw, cut the edges and ends of the panels at 10 degrees, leaving a small step where the blade exits the wood. If you have a hollow-ground planer blade, use it for this operation—it leaves the beveled edges of the panels very smooth, so that little sanding

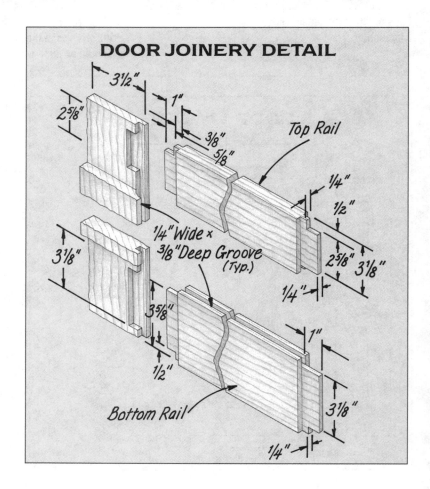

DOOR JOINERY DETAIL

will be necessary. For more on raising panels, see "Raising Panels on the Table Saw" on page 200.

4 **Assemble and hang the door.** Drill a 9/16-inch-diameter hole for the door pull through the left stile, as shown in the Door Layout. Finish sand the door rails, stiles, and panel.

Glue the rails and stiles together. As you assemble them, slide the panel into the grooves, but do not glue it in place. Let it float in the grooves so that it can expand and contract with changes in humidity and temperature. As you clamp the parts together, check that the door frame is flat and square.

When the glue is dry, reinforce the mortises and tenons with pegs the same way you reinforced the top face frame joinery. Attach the door to the right face frame stile with H-shaped hinges.

5 **Make and install the door pull and latch.** Turn the door pull to the shape shown in the Door Pull Layout. Also, drill a 7/16-inch-diameter hole near one end

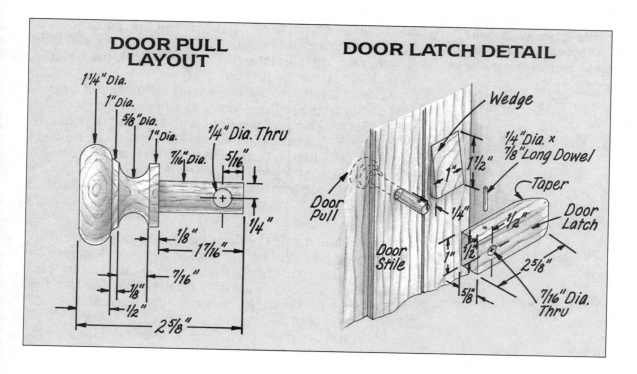

DOOR PULL LAYOUT

DOOR LATCH DETAIL

Left: When making small moldings, always shape the edge of a wide board, then rip the molding from it. If you try to shape a narrow strip, it may crack or splinter. *Right:* Round-over the area near the edge by making repeated passes with a hand plane. The bead and cove should blend together, making an S-curve.

of the latch and taper the other end, as shown in the Door Latch Detail. Insert the pull through the hole in the left door stile, and glue the latch to the small (inside) end of the pull. Be careful not to get glue on the pull shaft where it passes through the hole—you want the assembled pull and latch to turn freely. When the glue dries, reinforce the assembly by drilling a $1/4$-inch-diameter hole through the latch and the pull. Glue a $1/4$-inch-diameter, $7/8$-inch-long dowel in this hole.

Glue the wedge to the inside surface of the left stile, just opposite the pull assembly, as shown in the Door Latch Detail. Also glue the door stop to the underside of the counter. The front edge of this stop should be flush to and parallel with the back surface of the face frame stiles. Reinforce the stop by driving finishing nails up through the stop and into the counter. Set the heads of the nails.

6 Make and apply the door bead molding. Make the door bead molding from a wide piece of $1/4$-inch-thick stock. Cut the quarter-round profile on a table-mounted router. Rip the molding to width on the table saw. Run the wider, waste portion of the stock against the fence as shown in the photo.

Miter the door bead moldings to fit around the inside of the door frame. Nail the moldings to the door frame.

Apply the crown molding and the finish.

The final step in building this cupboard is to add a wide crown molding around the top. Rather than mill the profile from a single wide piece of wood, the crown molding is made of three separate pieces. Triangular glue blocks attach it to the case.

1 **Make the large ogee molding.** To make the large ogee molding, you cut both a bead and a cove in the same face of the stock. These should blend together, forming an S-curve or ogee. First, lay out the ogee on one end of the stock. Then cut the wide cove by passing the wood over the table saw at an angle to the blade. For more information on cove cutting, see "Cove Cutting on the Table Saw" on page 361. Finally, create the bead by rounding over the stock with a hand plane as shown in the photo. Bevel the edges of the large ogee stock on a table saw, as shown in the Large Ogee Molding Detail.

2 **Make the small moldings.** To make the top bead molding and the small ogee molding, cut the shapes

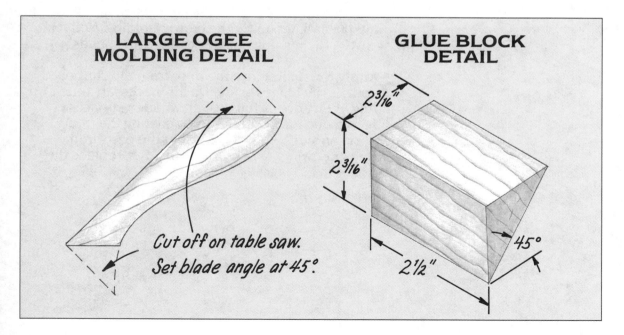

LARGE OGEE MOLDING DETAIL

Cut off on table saw.
Set blade angle at 45°.

GLUE BLOCK DETAIL

2³⁄₁₆"

2³⁄₁₆"

2½"

45°

in the edges of a wide board with a table-mounted router. Then rip the molding from the board on a table saw as you did for the door beads. Remember to bevel the edge of the top bead molding, as shown in the Top Molding Profile.

3 **Glue up the molding.** Glue the top bead molding to the large ogee molding. Use #6 × 1-inch roundhead wood screws to help clamp the pieces together. When the glue dries, remove the screws so you do not accidentally cut them when mitering the molding. Finish sand the molding stock. Make the glue blocks as shown in the Glue Block Detail, and attach them to the inside of the crown molding as shown in the Top View. The top edge of each glue block should be flush with the top of the crown molding.

4 **Install the moldings.** The crown molding is wrapped around the top of the cabinet with miter joints at the corners. These joints are cut on the table saw with the miter gauge. This procedure is explained in detail in "Mitering and Installing Crown Molding" on page 110.
   Miter the crown molding stock to fit around the case. Nail the molding into place around the top of the cabinet with 6d finishing nails. Miter the small ogee molding to fit around the cabinet under the crown molding. Nail it into place with 4d finishing nails. Set all the nail heads.

5 **Apply finish.** Remove the door from the cupboard and set the hinges aside. Do any necessary touch-up sanding, then apply a finish to all wooden surfaces, inside and out, back and front. (By coating the wood evenly on all sides, you help prevent the parts from warping or bowing.) When the finish dries, replace the door.

HANGING CUPBOARD
by Michael Dunbar

This closed hanging cupboard is a piece I originally designed for a traditional joinery and hand woodworking class. The project had to meet several criteria. It had to incorporate as many different joinery techniques as possible—open and blind mortises and tenons, dovetails, miter joints, frame and panel, and so on. It also had to introduce as many tools as possible—hand planes, back saw, and mortise gauge among them.

I taught the class in Ohio, where students from all over the country gathered to spend a week building and learning. Therefore the cupboard had to be small enough for students to carry back on a plane, and it had to be something they could build in a week. Furthermore, the piece had to be something the students would want to make and be proud to take home. They were going to be a diverse lot, so it had to blend with many decors.

While teaching the course, I made a cupboard along with the class. My wife liked it enough to hang it in her kitchen where it holds spices and condi-

ments. I made the cupboard in eastern white pine because it works easily. Pine has a very bland and even grain, so I painted my cabinet with a red milk paint rather than using a natural finish. However, there is no reason why you couldn't make yours out of any wood you wish and then finish the piece to your liking.

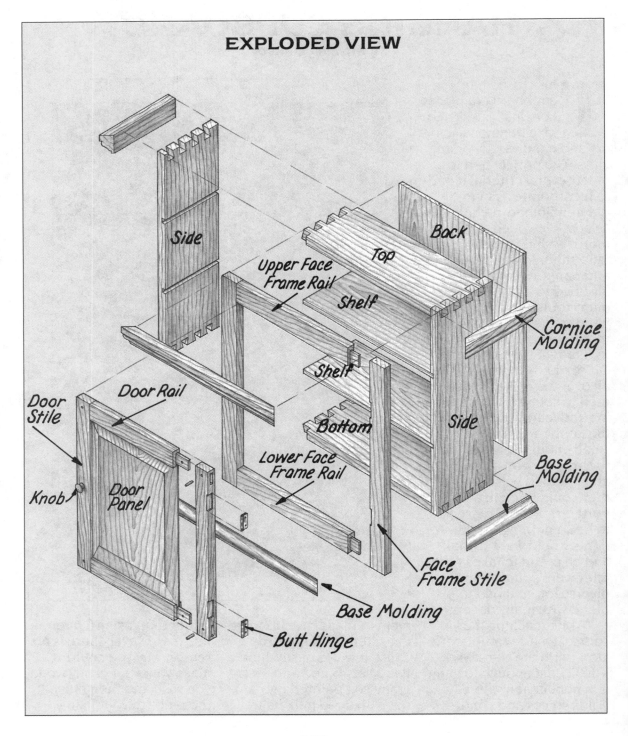

EXPLODED VIEW

Side

Back

Top

Upper Face Frame Rail

Shelf

Cornice Molding

Shelf

Door Rail

Door Stile

Side

Knob

Door Panel

Bottom

Lower Face Frame Rail

Base Molding

Face Frame Stile

Base Molding

Butt Hinge

Make the case.

1 Cut the pieces to size. Joint, rip, and cut all the parts except for the back and door panel to the dimensions given in the Materials List. Notice that the top and bottom of the case are ³/₈ inch narrower than the sides. This creates space for the back boards, which are hidden by the wider sides. I hand planed all the exposed surfaces of this cupboard for visual effect. Before continuing, hand plane both inside and outside surfaces. If you don't have much experience with hand planing, see "Planing Wood by Hand" on page 52.

2 Cut the shelf dadoes. The dadoes are cut into the inside surfaces of the case's sides as shown in the Side View. Cut the dadoes with a router or on a table saw. You can also cut the dadoes with a backsaw and pare out the waste with a chisel. As designed, the cupboard has only two shelves, which divide the inside into three separate storage areas. You can include as many shelves as you want, however, and space them to suit whatever you intend to store in the cupboard.

3 Cut the dovetails. Fashion the dovetails and pins by hand or with a router using a dovetail template. If you haven't done much dovetailing, see "Cutting Through Dovetails" on page 81. If you are cutting the dovetails

---

MATERIALS LIST

Part	Dimension	Part	Dimension
Sides (2)	³/₄" × 6" × 19"	Door rails (2)	³/₄" × 1³/₈" × 12"
Top and bottom (2)	³/₄" × 5⁵/₈" × 15"	Panel (raised)	¹/₂" × 9⁵/₈" × 13¹/₄"
Face frame stiles (2)	³/₄" × 1¹/₂" × 19"	Knob	⁷/₈" × ⁷/₈" × 2"
Upper face frame rail	³/₄" × 1³/₄" × 13³/₄"	Latch	¹/₄" × ³/₄" × 2"
Lower face frame rail	³/₄" × 1⁵/₈" × 13³/₄"		
Shelves (2)	³/₈" × 5⁵/₈" × 14¹/₄"	**HARDWARE**	
Back board (3)	³/₈" × 5" × 19"	2 brass butt hinges, 1¹/₂" × 1"	
Cornice molding stock	³/₄" × 1³/₄" × 36"	As needed, 4d finishing nails	
Base molding stock	³/₄" × ³/₄" × 36"	As needed, 2d finishing nails	
Door stiles (2)	³/₄" × 1³/₈" × 15⁵/₈"	1 pair hangers	

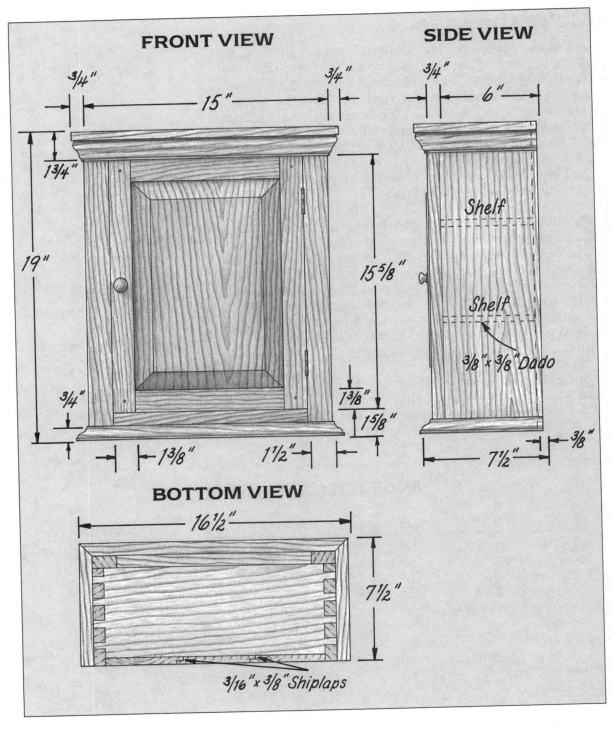

FRONT VIEW

SIDE VIEW

BOTTOM VIEW

with a router and a commercially available dovetail jig, follow the manufacturer's directions. The spacing and size of the dovetails does not matter. However, the case top and bottom are narrower than the sides, so the rear half-tails should be wide enough to accommodate this, as shown in the Dovetail Layout.

4 **Assemble the case.** When you've cut the tails and pins, test their fit, and make any necessary adjustments. Spread glue on the dovetails and assemble the case. Before the glue sets, make sure that the case is square by measuring diagonally from corner to corner. If the distances are equal, the cabinet is square. Make any necessary adjustments.

When the glue is dry, level and smooth the dovetail joints with a block plane. Because the ends of the pins and tails are end grain, make sure that your blade has a razor-sharp edge.

Make the face frame.

1 **Cut the joinery in the frame stiles and rails.** The face frame is held together by mortises and tenons.

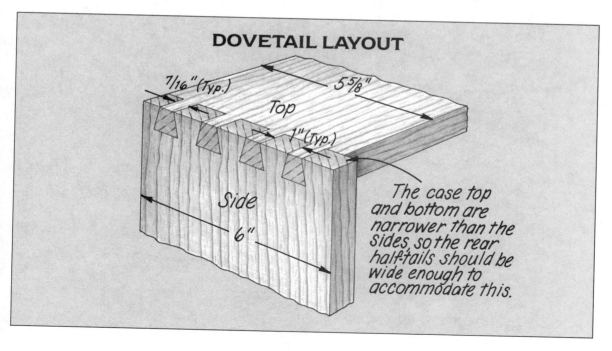

DOVETAIL LAYOUT

7/16" (Typ.) 5⅝"

Top

1" (Typ.)

Side

6"

The case top and bottom are narrower than the sides, so the rear half-tails should be wide enough to accommodate this.

Cut tenons on each end of the frame rails with a dado cutter set up in a table saw. Set up the table saw fence as a stop, and guide the stock with a miter gauge as you cut.

Lay out mortises on the stiles as shown in the Joinery Detail. To make the mortises, drill a series of ¼-inch-diameter × ⅞-inch-deep holes within the layout lines, and clean out the waste with a chisel.

Cut ¼ × ⅞ × ⅞-inch tenons on each end of the frame rails with a dado cutter set up in a table saw. Set up the table saw fence as a stop, and guide the stock with a miter gauge as you cut. Check the fit of the tenons in their mortises, and make any necessary adjustments.

2 Assemble the face frame. Glue together the stiles and rails. Clamp the frame together, and make sure that it is square by measuring from corner to corner as you did with the case. Allow the glue to dry.

After removing the clamps, plane out any ridges between the frame joints with a hand plane, removing any tool marks and glue stains in the process.

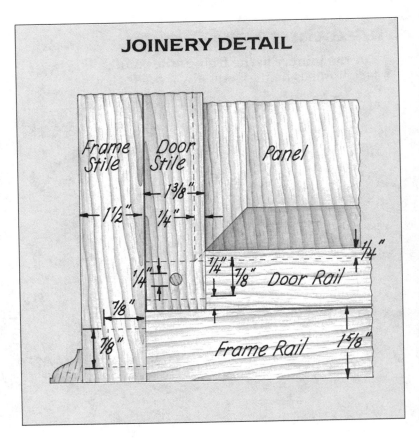

JOINERY DETAIL

Frame Stile · Door Stile · Panel · Door Rail · Frame Rail

Assemble the face frame and case, and install the shelves.

1 **Nail the face frame to the case.** Attach the face frame to the case with 4d finishing nails. Set the nails with a nail set, and fill the holes with wood putty. If you are planning to use a natural finish, use putty tinted the same color as the wood.

2 **Trim the face frame's outer edges.** The face frame and case sides probably do not meet perfectly. Even up the edges with a hand plane. Secure the case in a vise as you trim the frame edge.

3 **Fit the shelves into the dadoes.** Simply slide the shelves into the dadoes. They will be held in place by the face frame and the back boards, so no glue is necessary.

Make the back.

1 **Choose the backing material and make the back.** I made the back on the original from solid wood, and if you want to do the same, you must give the wood the opportunity to expand and contract naturally. Allow for expansion by making the back from three boards and cutting $3/16 \times 3/8$-inch shiplaps where they meet, as shown in the Bottom View. When you attach the back boards, leave a $1/16$-inch gap between the boards. This choice also gives you the opportunity to use up some scrap wood.

If you prefer, make the back from plywood. You can simply cut it to fit in the back opening.

2 **Install the back.** If you used plywood, nail the back in place with 2d finishing nails. If you used solid wood, nail the boards in one at a time with 2d finishing nails, and leave about $1/16$ inch between the boards for expansion. Cut the last board to fit into its space.

Make and attach the moldings.

1 **Select the moldings.** If you are making your cupboard of pine or you are planning on painting it, you can buy a stock molding at a lumberyard. If you are

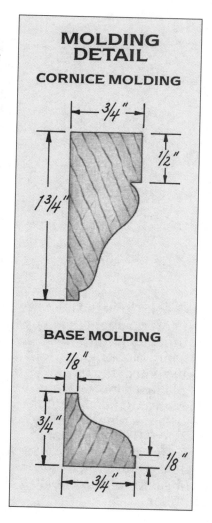

MOLDING DETAIL

CORNICE MOLDING

BASE MOLDING

223

Trim the miters with a razor-sharp block plane. Hold the end of the block plane against your sternum and pull the mitered stock over the plane's cutting edge.

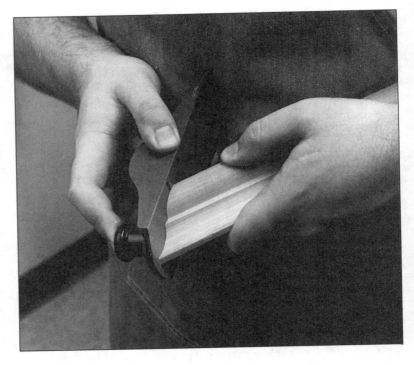

making your cupboard from a hardwood and want a natural finish, you will have to make your own molding.

You can make your own molding with a table-mounted router and your choice of bit. The molding doesn't have to look like mine, but the cornice molding should be 1 3/4 inches wide and the base molding should be 3/4 inch wide, as shown in the Molding Detail.

Quick Tip: If the miter joints do not fit perfectly, trim them with a razor-sharp block plane. Hold the end of the block plane against your sternum and pull the miter over the plane's cutting edge. This block plane technique provides excellent control when making fine adjustments to a miter.

2 Miter and attach the moldings. Miter the moldings to fit around the cupboard. Attach the cornice molding to the cupboard with 4d finishing nails, and attach the base molding with 2d finishing nails. Set the nails and fill the holes with wood putty.

Make and hang the door.

1 Cut the panel slot. The door is a frame-and-panel door: A beveled panel fits in a groove cut into the top and bottom of the door. Cut a 1/8 × 1/4-inch-deep groove along the inside edges of the rails and stiles as shown in the Frame and Panel Detail. The grooves can run along

224

Cut the mortises on the drill press by drilling a series of holes within the layout lines and completely through the stile.

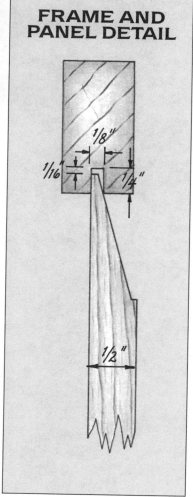

FRAME AND PANEL DETAIL

the rails' entire length, but only from mortise to mortise on the stiles. Make these cuts on the table saw with a standard blade.

2 **Lay out and cut the joinery in the door parts.** Lay out the through mortises on both edges of the door stiles as shown in the Joinery Detail. Cut the mortises on the drill press by drilling a series of holes within the layout lines and completely through the stile. Trim away any excess waste from each edge of the mortise with a chisel.

Lay out the tenons in the door rails as shown in the Joinery Detail. Cut the $1/4 \times 7/8 \times 1\,3/8$-inch tenons with a dado cutter on the table saw in the same way that you cut the tenons in the frame rails.

Test fit the stiles and rails, and pull the joints together with a pair of bar clamps. Make any necessary adjustments to the tenons.

3 **Cut the panel to size.** The panel's fit is critical and you should measure from your assembled door rather than relying totally on the Materials List. The

Quick Tip: You can easily substitute a flat panel for a raised panel. Plane a piece of wood to 1/4 inch, and cut it to the dimension of the panel. Hand plane a bevel in the edges of the flat panel to fit in the panel slot in the door frame. Install the panel so that the beveled edge of the panel is on the back of the door.

grooves in the door rails and stiles are 1/4 inch deep; however, to allow for expansion of the edges of the panel, they should only drop about 3/16 inch into the grooves. Measure the opening in the door frame and add 3/8 inch to the length and width. Cut the panel to the resulting dimensions.

4 Hand plane the panel. Hand plane the front and back of the panel to remove all the milling marks.

5 Raise the panel. Raise the panel by cutting a bevel in it as shown in the Frame and Panel Detail. I raised the panel with a panel-raising plane, and if you have one of these planes, you can do the same. If not, raise the panel on the table saw as explained in "Raising Panels on the Table Saw" on page 200.

6 Assemble the door. Pull the stiles and rails apart. Put some glue in the mortises, and reassemble the stiles and rails around the panel.

Reinforce the joint with pins. To do this, drill a 1/4-inch hole in each corner of the frame, piercing both the mortise and the tenon. When drilling, place a piece of scrap wood behind the joint to prevent tearout. Whittle 1/4-inch pins from scrap wood, and tap a pin into each hole with a hammer.

Hand plane the front and back surfaces of the door frame to remove any tool marks and even up the joints and pins.

7 Fit the door. When you put the door in its opening, there should be a 1/16-inch gap between the door and the face frame. If necessary, trim stock from the edges of the door with a hand plane or on the jointer until the door fits properly.

8 Hang the door. Lay out the hinge mortises where shown in the Front View. Cut the hinge mortises in the door and face frame with a router or chisel, and hang the door.

Make and install the knob.

1 Turn the knob. You can purchase a knob, or you can make your own. The knob for this cabinet is quite small and can be made out of a piece of scrap hardwood. Turn the knob on a lathe to the shape and size shown in the Knob Detail.

2 **Make the latch.** The latch fits on the end of the knob stem and holds the door closed. Make the latch from a piece of ¼-inch hardwood, and cut it to the size and shape shown in the Latch Detail with a coping saw or band saw. Drill a ⅜-inch-diameter hole through the latch as shown.

3 **Mount the knob.** Drill a ⅜-inch-diameter hole centered in the left door stile to position the knob as shown in the Front View. Insert the knob's stem through the hole in the door stile and through the one in the latch.

4 **Secure the knob.** Drill a ³⁄₃₂-inch-diameter hole through the edge of the latch and the knob's stem. Whittle a thin hardwood pin or use a round toothpick to act as a cotter. Put a spot of glue on the pin and insert it through the hole. Use a chisel to trim the pin flush with the edges of the latch. Use a dovetail saw to trim the end of the knob's stem flush with the latch. When the door is closed and the knob is turned, the latch will slide behind the face frame. To open the door, simply turn the knob one-quarter turn.

Finish the cupboard.

1 **Prepare the surface and apply the finish.** Sand lightly with 220-grit paper. Since you have hand planed every visible surface, the cupboard should need no more preparation than this. If you made your cabinet from hardwood, apply a clear oil and sealer. If your cabinet is pine, apply traditional milk paint.

2 **Hang the cupboard.** Screw two hangers to the upper back edge of the cupboard, and hang it on the wall.

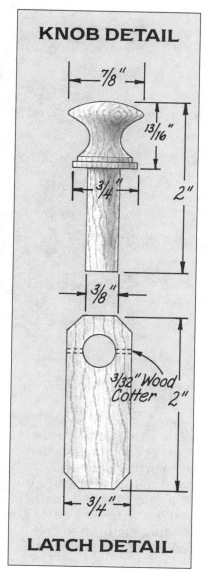

KNOB DETAIL

⅞"

13/16"

¾"

2"

⅜"

³⁄₃₂" Wood Cotter 2"

¾"

LATCH DETAIL

DIETERS' RECIPE BOX

by Paul Good

A box makes a wonderful gift; that special person will think of you each time it is opened. Making this particular box is a great chance to stretch your skills. Because it's small, you're risking only a small amount of time and materials. It's the perfect chance to try dovetails, and the intricate-looking top is easier than you'd think.

I made this recipe box for my wife on our wedding anniversary, and since we are both on the heavy side, I added the lock and we call it the "Dieters' Recipe Box."

I made the box from cherry, with the background panel of the top in walnut for contrast. Whatever hardwoods you use, make the effort to find that special board that will really stand out.

To make this box, I built a sealed container, and then cut the lid off with a table saw. The drawings and Materials List allow extra wood for this cut.

EXPLODED VIEW

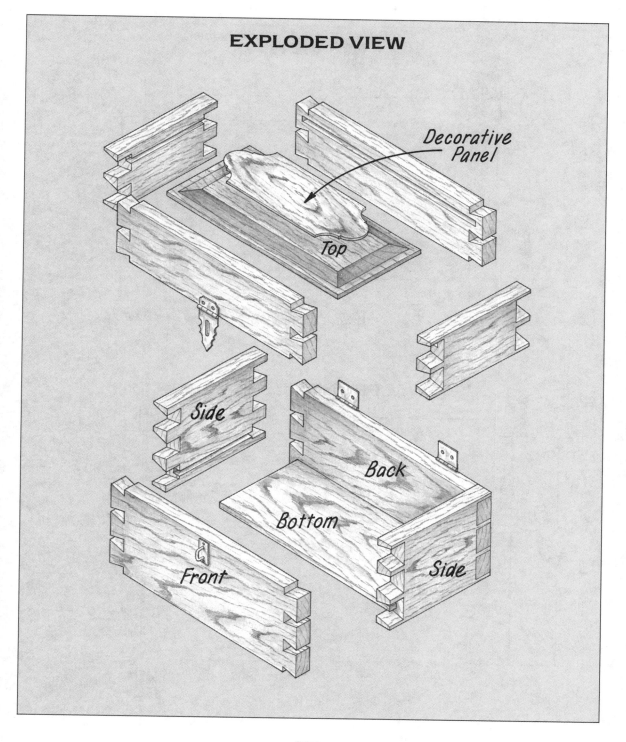

Decorative Panel

Top

Side

Back

Bottom

Side

Front

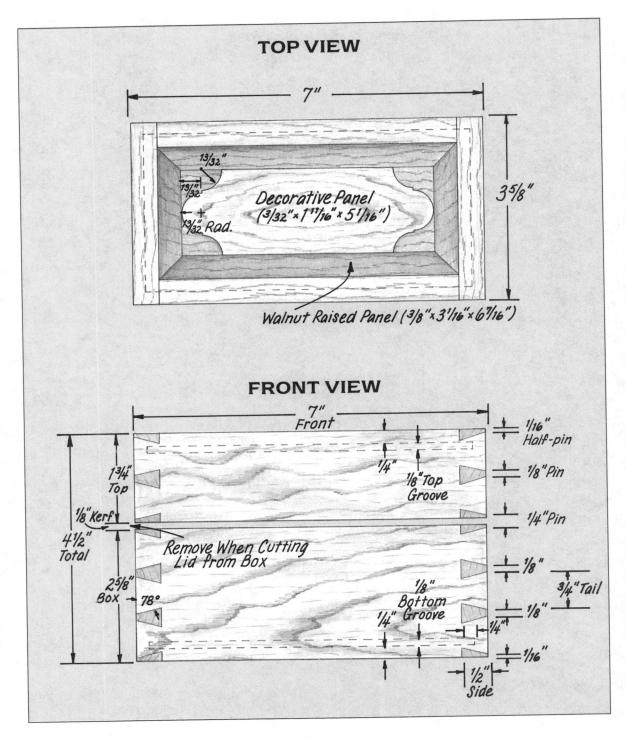

TOP VIEW

7"

3⁵/₈"

¹³/₃₂"

¹³/₃₂"

¹³/₃₂" Rad.

Decorative Panel
(³/₃₂" × 1¹¹/₁₆" × 5¹/₁₆")

Walnut Raised Panel (³/₈" × 3¹/₁₆" × 6⁷/₁₆")

FRONT VIEW

7"
Front

¹/₁₆"
Half-pin

¹/₄"

¹/₈"Top
Groove

¹/₈" Pin

1³/₄"
Top

¹/₄"Pin

¹/₈" Kerf

Remove When Cutting
Lid from Box

4¹/₂"
Total

¹/₈"

¹/₈"
Bottom
Groove

³/₄"Tail

2⁵/₈"
Box

78°

¹/₄"

¹/₈"

¹/₄"

¹/₁₆"

¹/₂"
Side

Make the front, back, and sides.

1 **Prepare the stock.** Joint, plane, and rip a single board to $1/2 \times 4\,1/2 \times 24$ inches from which you'll make the front, back, and sides. Joint, plane, rip, and cut the other parts to the sizes given in the Materials List.

2 **Cut the front, back, and sides to length.** With a little planning, you can build this box so that the grain flows around it. To do so, cut one side first, followed by the front, the second side, and then the back. The outside surfaces should all come from the same face of the board; so before cutting, mark which face that will be. As you cut, mark the pieces so you'll know which is which. Use a stop on the radial arm saw or table saw to ensure that both the front and back are the same length and that the sides are the same length.

Quick Tip: You can cut all four pieces without resetting the stop. First set the stop to cut a 7-inch-long piece for the front. Make a $3\,3/8$-inch spacer that butts against the stop. Cut the front without the spacer. To cut the side, put the spacer against the stop, and the stock against the spacer. The resulting piece should be exactly $3\,5/8$ inches long. Add and remove the spacer so you can cut the remaining pieces in the desired order.

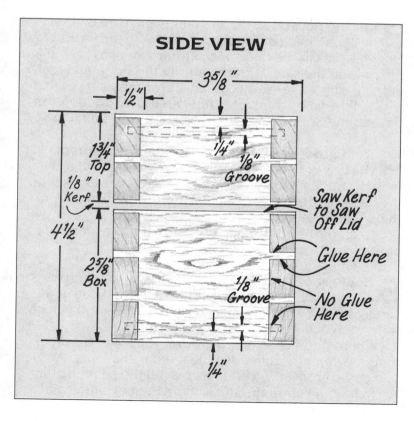

SIDE VIEW

$3\,5/8$ "
$1/2$ "
$1\,3/4$ " Top
$1/8$ " Kerf
$4\,1/2$ "
$2\,5/8$ " Box
$1/4$ "
$1/8$ " Groove
$1/4$ "
$1/8$ " Groove
Saw Kerf to Saw Off Lid
Glue Here
No Glue Here

Lower the stock onto the spinning bit to begin the cut.

3 Cut the dovetails. Cut the tails, which are on the front and back of the box, as shown in the Front View. Once you've cut the tails, trace around them to lay out the pins on the sides. Cut the pins in the sides, and test fit the parts. Make any necessary adjustments by paring with a chisel. For complete step-by-step instructions on dovetailing, see "Cutting Through Dovetails" on page 81.

4 Rout grooves in the sides. The top and bottom of the box fit in grooves routed in the sides. Put a 1/8-inch straight bit in a table-mounted router, and set up the table to rout a groove 1/4 inch deep and 1/4 inch from the edge of the stock.

Rout grooves for both the top and bottom along the entire length of each side.

5 Rout grooves in the front and back. These grooves are also for the top and bottom. Unlike those in the sides of the box, however, each groove must stop 1/4 inch from each end of the stock.

When routing a stopped groove, you lower the stock onto the spinning bit and guide it along the fence. At the end of the groove, you lift the stock off the spinning bit. To help position the stock, mark the beginning and

Carefully lift the stock end off the bit at the end of the cut.

end of the groove on the *outside* of the stock. Then with a square, transfer the location of the router bit to the fence. Make two marks, one indicating the leading edge of the cutter, the other marking the trailing edge.

To start the cut, line up the mark at the beginning of the groove with the mark indicating the trailing edge of the router bit. Carefully lower the stock onto the spinning bit, then move the stock forward. When the mark at the end of the groove reaches the mark indicating the leading edge of the bit, carefully lift the stock off the bit.

Make the top and bottom.

1 **Lay out and raise the top panel.** Raise the panel in a series of cuts. First, cut a $1/4 \times 1/4$-inch rabbet around the edges of the top. The rabbets produce a $1/8$-inch-thick tongue that fits into the groove for the top, as shown in the Raised Panel/Cross Section.

To lay out the edge of the bevel, draw a pencil line $11/16$ inch from the edge all the way around the top. Raise the panel by planing between the pencil lines and the edge of the rabbet with a rabbet plane. Bevel the ends of the panel first, because the splintered end grain at the board's edge will be removed when you bevel the sides.

Raise the panels with a rabbet plane. Hold the plane on an angle, as shown, to create the bevels on the panel's edges.

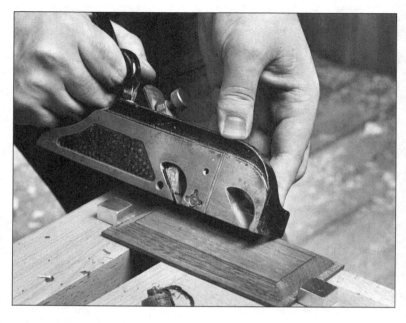

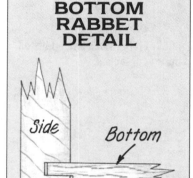

BOTTOM RABBET DETAIL

Side

Bottom

2 **Cut the bottom rabbet.** Cut the rabbet to the profile shown in the Bottom Rabbet Detail. Adjust the size of the rabbet so that the tongue produced fits into the bottom groove in the front, back, and sides.

3 **Make the decorative panel.** Trim the decorative panel to fit the box top, if necessary. Lay out the curves shown in the Top View with a compass. Cut out the shape on a scroll saw or with a coping saw. Sand the

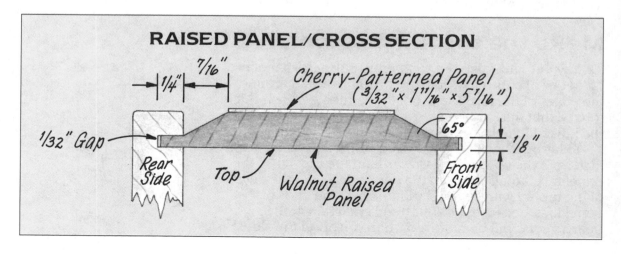

RAISED PANEL/CROSS SECTION

7/16"
1/4"
Cherry-Patterned Panel
(3/32" × 1"/16 × 5 1/16")
1/32" Gap
65°
1/8"
Rear Side
Top
Walnut Raised Panel
Front Side

edges and glue the decorative panel to the walnut raised panel.

Assemble the box.

1 **Sand the parts.** Clean up any glue that may have squeezed out around the top panel, and carefully sand the top. Also sand the inside of the box pieces before assembly. Avoid sanding any surface that will be part of a joint.

2 **Assemble the box.** Put glue on the pins and tails. Don't put glue on the end grain, as it won't hold and would just squeeze into the inside of the box. Also, don't glue in the grooves for the top and bottom; they must be free to expand and contract with changes in humidity. Assemble the two sides and the back, then slip the top and bottom into place. Put the front on the box, and clamp the box to pull the joints shut. Check that the box is square.

3 **Clean up the dovetails.** When the glue has dried, remove the clamps and carefully sand the box to clean up the excess glue and any protrusion of the pins.

Cut open the box.

1 **Cut off the lid.** Guide the box along the table saw rip fence to remove the lid. Adjust the fence so that when the bottom of the box is against the fence, the blade is centered in the second full pin, as shown in the Front

Quick Tip: Fill small gaps by mixing 5-minute epoxy and some sanding dust from the wood you are using. Put the mixture in place with a putty knife. Scrape and sand the epoxy flush after it dries.

MATERIALS LIST

Part	Dimension
Front	$1/2" \times 4 1/2" \times 7"$
Back	$1/2" \times 4 1/2" \times 7"$
Sides (2)	$1/2" \times 4 1/2" \times 3 5/8"$
Bottom	$1/4" \times 3 1/16" \times 6 7/16"$
Top	$3/8" \times 3 1/16" \times 6 7/16"$
Decorative panel	$3/32" \times 1 11/16" \times 5 1/16"$

HARDWARE

2 brass butt hinges, $3/4" \times 1"$. Available from The Woodworkers' Store, 21801 Industrial Blvd., Rogers, MN 55374. Part #27698.

1 hasp. Available from The Woodworkers' Store. Part #27771.

Guide the box along the table saw rip fence, as shown, to remove the lid.

and Side Views. Raise the saw blade so that it is slightly more than $1/2$ inch high.

Cut the sides of the box first. Make the final cuts on the front and back, which are longer and more stable. Guide the bottom portion of the box with a push stick. On the final cut, make sure the bottom portion of the box is clear of the blade before reaching for the top.

Plane or sand off the saw marks and check to see that the lid rests evenly on the box. Sand and plane to make any necessary adjustments.

2 Install the hinges. Cut mortises for the hinges listed in the Materials List. Lay out the mortises by tracing the outline of the hinge directly on the wood with a knife. The mortises should be the thickness of the hinge leaf. Cut away most of the waste with a straight bit in a router, and then chisel the corners square. When the mortises have been cut, apply an oil finish and screw the hinges into place.

After you've attached the hinges to the box, add the "use at your own risk" hasp on the front if you want to. Note that locks vary: The one in the Materials List simply nails into place.

Quick Tip: For super-tight dovetails, clamp the dovetails between glue blocks which are notched around the pins. The notched glue blocks apply pressure directly to the tails and push them against the pins, as shown in the Clamping Detail.

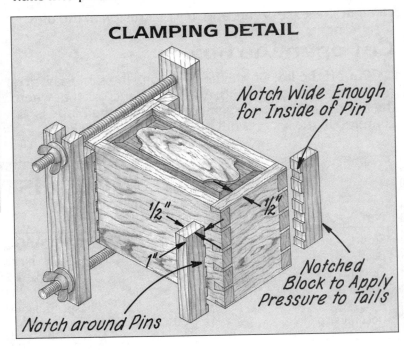

CLAMPING DETAIL

Notch Wide Enough for Inside of Pin

$1/2''$

$1/2''$

$1''$

Notched Block to Apply Pressure to Tails

Notch around Pins

HANGING CORNER CABINET
by Tom Groller

From triangular-leafed tables to three-legged chairs to V-shaped china cupboards, furniture makers have long sought to make good use of the awkward space created by the meeting of walls. This hanging corner cabinet is a classic contribution to that effort, elegantly displaying collectibles behind a fitted glass door. Below the door is a small open shelf for a plant or a dried flower arrangement.

Built of cherry with traditionally inspired scroll work and trim, this cabinet blends well with most decors. Its straightforward construction and modest proportions make it easy and relatively inexpensive to build.

EXPLODED VIEW

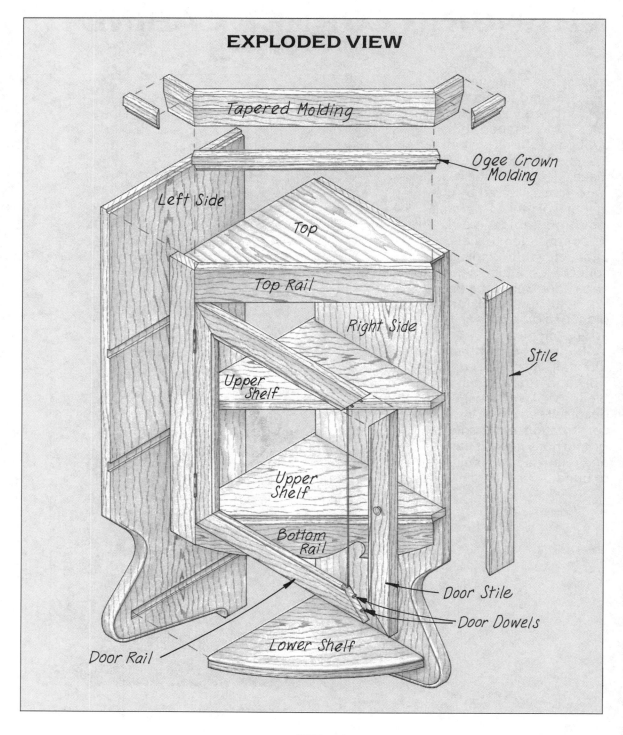

Tapered Molding

Ogee Crown Molding

Left Side

Top

Top Rail

Right Side

Stile

Upper Shelf

Upper Shelf

Bottom Rail

Door Stile

Door Dowels

Door Rail

Lower Shelf

Make the sides.

1 **Choose the stock and cut the parts.** Joint, plane, rip, and cut the sides and stiles to the sizes given in the Materials List. Mill the remaining parts, except for the shelves, to the thickness and width listed, but leave them an inch longer than called for.

You will mill the shelves in the next few steps.

2 **Rough-cut the top and shelves.** To save wood, cut the upper shelves and lower shelf from a single length of wood, as shown in the Shelf-Cutting Diagram. Lay out their shapes according to the Upper and Lower Shelf Details. Cut just outside the layout lines with a jigsaw or band saw. For now, leave the top shelves triangular.

Cut the top, which is identical to the upper shelves, from a piece of ¼-inch plywood. Lay out the top so that the rear corner comes from the corner of the plywood sheet. This assures a 90-degree angle, which will be

> **Quick Tip:** When gluing up stock, ensure a good grain match by cutting all the adjacent boards from the same piece of stock.

MATERIALS LIST

Part	Dimension
Case	**HARDWARE**
Left side	¾″ × 13⅜″ × 40½″ — 1 piece glass, ⅛″ × 13¼″ × 16″
Right side	¾″ × 12⅝″ × 40½″ — As needed, #8 × 2½″ drywall screws
Upper shelves (2)	¾″ × 10½″ × 18¼″ — As needed, #8 × 1½″ drywall screws
Lower shelf	¾″ × 10½″ × 18¾″ — 2 H-hinges. Available from Garrett Wade, 161
Top	¼″ × 10½″ × 18¼″ — Avenue of the Americas, New York, NY 10013.
Frame	Part #D18.01.
Top rail	¾″ × 2¾″ × 16⅝″ — 1 bullet catch. Available from Garrett Wade.
Bottom rail	¾″ × 3″ × 16⅝″ — Part #1.02.
Stiles (2)	¾″ × 2⅜″ × 23¾″ — 8 brass glass retainer clips
Molding	2 cherry furniture plugs, ⅜″ dia. Available from
Tapered molding stock	½″ × 6″ × 30″ — The Woodworkers' Store, 21801 Industrial
Ogee crown molding stock	¾″ × 6″ × 30″ — Blvd., Rogers, MN 55374. Part #B1035.
Door	As needed, 4d finishing nails
Door rails (2)	¾″ × 2″ × 16½″ — As needed, 2d finishing nails
Door stiles (2)	¾″ × 2″ × 19¼″ — As needed, ¾″ brads
Door dowels (8)	⅜″ dia. × 1″

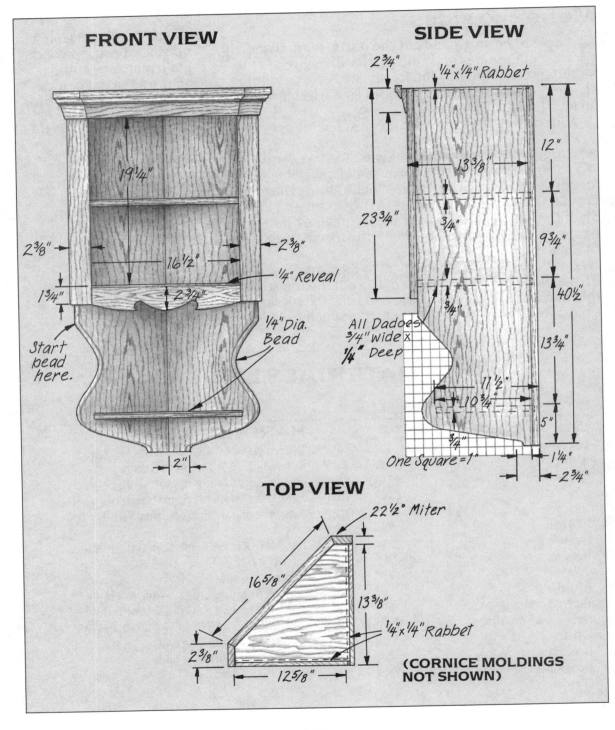

FRONT VIEW

19¼"

2⅜"   2⅜"

16½"

¼" Reveal

1¾"   2¾"

¼" Dia.
Bead

Start
bead
here.

2"

SIDE VIEW

2¾"

¼" x ¼" Rabbet

12"

13⅜"

23¾"

¾"

9¾"

¾"

40½"

13¾"

All Dadoes
¾" wide x
¼" Deep

11½"

10¾"

5"

¾"

One Square = 1"

1¼"

2¾"

TOP VIEW

22½° Miter

16⅝"

13⅜"

¼" x ¼" Rabbet

2⅜"

12⅝"

**(CORNICE MOLDINGS
NOT SHOWN)**

important in the next step. Carefully lay out the front
edge. Cut along the layout line as before. True up the cut
with a block plane. For now, leave the top triangular, too.

3 Trim the shelves. Use the top as a pattern to trim the
shelves with a router and flush trimming bit. This
assures that the back corner of each shelf is 90 degrees,
and that the cabinet will go together as designed.

Tack the top to the underside of a shelf. Guide the
bearing of the flush-trimming bit against the edge of the
top. Flush trim all three edges of each shelf.

4 Cut the shelves to shape. Lay out a 24-inch-radius
curve on the lower shelf, as shown in the Upper and
Lower Shelf Details. Cut out the curve with a jigsaw, and
sand the sawed edge.

Trim the corners of the remaining shelves and the top
on the table saw. First set the fence to make a 12⅞-inch
rip. Guide a back edge of the shelf against the fence to
trim off one front corner. Guide the other edge against

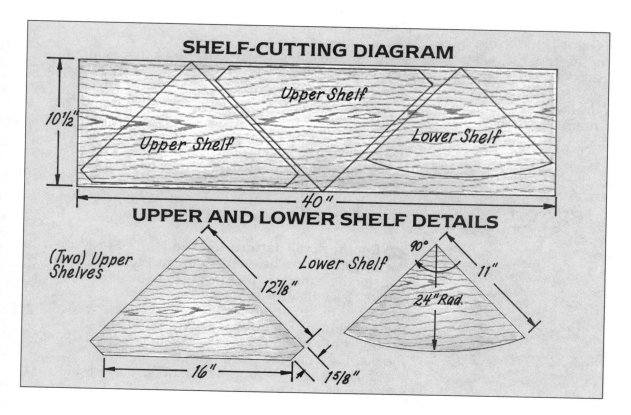

SHELF-CUTTING DIAGRAM

10½"

Upper Shelf

Upper Shelf

Lower Shelf

40"

UPPER AND LOWER SHELF DETAILS

(Two) Upper Shelves

Lower Shelf

90°

12⅞"

11"

24" Rad.

16"

15/8"

Clamp a straightedge to the side to guide the router as you rout the dado.

Quick Tip: To avoid splintering the stock when rabbeting or dadoing across the grain, score the layout lines with a sharp utility knife.

BEAD/CROSS SECTION

¼" Dia. Bead

¾"

the fence to trim off the other corner. Repeat on the remaining shelves and the top.

5 Dado the sides. Choose the best surfaces for the inside of the cabinet. Lay out three dadoes in each side to house the shelves, as shown in the Side View. Note that the dadoes for the upper shelves run all the way across the sides, while the lower shelf dadoes stop. The lower shelf dadoes are also different lengths: The right dado is 10¾ inches long, while the left dado is 11½ inches long. Position the dadoes as shown in the Side View.

Rout the dadoes with a ¾-inch straight bit, guiding the router against a straightedge as you work.

6 Cut the scroll pattern and bead the edge. Make a pattern of the curves shown in the Side View, and transfer the pattern to the sides. Cut to the layout lines with a jigsaw. Saw the sanded edge smooth.

When you've cut the sides to shape, rout a bead along them as shown in the Front View and Bead/Cross Section. Put a ¼-inch beading bit in the router, and guide the bearing along the stock.

Rout a bead in the upper edge of the curved shelf with the same setup.

7 Rabbet for the top. On the router table, cut a ¼ × ¼-inch rabbet in the top of the sides. Use a ½- or ¾-inch straight bit, and adjust the fence to control the width of the cut. Cut the rabbets across the whole width of the sides, as shown in the Side View.

Assemble the cabinet.

1 Predrill the cabinet sides and shelves. Test fit the cabinet sides and the two upper shelves. Predrill and countersink for #8 × 1 ½-inch drywall screws through the left side and into the edge of the right side. Predrill and countersink through both sides and into the edges of the shelves for the same size screws.

Insert a few screws to hold the cabinet together while you position the lower shelf. Drill and countersink for the screws that attach the sides into the lower shelf.

Disassemble the cabinet and sand all the surfaces that will be seen.

2 Glue up the cabinet. Put glue in the dadoes and adjoining surfaces. Assemble the cabinet and screw it together.

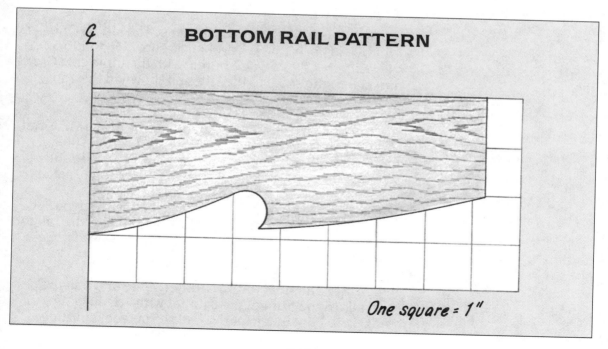

BOTTOM RAIL PATTERN

One square = 1"

Guide the rails on the table saw with the miter gauge set at 90 degrees. Gradually remove the stock until the rails fit between the stiles.

Make and assemble the face frame.

1 Bevel the stiles and glue them to the sides. One edge of each stile is beveled, as shown in the Top View. Rip the 22½-degree bevels with the table saw. Glue and clamp the stiles to the sides as shown in the Top View and Side View.

2 Cut rails to length and shape the bottom rail. Miter the top and bottom rails to fit between the stiles. Make the cut on the table saw with the saw blade still at 22½ degrees. Guide the cut with the miter gauge set at 90 degrees.

Enlarge the Bottom Rail Pattern on a piece of paper, and transfer the pattern to the bottom rail. Cut the rail to shape with a jigsaw or band saw. Sand the sawed edge smooth.

3 Attach the rails to the cabinet. Glue and nail the rails to the front of the cabinet with 4d finishing nails. Drill pilot holes for the nails to prevent splitting.

When the glue is dry, sand the bottom edge of the shaped rail to ease the transition between the rail and the stile.

4 **Attach the top.** Put the top into its rabbet and tack it into place with ¾-inch brads.

5 **Round-over the shaped rail.** Put a ¼-inch-radius roundover bit in your router and round-over the bottom edges of the shaped rail. Continue routing across the width of the adjoining stiles.

Make and attach the moldings.

The crown molding is made of two pieces, as shown in the Molding Detail. A tapered molding attaches directly to the cabinet; an ogee molding attaches to the tapered molding.

1 **Make the tapered molding.** The edge of this molding is tapered on the table saw. For safety in cutting, work on a piece of 6-inch-wide stock. Once you've tapered the stock, rip it to size.

First, tilt the saw blade 15 degrees away from the

Quick Tip: The stile end grain is likely to tear out when you rout it. To prevent this, rout from the edges of the cabinet toward the center.

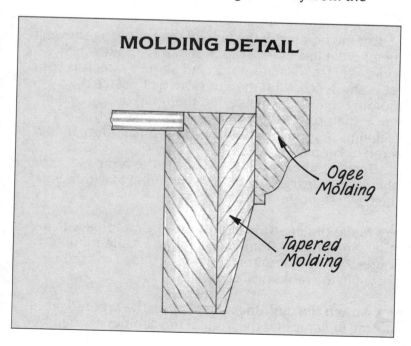

MOLDING DETAIL

Ogee Molding

Tapered Molding

Position the scrap on the top of the fence, and clamp it to the molding stock. Run the stock through the blade keeping steady pressure on the top of the scrap.

fence. On most saws, this means you'll have to put the fence to the left of the blade. Set the blade 1/8 inch from the fence and 2 inches high.

Cut the taper with the help of the simple jig shown in the photo. Find a piece of scrap that is about 2 inches wide, at least 30 inches long, and about as thick as your table saw fence. With the saw turned off, place the molding against the fence. Put the scrap on top of the fence. Clamp the scrap and the molding together with C-clamps. As you taper the molding, push down on the scrap to keep the stock from tipping.

Unclamp the molding stock from the scrap. Set the blade at 90 degrees, and rip the molding to width. Sand the bevel smooth.

2 Make the ogee molding. Rout the molding with a 1/4-inch-radius Roman ogee bit in a table-mounted router. Adjust the router height to produce the profile shown in the Molding Detail.

3 Attach the moldings. First, miter the tapered molding to fit around the front of the cabinet. Remember, these are 22½-degree miters. Attach the tapered moldings to the top rail with 2d finishing nails. Drive in the nails above the taper so that they will be covered by the ogee molding.

Next, miter the ogee molding to fit around the tapered molding. Position the ogee molding as shown in the Molding Detail, and attach it with glue and 4d finishing nails.

Make the door.

1 **Rabbet and bead the stiles and rails.** Rout a ³/₈ × ³/₈-inch rabbet for the glass on the back of the rails and stiles, as shown in the Door Detail.

With a ¼-inch-diameter beading bit in a table-mounted router, rout a bead on the front of the rails and stiles, as

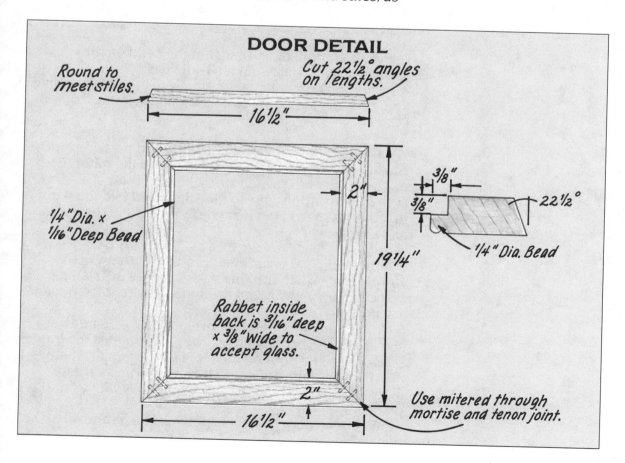

DOOR DETAIL

Round to meet stiles.

Cut 22½° angles on lengths.

16½"

¼" Dia. × ¹/₁₆" Deep Bead

2"

³/₈"

³/₈"

22½°

¼" Dia. Bead

19¼"

Rabbet inside back is ³/₁₆" deep × ³/₈" wide to accept glass.

2"

16½"

Use mitered through mortise and tenon joint.

Put the outside edge of a mitered frame on masking tape to align the pieces for clamping. Apply glue and fold the pieces together.

shown. Rout both the rabbet and the bead on the table-mounted router, guided by a fence.

Miter the door frame to fit snugly in the door opening. Reinforce the joint with dowels, as shown in the Door Detail.

2 Glue up the door. A band clamp and masking tape make mitered glue-ups easy. Spread the mitered parts end-to-end, along a strip of masking tape, as shown in the photo. Apply glue to the joints, and fold the parts together as shown. Put a band clamp around the door and tighten it.

3 Bevel the sides of the doors and fit them to the cabinet. When the glue dries, remove the clamps and clean up and smooth the surfaces with a scraper and a sander.

The door stiles must be beveled at $22\frac{1}{2}$ degrees, as shown in the Door Detail, in order to fit against the frame stiles. Bevel the door on the table saw, gradually removing stock until the door fits with about a $\frac{1}{16}$-inch gap along each stile. If necessary, trim the rails with a hand plane.

When the door fits in its opening, finish sand all of the door surfaces.

4 **Lay out and install the H-hinges and catch.** Because the door stiles are 45 degrees from the frame stiles, you may have to bend your hinges slightly to fit. Lay the cabinet on its left side, and put the door in its opening. Make sure the door is centered up and down, and put a 1/16-inch shim between the left door stile and the frame stile. Lay out the hinge screw holes, predrill for the screws, and install the hinges.

When the door is hinged, lay out and install the bullet catch. Set the cabinet vertically and test the motion and fit of the door and catch. When satisfied, remove the hardware in preparation for final finishing.

Complete the hanging corner cabinet.

1 **Apply a penetrating oil finish.** I wanted to achieve an early-American look, so I mixed and applied equal parts of Watco Danish Oil, dark walnut stain, and fruit wood stain. You can do the same, but you may want to try your own mixture. To protect the finish, apply a wax such as Watco's Satin Wax after two days. Rub it on with 400-grit wet-and-dry sandpaper, let it dry, and buff with a soft cotton rag.

2 **Install the glass.** Cut a piece of glass 1/16 inch shorter and narrower than the opening. Install the pane with brass glass retainers.

3 **Reinstall the door hardware.** Reattach the hinges and bullet catch. To make the door close more tightly, put an awl or brad into the hole in the side of the ball and turn it counterclockwise.

4 **Hang the cabinet on the wall.** If you are hanging the cabinet on a stud wall, you should find studs on either side of the wall corner. Transfer the stud locations inside the cabinet just below the top panel. Drill and countersink screw holes in the cabinet sides. Counterbore the holes to accept 3/8-inch-diameter furniture plugs, and put the cabinet against the wall. Check that the cabinet is plumb and then attach it to the wall with #8 × 2 1/2-inch drywall screws. Put the furniture plugs into the counterbores to cover up the drywall screws.

CUP SHELVES
by Ron Day

At the turn of the century, people often exchanged small mugs as presents. Some were merely decorative, others had mottoes on them. A man might give his sweetheart a mug that said "Love the Giver." A child might receive a mug that said "Little Shaver," or one that had his name on it.

The variety of mugs was endless, and when my wife discovered them several years ago, she began collecting them.

I made these shelves—three sets of them—to house her collection. I designed the shelves myself: I knew the size of the cups, what would hold them, what would look good, and I went from there.

The shelves fit into the sides on sliding dovetails. I was fascinated by dovetails at the time—you might say it was my dovetail period. You could dado the shelves in place, but I think the dovetails lend it some charm.

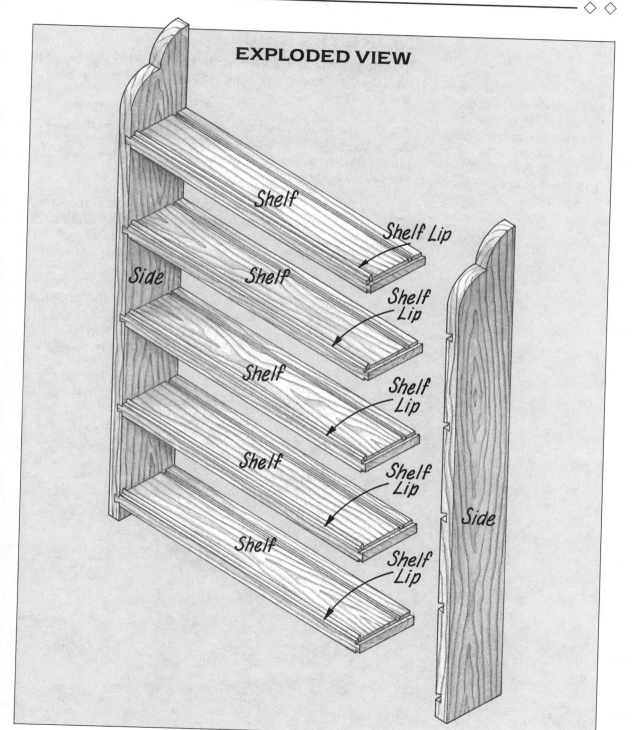

EXPLODED VIEW

Shelf

Shelf

Side

Shelf

Shelf

Shelf

Shelf

Shelf Lip

Shelf Lip

Shelf Lip

Shelf Lip

Shelf Lip

Side

Make the sides.

1 **Choose the stock and cut the parts.** Choose straight, flat stock, and cut the parts to the sizes given in the Materials List.

2 **Cut the sides to shape.** Lay out the radii at the top of the sides with a compass as shown in the Side View. Cut the radii with a jigsaw or band saw, and sand the sawed edges smooth.

3 **Lay out and cut the dovetail slots.** In order to get slots on one side which align with the slots on the other, I rout both sides in one pass. Lay the sides edge-to-edge, and clamp them to two pieces of scrap as shown.

Next make a T-square from some scraps of straight, flat, ³/₄-inch-thick wood. Cut the scraps to the dimensions shown in the Dovetail Slot Setup, and fasten them together with glue and #8 × 1¹/₄-inch drywall screws.

Lay out the centerlines of the shelves on the sides as

Quick Tip: To get two pieces with identical curves, cut both at once. First, stack the pieces together and secure them by putting double-sided tape between them. Then cut the two pieces in one operation to get two identical profiles.

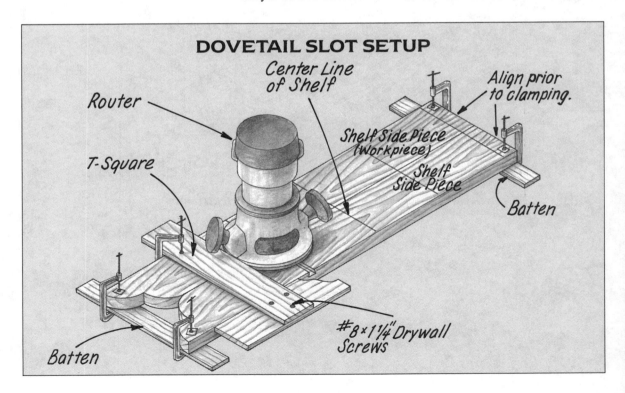

DOVETAIL SLOT SETUP

Center Line of Shelf

Router

Align prior to clamping.

Shelf Side Piece (Workpiece)

Shelf Side Piece

T-Square

Batten

Batten

#8 × 1¹/₄" Drywall Screws

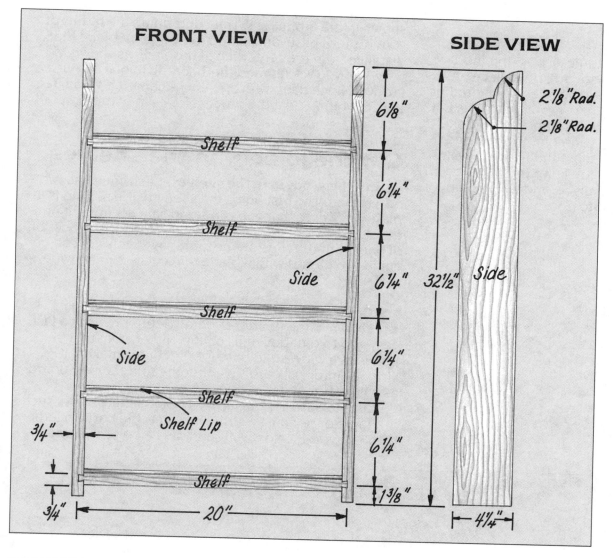

FRONT VIEW

SIDE VIEW

Shelf

Shelf

Side

Shelf

Side

Shelf

Shelf Lip

Shelf

3/4"

3/4"

20"

6⅛"

6¼"

6¼"

6¼"

6¼"

1⅜"

32½"

2⅛"Rad.

2⅛"Rad.

Side

4¼"

MATERIALS LIST

Part	Dimension
Sides (2)	¾" × 4¼" × 32½"
Shelves (5)	¾" × 4¼" × 20"
Shelf lips (5)	¼" × ⅜" × 19¼"

HARDWARE

2 brass hangers. Available from The Woodworkers'
Store, 21801 Industrial Blvd., Rogers,
MN 55374. Part #D3009.

Quick Tip: In order to quickly position the T-square, rip a piece of scrap to equal the radius of your router's base. Lay the scrap along the shelf center layout line, and move the T-square against it. Clamp the T-square in place, and you're ready to rout.

shown in the Front View. Then determine the radius of your router's base, and clamp the T-square blade that distance from the centerline of the shelf, as shown.

When you've clamped the T-square in place, rout a groove ³/₈ inch deep with a ⁹/₁₆-inch-diameter, 15-degree dovetail bit. Repeat the process for each of the dovetail slots.

Cut the joinery in the shelves.

1 **Cut the grooves in the shelves.** Each shelf has two grooves. The first holds the shelf lip; the second is a plate groove, so that you can stand saucers upright on the shelf. Lay out the slots as shown in the Cross Section of Shelf. Cut the slots on the table saw. Each slot can be cut in two passes with a blade that cuts a ¹/₈-inch-wide kerf.

2 **Cut the sliding dovetails in the shelves.** The jig shown in the Routed Dovetail Setup provides a fast, easy way to rout dovetails on the end of a board. It provides a wide, solid base for the router, making it virtually impossible to tip either the router or the board as you work.

Cut the parts for the jig from a stable hardwood, such as maple or poplar. Predrill and screw the parts together with #8 × 1¹/₄-inch drywall screws. The ¹/₄-inch-diameter

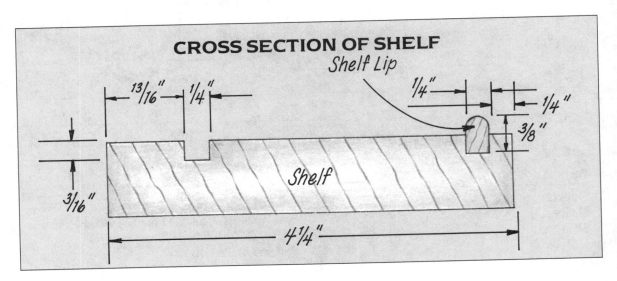

CROSS SECTION OF SHELF

Shelf Lip

Shelf

¹³/₁₆"   ¹/₄"   ¹/₄"   ¹/₄"

³/₁₆"   ³/₈"

³/₁₆"

4¹/₄"

holes in the fence allow you to adjust the fence by loosening the screws.

Set the cut up on a piece of scrap the exact thickness of the shelves. Clamp the jig to the scrap, as shown in the drawing, and guide the router against the fence to rout one side of the tail.

Clamp the jig to the other side of the board to rout the other side of the tail.

Test fit the resulting dovetail in one of the dovetail grooves. If you need to adjust the size of the tail, loosen the fence screws and move the fence. Move the fence closer to the board if the tail is too wide. Move the fence away from the board if the tail is too narrow. Always keep the fence parallel to the shelf. Tighten the screws gently and make sure the fence won't slip. When the dovetail fit is right, rout the dovetails in the ends of the shelves.

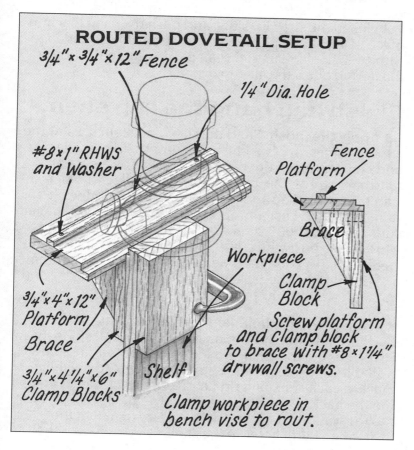

ROUTED DOVETAIL SETUP

3/4" x 3/4" x 12" Fence

1/4" Dia. Hole

#8 x 1" RHWS and Washer

Fence Platform

Brace

Workpiece

3/4" x 4" x 12" Platform

Brace

Clamp Block

3/4" x 4 1/4" x 6" Clamp Blocks

Shelf

Screw platform and clamp block to brace with #8 x 1 1/4" drywall screws.

Clamp workpiece in bench vise to rout.

Assemble the cup shelf.

1 Assemble the sliding dovetails. Spread a thin coat of glue in the dovetail slots with a glue brush or small stick. Carefully slide the shelf dovetails into the dovetail slots. Make sure the plate grooves face upward, and that the shelf lip grooves are at the front of the shelf.

If the dovetails don't slide into their slots easily, hold a piece of scrap wood against the shelf front and gently tap the dovetail with a wooden or rubber mallet. If the dovetail still won't slide into its groove, clean the glue away from the dovetail and trim along the edges of the dovetail with a chisel.

When the shelves have been joined to the sides, clean away any excess glue with a damp cloth.

2 Attach the shelf lips. Measure the distance between the sides, and if necessary, trim the shelf lips to fit. Put glue in the shelf lip slots, and push the shelf lips into place. If the shelf lips are too tight, trim along their edge with a block plane until they fit easily. Clamp the lips in place, and allow the glue to dry.

Finish and hang the cup shelf.

1 Apply the finish. Sand the shelf and stain it. After the stain dries, apply a finish. I've always liked shellac, and I mix my own from the liquid shellac available at hardware stores. Mix two parts white shellac with one part orange shellac and three parts shellac thinner. It's a thin finish, and I usually apply four coats. Rub the shellac surfaces with #0000 steel wool between each coat and wipe off the dust with a rag. For the last coat, dip the steel wool in a good hard wax with high carnuba content, and smooth the shellacked surfaces. Let the wax dry, and buff with a dry cloth.

2 Hang the cup shelf. Rather than use hangers, I hang the shelf directly from nails. Find two wall studs that will be behind the shelf. (An inexpensive stud-finder is available at most hardware stores.) Drive a 4d finishing nail into each stud, and drill corresponding $1/8$-inch holes into the back of one of the shelves. I angle the nails down into the wall when I drive them, and try to match the angle when I drill holes in the shelf. This keeps the shelf from slipping.

CABINETS FOR THE KITCHEN AND BATH

KITCHEN CABINET DESIGN

by William Draper and Robert Schultz, DBS Custom Cabinetry

We all spend a lot of time in the kitchen, and in these fast-paced days it may be one of the few places where our families actually spend any time together. The kitchen should be a refuge where we can gather three or four times a day for food and fellowship. So a kitchen should feel comfortable and familiar. We try to give our cabinets an authentic, artistic country character. All of the exterior parts of the cabinets are made from solid wood. The doors feature solid raised panels that float in the door frame. Traditional mortise-and-tenon joints are cut to join the stiles and rails, and the drawers are joined with dovetails. For ease of operation, the drawers glide on modern ball bearing drawer slides.

We design and build our kitchens along with our skilled designers and craftsmen in Bucks County, Pennsylvania. Unlike most kitchen manufacturers, who produce modular kitchen cabinets that don't always meet a kitchen's special needs, our kitchen cabinets are custom-designed to fit into unique kitchen spaces. The kitchen layout shown here was designed by Marchell Goll of Living Quarters Designs, Inc.

Obviously, the exact cabinets that we

describe building in the following two chapters may or may not fit into your kitchen. Your kitchen space is unique, so you will need to design your cabinets to fit your space. The cabinets that we describe in these chapters give you the basics necessary to design and build your own kitchen. First we'll look at kitchen design and some options that you might consider for your kitchen; then you will learn how to build a base cabinet with drawers and a sink base with a raised-panel door; and

finally, we'll show you how a basic wall cabinet with glass doors is assembled.

Designing Your Best Kitchen

When people look at a kitchen, they should see it as a whole; but it is actually made up of a number of different cabinets that are put together like a puzzle. As you lay out your puzzle, you must fit it in and

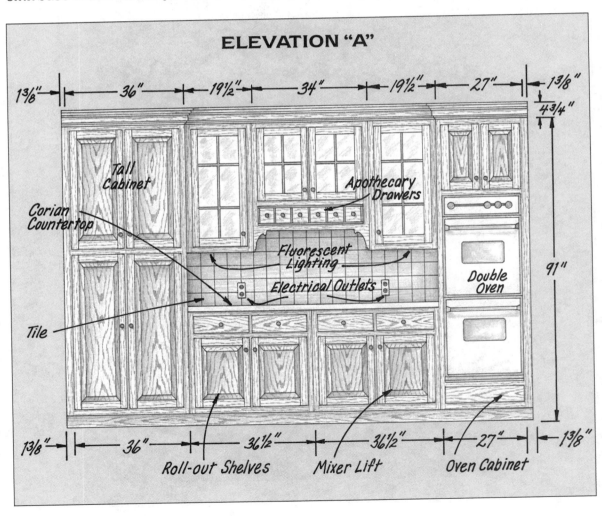

ELEVATION "A"

13/8" 36" 19½" 34" 19½" 27" 13/8"
4 3/4"

Tall Cabinet

Apothecary Drawers

Corian Countertop

Fluorescent Lighting

Double Oven

91"

Electrical Outlets

Tile

13/8" 36" 36½" 36½" 27" 13/8"

Roll-out Shelves   Mixer Lift   Oven Cabinet

Rollout shelves extend on full-extension slides and provide easy access to mixing bowls and pots and pans.

A mixer lift frees up counter space and provides easy access to a stationary mixer.

around things like ovens and stoves, vents, dishwashers, a sink and its plumbing, and windows and doors . . . not to mention your lifestyle. Electricity is another important part of planning your kitchen. The electrical outlets and light fixtures need to be positioned where they will do the most good. All of the water pipes and electrical wires need to be roughed-in before you install your kitchen.

This puzzle has to be put together on paper before you can ever start building the cabinets. None of us can be experts at everything, so get help in planning the parts of your kitchen that you don't feel qualified to plan by yourself.

Kitchen installation isn't discussed much here or in the following two chapters. For detailed instructions on installing fixed cabinets, see the chapter Installing Cabinets on page 293.

Questions of Design

Looking at three different parts of this kitchen will give you an idea of some options that you could include in your kitchen. It may also help you think of some questions you should be asking yourself as you design your kitchen.

Let's start by looking at Elevation "A." The customer for whom this kitchen was designed enjoys baking and wanted a space designed especially for baking. Elevation "A" provides a double oven which is contained in an oven cabinet. An oven vent runs through the top of the cabinet and to the outside. The drawer at the bottom of the cabinet provides space for cookie sheets and flat pizza trays. Electrical wires (and possibly gas lines) need to be roughed-into the wall for the oven. The left base cabinet has rollout shelves that provide easy access to heavy mixing bowls. Rollout shelves are wide, shallow drawers that take the place of shelves in a cabinet. The shelves pull out on full-extension drawer slides. (Accuride full-extension box drawer slides. Available from The Woodworkers' Store, 21801 Industrial Boulevard, Rogers, MN 55374. Several lengths available.)

The right base cabinet has a divider in the middle where the doors meet. There's an adjustable shelf behind the left door,

but the right-hand door opens to reveal a mixer lift. The mixer lift is a shelf that swings up in front of the drawer with spring tension. It easily holds a stationary mixer to free up space on the countertop. (Swing Up Mixer Shelf. Available from The Woodworkers' Store. Part #29405.) If you plan to install a mixer lift, you must remember to install an electrical outlet within the cabinet to provide power for the mixer.

In a baking area like this it is important

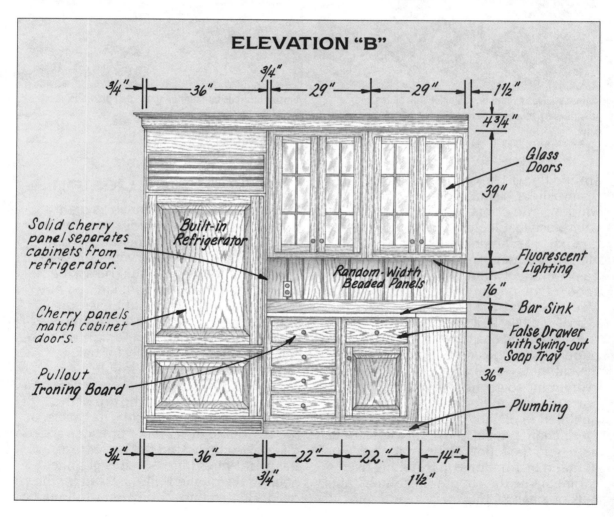

ELEVATION "B"

Solid cherry panel separates cabinets from refrigerator.

Built-in Refrigerator

Random-Width Beaded Panels

Glass Doors

Fluorescent Lighting

Bar Sink

Cherry panels match cabinet doors.

False Drawer with Swing-out Soap Tray

Pullout Ironing Board

Plumbing

Little dovetailed apothecary drawers add interest to the kitchen and provide storage space for baking ingredients.

Hidden in a drawer, the pullout ironing board provides quick, convenient access to a substantial ironing board.

to provide a flat surface for rolling out dough for cookies or pie crusts. A plastic laminate like Formica, or a solid plastic product like Corian, provides a very smooth and flat working surface. Tile, which can have bumps and ridges, would be a poor choice for a baking area surface. It is, however, an attractive and sensible wall covering for the baking area: Spills and splashes can easily be wiped off the tile.

The small dovetailed apothecary drawers, besides adding visual interest, provide an excellent place for storing baking ingredients. In a work space like this you might want to include some fluorescent lights and some electrical outlets under the the wall cabinets. If so, don't forget to rough-in the electrical power supply.

The tall cabinet on the left side of Elevation "A" serves as a pantry, and can hold the bulkier baking supplies. A tall

cabinet is basically a stretched-out base cabinet. The construction techniques are the same except for the added shelf, which is dadoed in place to separate the top and bottom portions of the cabinet. A frame rail also separates the two sets of doors. You should note that the upper pair of doors on the tall cabinet match the height of the wall cabinet doors. This is an important visual element that helps the cabinets flow across the wall.

The cabinets in Elevation "B" serve several useful functions. The base cabinet on the right is designed to hold a small "bar sink." Because of the sink there is no room for a real drawer. What appears to be a drawer on this cabinet is actually a drawer front or false drawer that tilts down on hinges to reveal a soap tray. Before you can install a cabinet like this, all of the plumbing must be planned and roughed-in.

The drawer base cabinet on the left has a surprise behind the top drawer front. The top drawer is really a pullout ironing board. (Pullout Ironing Board. Available from The Woodworkers' Store. Part #30544.) If you include this handy space-saver in your kitchen, you may never have to set up a bulky ironing board again. This option almost makes ironing clothes enjoyable.

The base cabinets in Elevation "B" are topped with a tile counter; the tile surface is fine since you won't be rolling out any dough here. There's a tile splashboard at the back of the counter, and random-width, beaded cherry boards above that.

Two glass-door wall cabinets above the counter provide a place to display goblets, glasses, and decanters. Electrical wiring needs to be roughed-in for fluorescent lights, which are mounted beneath each wall cabinet.

The built-in refrigerator is separated from the cabinets by a solid cherry panel.

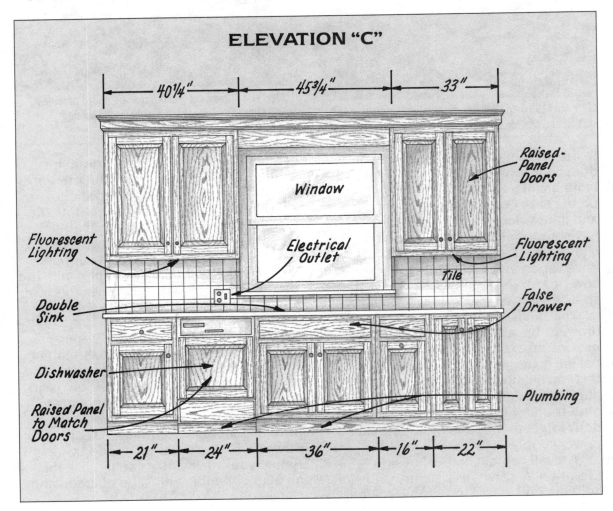

ELEVATION "C"

A trash can pullout provides quick, convenient access to a hidden trash receptacle.

If you have the room, a kitchen island can provide extra counter space or room for a stove.

The refrigerator doors are disguised with panels that match the cabinet doors. Electrical outlets should be roughed-in behind the refrigerator.

The cabinets in Elevation "C" are arranged around two elements: a window and a dishwasher. As in many kitchens, the main sink cabinet is directly below a large window. The window lets in natural light to illuminate the sink and counter, and it gives you an eye to the world outside. When it's dark outside, a light installed above the window illuminates the countertop.

The dishwasher is next to the sink for easy rinsing and loading. The dishwasher fills the space where another cabinet could go, and like the refrigerator, the dishwasher's front door is hidden by a cherry panel that matches the cabinet doors. Both the sink base and dishwasher require plumbing which must be roughed-in before they are installed. The dishwasher also needs an electrical hookup.

The cabinet on the right of the sink contains a trash can pullout. As you can see in the photo, a trash can pullout is really a drawer with a door attached to its front. The drawer is installed upside down, and a hole is cut in its "bottom" to hold the trash can. The trash can pullout is mounted on full-extension drawer slides that allow the trash can to clear the front of the cabinet. If you decide to design a trash can pullout for your kitchen, make sure that there is a plastic trash can available that will accommodate your design.

The wall cabinets on either side of the window have raised-panel doors behind which you can hide the Cap'n Crunch, corn flakes, and peanut butter.

Another element you might want to design into your kitchen is an island. An island is a group of cabinets positioned somewhere in the middle of the kitchen. It is topped with a counter and can include a built-in range or a sink. Include an island only if there will be plenty of room to work around it; an island isn't really appropriate for a small kitchen where it will just get in the way.

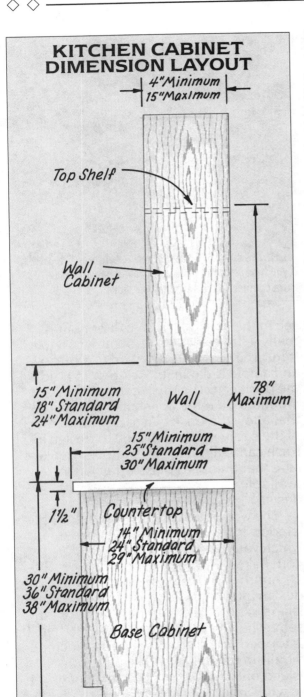

KITCHEN CABINET DIMENSION LAYOUT

4"Minimum
15"Maximum

Top Shelf

Wall Cabinet

15" Minimum
18" Standard
24" Maximum

Wall

78" Maximum

15" Minimum
25" Standard
30" Maximum

1½"

Countertop

14" Minimum
24" Standard
29" Maximum

30" Minimum
36" Standard
38" Maximum

Base Cabinet

Floor

Kitchen Standards

Conformity isn't easy, especially when you're a do-it-yourselfer, but there are a few standards you should keep in mind as you plan, design, and build your kitchen. As long as your electrical wiring meets local requirements, no one will stop you from designing and building kitchen cabinets that don't conform to these standards. However, if you ever plan to sell your house you should be aware that varying too much from the standard can decrease your home's resale value.

As shown in the Kitchen Cabinet Dimension Layout, base cabinets are generally 34½ inches high, and are topped with a 1½-inch-thick countertop. This combination produces a standard 36-inch counter height. Standard base cabinet depth is 24 inches and standard countertop depth is 25 inches, allowing a 1-inch overhang. Sink bases, designed for a standard double kitchen sink, should be 36 inches wide. In general, base cabinet drawers shouldn't be more than 33 inches wide. Instead of building a cabinet with a 40-inch-wide drawer, build your cabinet to hold two drawers 19¼ inches wide with a 1½-inch-wide rail between them. Remember, these design rules can be broken in special situations. If you need the storage space of a 40-inch-wide drawer, you can build it, but it should be mounted on heavy-duty slides.

Wall cabinets don't have as many standards as base cabinets. They can be anywhere from 4 to 15 inches deep, but a 4-inch-deep cabinet obviously has some limitations. When mounting a cabinet onto the wall, the top shelf shouldn't be any higher than 6½ feet, but the bottom of the wall cabinet should be at least 15 inches above the countertop.

DRAWER BASE AND SINK BASE CABINETS

by William Draper and Robert Schultz, DBS Custom Cabinetry

The cherry base cabinets shown here are designed to sit under and support a standard 36-inch-high counter. The sides, top, bottom, and back of these cabinets are made from birch plywood; but the frames, door, and drawers are made from solid wood (except for the drawer bottom). Although one of these cabinets is a sink base and the other is a drawer base, their basic construction is very similar. The case parts and their construction are almost identical, and the face frames are made with identical joinery techniques. When we build a kitchen in our shop, we cut out all of the case parts at one time. Then we cut out and assemble the frame parts, door parts, and drawer parts. So for these two cabinets we'll tell you how to build the cases first, then the frame, the door, and finally the drawers.

The drawer base cabinet has three drawers that are supported by epoxy-coated metal drawer slides. The top drawer front hides a commercially available pullout ironing board that is quite simple to install.

The base cabinet that supports the sink has one raised panel door and a false drawer front that tilts down to reveal a soap tray. If you were building a cabinet 3 to 4 inches wider than this one, we'd suggest designing it for two side-by-side drawers and two side-by-side doors. The top of the sink base is cut away during installation to make room for the sink.

EXPLODED VIEW

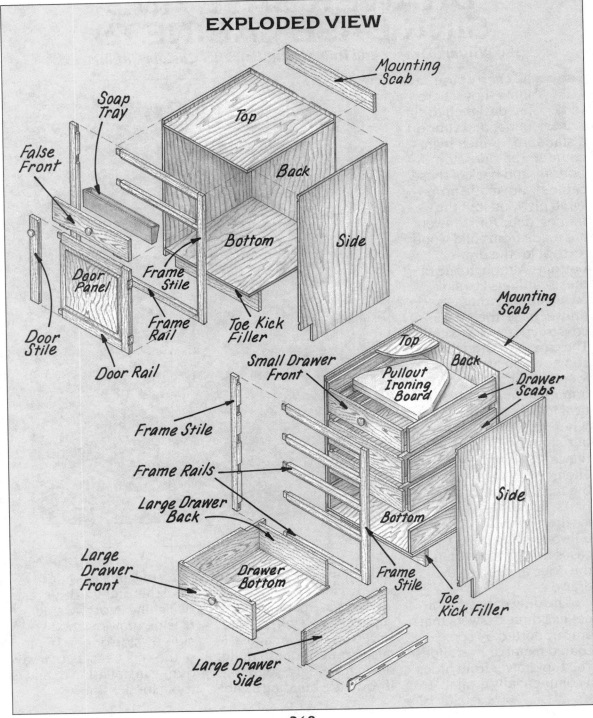

Mounting Scab

Top

Back

Side

Soap Tray

False Front

Door Panel

Frame Stile

Frame Rail

Door Stile

Door Rail

Bottom

Toe Kick Filler

Mounting Scab

Top

Back

Pullout Ironing Board

Drawer Scabs

Small Drawer Front

Side

Frame Stile

Frame Rails

Large Drawer Back

Bottom

Frame Stile

Large Drawer Front

Drawer Bottom

Toe Kick Filler

Large Drawer Side

Make the cases.

1 **Cut out the case parts.** All of the parts for the shells or cases of these two base cabinets are made from birch plywood. Rip and cut the case parts to the sizes given in the Materials List. You won't be installing the drawer scabs right away, so cut them out and set them aside for future use. As you cut the sides to size, cut out the notches in their front bottom corners as shown in the Side Views.

> **Quick Tip:** If one or both of the sides of a base cabinet will be exposed, make the exposed side or sides from a plywood that matches the face frames. Or, make the side from several random-width beaded boards.

MATERIALS LIST

Part	Dimension
Case	
Sides (4)	$3/4'' \times 22\,3/4'' \times 34\,1/2''$
Tops/bottoms (4)	$3/4'' \times 22\,1/2'' \times 21\,1/8''$
Backs (2)	$1/4'' \times 21\,1/8'' \times 30\,1/2''$
Drawer scabs (8)	$3/4'' \times 5'' \times 22''$
Catch block	$1'' \times 1'' \times 4''$
Toe kick fillers (2)	$3/4'' \times 4'' \times 20\,3/8''$
Mounting scabs (4)	$1/2'' \times 4'' \times 21\,3/4''$
Frames	
Rails (8)	$3/4'' \times 1\,1/2'' \times 21\,1/2''$
Stiles (4)	$3/4'' \times 1\,1/2'' \times 30\,1/2''$
Door	
Rails (2)	$3/4'' \times 2'' \times 17\,1/2''$
Stiles (2)	$3/4'' \times 2'' \times 21''$
Panel	$3/4'' \times 16'' \times 18''$
Drawers	
Small fronts (3)	$3/4'' \times 4\,13/16'' \times 18\,7/8''$
Small sides (4)	$1/2'' \times 4\,13/16'' \times 22\,1/2''$
Small backs (2)	$1/2'' \times 3\,1/4'' \times 17\,3/8''$
Large front	$3/4'' \times 7\,13/16'' \times 18\,7/8''$
Large sides (2)	$1/2'' \times 7\,13/16'' \times 22\,1/2''$
Large back	$1/2'' \times 6\,5/16'' \times 17\,3/8''$
Bottoms (3)	$1/4'' \times 21\,1/2'' \times 17\,3/8''$
False front	$3/4'' \times 4\,7/8'' \times 18\,7/8''$

As needed, #8 × 1 1/2" drywall screws
As needed, #8 × 1 1/4" drywall screws
4 no-mortise hinges. Available from Paxton Hardware Ltd., 7818 Bradshaw Rd., Upper Falls, MD 21156. Part #4168.
2 brass ball catches. Available from The Woodworkers' Store, 21801 Industrial Blvd., Rogers, MN 55374. Part #D3910.
6 birch disk knobs. Available from Constantine's, 2050 Eastchester Rd., Bronx, NY 10461. Part #94V5B.
3 sets 22" Alfit epoxy-coated drawer slides, 100-lb. capacity. Available from Woodworker's Supply of New Mexico, 5604 Alameda Place, Albuquerque, NM 87113. Part #801-695
As needed, 6d nails
As needed, 4d nails
1 adhesive-backed edge banding, 13/16" × 21 1/8" × 8'. Available from The Woodworkers' Store. Part Edgemate #A2302 Birch.
1 pullout ironing board. Available from The Woodworkers' Store. Part #30544.
1 soap tray, 36" (cut to fit). Available from The Woodworkers' Store. Part #63149.

HARDWARE

As needed, #5 × 5/8" flathead wood screws
As needed, #5 × 3/4" roundhead wood screws

2 Dado and rabbet the sides. Set up a ³/₄-inch-wide dado cutter in the table saw, and dado the sides to accept the tops and bottoms. Lay out the dadoes as shown in the Sink Base Interior/Side View and Drawer Base Interior/Side View. Notice that the bottoms are positioned slightly differently in each case: In the drawer base the bottom is ¹/₄ inch below the bottom frame rail, but in the sink base the bottom protrudes ³/₈ inch above the bottom frame rail to act as a door stop.

Before cutting the dadoes in the sides, cut a test dado in a piece of scrap, and test fit the plywood in it. The plywood should fit easily, but not sloppily, into the dado. Make any necessary adjustments to the width of the blade, and then adjust the height of the blade to cut ³/₈-inch-deep dadoes in the sides.

Next, cut a ¹/₄ × ³/₈-inch rabbet along the back edge of the sides as shown. Use the same dado setup to cut the

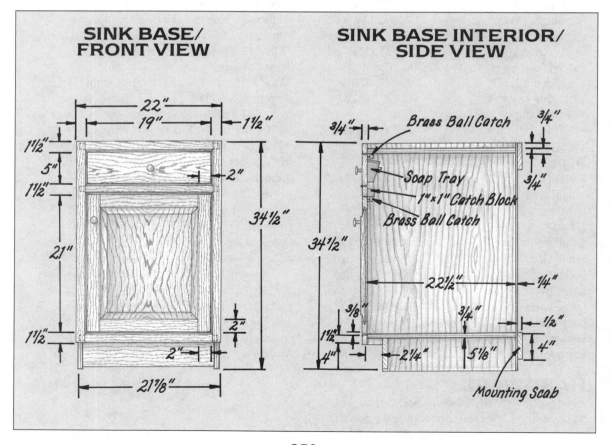

SINK BASE/
FRONT VIEW

SINK BASE INTERIOR/
SIDE VIEW

rabbets, with the help of a wooden auxiliary fence attached to the rip fence. Bury part of the blade in the fence to get the proper-width rabbet.

3 **Edge-band the sink base bottom.** Because the edge of the sink base's plywood bottom is exposed above the bottom frame rail, it is covered with edge banding. The edge banding listed under Hardware in the Materials List is backed with a heat-activated adhesive. Cut a piece 22 inches long and lay it on the front edge of the sink base bottom. Run a hot iron over the edge banding to adhere it to the plywood. Trim its edges flush with a utility knife.

4 **Assemble the case.** Glue the tops and bottoms into place between the sides, and then nail through the sides and into the tops and bottoms with 6d common

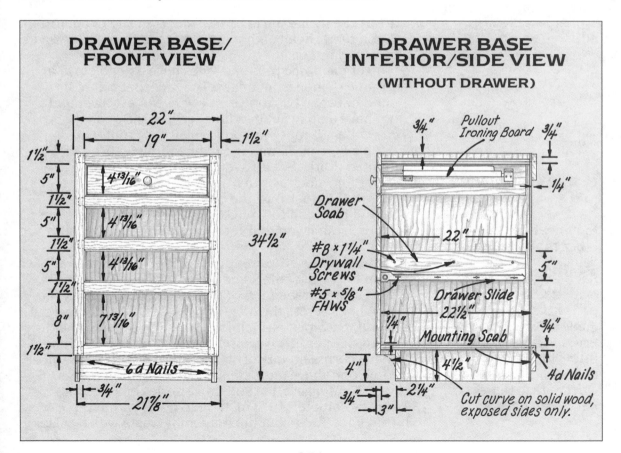

nails. Glue the back into its rabbets, and then secure it with 4d common nails.

The toe kick filler will give support to the toe kick after the cabinets have been installed. Nail the toe kick fillers between the sides and below the bottom with 6d common nails as shown in the Front Views. When the toe kick fillers are in place, attach the mounting scabs to the backs of the cabinets with glue and 4d common nails as shown in the Side Views. When you install the cabinets, you will screw through the mounting scabs and into the wall.

Make the frames.

Both cabinets have frames applied over the case. The shape and size varies, but the construction is the same.

1 Cut the frame parts to size and rout the bead. Rip and then cut all of the frame parts to the sizes given in the Materials List.

All of the frame rails and stiles have a bead cut in at least one of their front edges. The rails that are positioned between two drawers or between a drawer and a door have a bead cut in both edges, as shown in the Drawer Base/Front View and Sink Base/Front View.

Put a ¼-inch-diameter edge-beading bit in a table-mounted router. Set up a fence on the router table to support the stock as you rout.

Feed the stock past the bit at a moderate speed. If you rout the bead too quickly, small ridges will appear on the bead, but if you rout too slowly, the wood will burn.

2 Mortise the stiles. Lay out the position of the rails on the back of the stiles where shown in the Sink Base/Front View and Drawer Base/Front View. Carry the layout lines across the edge of the stiles, and then lay out the 5/16-inch-wide × 1-inch-long mortises centered within the layout lines. In my shop I have a mortising machine that makes quick work of cutting mortises. However, most people don't have mortising machines in their home shops, so I suggest that you drill a series of adjacent 5/16-inch-diameter × 1¼-inch-deep holes within the layout lines. Clean out the remaining waste with a chisel.

3 **Tenon the rails.** Cut ⁵/₁₆-inch-thick tenons on the ends of the rails with a dado cutter set up in a table saw. Adjust the blade height so that the resulting tenons will fit snugly in their mortises. All of the tenons should have ¹/₄-inch shoulders, as shown in the Frame Joinery Detail. Guide the stock with a miter gauge as you cut the tenons.

4 **Miter the bead.** As shown in the Frame Joinery Detail, the bead is mitered at 45 degrees so that the rails can nestle into the stiles. To set up the cut, tilt the table saw blade at 45 degrees and raise it high enough so that it cuts through the bead and just up to the shoulder

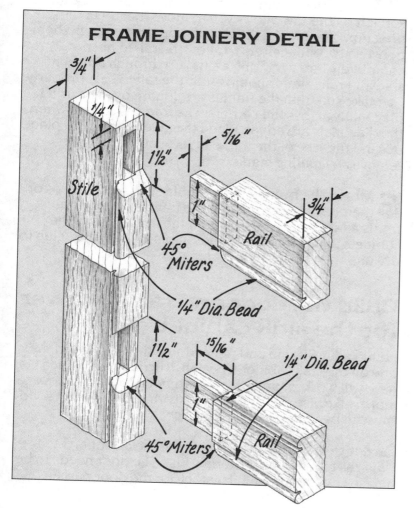

FRAME JOINERY DETAIL

beyond the bead, as shown in the Frame Joinery Detail. For complete step-by-step directions on mitering beads, see "Mitering a Beaded Frame" on page 70.

After the bead has been mitered, hand plane the edge of the frame stiles and rails to remove any saw marks.

5 **Assemble the base cabinet frames.** Apply a small amount of glue to the mortises, insert the tenons, and clamp the rails between the stiles. Measure the distance between the rails to make sure that the drawer and door openings are accurate and that the rails are parallel. While the frame is in the clamps, you can make slight adjustments to the position of the rails by slicing down through the miters with a dovetail saw. The thin kerf left by the saw allows you to move the rail in the direction of the kerf. Likewise, if there isn't enough room between two stile miters to allow the rail to nestle completely into it, cutting a saw kerf through adjacent stile and rail miters should allow the rail to seat properly.

Make sure that the frames are square by measuring diagonally across the corners. The frame is square when the diagonals are equal. When the glue is dry, hand plane or sand the face of the frame to level out joints and remove any milling marks.

6 **Attach the frames to the cabinets.** Lay the cases on their backs, and position the frames on the case fronts as shown. Spread glue on the front edge of the cabinets and clamp the frames in place. Allow the glue to dry, and then remove the clamps.

Build the door and false drawer for the sink cabinet.

I build all my frame and panel doors the way I build the one on the sink cabinet. The construction techniques here will work for any kitchen cabinet door you choose to make. Likewise, the false drawer with the swing-out soap tray can be added to any sink base.

1 **Cut the door parts.** Rip and cut the door parts to the sizes given in the Materials List. The door needs to be flat, so choose straight, flat stock for the door parts.

274

2 **Make the mortises in the stiles.** Lay out the mortises as shown in the Door Detail. All of the mortises are ½ inch from the ends of the stiles, and all are centered on the stiles' inside edges. Cut the mortises by drilling a series of 1¼-inch-deep, ⁵⁄₁₆-inch-diameter holes within the layout lines. Clean away the remaining waste with a chisel.

3 **Tenon the rails.** As shown in the Door Detail, all of the tenons are ⁵⁄₁₆ inch thick and 1¼ inches long, and have ½-inch shoulders. Tenon the ends of the rails with a dado cutter set up in a table saw. Make a cut on each face of the rail. Adjust the blade height so that the resulting tenons will fit snugly in their mortises. Guide the rails with a miter gauge as you cut the tenons.

4 **Rout the panel groove in the stiles and rails.** Cut a ½-inch-deep × ¼-inch-wide groove in the inside edge of the rails and stiles with a ¼-inch slotting cutter in

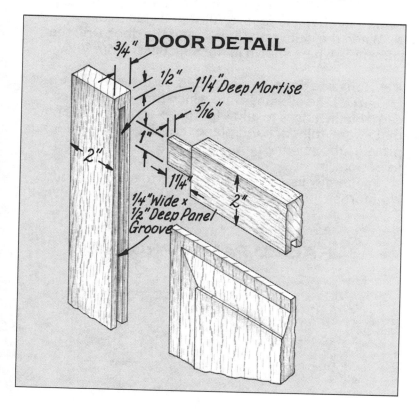

DOOR DETAIL

¾"

½"

1¼" Deep Mortise

⁵⁄₁₆"

1"

2"

1¼"

2"

¼"Wide × ½"Deep Panel Groove

a table-mounted router. The groove should run along the entire edge of the rails, but only between the mortises on the stiles. Hand plane the grooved edge to remove any saw marks.

Quick Tip: Before assembling the door, joint or hand plane 3/32 inch from each side of the panel. The extra space created will allow the door panel to expand freely within the door frame with changes in humidity.

5 **Raise the panel.** I raise my door panels on the shaper to the shape shown in the Raised Panel Profile. You can rout a similar profile with a vertical or horizontal router bit, or you can raise the profile on the table saw as explained in "Raising Panels on the Table Saw" on page 200.

Whatever method you choose, make sure that the resulting profile slips into the 1/4-inch groove in the stiles and rails. Finish sand the panel before you assemble the door. Once the panel is in its frame, it is impossible to sand it thoroughly.

6 **Assemble the door.** Put glue in the mortises and assemble the stiles and rails around the panel. Do *not* glue the panel in place. Clamp the door together, and make sure that it is square. Allow the glue to dry.

When the glue is dry, finish sand the door. Drill the knob hole where shown in the Sink Base/Front View.

7 **Hang the door.** I always build my doors to the exact size of the openings into which they will fit. Then I can trim the edges to allow for the exact amount of play that I want. Joint or hand plane the edges of your door to provide about 1/8-inch total play, side to side and top to bottom.

I generally use no-mortise hinges to hang my doors. No-mortise hinges are quick and easy to install because

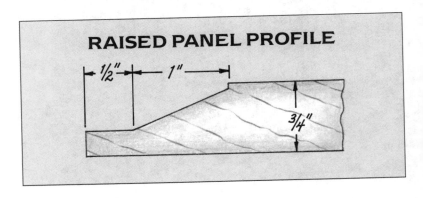

RAISED PANEL PROFILE

1/2"   1"   3/4"

you don't have to worry about scribing around the hinges and cutting mortises for them. Simply position the no-mortise hinges as shown in the Sink Base/Front View, and screw them to the door and face frame. After hanging the door, use #8 × 1 1/2-inch drywall screws to attach a block to hold the door catch onto the frame rail above the left door stile. Install the brass ball catch on the door.

8 **Hinge the false drawer front.** For the sake of consistency, all of my base cabinet frames are divided to leave a 5-inch-wide drawer opening just below the top frame rail (unless a customer makes a special request). This includes sink base cabinet frames, but because the sink takes up all of the space, a real drawer can't be installed. One solution to this problem is to mount a piece of 1/4-inch plywood behind the drawer opening and attach a false drawer front to it. I prefer, however, to hinge the false drawer front at the bottom and attach a soap tray to the back of it, as shown in the Sink Base Interior/Side View.

Attach the false front to its opening in the sink base with no-mortise hinges as shown in the Sink Base/Front View. When the false front has been hinged into place, attach the soap tray to the back of it with #5 × 3/4-inch roundhead wood screws. Add the brass ball catch centered along the top edge of the false drawer.

Build the drawers for the drawer cabinet.

The drawer cabinet shown here requires three regular drawers and one drawer front that attaches to a pullout ironing board. Although one of the regular drawers is slightly deeper than the others, the construction technique is the same. In fact, every drawer in this kitchen is built exactly like these drawers.

1 **Cut the drawer parts to size.** The drawer fronts should all be cut from the hardwood from which you made the frames and doors. The drawer sides can be made from a secondary, less expensive wood like pine or poplar. Make the drawer bottoms from 1/4-inch plywood. Rip and cut the drawer parts to the sizes given in the

Precede and follow the dovetail slot cut in the drawer fronts with pieces of scrap.

Quick Tip: In order to prevent the wood from splintering where the bit enters and exits the drawer fronts, precede and follow the cuts with pieces of scrap. The scraps, held firmly against the top and bottom edges of the drawer fronts, support the edges as the bit passes through them.

Materials List. Once all of the parts have been cut to size, mark and set aside the ironing board front and the false front.

2 Cut the dovetail slots in the drawer fronts. As shown in the Drawer/Top View, the drawer fronts and drawer sides are joined together with sliding dovetails. Put a 1/2-inch-diameter, 14-degree dovetail bit in a table-mounted router, and adjust the height of the bit so that it is 1/2 inch above the surface of the router table. Attach a fence to the router table and adjust it so the it is exactly 3/4 inch from the center of the bit. Set a drawer front face up on the router table with the end of the drawer front against the fence. Slowly and carefully guide the drawer front against the fence and into the bit to make the first dovetail slot. Reverse the drawer front and cut a matching slot along the opposite end. Cut the slot in the other fronts. Don't readjust the bit yet.

3 Cut the sliding dovetails on the drawer sides. Adjust the fence so that the bit is mostly buried in it, as shown in the Sliding Dovetail Setup. Rout a sliding dovetail in each end of several pieces of 1/2-inch-thick scrap, adjusting the fence until the sliding dovetails produced fit snugly in their slots. When the sliding dovetails seem to be fitting well, rout the sliding dovetails in the front edge of the drawer sides.

4 Cut the drawer bottom slots. The drawer fronts and drawer sides are slotted to accept the drawer bottoms. The 1/4 × 1/4-inch slots run along the entire length of the sides, but only between the dovetail slots on the drawer fronts. Make these slots as shown in the Drawer Interior/Side View with the 1/4-inch slotting cutter that you used to cut the panel slots in the doors. Put the cutter in a table-mounted router and adjust the fence to cut a 1/4-inch-deep slot where shown in the Drawer Interior/Side View.

5 Dado the sides. The drawer sides are dadoed to accept the back as shown in the Drawer/Top View. Cut these 1/4-inch-deep × 1/2-inch-wide dadoes with a dado cutter on the table saw or with a router and a 1/2-inch-diameter straight bit.

278

6 **Cut the clearance notch in the drawer sides.** As shown in the Drawer Interior/Side View, the drawer sides have a clearance notch in their back top corner. The clearance notch allows the drawer to hop over the drawer slide stop when the drawer is being installed or removed from the cabinet. Cut the notch with a jigsaw or band saw, and sand the cut smooth.

7 **Assemble the drawers.** First, put some glue in the dovetail slots in the drawer front. Slide the sliding dovetails into place so that the top edge of the sides is even with the top edge of the front. Next, apply glue to

Quick Tip: Before you assemble the drawers, joint about ¹/₁₆ inch off the bottom edge of the drawer sides. When you attach the drawer slides to the drawer sides, they will be recessed slightly behind the drawer front. I've found from experience that if you leave the drawer sides their full width, occasionally the slides will hit against the frame rails as you pull the drawers open.

DRAWER/TOP VIEW

4d Nails

¾" · ½" ¾"

½"

22½"

DRAWER INTERIOR/SIDE VIEW

¾" 5"

½"

¾" Clearance Notch ¾"

¼"

½"

4d. Nails

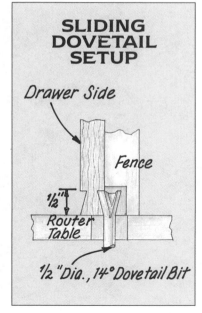

SLIDING DOVETAIL SETUP

Drawer Side

Fence

½"

Router Table

½" Dia., 14° Dovetail Bit

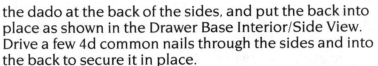

the dado at the back of the sides, and put the back into place as shown in the Drawer Base Interior/Side View. Drive a few 4d common nails through the sides and into the back to secure it in place.

When the drawer sides and back are in place, put the drawer upside down on your workbench and slide the bottom into place. Make sure that the drawer is square, and then nail the drawer bottom to the drawer back with 4d common nails.

Finish sand the drawers (including the ironing board front and the false front), and drill knob holes centered in the drawer fronts.

8 **Install the drawers in the drawer base.** Screw a pair of drawer scabs to the sides of the drawer base for each drawer (including the pullout ironing board) as shown in the Drawer Base Interior/Side View. Attach the drawer slide hardware to the drawer sides and their corresponding drawer scabs as recommended by the manufacturer. Install the drawers and adjust the hardware so that the fronts are centered in the drawer openings.

9 **Install the pullout ironing board.** It isn't difficult to install this pullout ironing board. Just buy the works from the source given in the Materials List, and screw it into place following the manufacturer's directions. The false drawer front simply screws into place.

BASIC KITCHEN WALL CABINET
by William Draper and Robert Schultz, DBS Custom Cabinetry

The cherry wall cabinet shown here is one of our standard glass-door wall cabinets. The side, top, and bottom are made from cherry plywood, but all of the other parts are made from solid cherry. The back is made up of several random-width beaded boards, and the shelves are adjustable. The door stiles and rails are rabbeted to hold the glass, and muntins are installed in front of the glass to divide it into six panes or "lights." If you choose, you could also make raised panel doors for this cabinet with the same methods described in the previous chapter. The frame and door joinery is identical to that used in the chapter Drawer Base and Sink Base Cabinets on page 267, because these cabinets are part of the same kitchen. As in the base cabinets, the top and bottom of this cabinet are dadoed into the sides. The top drops $3/8$ inch below the top frame rail, and the bottom rises $3/8$ inch above the bottom frame rail top to stop the door.

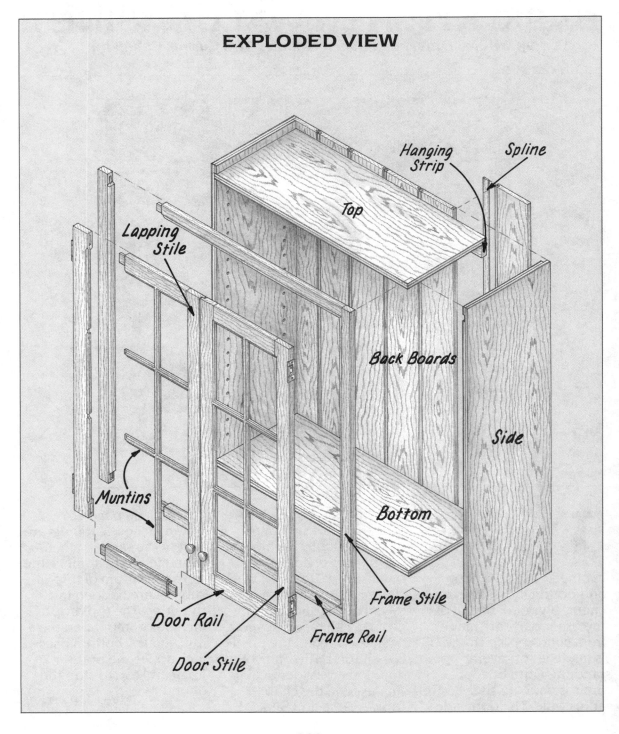

EXPLODED VIEW

Hanging Strip

Spline

Top

Lapping Stile

Back Boards

Side

Muntins

Bottom

Door Rail

Frame Stile

Door Stile

Frame Rail

Make the case.

1 **Cut out the wall cabinet case parts.** The sides, top, and bottom of this wall cabinet are made from cherry plywood. The back is made up of random-width, 5- to 6-inch-wide cherry boards. Rip and cut the side, top, and bottom pieces to the sizes given in the Materials List, and cut enough random-width boards to cover a 29-inch span.

2 **Cut the dadoes and rabbets in the sides.** Lay out the dadoes on the sides as shown in the Side View. Cut these dadoes on the table saw as you did for the base cabinets. Be sure to check the fit of the dado in some scrap before you cut the actual dadoes in the cabinet sides.

Next, cut a $1/2 \times 3/8$-inch rabbet along the back edge of the sides as shown in the Side View. Again, cut these rabbets the same as the rabbets in the base cabinet sides.

MATERIALS LIST

Part	Dimension
Case	
Sides (2)	$3/4'' \times 12\,1/4'' \times 39''$
Top/bottom (2)	$3/4'' \times 11\,3/4'' \times 28\,1/8''$
Back boards (5–6)	$1/2'' \times 5''$ to $6'' \times 39''$
Splines (4–5)	$1/8'' \times 3/4'' \times 39''$
Shelves (3)	$3/4'' \times 11\,1/4'' \times 27\,1/4''$
Filler strip	$3/4'' \times 1\,1/8'' \times 27\,3/8''$
Hanging strip	$3/4'' \times 1\,1/2'' \times 27\,3/8''$
Frames	
Rails (2)	$3/4'' \times 1\,1/2'' \times 28\,1/2''$
Stiles (2)	$3/4'' \times 1\,1/2'' \times 39''$
Glass Doors	
Rails (4)	$3/4'' \times 2'' \times 11\,1/2''$
Stiles (3)	$3/4'' \times 2'' \times 36''$
Lapping stile	$3/4'' \times 2\,3/8'' \times 36''$
Muntin stock	$3/8'' \times 9/16'' \times 10'$
Bead molding stock	$1/4'' \times 1/4'' \times 10'$

HARDWARE

2 glass panes, $1/8'' \times 9\,9/16'' \times 32\,9/16''$

As needed, #8 × 1" drywall screws

4 no-mortise hinges. Available from Paxton Hardware Ltd., 7818 Bradshaw Rd., Upper Falls, MD 21156. Part #4168.

2 brass ball catches. Available from The Woodworkers' Store, 21801 Industrial Blvd., Rogers, MN 55374. Part #D3910.

2 birch disk knobs. Available from Constantine's, 2050 Eastchester Rd., Bronx, NY 10461. Part #94V5B.

8 brass shelf pegs. Available from Woodworker's Supply of New Mexico, 5604 Alameda Place, Albuquerque, NM 87113. Part #801-629.

As needed, 6d nails

As needed, 6d finishing nails

◇ ◇ — ◇ ◇

Quick Tip: For perfectly aligned adjustable shelf holes, drill the holes with the help of a template. Make the template from a 3-inch-wide × 35-inch-long piece of scrap wood. Lay out and drill a series of holes centered on the width of the scrap. Start 1 1/2 inches from its bottom edge and space the holes 1 1/2 inches apart as shown in the Side View. Clamp the template on one of the sides so that its bottom edge is even with the bottom dado and its front edge is even with the front edge of the side. Label the front edge of the template "front," and label the top as "top." Drill the adjustable shelf holes in the sides by guiding the drill bit through the holes in the template and into the side. When you have drilled the first set of holes, remove the clamps and slide the template back along the side until it is even with the edge of the back rabbet. Clamp the template in place and drill the second set of holes. When the second set has been drilled, remove the clamps and repeat the process on the second side.

3 Drill the adjustable shelf holes. Adjustable shelf pegs hold the shelves in place between the sides. The shelf pins fit into 1/4-inch-diameter × 3/8-inch-deep holes in the sides. Lay out these holes as shown in the Side View, and drill the holes with a 1/4-inch-diameter drill bit. So that you don't drill too deep, attach a masking tape "flag" 3/8 inch above the point of the drill bit. When the masking tape reaches the wood, you know that the hole is 3/8 inch deep.

4 Bead the back boards and cut the spline grooves. As shown in the Front View, each back board has a 1/4-inch-diameter bead running along one of its edges. Cut the beads in the back boards with a 1/4-inch-diameter

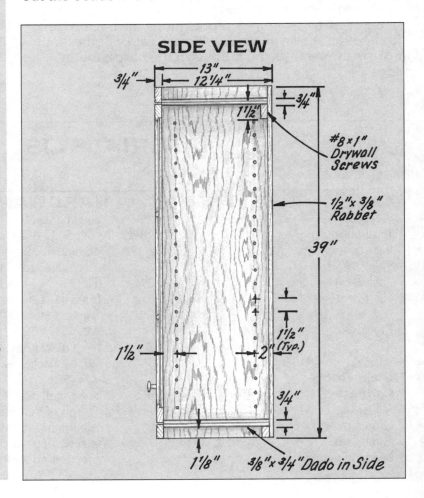

SIDE VIEW

13"
12 1/4"
3/4"
3/4"
1 1/2"
#8 × 1" Drywall Screws
1/2" × 3/8" Rabbet
39"
1 1/2" (Typ.)
1 1/2"
2"
3/4"
1 1/8"
3/8" × 3/4" Dado in Side

edge beading bit set up in a table-mounted router. Guide the stock against a fence as you rout.

Because the back boards are made from solid wood, some space has to be left between them to allow the wood to expand and contract freely. Fill the space between the boards with splines so that you won't be able to look through the space and see the wall behind. Cut the spline slots as shown in the Spline Detail on the table saw with a blade that cuts a $1/8$-inch-wide kerf (most standard table saw blades cut a $1/8$-inch-wide kerf). Position the kerf $1/8$ inch from the back of the back boards.

Rip the $1/8$-inch-wide $\times$ 30-inch-long splines from the edge of some $3/4$-inch-thick stock.

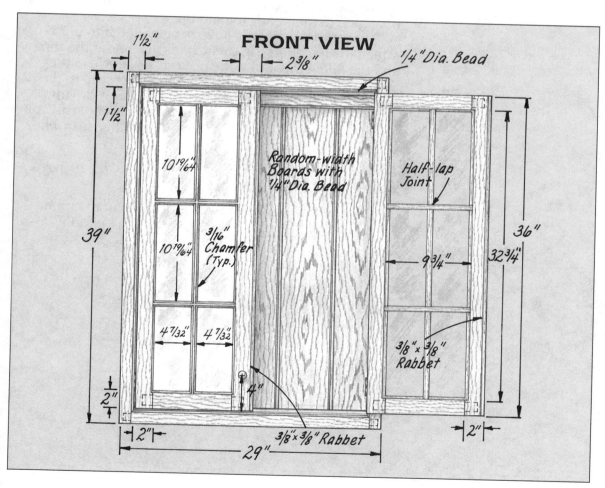

FRONT VIEW

Quick Tip: In order to make perfectly sized pre-drilled nail holes, drill the holes with one of the nails. Chuck one of the finish nails into a drill, and then drill the hole as if the nail were a drill bit. The nail will size the hole perfectly.

5 **Assemble the case.** Apply some glue to the dadoes in the sides and put the top and bottom in place. Drive 6d common nails through the sides and into the ends of the top and bottom.

When the top, bottom, and sides are assembled, lay the case face down on a flat surface and install the back boards. Install the back boards one at a time by driving one 6d finishing nail through each back board and into the top, and one into the bottom. Predrill holes for the nails to avoid splitting. As shown in the Spline Detail, leave a 1/16-inch space between the back boards. Rip the final back board to fit into its opening.

When all of the back boards have been nailed into place, slip the splines into their slots as shown in the Spline Detail. As you slide the splines into place, apply a little glue to their ends to hold them in place.

After the back boards have been nailed into place, attach the hanging strip to the back just under the top, and the filler strip under the bottom, as shown in the Side View. Glue the hanging strip and filler strip to the top and bottom, and secure them in place by driving #8 × 1-inch drywall screws through the back boards. You will screw through the hanging strip and filler strip when you attach the cabinet to the wall.

Make the frame.

1 **Cut the frame stock to size.** Rip and cut the frame stiles and rails to the sizes given in the Materials List.

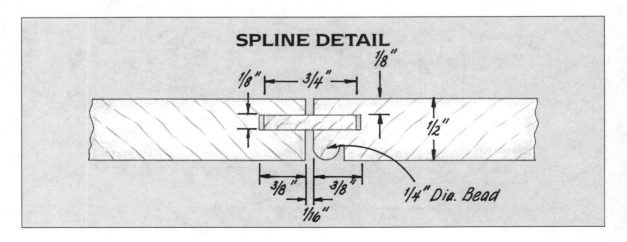

SPLINE DETAIL

2 Bead the stock and cut the joinery. Cut a
¼-inch-diameter bead in the front edge of the stiles
and rails as shown in the Front View. Bead this stock in
the same way that you beaded the stock for the base
cabinet frames.

Lay out the mortises at the ends of the stiles and the
tenons at the ends of the rails, and cut them as you did in
the base cabinet frames.

Miter the bead as explained in "Mitering a Beaded
Frame" on page 70.

3 Assemble the frame and attach it to the case. Put
glue in the mortises and clamp the rails between the
stiles with pipe clamps. Make sure that the frame is
square, and allow the glue to dry.

When the frame is dry, glue and clamp it to the front
of the case, positioned as shown in the Front View. The
frame is slightly wider than the case; it should overhang
the case sides by about ¹⁄₁₆ inch. Make sure that the
overhang is even and the case assembly is square. Allow
the glue to dry and remove the clamps.

Make the glass doors.

1 Choose the stock and cut the door parts to size. It is
very important to choose straight, flat stock for the
glass doors. Twisted or bowed stock will prevent the
doors from closing properly. Rip and cut the stiles and
rails to the sizes given in the Materials List. Rip the
muntins to width and thickness, but cut them to fit the
door later.

2 Cut the joinery in the rails and stiles. The glass
door rails have a ⁵⁄₁₆-inch-thick × 1¼-inch-long tenon
cut into each end, and the stiles have matching mortises.
Lay out and cut this joinery as you did for the base
cabinet door. *Do not* cut a panel slot in these stiles and
rails.

After the joinery has been cut, hand plane the inside
edge of the rails and stiles to remove any saw marks.

3 Rabbet the lapping stiles. As shown in the Front
View, the lapping stile and the stile that closes over it

have interlocking rabbets cut in their edges. One stile has a rabbet cut in its front side, and the other stile has a rabbet cut in its back side. Rout the $3/8 \times 3/8$-inch rabbets with a $3/8$-inch rabbeting bit.

4 **Assemble the rails and stiles.** Put glue in the mortises and clamp the rails between the stiles. Make sure that the doors are square, and allow the glue to dry.

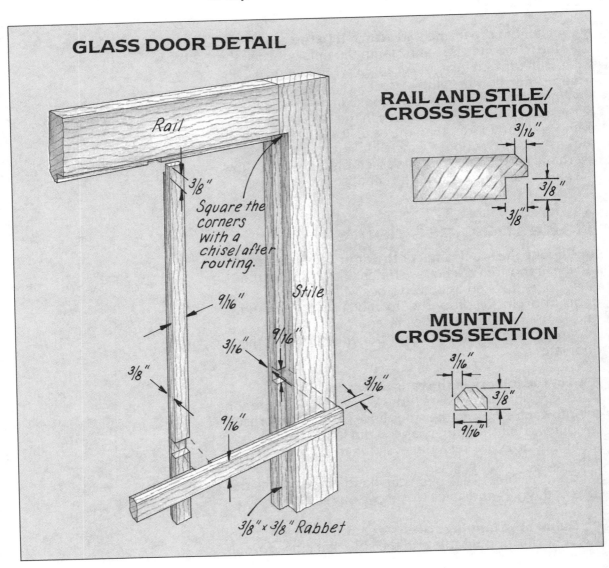

GLASS DOOR DETAIL

Rail

$3/8$"

Square the corners with a chisel after routing.

$9/16$"

$3/8$"

$3/16$"

$9/16$"

Stile

$9/16$"

$3/16$"

$3/8$" × $3/8$" Rabbet

RAIL AND STILE/ CROSS SECTION

$3/16$"

$3/8$"

$3/8$"

MUNTIN/ CROSS SECTION

$3/16$"

$3/8$"

$9/16$"

Guide the inside of the door against the rabbeting bit's bearing to rout the rabbet in the back of the door.

5 **Rabbet the doors to accept the glass.** As shown in the Glass Door Detail, the back inside perimeters of the doors are rabbeted to accept the glass. Cut the ⅜ × ⅜-inch rabbet with a ⅜-inch rabbeting bit set up in a table-mounted router.

Cut the rabbet in a piece of ¾-inch-thick stock, and make sure that after the rabbet is cut the remaining edge is ⅜ inch thick. Rout the rabbets in the doors by placing them one at a time on their backs on the router table, with the bit in the middle of the door opening. Move the door against the spinning bit and cut the rabbet in the back of the rails and stiles.

The bit will not produce square corners, so square them with a chisel when you're finished routing.

6 **Cut the muntins and lay out their position on the door.** As shown in the Front View, there are two muntins on each door that run from stile to stile and one muntin that runs from rail to rail. The muntins run across the width of the rabbets. Measure the door opening and rabbets, and cut the muntins to length. When the muntins have been cut to length, hand plane their edges to remove any saw marks.

After hand planing, lay the doors face down on a flat surface, and lay out the positions of the muntins in the rabbets as shown in the Front View. First, center the long

Guide the muntins with a miter gauge as you cut the half-lap notches.

vertical muntins between the door stiles, and then mark their position with a marking knife or sharp pencil. Next, space the horizontal muntins evenly between the rails, and mark their position.

7 Cut the half-laps in the muntins and door. As shown in the Glass Door Detail, the muntins have half-lap joints where they cross and where they meet the door frame. The door is notched, as shown, to accept the muntin.

First, chisel out the 3/16-inch-deep notches within the layout lines where the muntins meet the door frame, as shown.

Next, draw layout lines on the muntins where they cross each other. Cut 3/16-inch-deep notches at these points with a 9/16-inch-wide dado cutter set up on a table saw. Make test notches in some scrap and adjust the blade as necessary. Guide the cut with the miter gauge so that the blade passes between the layout lines.

When the half-lap notches have been cut where the muntins cross, notch the ends of the muntins where they meet the door. Lay out these 3/8-inch-long × 3/16-inch-deep notches and cut them on the table saw with a dado

Guide the door frame and muntins against the chamfer bit's bearing as you cut the chamfer.

cutter. Orient the notches as shown in the Glass Door Detail, so that when seen from the front, the vertical muntins will appear continuous from the top rail to the bottom rail.

8 **Glue the muntins in place.** Push the horizontal muntins into the matching half-laps in the vertical muntins, and then fit the muntins into the back of the door. The ends of the muntins should fit snugly in the notches in the door frame, and when they're all of the way in, they should be flush with the front surface of the door frame. Make any necessary adjustments.

Take the muntins out of the door frame, and take them apart at the half-laps. Put a spot of glue in the half-laps and notches, and reassemble the muntins and door frame. Clamp the glued surfaces together with small C-clamps, and allow the glue to dry.

9 **Chamfer the muntins and door frame.** When the glue is dry, remove the clamps and clean away any excess glue from the corners with a chisel. Put a 45-degree chamfer bit with a ball bearing guide in a table-mounted router. Adjust its height so that it removes

Slide the chisel flat along the chamfer to square the corners.

about ³/₁₆ inch of material. Lay the doors face down, one at a time, on the router table with the chamfer bit within one of the "lights" or openings made by the muntins. Move the door against the bit's bearing, and rout a chamfer along the muntins and door frame as shown in the Rail and Stile/Cross Section and Muntin/Cross Section. When one complete "light" has been chamfered, move on to the next.

As when routing the rabbet, the chamfer bit will not produce square corners. Chisel the corners square, and finish sand the doors.

10 **Drill the knob holes and hang the doors.** Drill knob holes in the doors, positioned as shown in the Front View. Fit the doors to their opening and hang them with no-mortise hinges. When the doors have been fit and hung properly, attach brass ball catches to the top of the doors and inside the cabinet.

11 **Install the shelves.** Put the shelf pins into place to support the four corners of the shelves. In general, I try to align the shelves with the horizontal muntins in the door.

INSTALLING CABINETS

by Bret Shaw and Ernie Kreider

Installing cabinets is slow, meticulous work. A bad installation can ruin a good cabinet. We've been installing kitchens for Living Quarters Designs, Inc. for several years now, and we've come to anticipate problems in advance and solve them as we work. The problems we face installing a kitchen are the problems you'll face installing even the simplest cabinet. Bear in mind two simple principles, and you'll have a successful installation: Install your cabinet so that it's square and level in all directions, and install it so that it fits against the wall with no gaps.

The tools of the trade are simple compared to those required by a cabinet shop. You'll need an accurate 4-foot level, a circular saw, an electric drill, a sharp block plane, a compass, a hammer, a small pry bar, a wide chisel, and a stud finder.

Before you begin an installation, make sure the room is ready. The electrical and plumbing rough-in must be complete. If there will be a new hardwood or tile floor, it should be installed before you begin. If there will be carpeting on the floor, that should be installed after the cabinets.

Look the room over before you start. You're going to be using screws to attach the cabinets to the studs, so mark their location on the wall.

See if the floor is level: Often the floor slopes away from the wall. If so, level the cabinets as you install them by slipping wooden shims under the front. Use a pry bar to lift the front edge of the cabinet as you insert the shims. If the floor rises or falls along the length of a run of cabinets, find the high spot. Begin installing at the high spot, and shim all the cabinets to that height.

If you are installing cabinets around a corner, see if the corner is square. Do this by measuring a "3-4-5" triangle. From the corner, measure 3 feet down one wall, and 4 feet down the other wall. The diagonal distance between these two points should be exactly 5 feet. If it isn't, your corner is out-of-square. If it is less than 5 feet, you have an acute angle, and your corner cabinet will need to be set farther out from the wall to compensate. If it is greater than 5 feet, you have an obtuse angle. The cabinets at the end of the run need to be shimmed farther from the wall. How much compensation you need is determined by how severely out-of-square the walls are.

To determine your cabinet placement in an out-of-square corner, begin by laying down lines, corresponding to the front edge of the cabinets, on the floor. You can use long, straight sticks, such as one-bys. Begin at the end of the run, where the cabinets will be snug against the wall. Adjust the sticks until you have a perfect 3-4-5 triangle. Then draw these lines on the floor and use them as guidelines for placing your base cabinets.

Once you have checked to make sure that your room is square and level, you can begin installing your base cabinets. Begin with an end cabinet, or a corner cabinet, if you have one. Place the cabinet on your layout lines and level it with wedge-shaped shims. Secure the cabinet to the wall by screwing through the cabinet's mounting scabs or mounting rail into the studs. Screws should penetrate the studs by at least 1 inch.

Install the neighboring cabinet. Screw the neighboring cabinet to the first cabinet before screwing the cabinet to the wall. Two similar cabinets can be screwed together and then set in place as a unit.

Once the base cabinets are installed, turn your attention to the wall cabinets. Temporarily screw a ledge to the wall on which you can rest the cabinets as you install them. The board should be level, and even with the bottom of the cabinets. Begin at the end or in a corner, as before. Rest the cabinets on the ledge and screw them to the studs. Plumb the cabinets by adding shims between the cabinets and wall if necessary.

Sometimes cabinets leave gaps when they meet the wall or each other. If so, you can scribe and trim the stiles slightly for a tighter fit.

A Few Tips

- When you remove the doors to install the cabinets, attach a masking tape label that matches them with their cabinet.
- If you need to pry cabinets away from the wall for shimming, make sure you pry against the stud, or else the drywall may cave in.
- Glue your shims to the floor or wall so that they don't slip once you've installed the cabinet.
- Before you drive the drywall screws into the cabinets and wall, lubricate them with beeswax.
- If you need to touch up a finish, apply a matching shoe polish. The kind with the foam applicator works best.

Installing Base Cabinets

Now that you know the general principles, here's a more detailed look at a recent kitchen installation.

1 When installing a run of base cabinets, it is easier and more accurate to screw two or more smaller cabinets together and install them as a unit. Predrill for screws through the stiles of one of the cabinets.

2 Remove the doors and hinges, and clamp the units together. With a level, check to be sure that the cabinets are even across their tops, and that the face frames are aligned. If necessary, shim between the cabinets in the rear to align the fronts.

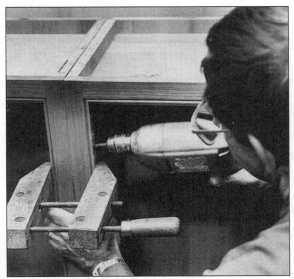

3 Screw the cabinets together.

5 When turning a corner, square the cabinets to each other, not to the wall, since the walls may not be square. When a cabinet must accommodate plumbing, measure the location of the pipes from the adjacent cabinet, and from the front of the cabinet you will install.

4 Put the cabinets into place, and check to make sure they are level, front to back and side to side. Level the cabinets, if necessary, by tapping thin wedge-shaped shims between the cabinet and the floor. Screw the cabinets to studs in the wall, and install the neighboring cabinet.

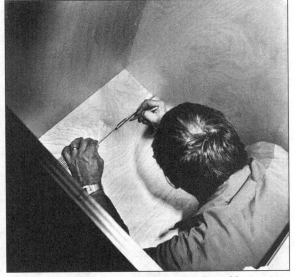

6 Transfer the location of the pipes to the cabinet floor. Remember to account for the space between the cabinets and the thickness of the sides when transferring the measurements to the inside of the cabinet. Drill for large pipes with a hole saw and for smaller pipes with a spade bit.

7 Be sure to level the top of the cabinet in all directions and in relation to the adjacent cabinet. Shim as necessary.

8 Trim the shims flush to the cabinet sides with a utility knife or a chisel, and install the next cabinet.

Installing Wall Cabinets

1 Draw a line along the wall indicating the bottom of the wall cabinets. Screw a temporary ledge along the line. Be sure to screw into the studs, and double-check to make sure the ledge is level.

2 As with base cabinets, attach two or more wall units together before hanging for an easier, more accurate installation.

3 Make sure the face frames are exactly aligned, adding shims in the rear as needed.

4 Hanging wall cabinets is a two-person job. Lift the cabinet onto the ledge. Slide it tightly against the wall, and hold it as level and plumb as possible.

5 Hang the cabinet by driving screws through the hanging strips. With a level, check for plumb. Shim from the bottom, if necessary. Then secure the bottom of the cabinet to the wall by screwing through the bottom rail into the studs. Trim the shims flush.

Scribing Cabinets

1 Sometimes, two cabinets leave a gap where they meet. Because the cabinet stiles are proud of the side, they can be trimmed to close the gap. If a gap exists, as shown here, measure the gap at its widest point.

2 Draw, or "scribe," a line on the stile that corrects for the gap. Begin the line at the end of the stile where the gap occurs. At this end, draw the line flush with the edge of the stile. Continue the line to the other end of the stile, where it is a gap's width from the stile edge.

297

3 Plane and sand to the scribed line.

4 When the cabinets fit tightly together, use a long straightedge to make sure the face frames are aligned. Screw the cabinets together through the stiles. Drill and countersink the screws where they will be hidden by the door hinges.

5 If there are gaps between the cabinet and the wall, set a compass to the amount of the maximum gap. Scribe a line down the side of the cabinet, with the point of the compass following the wall. Be sure the cabinet is level and plumb when you scribe.

6 Saw or plane to the line that's left by the compass pencil. Angle the cut toward the back of the cabinet, undercutting the edge slightly. This yields a snug fit and makes any final trimming easier.

BATHROOM VANITY
by Glenn Bostock

The folks I built this vanity for are renovating an old farmhouse. There is a lot of old pine trim in the house, and they wanted a vanity that would complement the country style. The design that I came up with is this simple pine and plywood cabinet. The pine gives the piece the right look; the plywood, which is hidden from view, simplifies construction.

One of the benefits of working with pine is that you can buy dimensioned pine from your local lumberyard. You don't have to plane the stock.

I use beaded frames and doors a lot in the cabinets I design. A bead adds a touch of class to a simple cabinet. It also helps hide any unevenness in the doors.

I chose a ready-made Corian top and sink for this vanity because it was easy to install. It looks great, but you could install a tile or plastic laminate top. Choose a top and sink for your vanity before you build it, and make sure that it will work with this design.

This cabinet was designed to fit into a right-hand corner of a bathroom. If you need a cabinet for a left-hand corner, simply reverse the design.

EXPLODED VIEW

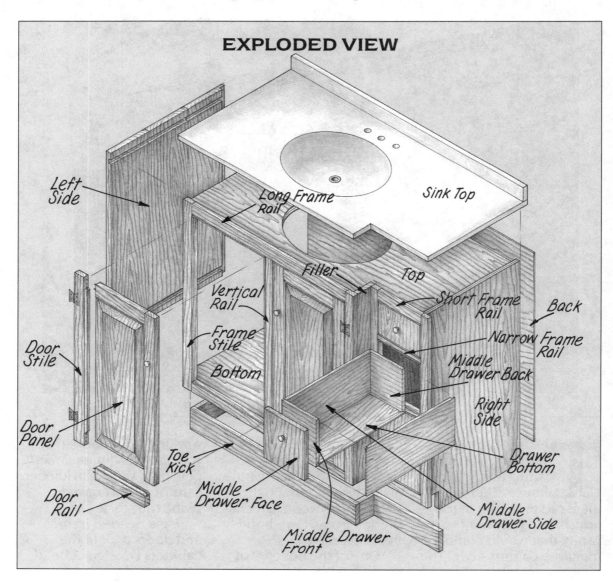

Left Side

Long Frame Rail

Sink Top

Filler

Top

Vertical Rail

Short Frame Rail

Back

Frame Stile

Narrow Frame Rail

Door Stile

Bottom

Middle Drawer Back

Right Side

Door Panel

Toe Kick

Drawer Bottom

Door Rail

Middle Drawer Face

Middle Drawer Side

Middle Drawer Front

Make the frame.

1 **Select the stock and cut the parts.** Number 2 common pine works well for this project. Choose ½-, ¾-, and 1-inch-thick stock that has small, tight knots (1¼-inch diameter or less), and avoid boards with knots on the edges. Purchase ¾-inch A-A interior-grade birch plywood for the top, bottom, and right side, and ¼-inch A-D interior-grade birch plywood for the back and drawer bottoms. Joint, rip, and cut the parts to the sizes listed in the Materials List.

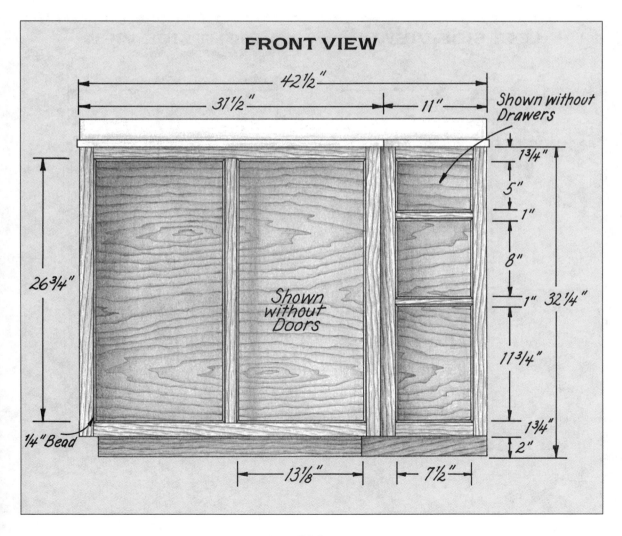

FRONT VIEW

42½"

31½"   11"

Shown without Drawers

1¾"

5"

1"

8"

1"   32¼"

26¾"

Shown without Doors

11¾"

¼" Bead

1¾"

2"

13⅛"   7½"

2 **Rout the bead.** All of the frame rails and stiles have a bead cut into at least one of their front edges. The narrow rails and vertical rail have a bead cut into both edges, as shown in the Front View.

Put an edge-beading bit in your table-mounted router. Set up a fence on the router table to support the stock as you rout.

Feed the stock past the bit at a moderate speed. If you rout the bead too quickly, small ridges will appear on the bead; however, if you rout too slowly, the wood will burn.

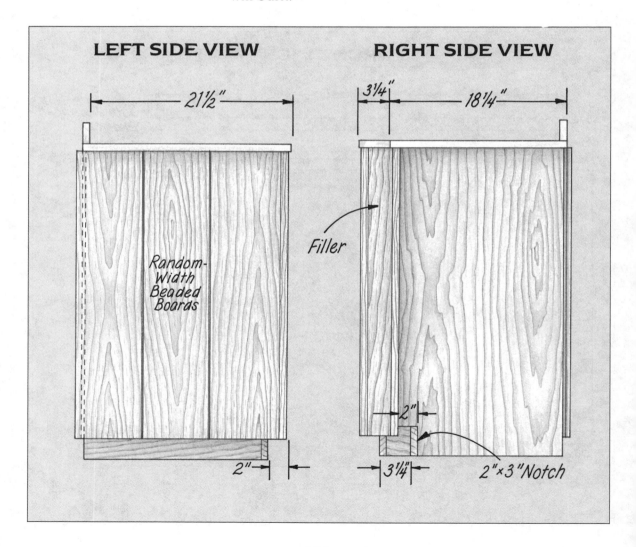

LEFT SIDE VIEW   RIGHT SIDE VIEW

21½"   3¼"   18¼"

Random-
Width
Beaded
Boards

Filler

2"

2"   3¼"   2"×3" Notch

3 **Miter the bead.** As shown in the Frame Joinery Detail, the bead is mitered at 45 degrees and then partially cut away so the frame can be doweled together. To set up the cut, tilt the blade to 45 degrees and raise it high enough so that it cuts through the bead and just up to the shoulder beyond the bead, as shown in the Frame Joinery Detail. For complete instructions on this technique, see "Mitering a Beaded Frame" on page 70.

4 **Assemble the frame.** The frame rails are doweled to the stiles. Lay out and drill 1/4-inch-diameter × 1-inch-deep dowel holes in the ends of the rails. To locate the holes in the stiles, put dowel centers into the

MATERIALS LIST

Part	Dimension
Face Frame	
Frame stiles (4)	3/4" × 1 3/4" × 30 1/4"
Long frame rails (2)	3/4" × 1 3/4" × 28 5/8"
Vertical rail	3/4" × 1 3/4" × 27 3/8"
Short frame rails (2)	3/4" × 1 3/4" × 8 1/8"
Narrow frame rails (2)	3/4" × 1" × 8 1/8"
Doors	
Door rails (4)	3/4" × 2" × 9 7/8"
Door stiles (4)	3/4" × 2" × 26 3/4"
Door panels (2)	9/16" × 9 7/8" × 23 1/2"
Drawers	
Top drawer face	3/4" × 4 7/8" × 7 3/8"
Top drawer front/ back (2)	1/2" × 4 7/8" × 6"
Top drawer sides (2)	1/2" × 4 7/8" × 16 1/2"
Middle drawer face	3/4" × 7 7/8" × 7 3/8"
Middle drawer front/ back (2)	1/2" × 7 7/8" × 6"
Middle drawer sides (2)	1/2" × 7 7/8" × 16 1/2"
Bottom drawer face	3/4" × 11 5/8" × 7 3/8"
Bottom drawer front/back (2)	1/2" × 11 5/8" × 6"
Bottom drawer sides (2)	1/2" × 11 5/8" × 16 1/2"
Drawer bottoms (3)	1/4" × 16" × 6"

Part	Dimension
Case	
Case top/bottom (2)	3/4" × 20 1/2" × 41 3/4"
Right side	3/4" × 17 1/4" × 32 1/4"
Left side boards (3–4)	3/4" × RANDOM × 30 1/4"
Back	1/4" × 30 1/4" × 42 1/8"
Partition	3/4" × 17 1/4" × 26 3/4"
Filler	3/4" × 3 1/4" × 30 1/4"
Toe kick stock	3/4" × 3" × 72"

HARDWARE

3 pairs 16" Grass full-extension European-style drawer runners. Available from Constantine's, 2050 Eastchester Rd., Bronx, NY 10461. Part #GR6040.

As needed, #8 × 1" flathead wood screws

As needed, #8 × 2" drywall screws

As needed, #8 × 1 1/2" drywall screws

4 butterfly hinges, 1 3/4". Available from The Woodworkers' Store, 21801 Industrial Blvd., Rogers, MN 55374. Part #25783.

As needed, 4d nails

As needed, 6d finishing nails

As needed, 4d finishing nails

holes in the rails. Put the rails in position against the stiles, and press the dowel center points into the stile to mark for matching dowel holes.

Glue and dowel the frame together. Clamp the frame securely, and make sure that it is square. Make any necessary adjustments, and allow the glue to dry.

Make the doors.

1 **Rout the bead in the stiles and rails.** The doors, like the frames, have a bead on the inside edges of the

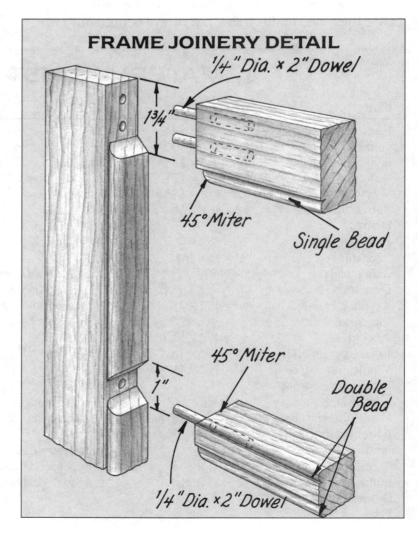

FRAME JOINERY DETAIL

1/4" Dia. × 2" Dowel

1 3/4"

45° Miter

Single Bead

45° Miter

Double Bead

1"

1/4" Dia. × 2" Dowel

rails and stiles. Rout a bead along one complete edge of all the stiles and rails.

2 **Cut the panel slot.** There is a ⅜-inch-deep panel slot routed into the rails and stiles as shown in the Door Detail. Put a ¼-inch slotting cutter in your table-mounted router. Set up a fence so that the slotting cutter is mostly buried in the fence. Adjust the fence and cutter height to cut a ⅜-inch-deep slot centered on the edge of the rails and stiles. Rout the slot along the entire length of the rails and stiles.

3 **Miter the rails and stiles.** Like the frames, the door beads are also mitered. But, as shown in the Door

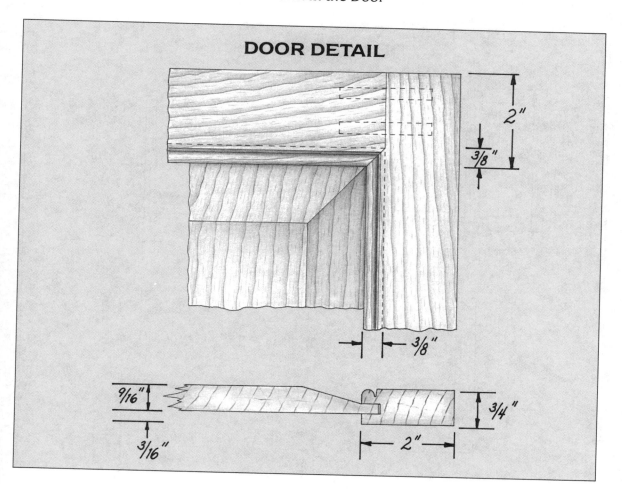

DOOR DETAIL

Detail, the miter is deeper: It cuts through the bead and into the rails and stiles. Adjust the blade to cut to the bottom of the panel slot. Once you've adjusted the blade, miter these beads the same way you mitered those in the frame.

Cut the miters at the ends of the rails first, and then cut the miters and rail clearance at the end of the stiles. Make sure that the stile miters begin exactly 2 inches from the end of the stiles, as shown in the Door Detail. Clean up the waste between the miters and stile ends as before.

4 Raise the panel. Raise the panels on the table saw. For complete step-by-step directions, see "Raising

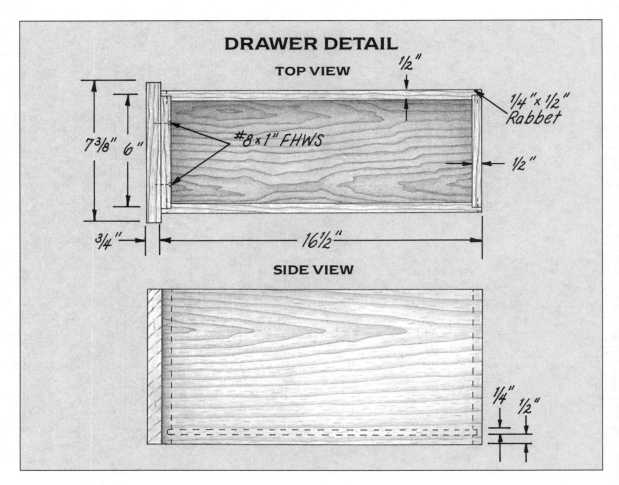

DRAWER DETAIL

TOP VIEW

½"

¼" x ½" Rabbet

7⅜"   6"

#8 x 1" FHWS

½"

¾"

16½"

SIDE VIEW

¼"   ½"

Panels on the Table Saw" on page 200. If you would prefer, raise the panels with a panel-raising bit in a table-mounted router.

5 **Assemble the doors.** The doors are doweled together as shown in the Door Detail. Lay out and dowel the doors as you did the frames.

Assemble the door frame around the panel. Do not glue the panel into place: The panel must float free in its slot, or else it may crack. Clamp the door securely, and make sure that it is square. Make any necessary adjustments, and allow the glue to dry.

Make the drawers.

1 **Cut the drawer joinery.** The drawers for this cabinet are basically rabbeted boxes with an attached face. Rabbets in the box sides accept the box front and back, and a slot in the sides, front, and back accepts the bottom.

First, cut $1/2 \times 1/4$-inch rabbets into the sides as shown in the Drawer Detail. Cut the rabbets with a dado cutter set up in a table saw.

Next cut a $1/4 \times 1/4$-inch slot for the bottom with a slotting cutter set up in a table-mounted router.

2 **Assemble the drawer boxes.** Assemble the sides, fronts, and backs around the bottoms. Glue and nail the fronts and backs into the rabbets. The bottoms should simply float free in their grooves. Make sure the drawer boxes are square. Set the drawer box on a flat surface to make sure it doesn't rock. If the drawer rocks, it is twisted—probably as a result of the pressure applied by the clamps. If necessary, remove the clamps. When you put them back on, make sure they are parallel to the top and bottom of the drawer, and apply no more pressure than absolutely necessary.

3 **Attach the drawer face.** The drawer face is screwed to the front of the drawer box with #8 × 1-inch flathead wood screws. Lay the drawer front on a flat surface, and center the drawer box on top of it. Predrill for the screws through the drawer front and into the drawer face. Screw the drawer face into place.

Quick Tip: Whenever you are framing a panel, it is always a good idea to leave some room for the panel to expand across the grain. After the panels have been raised, trim 1/16 inch from the edges of the panels that are parallel to the grain to allow for this expansion.

Make the case.

1 Cut the parts to shape. Lay out the notches in the top and bottom as shown in the Case Detail/Bottom View, and cut them out with a jigsaw.

Next lay out and cut the 2 × 2-inch notch in the right side as shown in the Right Side View.

2 Assemble the side boards. The left side of this vanity is made up of several random-width beaded boards. Each board has a bead along one of its edges. Rout the beads in the boards with a router and an edge-beading bit.

When all of the boards have been beaded, glue them together edge-to-edge. Clamp the boards together securely, and allow the glue to dry.

3 Dado the sides. Dado the sides for the top and bottom where shown in the Case Detail/Front View. Cut the dadoes on the table saw with a dado cutter, or with a router and straight bit.

4 Cut the rabbet in the left side. Cut the 3/8-inch-deep × 3/4-inch-wide rabbet for the back as shown in the Bottom View and in the Left Side View.

5 Assemble the case. Put glue into the dadoes of the plywood side and assemble the top, bottom, and sides. Drive several 6d finishing nails through the sides and into the top and bottom. Set the nails.

Next, lay out the position of the partition, and then fasten the partition into place by driving #8 × 2-inch drywall screws into it through the top and bottom.

When the partition has been fastened into place, make sure that the cabinet is square, and then attach the back with glue and 4d common nails.

Finally, fasten the frame and filler to the case with glue and 4d finishing nails as shown in the Case Detail and Right Side View.

6 Attach the toe kick. The whole cabinet is supported 3 inches off the floor by a toe kick. The toe kick is set back 2 inches from the front of the frame to allow room for the user's toes. Cut the toe kick to fit the bottom of the

> **Quick Tip:** When you are gluing beaded boards together, don't apply too much glue. Excess glue is *very* difficult to clean out of a beaded edge. Apply a little bit of glue to the edge as far away from the bead as possible.

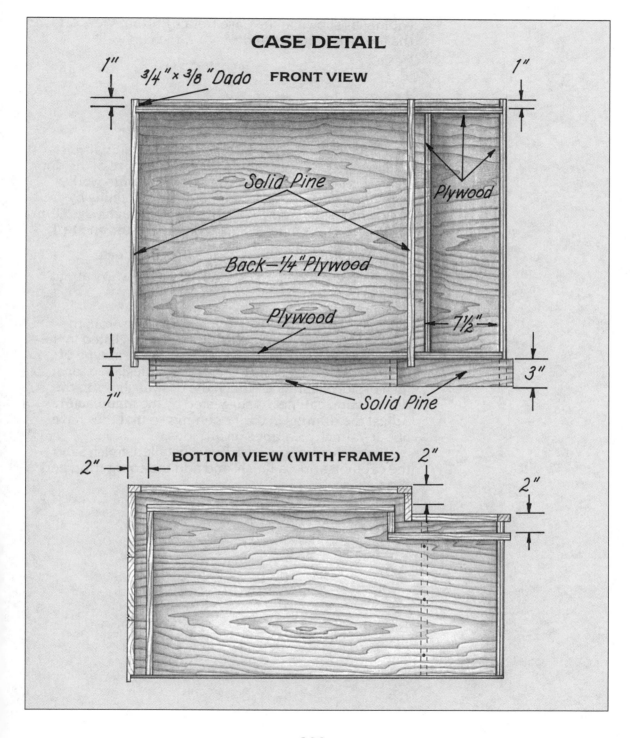

CASE DETAIL

1"
3/4" × 3/8" Dado   FRONT VIEW   1"

Solid Pine

Plywood

Back—1/4" Plywood

Plywood

7½"

1"

3"

Solid Pine

BOTTOM VIEW (WITH FRAME)

2"   2"   2"

cabinet as shown in the Case Detail/Bottom View. Attach the toe kick with glue and #8 × 1 1/2-inch drywall screws.

Hang the doors and install the drawers.

1 **Hang the doors.** If you followed the Materials List closely, the doors should be the exact size of the door openings in the frame. In order for the door to work correctly, you must custom-fit it into the opening by removing about 1/16 inch of material from each edge. Trim the edges with a hand plane or on the jointer, and test the door's fit in the opening.

Hinge the doors with butterfly hinges, which you simply screw into place. You don't have to worry about routing or chiseling the mortise.

2 **Install the drawers.** I hung the drawers from the commercially available drawer runners listed in the Materials List. If you decide to use a different type of drawer runner, make sure that they are designed for 1/2 inch of side clearance. Attach the drawer glides to the drawers and cabinet as suggested by the manufacturer. Adjust the drawers in their openings so that they have about 1/16-inch clearance on all sides.

When the drawers have been installed, finish sand the cabinet, apply a finish, and add the countertop and the sink.

CORNER VANITY

by Glenn Bostock

The customer for whom I built this piece needed a vanity for a guest bathroom. This bathroom was fairly small, so in order to conserve space I designed this cabinet to fit into the corner.

I designed the vanity to complement an antique cherry cabinet that is in the same house. As a result, I built the vanity out of cherry and ground a special scratch cutter to match the antique door molding. In keeping with the feel of the room, I built the sink with a wooden countertop, and fastened the sink to the underside of the countertop according to my client's wishes. Because of this design, the countertop is likely to get wet more often than usual, so I finished it with moisture-resistant lacquer. I added the ledge along the back edge of the top to keep water away from the wall.

I think brass hardware and cherry were meant to go together, so I chose solid brass knobs and brass butt hinges to finish off the piece.

Before you begin building this piece, choose and purchase a suitable sink. When it comes time to cut the sink holes in the counter and sub-top, lay out the cuts directly from the sink.

EXPLODED VIEW

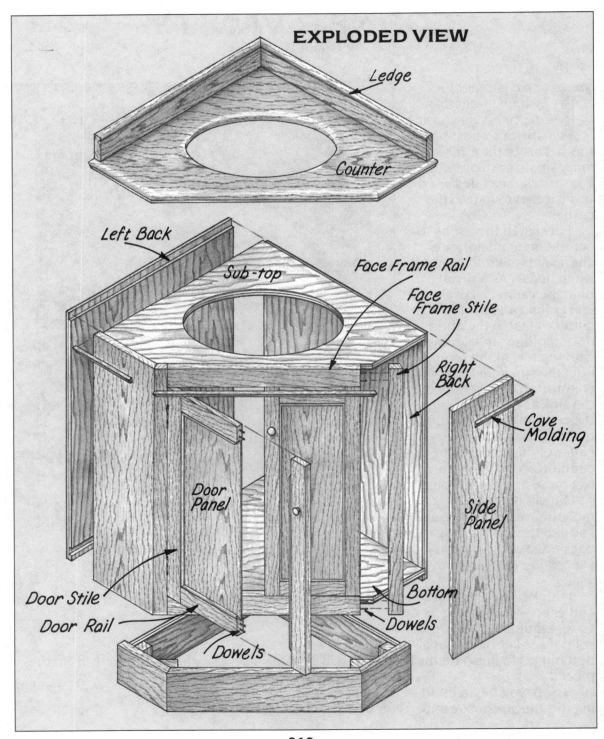

Ledge

Counter

Left Back

Sub-top

Face Frame Rail

Face Frame Stile

Right Back

Cove Molding

Door Panel

Side Panel

Door Stile

Door Rail

Dowels

Bottom

Dowels

Make the frame.

1 **Choose the stock and cut the parts to size.** You don't have to make your vanity from cherry—walnut, oak, or mahogany would also be good choices. The countertop should be made from a durable hardwood, so stay away from soft woods like pine. Joint, plane, rip, and cut all of the parts, except for the face frame stiles and side panels, to the sizes given in the Materials List. Cut the face frame stiles and side panels 1 inch wider than called for, to allow for the miters you'll make later. Glue together several boards to make the wider parts.

2 **Assemble the frame.** Assembly of the cabinet begins with the frame that holds the doors. The frame is doweled together with two $1/4$-inch-diameter × 2-inch-long dowels at each corner. Lay out and drill $1/4$-inch-diameter × 1-inch-deep dowel holes in the ends of the rails. To locate the holes in the stiles, put dowel centers into the holes in the rails. Put the rails into position against the stiles, and press the dowel center points into the stile to mark for matching dowel holes.

Glue and dowel the frame together, and clamp the frame securely. Make sure that it is square, and allow the glue to dry.

MATERIALS LIST

Part	Dimension	Part	Dimension
Face Frame and Panels		Sub-top/bottom (2)	$3/4" \times 23\,5/8" \times 23\,5/8"$
		Toe kick stock	$3/4" \times 4" \times 80"$
Rails (2)	$3/4" \times 2" \times 21\,1/2"$	**Counter Assembly**	
Stiles (2)	$3/4" \times 2" \times 27\,1/4"$	Counter	$3/4" \times 24\,1/8" \times 37\,1/4"$
Side panels (2)	$3/4" \times 7\,3/4" \times 27\,1/4"$	Ledges (2)	$3/4" \times 2\,5/8" \times 25\,1/2"$
Dowels (8)	$1/4"$ dia. $\times 2"$	Cove molding stock	$1/2" \times 1/2" \times 48"$
Doors			
Rails (4)	$3/4" \times 2" \times 7\,1/2"$	**HARDWARE**	
Stiles (4)	$3/4" \times 2" \times 23\,1/4"$	As needed, #8 × 1 1/2" drywall screws	
Panels (2)	$1/4" \times 7\,1/2" \times 20"$	As needed, #8 × 1 1/4" drywall screws	
Dowels (16)	$1/4"$ dia. $\times 2"$	4 ball-tip brass butt hinges, 2" × 1 1/2" (open)	
Case		As needed, 4d finishing nails	
Left back	$3/4" \times 24" \times 27\,1/4"$	As needed, 1" brads	
Right back	$3/4" \times 23\,1/4" \times 27\,1/4"$		

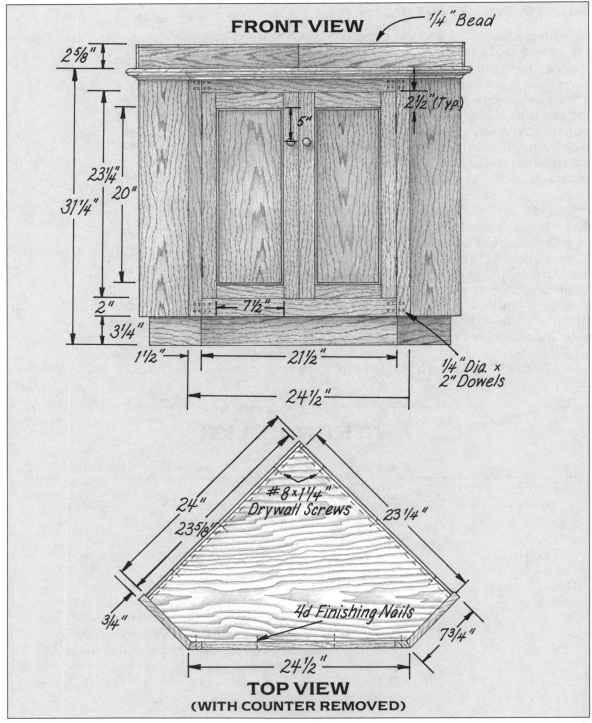

FRONT VIEW

1/4" Bead

2 5/8"

2 1/2" (Typ.)

5"

23 1/4"

20"

31 1/4"

2"

3 1/4"

7 1/2"

1 1/2"

21 1/2"

24 1/2"

1/4" Dia. x
2" Dowels

#8 x 1 1/4"
Drywall Screws

24"

23 5/8"

23 1/4"

3/4"

4d Finishing Nails

24 1/2"

7 3/4"

TOP VIEW
(WITH COUNTER REMOVED)

Make the doors.

1 **Cut the profile in the door stiles and rails.** The doors are frame-and-panel construction, and are also doweled together. Begin work on the doors by cutting a molded shape, called an ogee, along the inside edge of the rails and stiles as shown in the Door Detail. The ogee was custom-made to match the molding on the antique cabinet in the bathroom.

To make your own custom molding, make a simple tool called a scratch stock. First, file the profile of the molding into an old scraper or bandsaw blade. Fasten the scraper onto a block of wood, as shown in the Scratch Stock Detail, and cut the molding by repeatedly drawing the block of wood and the blade across the edge of the board. The work goes surprisingly quickly.

If you choose, you could match your vanity door profile to one of your antiques. The simplest alternative to the scraped door profile is to substitute a routed

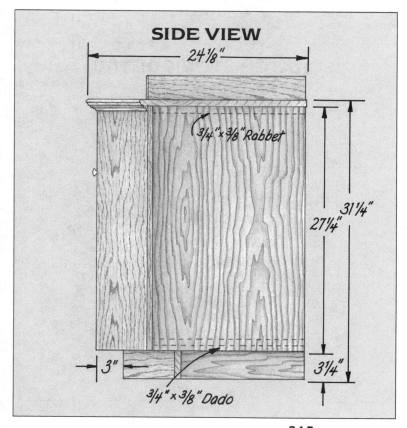

SIDE VIEW

24⅛"

¾" x ⅜" Rabbet

31¼"

27¼"

3"

3¼"

¾" x ⅜" Dado

¼-inch bead. Simply rout a bead along one complete edge of all the stiles and rails.

2 **Cut the panel slot.** Once you've shaped the rails and stiles, cut a slot in them to hold the door panel, as shown in the Door Detail. Put a ¼-inch slotting cutter in a table-mounted router, and rout the ⅜-inch-deep groove centered on the edge of each rail and stile.

3 **Miter the rails and stiles.** Assembly of the door requires that the ends of the ogee molding be mitered to fit together, as shown in the Door Detail. Set the table saw blade at 45 degrees, and raise it until it cuts through the bottom of the panel slot.

Miter the profile on the ends of the rails first. Clamp a wooden fence to your table saw fence, and adjust it so that the top of the blade just cuts into the fence as shown in the Door Miter Setup/Mitering the Rail. To miter the bead or profile, guide the end of the rail along the fence with a miter gauge set at 90 degrees.

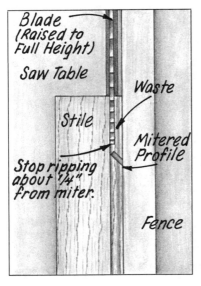

Blade (Raised to Full Height)

Saw Table

Stile

Waste

Mitered Profile

Stop ripping about ¼" from miter.

Fence

Quick Tip: When mitering the profile on a door or frame stile, remove most of the waste between the miter and end of the stile with the table saw blade. Set the blade at 90 degrees, and raise it to its full height. Adjust the table saw fence as shown so that when you guide the stile against it the blade will rip away the waste. Stop the cut about ¼ inch from the miter, and chisel away the remaining waste.

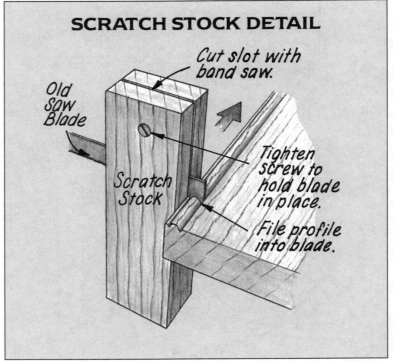

SCRATCH STOCK DETAIL

Cut slot with band saw.

Old Saw Blade

Scratch Stock

Tighten screw to hold blade in place.

File profile into blade.

When the miters have been cut in the rails, miter the bead or profile at the end of each stile. Guide the cut with both the miter gauge and rip fence. Adjust the rip fence so that the cut will start exactly 2 inches from the end of the stiles to accommodate the width of the rails, as shown in Door Miter Setup/Mitering the Stile. Guide the stock with a miter gauge as you cut. Clean away the waste between the miter and the end of the stile with a backsaw and chisel.

4 **Assemble the doors.** The doors are doweled together as shown in the Door Detail. Lay out and dowel the doors as you did the frames. Make sure that the miters are tightly closed in the corners of the door frame.

Assemble the door frame around the panel. Do not

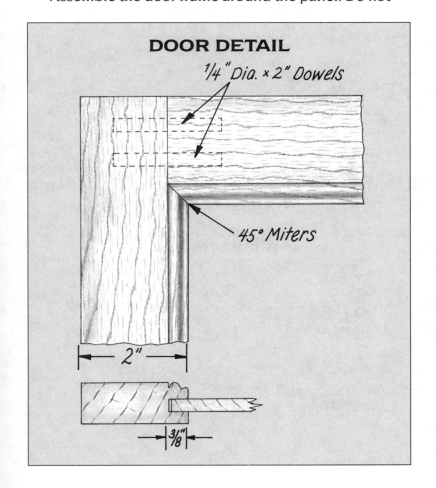

DOOR DETAIL

¼" Dia. × 2" Dowels

45° Miters

2"

3/8"

glue the panel in place. The panel must float freely in its slot, or else it may crack. Clamp the door securely, and make sure that the miters are tightly closed in the corners of the door frame. Make any necessary adjustments, and allow the glue to dry.

Cut and assemble the case.

1 **Cut the dadoes and rabbets in the backs.** To build the case, you'll assemble the backs to form a right angle, and then attach the bottom and the sub-top. Next, you'll attach the face frame and side panels.

Before assembling the back, cut dadoes and rabbets

DOOR MITER SETUP
MITERING THE RAIL

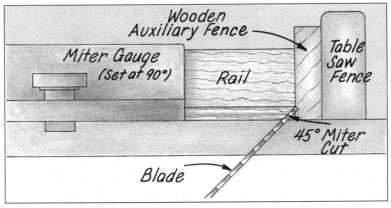

MITERING THE STILE

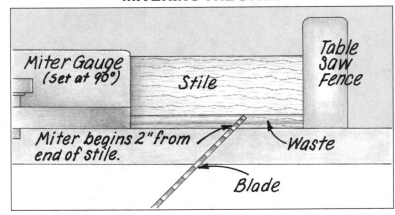

for the bottom and sub-top in the backs as shown in the Side View. You can cut these joints on the table saw with a dado cutter, or with a router and a ³/₄-inch straight bit.

2 Cut the sub-top and bottom to shape. Cut the angle in the sub-top and bottom as shown in the Top View. The easiest way to make this angle cut is with a hand-held circular saw. Lay out the cut on the stock, and clamp a straightedge to the stock to guide the circular saw as you cut.

3 Assemble the backs, sub-top, and base. First, attach the left back to the right back with glue and #8 × 1 ¹/₂-inch drywall screws. There isn't any special joinery needed here, just a simple butt joint.

Next, spread glue in the dado and rabbet, and put the sub-top and bottom in place. Finally, screw through the backs and into the bottom and sub-top with #8 × 1 ¹/₄-inch drywall screws.

4 Bevel the side panels and frame, and attach them to the case. The side panels and face frame meet at a 22¹/₂-degree bevel, as shown in the Top View. Lay out the bevels in the frame directly from the sub-top. Center the frame on the front edge of the sub-top, and mark the locations of the bevels on it.

Set the table saw blade to 22¹/₂ degrees, and rip the bevels in the face frame. Guide the face frame against the table saw fence as you cut. Attach the face frame to the case with glue and 4d finishing nails as shown in the Top View. Set the nails, and fill the holes with wood putty.

After you've attached the face frame, rip the bevels in the side panels. Adjust the width of the side panels as needed so that they overhang the backs of the case by ¹/₄ inch. Attach the side panels to the case with glue and 4d finishing nails. Set the nails and fill the holes.

5 Hang the doors. Use a hand plane or the jointer to trim the doors to fit the face frame. Trace around the hinges to lay out the hinge mortises. Cut the mortises with a chisel or a router and straight bit, and hang the door.

When you have hung the doors, drill and add door pulls of your choice.

Quick Tip: Since the sub-top and bottom are identical, you can save time by cutting both parts at the same time. Stack the two together, and clamp the straightedge to them. The clamps that hold the straightedge will keep the parts from sliding out of position as you cut.

Make the angle cut on the sub-top with a hand-held circular saw. Lay out the cut on the stock, and clamp a straightedge to the stock to guide the circular saw as you cut.

Make the counter and install the sink.

1 Cut the counter to shape. The counter is the same shape as the sub-top. The top is, however, slightly larger, and the wood grain runs parallel to the front of the cabinet, as shown in the Counter Layout. Lay out the shape directly on the counter stock from the dimensions shown in the Counter Layout. As with the sub-top and bottom, clamp a straightedge to the top, and guide a circular saw against it to cut the angles in the top.

2 Cut the sink access hole in the counter. Lay out the sink access hole in the counter as shown in the Counter Layout. The sink access hole corresponds to the sink that will be installed in your vanity. Drill a blade access hole within the layout lines, and then cut out the hole with a jigsaw. Sand the sawed edge smooth.

3 Rout the profiles in the sink access hole and counter edge. The profile in the edge of the sink access hole is a simple roundover. Rout the 1/2-inch-radius roundover in the top edge of the sink access hole as shown in the Sink Mount Detail.

The profile in the front edges of the top is a bit more complicated . . . but not much. First, rout a ³/₈-inch roundover in the front edges of the top as shown in the Counter Edge Detail. Next, put a ³/₈-inch beading bit in your router, and rout the bottom of the front edges of the counter as shown. A beading bit is really a roundover bit with a smaller bearing. The smaller bearing causes the step shown in the Counter Edge Detail.

4 **Finish sand the counter.** Give the top a good sanding at this point before you attach it to the case.

5 **Bead and miter the ledges, and screw them to the top.** Rout a ¹/₄-inch bead in the face of each ledge as shown in the Front View. Once you've routed the bead, miter one end of each ledge, and clamp them to the back edges of the counter as shown in the Counter Layout. Predrill holes through the bottom of the counter and into the ledges for several #8 × 1¹/₂-inch drywall screws. Drive the screws, and remove the clamps.

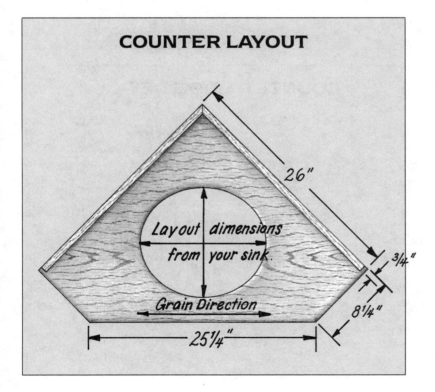

COUNTER LAYOUT

26"

Layout dimensions from your sink.

Grain Direction

³/₄"

8¹/₄"

25¹/₄"

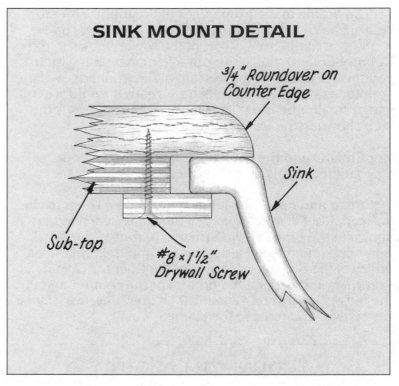

SINK MOUNT DETAIL

3/4" Roundover on Counter Edge

Sink

Sub-top

#8 × 1 1/2" Drywall Screw

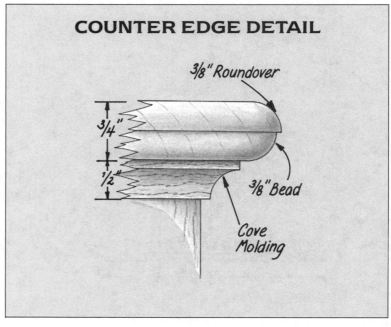

COUNTER EDGE DETAIL

3/8" Roundover

3/4"

1/2"

3/8" Bead

Cove Molding

6 **Cut a sink clearance hole in the sub-top.** Put the counter into position on top of the case. Trace around the edge of the sink access hole onto the sub-top. Remove the counter, and draw a second line 1 1/2 inches to the outside of the first line to provide clearance for the sink lip. Drill a saw blade access hole within the layout lines, and cut out the sink clearance hole in the sub-top with a jigsaw.

7 **Attach the top to the base.** Place the countertop back on the base, and fasten it into place by driving #8 × 1 1/4-inch drywall screws through the sub-top and into the countertop.

8 **Fasten the sink to the top.** Attach the sink to the underside of the countertop as shown in the Sink Mount Detail. Hold the sink in place with a piece of scrap that is screwed to the sub-top with #8 × 1 1/2-inch drywall screws. You may have to modify this procedure to hold your particular sink, depending on the width and thickness of the sink lip.

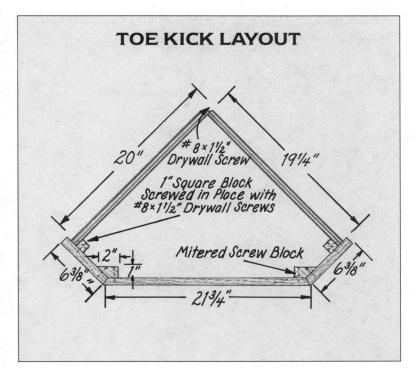

TOE KICK LAYOUT

20"

19 1/4"

#8 × 1 1/2" Drywall Screw

1" Square Block Screwed in Place with #8 × 1 1/2" Drywall Screws

Mitered Screw Block

2"

1"

6 3/8"

6 3/8"

21 3/4"

Quick Tip: When you need to rout small moldings, keep your hands away from the cutter by routing the desired profile into the edge of stock that is 3 to 4 inches wide. After you've routed the molding, rip it on the table saw to the width needed. Set up the cut so that the scrap, rather than the molding, is between the fence and the blade.

Finish sand the cove molding. Cut 22 1/2-degree miters in the cove molding to fit around the face frame and side panels as shown in the Front View and Counter Edge Detail. Tack the molding into place with 1-inch brads.

9 Attach the cove molding. If cove molding isn't available at the local lumberyard in the wood species you want, make your own. Rout a 3/8-inch-radius cove in the edge of some 1/2-inch-thick stock to produce the profile shown in the Counter Edge Detail.

10 Cut the toe kick to fit the bottom of the cabinet. The case rests on the toe kick, and the toe kick is set back to provide room for the user's toes. Lay out and assemble the toe kick as shown in the Toe Kick Layout.

11 Finish sand the corner vanity. Sand the assembled vanity case with 180-grit sandpaper. Apply a finish of your choice.

12 Install the cabinet. Put the toe kick into place on the floor. Put the cabinet into place on the toe kick. Check to make sure that the cabinet is against the wall and that it is level. If necessary, insert shims between the toe kick and the cabinet to level the cabinet. When the shims are in place, and the cabinet is level, screw through the bottom and into the toe kick.

Attach your cabinet to the wall as shown in the chapter Installing Cabinets on page 293.

CABINETS
FOR THE
BEDROOM

CLOSET ORGANIZER
by Kenneth S. Burton, Jr.

Many homes lack adequate closet space, mine among them. In searching for a solution to this problem, I came to see that much of the space inside a typical closet is used inefficiently. By putting this space to better use, even a small closet can become an effective storage area. There are many commercially available systems for doing this, but I couldn't find one I liked. I decided I could design and build a nicer unit myself.

I designed this organizer to be a simple plywood project using basic woodworking techniques, a minimum of materials, and a limited amount of time. Too often, however, quick-and-easy projects lack something in the way of design. I tried to add a certain amount of style and detail to help lift this organizer out of the realm of the ordinary.

The organizer has cantilevered shelves supported by triangular brackets. The upright, made from two layers of plywood with a thin piece of trim between them, adds strength and rigidity as well as visual

appeal. I positioned the shelves to accommodate shoes and boots toward the bottom and sweaters and shirts at the top. Clothes bars can be added at heights most useful to the

person for whom you are creating this. As your closet is probably different from mine, you may need to change some of the dimensions slightly for a perfect fit.

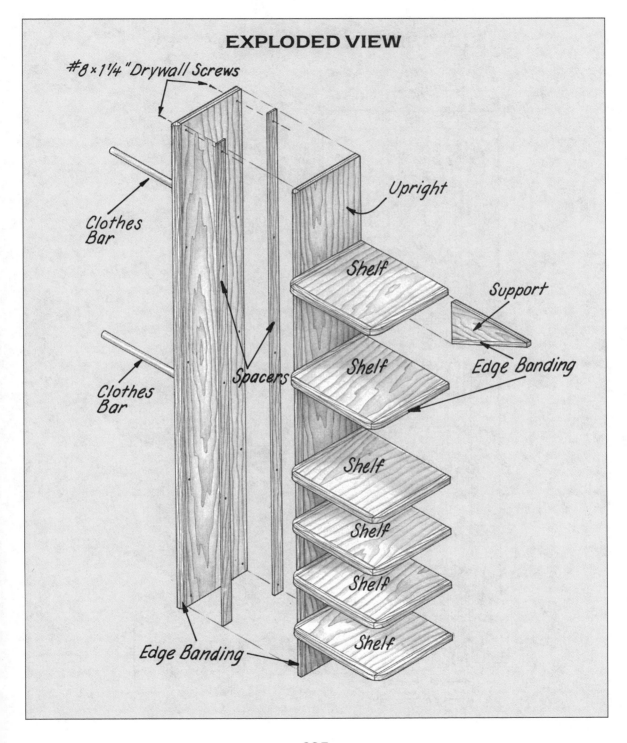

EXPLODED VIEW

#8 × 1¼" Drywall Screws

Clothes Bar

Clothes Bar

Spacers

Edge Banding

Upright

Shelf

Shelf

Shelf

Shelf

Shelf

Shelf

Support

Edge Banding

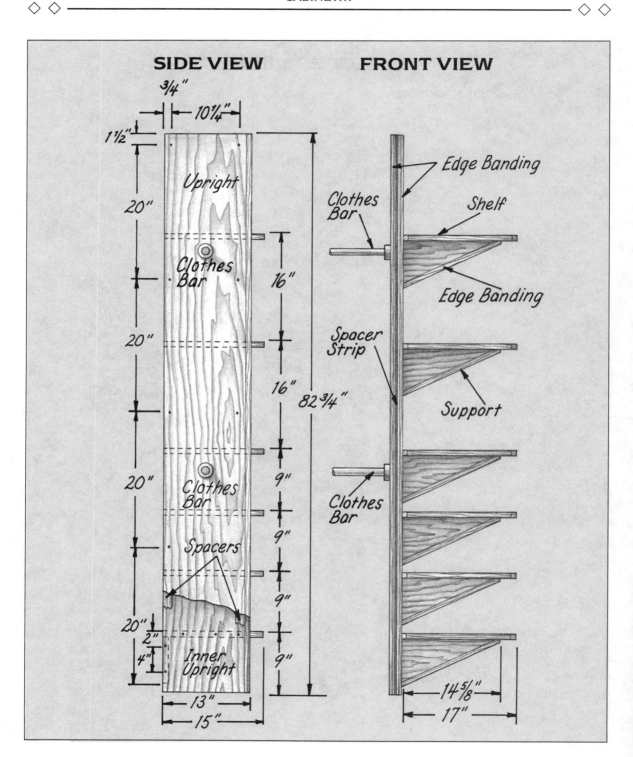

SIDE VIEW

3/4"
10¼"
1½"
Upright
20"
Clothes Bar
16"
20"
16"
20"
9"
Clothes Bar
9"
Spacers
9"
20"
2"
4"
Inner Upright
9"
82¾"
13"
15"

FRONT VIEW

Edge Banding
Clothes Bar
Shelf
Edge Banding
Spacer Strip
Support
Clothes Bar
14⅝"
17"

Prepare the parts.

1 **Cut the parts to size.** All the main parts for this organizer can be cut from a single 4×8-foot sheet of ³/₄-inch A-A interior-grade birch plywood, as shown in the Plywood Layout. Cut the parts to the sizes listed in the Materials List.

2 **Cut the supports to shape.** Cut the triangular supports to shape with the jig shown in the Support Jig Layout. Make the jig from some scrap ³/₄-inch plywood, and then cradle the shelf support in it. Guide the jig against the table saw fence for a straight and safe diagonal cut.

3 **Apply the edge banding.** To give the edges of plywood a more finished appearance, most cabinet-makers cover them with a strip of wood called edge banding. The edge banding for this project is slightly thicker and longer than needed. The overhang is trimmed flush after the glue dries.

Apply edge banding to the uprights first. Cut the banding to the width and thickness in the Materials List, but leave it about ¹/₂ inch longer than needed. Apply glue to the edge banding and to the edge of the plywood that will be exposed once the organizer is installed. Put a ³/₄-inch-thick piece of scrap wood on top of the banding to protect it, and clamp the edge banding in place. Space the clamps no more than 12 inches apart to get adequate pressure.

When the glue is dry, trim away the excess length with

Cradle the shelf support in the support jig as shown, and guide the jig against the table saw fence for a straight and safe diagonal cut.

MATERIALS LIST

Part	Dimension	
Supports (6)	³/₄" × 6" × 13³/₄"	**HARDWARE**
Edge banding	⁷/₈" × ³/₄" × 40'	2 pairs of clothes bar hangers
Uprights (2)	³/₄" × 12¹/₄" × 82³/₄"	As needed, #8 × 1³/₄" drywall screws
Shelves (6)	³/₄" × 14¹/₄" × 16¹/₄"	As needed, #8 × 1¹/₄" drywall screws
Spacers (2)	¹/₄" × 1¹/₂" × 82³/₄"	2 finishing nails, 6d
Clothes bars (2)	(dimensions vary)	

Quick Tip: Cutting a full sheet of plywood alone on a table saw can be very difficult and dangerous. Cut oversized pieces with a hand-held saber saw or circular saw, and then trim them to final size on the table saw.

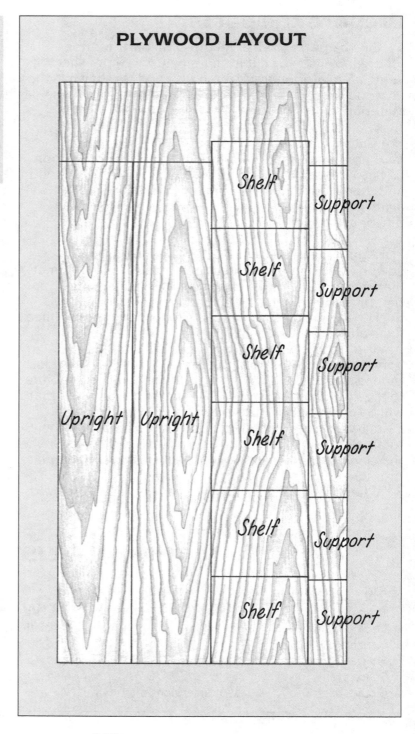

PLYWOOD LAYOUT

Upright Upright

Shelf

Shelf

Shelf

Shelf

Shelf

Shelf

Support

Support

Support

Support

Support

Support

a handsaw. Plane or scrape the banding flush with the face of the plywood.

Edge-band the bottom of the shelf supports with the help of the jig you used to cut them on the table saw. Cradle the shelf support in the jig, and glue the edge banding in place by clamping across the shelf support to the far side of the jig.

Edge-band the shelves in stages. First glue up one edge, as before. When the glue dries, trim the overhang flush on both sides and on the ends, and then glue on the banding on an adjoining edge. Trim the banding flush when the glue dries.

Make the uprights.

1 **Rout the front edge of the uprights.** Mark the inside surface of the uprights with an X. Rout a $^{5}/_{16}$-inch-deep

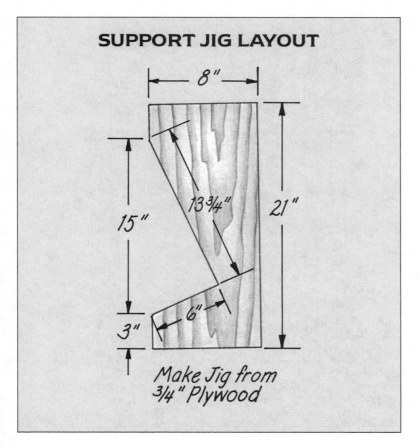

SUPPORT JIG LAYOUT

8"

15"

13¾"

21"

3"

6"

Make Jig from 3/4" Plywood

chamfer the entire length of the inside edge of the edge banding, as shown in Cross Section of Uprights. Sand the chamfers without rounding the corners.

2 **Attach the spacer strips.** Sand the edge of the spacers that will be exposed. Attach the spacer to the marked side of the left upright with glue and ³/₄-inch brads as shown in Cross Section of Uprights. Attach the other spacer so that it is flush with the back edge of the

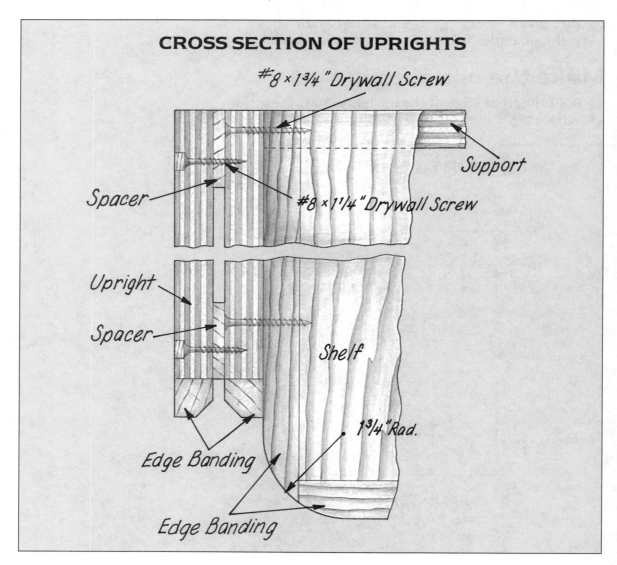

CROSS SECTION OF UPRIGHTS

#8 × 1³/₄" Drywall Screw

Support

Spacer

#8 × 1¹/₄" Drywall Screw

Upright

Spacer

Shelf

1³/₄" Rad.

Edge Banding

Edge Banding

upright. Attach the right-hand upright later, when installing the organizer.

Make the shelves.

1 Round the front corners. The front corners of the
shelves could be a hazard in a closet if they were left
square. I decided to round them off as shown in the
Cross Section of Uprights, to avoid unnecessary pain.
This also adds a bit of class to the finished piece. Mark a
1 3/4-inch radius on each corner (I used an empty tuna
can), and cut the corners to shape with a jigsaw or band
saw. Scrape and sand the sawed radius.

2 Trim the shelf supports. On the table saw, trim the
supports to the length shown in the Front View.
Guide the stock with a miter gauge as you cut. Sand the
supports where needed.

3 Attach supports to shelves. Predrill holes across
the back of each shelf for #8 × 1 3/4-inch drywall
screws as indicated on the drawing. Assemble by screwing a shelf support onto each shelf. Be sure to align the
supports with the back and with the edge-banded side of
the shelves.

Assemble the closet organizer.

1 Lay out the shelf positions on the upright. Lay out
the top of each shelf as shown in the Side View. On
the marked side only, draw a second set of lines 3/8 inch
below the first set, marking the center of each shelf. Lay
out the screw holes on the secondary lines as shown in
the Side View. Along the back edge, mark the holes for
the shelf supports. Predrill these holes for #8 × 1 3/4-inch
drywall screws.

2 Attach the shelves. Make sure the assembled unit
can be transported to the closet for which it is
intended. If not, carry the pieces separately and assemble the unit closer to the closet. When you are ready, have
a helper hold the top of each shelf in line with the line on
the upright. Drill pilot holes, and attach each shelf to the
uprights with #8 × 1 3/4-inch drywall screws.

Quick Tip: Drywall screws
save time and effort. They
often can be driven
quickly without pilot
holes by a power screw-
driver. In plywood, how-
ever, they often cause
the wood to split. To
avoid this, drill a 3/32-inch
pilot hole through both
pieces you will screw
together, and countersink
for the screw head. This
ensures a good tight fit
with no splitting.

3 **Attach the left-hand upright.** Carefully lay the organizer on the floor so that the upright is horizontal. Align the left-hand upright on top of the right-hand upright so that they are flush on all four sides. Drill pilot holes where shown in the Side View, and countersink the holes for 3/8-inch-diameter wood plugs. Glue and screw the two parts together with #8 × 1 1/4-inch drywall screws.

Install the closet organizer.

1 **Prepare the closet.** Before setting the organizer in place, prepare the closet. Remove the baseboard, the clothes bar, the existing shelf, and the shelf brackets before putting the organizer into place. Make sure the organizer is plumb, and then cut the baseboard and the shelf brackets to fit around it. Re-install the baseboard and shelf brackets in the closet. Put the baseboard back in its old location, and move the shelf brackets up so that they are flush with the tops of the uprights. Replace the old shelf and screw down through it with #8 × 1 3/4-inch drywall screws to hold the organizer firmly at the top. Toenail the uprights at the bottom to anchor the organizer in place using two 6d finishing nails.

Finally, install the clothes bars with your choice of the clothes bar hangers available at your local hardware store. The height of your clothes bars should suit the clothes that you want to hang on them.

2 **Apply finish.** I painted my organizer with a latex primer and two coats of winter white semi-gloss latex enamel. I sanded the unit lightly after the primer dried to eliminate some rough spots on the shelves. The top coats went on smoothly. I chose paint because it helped tie the organizer into the color scheme of its surroundings. The light color also helped brighten the inside of the closet. If you use a stain or clear wood finish, I recommend finishing the parts before assembly.

CEDAR-LINED CHEST
by Glenn Bostock

amilies have always passed their treasures from one generation to the next. If they are linens or quilts, they've often kept them in cedar chests. This chest was designed to be as much of a treasure as the things stored in it. The lid kept out the dust and mice, and the aromatic cedar repelled moths and kept the family treasures smelling fresh.

Cedar is preferable to moth balls, and it is easy to install. You can buy packs of aromatic cedar lining with a tongue milled in one side and a groove in the other. All you do is brad it into place. If you want the look of cedar, but not the high price, use 1/4-inch cedar veneer plywood. It looks good, but the cedar smell doesn't last as long.

I chose cherry and walnut for this piece because I like the way that the red of the cherry and the deep brown walnut complement each other. I work with cherry a lot because it is beautiful, durable, and readily available. Walnut is also a beautiful wood, but quality walnut is getting harder to find.

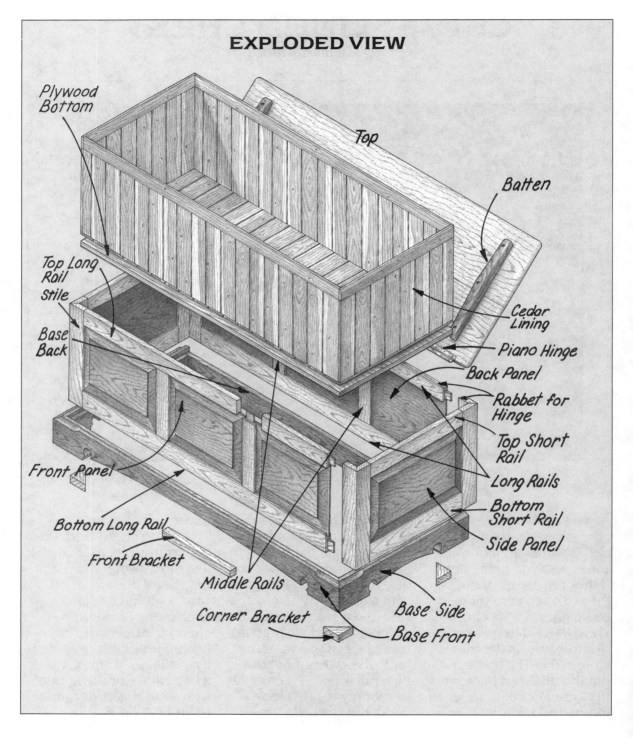

EXPLODED VIEW

Plywood Bottom

Top

Batten

Top Long Rail

Stile

Base Back

Cedar Lining

Piano Hinge

Back Panel

Rabbet for Hinge

Top Short Rail

Long Rails

Front Panel

Bottom Short Rail

Side Panel

Bottom Long Rail

Front Bracket

Middle Rails

Corner Bracket

Base Side

Base Front

Make the sides, front, and back.

1 Select the stock. Joint, plane, rip, and cut all of the parts except for the base front, base sides, and the bottom to the sizes given in the Materials List. Make the bottom of the chest from ³/₄-inch birch plywood, and cut it to fit the chest case. Cut the base front and sides about 1 inch longer than called for in the Materials List. Glue together several boards to make the top, bottom, and panels.

2 Mortise the stiles and long rails. Lay out the mortises on the stiles and rails as shown in the Mortise and Tenon Layout. Drill a series of adjacent ⁵/₁₆-inch-diameter × 1¹/₄-inch-deep holes between the layout lines. Clean out the rest of the waste with a chisel. If you have a plunge router, rout the mortises with a ⁵/₁₆-inch-diameter straight bit.

When the mortises have been cut, rip 45-degree miters in the outside edges of the stiles to form the mitered corners.

MATERIALS LIST

Part	Dimension	Part	Dimension
Stiles (8)	³/₄" × 2¹/₂" × 15"	Battens (2)	1" × 1¹/₂" × 17"
Top long rails (2)	³/₄" × 2" × 45¹/₂"	Cedar lining*	⁵/₁₆" × 15 sq. ft.
Bottom long rails (2)	³/₄" × 2¹/₂" × 45¹/₂"		
Top short rails (2)	³/₄" × 2" × 18¹/₂"		
Bottom short rails (2)	³/₄" × 2¹/₂" × 18¹/₂"		
Middle rails (4)	³/₄" × 2" × 13"		
Front/back panels (6)	³/₄" × 11¹/₂" × 14"		
Side panels (2)	³/₄" × 11¹/₂" × 17"		
Plywood bottom	³/₄" × 19¹/₂" × 46¹/₂"		
Base front	1¹/₂" × 3¹/₂" × 50"		
Base sides (2)	1¹/₂" × 3¹/₂" × 22"		
Base back	³/₄" × 3" × 48"		
Corner bracket stock	1" × 2" × 18"		
Front/back brackets (2)	1" × 1" × 12"		
Top	1" × 22" × 50"		

*Cedar lining can be purchased from The Woodworkers' Store, 21801 Industrial Blvd., Rogers, MN 55374.

HARDWARE

2 #8 × 2" roundhead wood screws
4 #8 × 1¹/₄" roundhead wood screws
4 #8 × 2" drywall screws
As needed, #8 × 1¹/₂" drywall screws
6 flat washers, ³/₈" dia.
1 piano hinge, 46¹/₂"
As needed, ³/₄" brads

FRONT VIEW

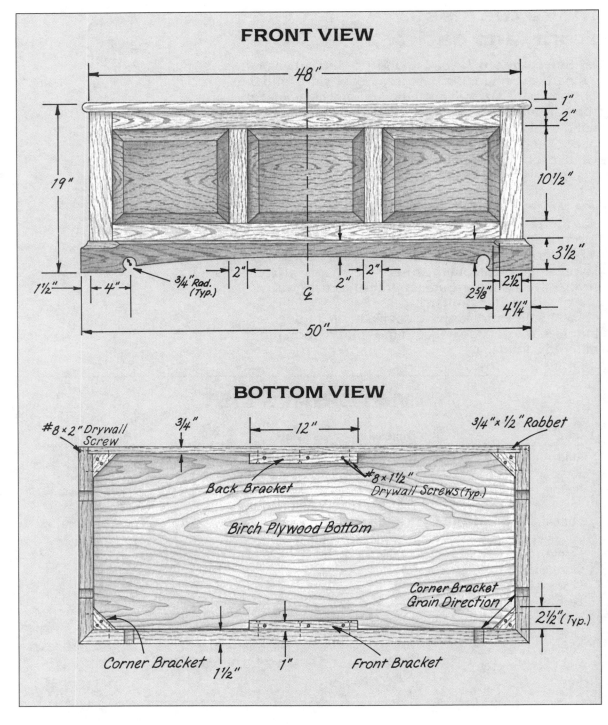

48"

1"
2"

19"

10½"

3½"

1½"

4"

¾" Rad.
(Typ.)

2"

2"

2"

⌀

2"

2⅝"

2½"

4¼"

50"

BOTTOM VIEW

#8 × 2" Drywall
Screw

¾"

12"

¾" × ½" Rabbet

Back Bracket

#8 × 1½"
Drywall Screws (Typ.)

Birch Plywood Bottom

Corner Bracket
Grain Direction

2½" (Typ.)

Corner Bracket

1½"

1"

Front Bracket

338

3 **Tenon the ends of the rails.** Cut the tenons on the ends of the stiles with a dado cutter set up in a table saw. Adjust the blade height so that the resulting tenons will fit snugly in their mortises. All of the tenons should have 1/2-inch shoulders, as shown in the Tenon Detail.

Left: Drill a series of adjacent holes within the mortise layout lines. *Right:* Guide the rails with the miter gauge as you cut the tenons.

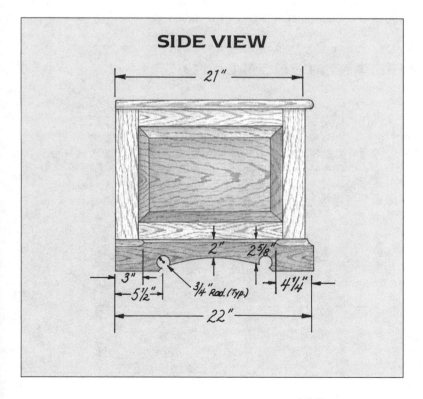

SIDE VIEW

21"

2" 2⅝"

3" ¾" Rad. (Typ.) 4¼"

5½"

22"

Quick Tip: Put a fence on the router table to help guide the cut. Make the fence from a piece of flat, straight wood. Cut a semicircle in the edge of the fence that fits around the cutter. Clamp the fence to the table, and move it in and out to adjust the depth of cut.

4 Rout the panel slots. Put a ¼-inch slotting cutter with a ball bearing guide in your table-mounted router. Adjust the setup to cut a groove centered in the rails and stiles. Rout a slot along the entire length of the rails, and from mortise to mortise in the stiles. Cut grooves on both sides of the middle rails.

5 Sand the panels flat. Sand the panels to remove any excess glue from the glue joints, and at the same time make sure that the joints are flush along their entire length. Any excess glue or unevenness will result in irregularities when you raise the panel.

6 Raise the panels. Cut the bevels in the front surface of the panels as shown in "Raising Panels on the Table Saw" on page 200. Several bits are also available for routing raised panels, but the profile they produce is slightly different from the one shown here.

Whenever you are framing a panel, it is always a good idea to leave some room for the panel to expand across the grain. After the panels have been raised, trim $3/32$ inch from the edges of the panel that are parallel to the grain.

MORTISE AND TENON LAYOUT

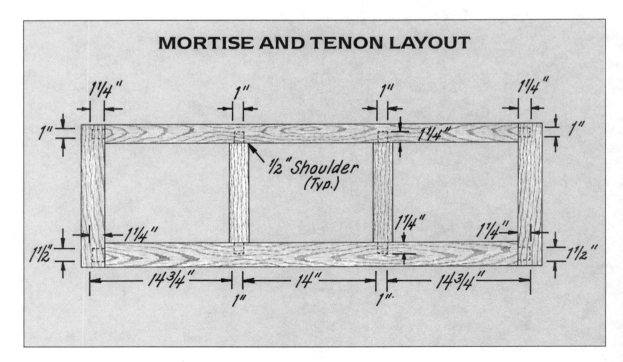

7 **Assemble the sides, front, and back.** First, test fit the sides, front, and back. Position the panels as shown in the Front and Side Views, and make sure that everything fits properly. The panels should be snug in the panel slots, but not so tight that they might cause the rails and stiles to split. The tenons should also be snug but not overly tight. Make any necessary adjustments.

Assemble the frames and panels. Measure diagonally from corner to corner. If measurements are equal, the assembly is square. If not, make any necessary adjustments. Make sure that you don't get any glue in the panel slots or on the lip of the panels. If the panels get glued into their slots, they are almost guaranteed to split.

Allow the glue to dry.

Assemble the chest case.

1 **Test fit the sides, front, and back assemblies.** It can be rather tricky aligning these large mitered corners to create the chest case. I suggest that you lay the front panel and one of the sides edge-to-edge on your workbench with their inside surfaces facing up, and run a wide strip of adhesive tape along the outside of the joint. With the tape in place, you can fold the parts together to form a tight and perfectly aligned corner. Repeat the process with the back and remaining side, and then clamp the whole case together with two band clamps. Make sure that the assembly is square, and then measure the inside for the bottom.

Don't apply glue to any of the joints yet.

2 **Cut the bottom to fit.** Measure the inside width and length of the chest, and cut the bottom to fit.

3 **Glue and screw the chest case together.** Remove the band clamp from the chest case. Spread glue on the miters at the corners, and reclamp the chest case.

Next, slide the clamped case over the bottom, and drill pilot and countersink holes for #8 × 1½-inch drywall screws within ½ inch of the bottom edge of the chest case. Drive the screws, but don't bother plugging the holes because the base will cover them later.

Allow the glue to dry.

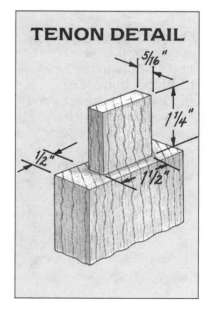

TENON DETAIL

5/16"

1 1/4"

1/2"

1 1/2"

341

Quick Tip: For the cleanest results, rout the rabbet in two passes—one with the bearing about 1/4 inch away from the stock, and one with the bearing riding against the stock.

Quick Tip: The best bit to use when drilling a large-diameter hole through thick stock is a Forstner bit. Forstner bits cut clean, smooth holes, and are available in large diameters.

Quick Tip: Draw the curves on the base front and sides with the help of a long, thin, flexible piece of scrap wood. Hold the scrap even with the ends of the proposed arc. Slowly bring your hands together, forcing the center of the scrap to arc upward on the stock. When the bend of the scrap reaches the top of the arc, have a helper draw a line following the bend of the scrap.

Make the base.

1 **Rout a 1/2-inch-square rabbet in the base stock.** Put a 1/2-inch rabbeting bit in your table-mounted router. Adjust the height of the bit to cut a 1/2-inch-square rabbet in one edge of the base stock.

2 **Miter the stock.** Miter the base stock on the table saw to fit around the front and sides.

3 **Rout the small and large coves.** Rout a cove along the top of the base with a 3/8-inch cove bit in your table-mounted router.

Next, replace the 3/8-inch cove bit with a 3/4-inch cove bit, and rout the coves at the ends of the front and side base pieces. Guide the stock against a fence as you rout. Stop the coves as shown in the Front and Side Views.

4 **Drill holes in the base front and sides.** Locate and drill the 1 1/2-inch-diameter holes in the base front and sides as shown in the Front and Side Views.

5 **Cut the curves in the base.** Lay out the curves on the base front and sides as shown in the Front and Side Views. Cut the base front and sides to shape with a band saw or jigsaw. Sand away any saw marks.

6 **Rabbet the base sides.** The base back fits into rabbets cut in the base sides. Put a 3/4-inch-wide dado cutter in your table saw. Adjust the fence and blade height to cut a 3/4 × 1/2-inch rabbet on the inside back edge of the base sides, as shown in the Bottom View.

7 **Assemble and attach the base.** Test fit the base sides and base back. Drill pilot, recess, and plug holes through the base sides and into the ends of the base back for #8 × 2-inch-inch screws. Glue and screw the base together, and plug the screw holes.

Next, turn the chest case upside down on a low, flat surface, and glue and clamp the assembled base sides and base back to it. When the sides and back assembly are in position, spread some glue on the base front's rabbet and miters, and put the base front into position on the chest case. Clamp the parts of the base together

Lay out a long curve with a thin, flexible piece of scrap.

with a band clamp, and clamp the assembled base to the chest case.

While the parts are still clamped together, secure the base to the chest case with front, back, and corner brackets as shown in the Bottom View. Cut the corner brackets to the profile shown. Drill pilot and clearance holes through the brackets, and attach them to the chest bottom and base with glue and #8 × 1 1/2-inch drywall screws as shown in the Bottom View.

Make the top.

1 Round the front and side edges. Round the edges with a 3/8-inch roundover bit in a table-mounted router. Set up a fence to support the stock as you rout. Rout the front and side, and then flip the top over and repeat the process to create totally rounded edges.

2 Cut the battens to shape. Use a band saw to cut the battens to the shape shown in the Batten Detail. Sand the sawed edges smooth.

3 Attach the battens. The battens are held in place with screws which run through oversized pilot holes. The oversized holes allow the wood of the chest top to expand and contract freely with changes in the weather. Flat washers keep the screws from pulling through the holes.

Quick Tip: When routing across end grain, the wood often splinters at the corners. To eliminate this splintering, rout the end grain first. As you rout the other sides, any splintering should be cut away.

343

First, lay out and drill $1/4$-inch-diameter screw clearance holes through the battens as shown in the Batten Detail. Next, drill $7/16$-inch-diameter × $1/4$-inch-deep holes for the washers. Finally, secure the battens to the top with #8 × 1$1/4$- and 2-inch roundhead wood screws and $3/8$-inch flat washers as indicated in the Batten Detail.

4 Hinge the top. The top is hinged with a 46$1/2$-inch-long piano hinge. The hinge fits into a mortise cut in the top edge of the back. Cut the hinge to length with a hacksaw and file away any sharp corners. Put the hinge into position on the back of the cabinet, and lay out the mortise by tracing around it with a marking knife.

Next, put a $1/2$-inch straight bit in your router and adjust the bit to cut a mortise as deep as the thickness of the closed hinge. Attach the router fence to the router, and adjust it so that the blade cuts up to your layout lines. Rout the mortise in two passes if necessary. Square the corners with a chisel, and screw the hinge in place.

Attach the cedar lining.

1 Fit the cedar lining to the bottom. You can buy tongue-and-groove cedar lining for your chest at most lumber stores. If you cannot find it locally, purchase it through the mail from the source given in the Materials List.

Cut several lengths of the cedar lining to fit the width of the plywood bottom. Make sure that you don't cut

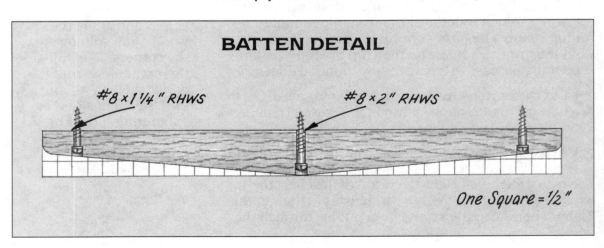

BATTEN DETAIL

#8 × 1$1/4$" RHWS

#8 × 2" RHWS

One Square = $1/2$"

more than you need for the bottom. Place the cedar lining boards into the bottom of the chest one at a time, and tack them into place with ³/₄-inch brads. Leave approximately ¹/₃₂-inch gap between each piece to allow the wood to expand.

2 Fit and attach the cedar lining to the front, back, and sides. When the cedar lining has been attached to the bottom, install the cedar lining for the sides vertically, with a narrow band of cedar lining running horizontally along the inside top edge of the sides, as shown in View through Side.

Cut the vertical boards into 12¹/₂-inch-long pieces, and install them with ³/₄-inch brads. Rip the corner pieces to fit.

Finally, measure the distance from the top edge of the chest to the vertical lining, and fill that space with horizontal strips of cedar lining. Again fasten these strips with ³/₄-inch brads.

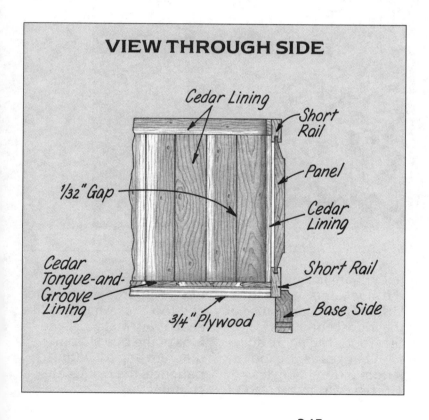

VIEW THROUGH SIDE

Cedar Lining

Short Rail

Panel

Cedar Lining

¹/₃₂" Gap

Cedar Tongue-and-Groove Lining

Short Rail

Base Side

³/₄" Plywood

CHEST OF DRAWERS

by Edward J. Schoen

I made this chest of drawers from tiger maple, a favorite wood of colonial cabinetmakers. The most difficult part of working with tiger maple is choosing the wood. It's tough to match the contin-ually changing grain along the glue joints. It's particu-larly frustrating because of the iridescent quality of the wood. The figure actu-ally changes as you look at it from different angles. The best way to get a good grain match is to spread out the boards for the sides and top. Pick what look like good grain matches, and look at the board from different angles. With patience, the results are stunning.

EXPLODED VIEW

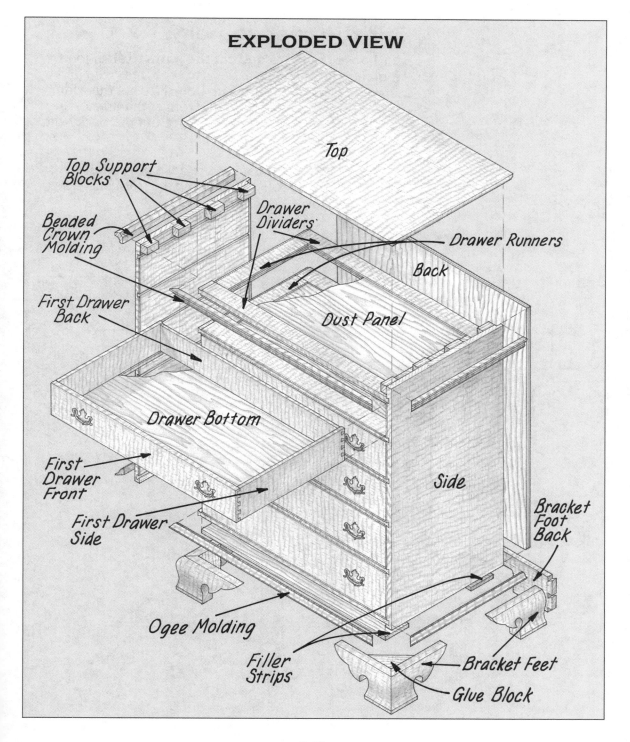

Top

Top Support Blocks

Drawer Dividers

Beaded Crown Molding

Drawer Runners

Back

First Drawer Back

Dust Panel

Drawer Bottom

Side

First Drawer Front

First Drawer Side

Bracket Foot Back

Ogee Molding

Filler Strips

Bracket Feet

Glue Block

Cut the case joinery.

1 **Choose the stock and cut the parts to size.** Joint, plane, rip, and cut the parts to the sizes given in the Materials List. When gluing up boards to get the wider parts, glue up a panel wider and longer than necessary. Trim to final size when the glue is dry. Cut the back from hardwood plywood.

2 **Round the top and sand the case parts.** Rout a 1/2-inch-radius roundover along the front and side edges of the top.

3 **Bead the sides and drawer dividers.** As shown in the Front View, the drawer openings are framed by a

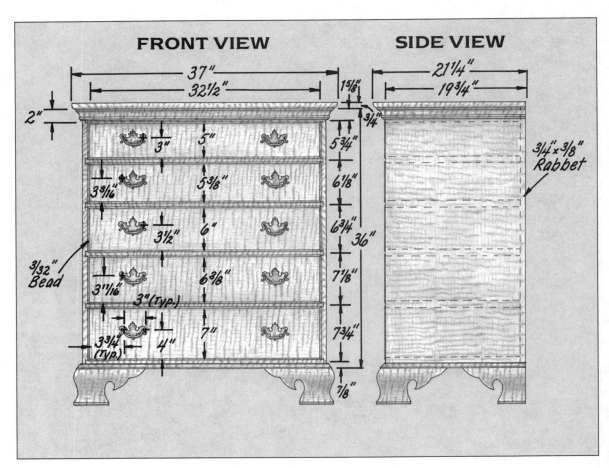

³/₃₂-inch-diameter bead which protrudes from the front edges of the sides and front drawer dividers. You have a couple of options when making these beads.

I took a ¹/₂-inch-diameter straight bit to a local blade sharpener, and asked him to grind two ³/₃₂-inch-diameter coves into it as shown in the Custom Beading Setup. To make the cut with this bit, set up the bit in the router table as shown and rout the beads in the front edge of the sides and front drawer dividers. When the beads have been cut, one bead should be trimmed away from the front edge of the sides and top and bottom drawer dividers, as shown in the Front View. These excess beads can be trimmed away with a flush trim bit in a router.

Another option is to cut the bead with the combination of a rabbeting bit and a homemade scratch stock.

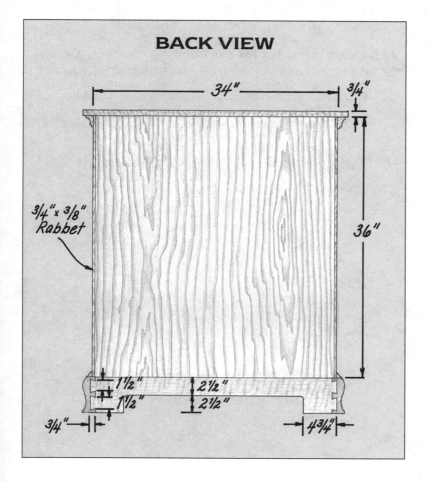

First, set up a rabbeting bit (with a ½-inch cutting length) in a table-mounted router, and cut a ¹⁄₁₆-inch-deep trough centered in the edges of the sides and front drawer divider stock, as shown in the Scratched Bead Detail. Bury the bit in the fence and guide the stock against the fence as you cut. Since the sides and top and bottom drawer dividers have only one bead, lower the bit and cut away one of the trough edges on these parts.

Next, make a scratch stock like the one shown in the Scratched Bead Detail from an old hacksaw blade. Break off a piece of blade about 6 inches long. Scribe the profile of the bead on the blade and file or grind it to shape. Insert the blade into a piece of scrap, as shown. When the blade has been tightened down, hold the scratch stock firmly and draw it along the stock as shown in the Scratched Bead Detail. Remove a shaving of wood with each pass until the bead is complete.

4 Rabbet the sides for the back. Lay out and rout a rabbet for the back with a ¾-inch-diameter straight

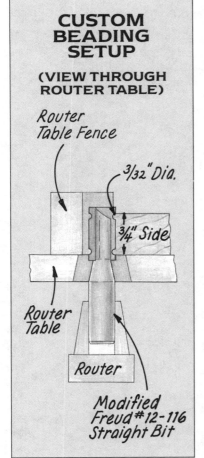

CUSTOM BEADING SETUP

(VIEW THROUGH ROUTER TABLE)

Router Table Fence

³⁄₃₂" Dia.

¾" Side

Router Table

Router

Modified Freud #12-116 Straight Bit

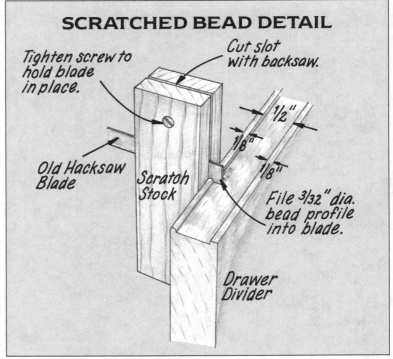

SCRATCHED BEAD DETAIL

Tighten screw to hold blade in place.

Cut slot with backsaw.

Old Hacksaw Blade

Scratch Stock

½"

⅛"

⅛"

File ³⁄₃₂" dia. bead profile into blade.

Drawer Divider

Guide the drawer dividers and sides against the fence as you rout the trough.

MATERIALS LIST

Part	Dimension	Part	Dimension
Case		Fifth drawer front	$3/4'' \times 6^7/8'' \times 32^3/8''$
Top	$3/4'' \times 21^1/4'' \times 37''$	Fifth drawer sides (2)	$1/2'' \times 6^7/8'' \times 18^1/2''$
Sides (2)	$3/4'' \times 19^3/4'' \times 36''$	Fifth drawer back	$1/2'' \times 6'' \times 32^3/8''$
Back	$3/4'' \times 36'' \times 33^1/4''$	Drawer bottoms (5)	$1/4'' \times 18^1/4'' \times 32^7/8''$
Drawer dividers (12)	$3/4'' \times 2^1/2'' \times 33^1/4''$	**Bracket Feet and**	
Drawer runners (12)	$3/4'' \times 2^1/2'' \times 16^1/2''$	**Molding**	
Dust panels (5)	$1/4'' \times 15'' \times 29^1/4''$	Beaded crown molding	
Top support blocks (8)	$1'' \times 1'' \times 2''$	stock	$3/4'' \times 1^3/4'' \times 84''$
Filler strips (2)	$1/2'' \times 4'' \times 32^1/2''$	Ogee molding stock	$3/4'' \times 3/4'' \times 84''$
Drawers		Bracket foot stock	$1^3/4'' \times 5'' \times 48''$
First drawer front	$3/4'' \times 4^7/8'' \times 32^3/8''$	Bracket foot back	$3/4'' \times 5'' \times 34^1/2''$
First drawer sides (2)	$1/2'' \times 4^7/8'' \times 18^1/2''$	Glue block stock	$1^1/4'' \times 3^1/2'' \times 30''$
First drawer back	$1/2'' \times 4'' \times 32^3/8''$		
Second drawer front	$3/4'' \times 5^1/4'' \times 32^3/8''$	**HARDWARE**	
Second drawer sides (2)	$1/2'' \times 5^1/4'' \times 18^1/2''$	As needed, #8 × 2" drywall screws	
Second drawer back	$1/2'' \times 4^3/8'' \times 32^3/8''$	As needed, #8 × 1 1/2" drywall screws	
Third drawer front	$3/4'' \times 5^7/8'' \times 32^3/8''$	10 Chippendale plate pulls. Available from	
Third drawer sides (2)	$1/2'' \times 5^7/8'' \times 18^1/2''$	Horton Brasses, Nooks Hill Rd., P.O. Box 95,	
Third drawer back	$1/2'' \times 5'' \times 32^3/8''$	Cromwell, CT 06416. Part #CH-8.	
Fourth drawer front	$3/4'' \times 6^1/4'' \times 32^3/8''$	As needed, 3d finishing nails	
Fourth drawer sides (2)	$1/2'' \times 6^1/4'' \times 18^1/2''$	As needed, 2d finishing nails	
Fourth drawer back	$1/2'' \times 5^3/8'' \times 32^3/8''$	As needed, 3/4" brads	

bit in a router. Adjust the router and router fence attachment to cut a ³/₈ × ³/₄-inch rabbet along the inside back edge of the sides.

5 **Dado for the drawer runners.** The drawer runners fit into dadoes routed into the sides. But the story doesn't end there. The drawer dividers—the parts that you see between the drawers—fit into dovetail slots, which you'll also need to cut. It pays to miter the beads in the side where they meet the beads in the drawer runners, while you're at it. All three are simple router operations.

Guide the router against a straightedge to cut the dado. You'll make the job easier if you clamp together the sides so that you can rout both in one pass. Position the sides edge-to-edge, with the layout lines facing up. Adjust them so that the corresponding layout lines meet, and clamp the sides together.

Clamp a straightedge to the sides, and guide the router along it to rout a ¹/₂-inch-wide × ³/₈-inch-deep dado.

6 **Rout the dovetail slot.** Before you move the straightedge, rout the dovetail slot for the front rail. Put a ³/₄-inch-diameter dovetail bit in the router. Guide the router against the fence to cut a 3-inch-long × ³/₈-inch-deep dovetail slot at the front edge of each side. Leave the straightedge in position when you are done with this cut.

7 **Miter the bead on the sides.** The bead along the edge of the side is mitered to meet with the bead on the front drawer dividers, as shown in the Joinery Detail. Cut the miter with a V-grooving bit in the router. Adjust the depth of the bit so that the chamfer created just cuts through the bead.

After you cut the chamfer, move the straightedge to the next dado. Dado, dovetail, and miter for each drawer.

Make the web frames.

The heart of the case is the web frames which support the drawers. Each frame has four parts: a drawer divider, which you see from the front of the chest; two runners, on which the drawers travel; and a rear rail across the back

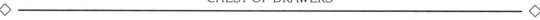

of the chest. Each frame also has a dust panel, which fits inside the frame.

1 **Tenon the drawer runners.** The web frames are mortised and tenoned together. Lay out the drawer runner tenons as shown in the Divider and Runner Detail. Cut the tenons with a tenoning jig on the table saw. For more information on this technique, see "Tenoning Jig" on page 375.

2 **Mortise the drawer dividers.** Lay out the mortises on the front and back drawer dividers as shown in the Divider and Runner Detail. Make the mortises with the drill press by drilling a series of $5/16$-inch-diameter $\times$ $1\,5/16$-inch-deep holes within the layout lines. Clean out the waste to the layout lines with a sharp chisel.

3 **Cut slots for the dust panels.** The web frames have panels in them designed to keep out the dust. Rout grooves for these panels on the router table.

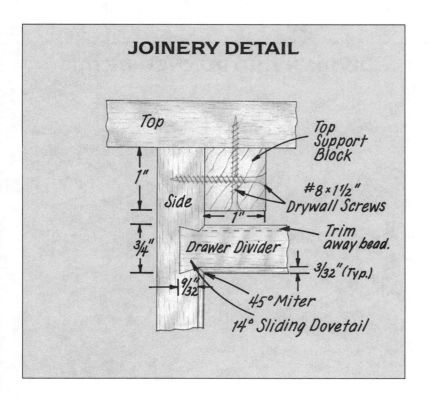

JOINERY DETAIL

Top

Top Support Block

Side

#8 × 1½" Drywall Screws

1"

1"

Trim away bead.

¾"

Drawer Divider

3/32" (Typ.)

9/32"

45° Miter

14° Sliding Dovetail

To rout a stopped groove on the rail, lower the mortise over the bit. Guide the cut along the fence until you reach the second mortise, and then lift the rail off the cutter.

Put a ¼-inch straight bit in the router, and adjust the router table fence to position the groove as shown in the Divider and Runner Detail. Rout a groove the entire length of the drawer runners. On the dividers, the groove runs from mortise to mortise. To rout a stopped groove like this, lower the mortise over the bit, as shown in the photo. Rout until you reach the other mortise, and then lift the divider off the bit.

4 Cut the tongue on the drawer runners and back drawer dividers. The drawer runners have a tongue cut along their edge as shown in the Divider and Runner Detail, and the back drawer dividers have matching tenons cut into each end. These tongues and tenons fit into the ½-inch-wide dadoes that were cut in the sides. Cut the ½-inch-thick × ⅜-inch-wide tongues and the ½-inch-thick × ⅜-inch-long tenons with a dado cutter on the table saw.

5 Dovetail the front drawer dividers. Rout the dove-tails in the ends of the front drawer dividers with the

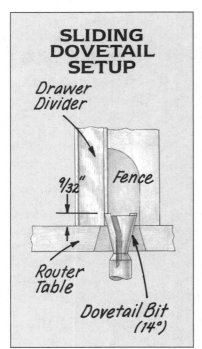

SLIDING DOVETAIL SETUP

Drawer Divider

Fence

⁹⁄₃₂"

Router Table

Dovetail Bit (14°)

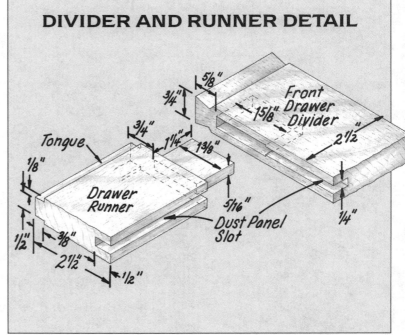

DIVIDER AND RUNNER DETAIL

Front Drawer Divider

⅝"

¾"

1⁵⁄₈"

2½"

Tongue

¾"

1¼"

1⅜"

⅛"

Drawer Runner

½"

⅜"

2½"

½"

⁵⁄₁₆"

Dust Panel Slot

¼"

same bit you used to cut the dovetail slots in the sides. This time put the dovetail bit in a table-mounted router. Set up the cut as shown in the Sliding Dovetail Setup, with the bit buried in the fence, and the drawer divider standing on its end. For stability, back up the drawer divider with a piece of scrap as you rout. Cut the sliding dovetail in both ends of all the front drawer dividers.

6 Miter the bead. As shown in the Joinery Detail, the beads on the front drawer dividers are mitered where they meet the beads on the sides.

Miter the drawer divider beads on the table saw as shown in the photo. Set the table saw blade at 45 degrees. Put one of the drawer dividers flat on the saw table and adjust the blade so that as it cuts the miters it will just touch the dovetail. Adjust the fence so that you can guide the end of the rail against it to position the cut. Guide the drawer dividers with a miter gauge as you cut.

7 Assemble the case. Install the drawer divider, drawer runner, and dust panel assemblies one at a time, starting at the bottom of the sides and moving toward the top. Lay the cabinet on its back and glue the bottom back drawer dividers into their dadoes. Next

Left: Hold the drawer dividers on end and guide them against the fence as you rout the sliding dovetails. Support the drawer dividers by following them with a piece of scrap as you rout. *Right:* Guide the drawer dividers with a miter gauge as you miter the bead. Adjust the fence to determine the position of the cut.

install the drawer runners and dust panel without glue, and complete the assembly by gluing the front drawer dividers' sliding dovetails into the dovetail slots in the sides. Gently tap the drawer dividers into place until they are even with the front edges of the sides.

Continue by adding the other drawer dividers, runners, and dust panels, but attach the top to the cabinet before you install the top drawer divider frame. Predrill two clearance holes in the top support blocks for #8 × 1 1/2-inch drywall screws; orient the screws as shown in the Joinery Detail. Evenly space four support blocks along the top edge of each side, and screw the top to the sides. When the top is in place install the final drawer divider frame. Screw the plywood back into place with #8 × 1 1/2-inch drywall screws.

Make and fit the drawers.

The drawer fronts are joined to the sides with half-blind dovetails, and the sides to the backs with through dovetails. The bottoms rest in grooves in the sides and fronts.

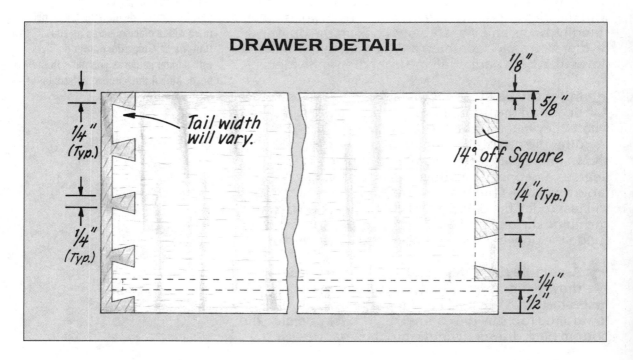

DRAWER DETAIL

Tail width will vary.

1/4" (Typ.)

1/4" (Typ.)

1/8"

5/8"

14° off Square

1/4" (Typ.)

1/4"

1/2"

As you will see in the Drawer Detail, I have given the exact size for the pins, but not for the tails. In my opinion, dovetails on the side of a drawer don't all need to be uniform. If I see a drawer that has a row of identical tails, I tend to think that it was factory-made. Give your drawers a handmade look by spacing them with a craftsman's eye rather than with a ruler.

1 **Cut the drawer parts.** Because of construction variations, the drawers may differ slightly from the dimensions given in the Materials List. Use the Materials List as a guide, but measure directly from the cabinet for final dimensions. Cut the drawer parts to leave $1/16$-inch clearance above each drawer, and a total of $1/8$-inch side-to-side clearance.

2 **Cut the dovetails.** Lay out the dovetails on the side of the drawer as shown in the Drawer Detail. Cut the tails with a dovetail saw, and chisel out the waste. Trace around the tails to lay out the pins in the drawer front. Saw and chisel away the waste. For more on drawer joinery, see "Cutting Through Dovetails" on page 81 and "Cutting Half-Blind Dovetails" on page 155.

3 **Assemble the drawers.** Finish sand the parts of the drawers, and test fit them. When you're sure that they fit properly, glue the fronts, sides, and backs together. Slide the bottoms into the grooves, but do not glue them in place—let the bottoms float in the grooves. Drive a single 3d finishing nail up though each bottom and into the back to keep the bottom in place.

Sand the drawer joints clean and flush, and install drawer pulls. Fit the drawers to their openings, sanding or planing the assemblies until they slide smoothly.

Make the bracket feet and moldings.

1 **Cut the cove in the bracket foot stock.** Cut stock for the bracket feet to the thickness and width given in the Materials List, but leave the stock about 1 inch longer than specified. Lay out the profile of the Bracket Foot Pattern on the end of the stock.

Cut the large cove on the bracket feet by running the stock diagonally across the table saw blade, as explained in "Cove Cutting on the Table Saw" on page 361.

Scrape away the saw marks with a gooseneck scraper and sandpaper.

2 **Cut the top radius in the bracket feet.** Create the curve on the top of the bracket by cutting adjoining bevels on the stock. First, set the table saw blade at 15 degrees, and adjust the fence so that the blade just touches the radius layout lines. Cut the bevel on the stock and readjust the blade to 30 degrees. Adjust the fence and rip away more waste.

Smooth out the radius with a hand plane, scraper, and sander.

3 **Miter the bracket feet and cut them to shape.** Miter the appropriate corners of the foot blanks and cut the feet to length.

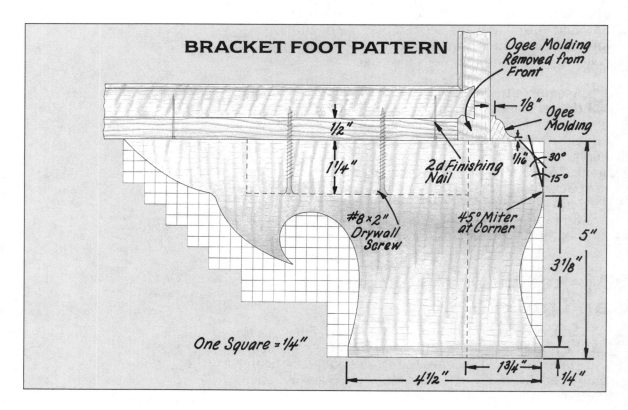

BRACKET FOOT PATTERN

Ogee Molding Removed from Front

⅛"

Ogee Molding

½"

1¼"

2d Finishing Nail

#8 x 2" Drywall Screw

45° Miter at Corner

1/16"

30°

15°

5"

3⅛"

¼"

One Square = ¼"

4½"

1¾"

Make a grid of ¼-inch squares, and enlarge the bracket foot shape on it. Transfer the pattern to the back of the bracket foot blanks, and cut them to shape on the band saw. Sand the sawed edges smooth.

4 Assemble the front corners. Cut the triangle glue blocks to the shape shown in the Bracket Foot Assembly Detail. Set your table saw miter gauge to 45 degrees, and guide the glue block stock with it as you cut. Begin by making a 45 degree-cut in the end of the stock, and then roll the stock over to make the second 45-degree cut to complete the first glue block. Continue by rolling the stock to cut successive triangular glue blocks.

Drill pilot holes in the glue blocks for #8 × 2-inch drywall screws as shown in the Bracket Foot Assembly Detail. Assemble the bracket feet for the front corners first. Spread glue on the miters and screw the bracket feet to the glue blocks as shown.

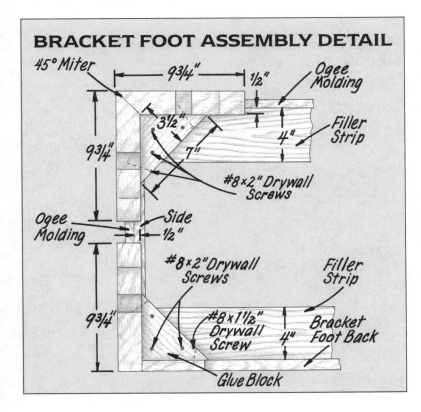

BRACKET FOOT ASSEMBLY DETAIL

5 **Dovetail the back feet.** The skirt that connects the two rear feet is dovetailed into place, as shown in the Back View.

Lay out and cut the half-blind dovetails in the bracket foot back as you did for the drawers. Assemble the dovetails and screw the glue blocks into place as shown in the Bracket Foot Assembly Detail.

6 **Attach the bracket feet.** Attach filler strips to the bottom of the cabinet with glue and 2d finishing nails, as shown in the Bracket Foot Pattern. Attach bracket feet to the bottom of the chest, as shown in the Bracket Foot Assembly Detail, with glue and #8 × 2-inch drywall screws.

7 **Make and attach the ogee molding.** Rout the ogee molding to the profile shown in the Bracket Foot Pattern with a 1/4-inch-radius ogee bit. Miter it to fit around the case just above the bracket feet, and nail it into place with 3/4-inch brads.

8 **Mill and attach the crown molding.** Mill the beaded crown molding stock as shown in the Crown Molding

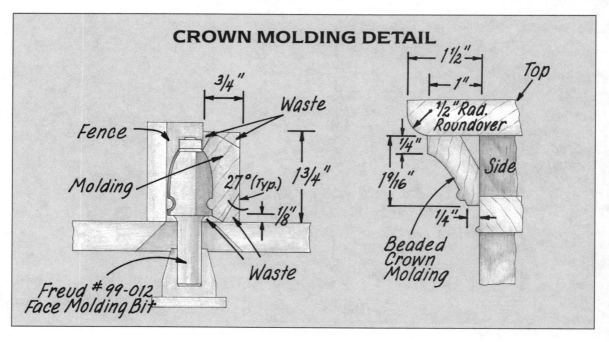

CROWN MOLDING DETAIL

Fence

Molding

Waste

3/4"

27°(Typ.)

1 3/4"

1/8"

Waste

Freud #99-012 Face Molding Bit

1 1/2"

1"

Top

1/2" Rad. Roundover

1/4"

1 9/16"

Side

1/4"

Beaded Crown Molding

Detail. After cutting the profile, set the table saw blade at 27 degrees and cut away the waste where shown.

Miter the crown molding to fit around the case, and attach it with ³/₄-inch brads as shown in the Crown Molding Detail.

Sand and finish the chest of drawers.

COVE CUTTING ON THE TABLE SAW

Cutting a cove was done with a hand plane in the old days. The easiest way to do it these days is to feed the stock at an angle across the table saw blade.

Draw the cove on a piece of scrap about 2 feet long and the exact width and thickness of the finished molding.

With the saw turned off, lay the sample piece on the table with what will be the molded face down. Raise the blade as high as the deepest section of the cove. Sight along the blade at the sample. Vary the angle of the sample relative to the blade until the blade obstructs your view of the entire cove. Draw a pencil line along each edge of the sample, and clamp a fence along each line as shown.

Make the first cut with the blade very low. Run all the stock across the blade, and then raise the blade slightly for the next pass. Continue until you reach the layout line.

Compare the scrap with the desired profile. If necessary, adjust the angle of the fence to change the shape of the cove. Increasing the angle at which the stock crosses the blade makes the cove more circular. Decreasing it makes its curve flatter.

If you change the angle of the fence, cut another test piece. Always cut the cove in a series of passes, to avoid possible damage to the saw's motor.

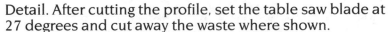

COVE CUT SETUP

Push stock across blade to cut cove.

Bracket Foot Stock

Fence

Fence

SARAH'S LOOKOUT
by David Page

This project was designed for a two-year-old girl who loved to look out of her bedroom window. Her parents commissioned me to make a piece of furniture that she could sit upon, and which could also serve as a storage unit. They suggested a ladder on one side so she could reach the top, but I wanted something more integral to the piece. A ladder, after Sarah gets a few years older, will be in the way.

I also wanted to build a piece which would fit into a young girl's room, and later into a teenager's room, and which this two-year-old would one day be proud to hand down to her own two-year-old. The stair-step drawers solve the problem and give the piece a strong personal presence. Though it is strong and sturdy, the top railing is only screwed into place, and later Sarah can remove it if she likes. For now, it gives Sarah and

EXPLODED VIEW

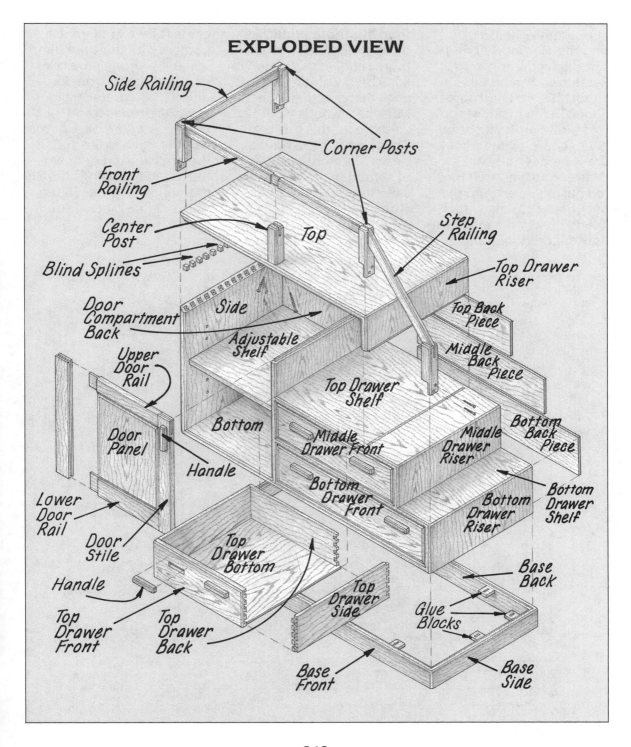

Side Railing

Corner Posts

Front Railing

Center Post

Blind Splines

Top

Step Railing

Top Drawer Riser

Door Compartment Back

Side

Top Back Piece

Adjustable Shelf

Middle Back Piece

Upper Door Rail

Top Drawer Shelf

Door Panel

Bottom

Middle Drawer Front

Middle Drawer Riser

Bottom Back Piece

Handle

Bottom Drawer Front

Lower Door Rail

Door Stile

Bottom Drawer Riser

Bottom Drawer Shelf

Handle

Top Drawer Bottom

Base Back

Top Drawer Side

Glue Blocks

Top Drawer Front

Top Drawer Back

Base Front

Base Side

her parents a sense of security. Her mother tied a soft rug on the top, and Sarah was perched there almost before I had it positioned beneath her window.

I built Sarah's lookout out of cherry, with red oak drawer sides and backs. Drawer bottoms are ¼-inch red oak plywood, and the back of the case is ¼-inch cherry plywood. I made the drawer and door handles from air-dried walnut. Air-dried walnut has a much more reddish color than kiln-dried walnut, and it goes better with the cherry. Most hardwoods would be suitable for this project. The chamfers are both a design element and a way of softening the piece for safer interaction with a young child.

When constructing this piece, build the drawer cabinet first. I joined the corners with multiple blind splines, although the corners could easily be dovetailed if you prefer. Inside joints are tongue-and-groove. Add the base to the cabinet, then make and fit the drawers and door to the cabinet openings. Attach the railing last, even after finishing the piece if you wish.

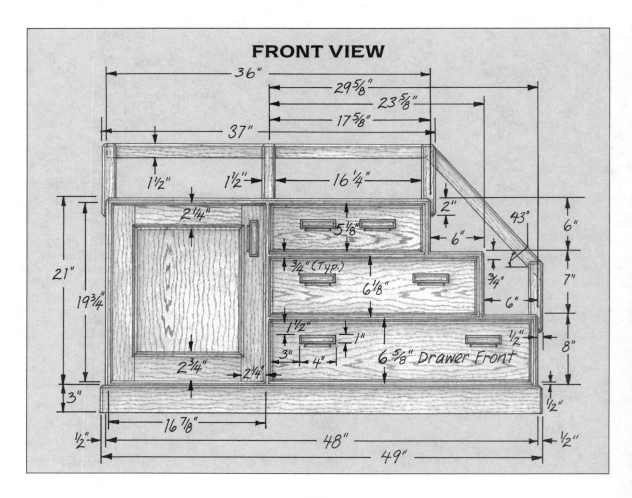

FRONT VIEW

Build the drawer cabinet and base.

1 **Choose the stock and cut the parts.** Plane and glue up wood to the dimensions in the Materials List for the base, top, bottom, side, risers, drawer shelves, divider, and adjustable shelf. Cut and joint the pieces to width, but for now leave them about 1 inch longer than called for. Cut all the other parts except for the drawer parts to the sizes given in the Materials List. You'll cut the drawer parts later, when you make the drawers.

2 **Miter the drawer cabinet and base.** Set the table saw blade at 45 degrees, and crosscut the corner

Quick Tip: Wide boards stay flattest when both surfaces receive the same airflow. Do not leave your case parts lying overnight on the bench, where air can reach the one surface but not the other. Set these pieces against a wall where air circulates freely around both faces, or stack them tightly on top of each other between two pieces of plywood so that air cannot reach the face surfaces.

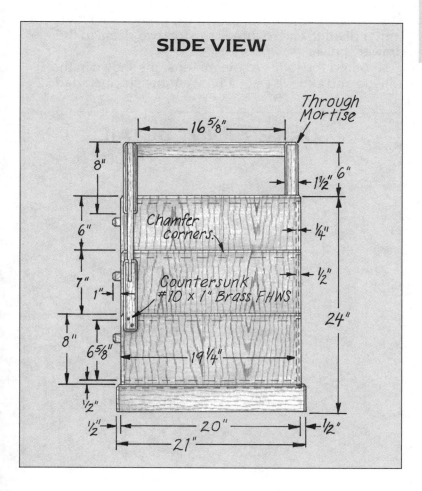

SIDE VIEW

Through Mortise

16 ⅝"

8"

1½" · 6"

Chamfer corners.

¼"

6"

½"

7"

Countersunk #10 × 1" Brass FHWS

1"→

24"

8"

6⅝"

19¼"

½"

½"→

20"

½"

21"

Guide the router against a straight-edge clamped across the cabinet pieces.

miter joints in the drawer cabinet parts and in the base parts. Cut the pieces to length as you cut the miters on the top, bottom, left side, first drawer riser, and base pieces. The other two risers, the divider, and the drawer shelves are still slightly long. Return the saw blade to 90 degrees and crosscut these pieces to final length.

3 **Cut the multiple spline joint in the mitered corners.** This joint is made with a router. Cut the joint in the mitered corners of the drawer cabinet and the base as shown in the Corner Joint Detail. For complete step-by-step directions, see "Multiple Blind Splines" on page 380.

4 **Rout the tongue-and-groove joints.** Cut tongue-and-groove joints to attach the drawer shelves to the center divider, and to attach the top two risers to the drawer shelves.

I routed the joints to the dimensions shown in the Tongue and Groove Detail. First cut the stopped dado

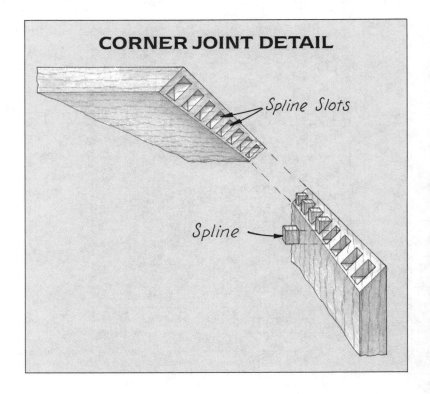

CORNER JOINT DETAIL

Spline Slots

Spline

grooves by guiding the router against a straightedge. Stop the dadoes at least ½ inch from the front edge of the cabinet pieces.

Lock a ¾-inch double-fluted router bit in the router. Guide the router along the end of the board with its fence attachment, and rout a rabbet on each surface of the board. Adjust the depth of cut so that the rabbets create ¼ × ¼-inch tongues that fit the grooves. Cut a ½-inch section off the front edge of the tongues to match the stopped dadoes.

MATERIALS LIST

Part	Dimension	Part	Dimension
Case		Middle drawer bottom	¼" × 19" × 22¼"
Top	¾" × 20" × 36"	Bottom drawer front	¾" × 6⅝" × 28¹³/₁₆"
Bottom	¾" × 20" × 48"	Bottom drawer sides (2)	½" × 6⅝" × 19"
Side	¾" × 20" × 21¼"	Bottom drawer back	½" × 5⅞" × 28¹³/₁₆"
Top drawer riser	¾" × 20" × 6¼"	Bottom drawer bottom	¼" × 19" × 28¼"
Middle drawer riser	¾" × 20" × 7¼"	**Door**	
Bottom drawer riser	¾" × 20" × 8¼"	Upper door rail	¾" × 2¼" × 16¾"
Top drawer shelf	¾" × 20" × 23⅞"	Lower door rail	¾" × 2¾" × 16¾"
Bottom drawer shelf	¾" × 20" × 29⅞"	Door stiles (2)	¾" × 2¼" × 19⅝"
Divider	¾" × 20" × 20¼"	Door panel	½" × 12¾" × 15¹/₁₆"
Adjustable shelf	¾" × 18½" × 16¹¹/₁₆"	Handles (7)	1" × 1" × 4"
Top back piece	¼" × 5¾" × 17⅜"	**Railing**	
Middle back piece	¼" × 6¾" × 23⅜"	Corner posts (4)	1½" × 1½" × 8"
Bottom back piece	¼" × 7¼" × 29⅜"	Center post	1½" × 1½" × 6"
Door compartment back	¼" × 17⅜" × 20¼"	Side railing	¹³/₁₆" × 1½" × 19"
Base front and back (2)	¾" × 3" × 49"	Front railing	¹³/₁₆" × 1½" × 36⅜"
Base sides (2)	¾" × 3" × 21"	Step railing	¹³/₁₆" × 1½" × 20"
Glue blocks (12)	¾" × 1½" × 1½"		
Drawers		**HARDWARE**	
Top drawer front	¾" × 5⅛" × 16¹³/₁₆"	As needed, #10 × 1" brass flathead wood screws	
Top drawer sides (2)	½" × 5⅛" × 19"	As needed, #8 × 1¼" brass flathead wood screws	
Top drawer back	½" × 4⅜" × 16¹³/₁₆"	As needed, #6 × ¾" brass flathead wood screws	
Top drawer bottom	¼" × 19" × 16¼"	As needed, #6 × ⅝" brass flathead wood screws	
Middle drawer front	¾" × 6⅛" × 22¹³/₁₆"	As needed, #8 × 1¼" roundhead wood screws	
Middle drawer sides (2)	½" × 6⅛" × 19"	with flat washers	
Middle drawer back	½" × 5⅜" × 22¹³/₁₆"	2 brass butt hinges, 1½"	

Quick Tip: Drill perfectly corresponding adjustable shelf holes with a drill guide. Make a drill guide from a 1 × 2 × 18-inch piece of wood. Lay out and drill the holes in this template, then clamp it into place on each piece to be drilled. Put a commercially available stop collar on your hand drill and drill through the guide into the cabinet piece. This assures perfectly aligned holes.

5 **Drill holes for the adjustable shelf.** Lay out two sets of shelf support holes in the side, and two sets in the divider. The holes are on 2-inch centers, beginning 6 inches above the bottom. I drilled the holes 2 1/2 inches in from the front and back edges of the cabinet. Drill the holes 1/2 inch deep with a 1/4-inch brad point drill bit.

Assemble the cabinet.

The order in which you work is an important part of this glue-up. First, attach each drawer riser to the piece above it, creating three L-shaped assemblies. Then glue the divider to the top and bottom and add the left side. While the glue is still wet, begin adding the riser assemblies to the cabinet.

1 **Make the riser assemblies.** Before gluing, sand the surfaces that make up the inside of the door cabinet. Then glue two of the drawer risers to the two drawer shelves and the third riser to the cabinet top. This gives

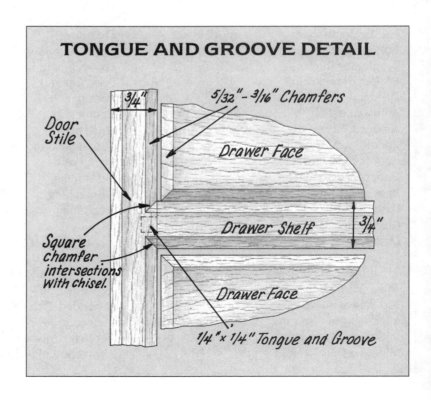

TONGUE AND GROOVE DETAIL

3/4"

Door Stile

5/32" - 3/16" Chamfers

Drawer Face

Square chamfer intersections with chisel.

Drawer Shelf

3/4"

Drawer Face

1/4" x 1/4" Tongue and Groove

you three separate L-shaped pieces. Make certain the assemblies form perfect 90-degree angles. Let this glue-up dry before going to the next step.

2 **Add the center divider, the bottom, and the side.** Glue the center divider into the top and riser assembly. Before clamping, add the bottom and then the left side. Check to make sure everything is square, and make any necessary adjustments.

3 **Add the steps.** While the glue is still wet, glue and clamp the lower step-and-riser into place, clamping the miter before clamping the tongue-and-groove joint. Then glue and clamp the remaining step-and-riser into place. Check again to make sure the cabinet is square. Sight along the front edge of the case to make sure it is not twisted.

4 **Rout the chamfers.** When the glue is dry, lay the cabinet on its back and rout a $3/16$-inch-wide chamfer

Quick Tip: Here's a good way to glue miters. Glue a triangular scrap of wood to the long face of each mitered piece, as shown below in the Miter Clamping Detail. Then clamp across these glue blocks to close the miter. To make it easier to remove the glue blocks after the joint has set, glue a strip of grocery bag paper between the glue blocks and the cabinet members. After gluing, a quick tap with a chisel pops off the glue blocks. Plane or scrape off the remaining glue and paper.

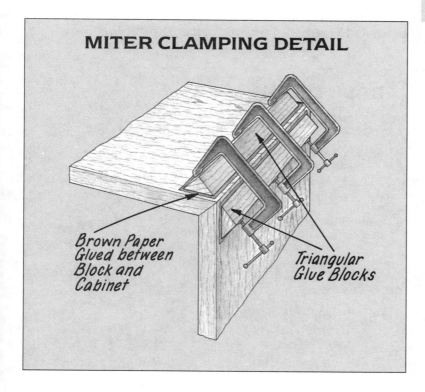

MITER CLAMPING DETAIL

Brown Paper Glued between Block and Cabinet

Triangular Glue Blocks

around the edges of the door and drawer openings and around the perimeter of the cabinet face, as shown in the Front View. Also rout a chamfer where the miters come together on the steps and top, as shown in the Front and Side Views. Rout the chamfers with a ball bearing chamfer bit in a hand-held router. Use a chisel to square the inside corners where the chamfers meet.

Chamfer the mitered corners, but first lay out the locations of the posts that hold the railing. Rout the chamfers, stopping them just short of the post layout lines.

5 Rabbet for the back. Each door and drawer opening has a separate back piece. Rout ½-inch-deep × ¼-inch-wide rabbets for these back pieces. Use a chisel to square the corners where the rabbets meet.

Assemble the base.

1 Rabbet and glue the base. Cut a ¼ × ¼-inch rabbet in the top inside edge of the front and side pieces of the base. Cut a ¼ × 7⁄16-inch rabbet in the back piece. The extra wide rabbet in the back gives the cabinet parts

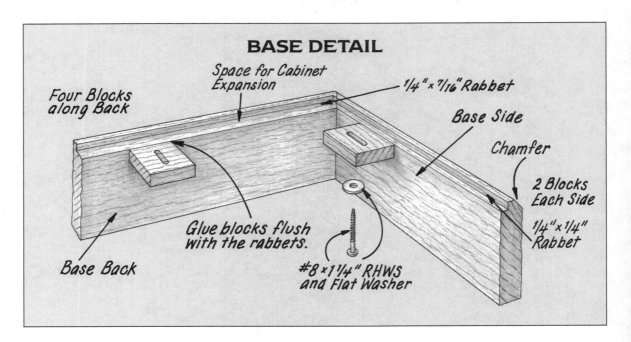

BASE DETAIL

Four Blocks along Back

Space for Cabinet Expansion

¼" × 7⁄16" Rabbet

Base Side

Chamfer

2 Blocks Each Side

¼" × ¼" Rabbet

Glue blocks flush with the rabbets.

Base Back

#8 × 1¼" RHWS and Flat Washer

some room for expansion in humid weather. Glue the base together, clamping across the miters as before. Check to make sure the base is square.

2 Chamfer the edges. Rout a ³/₁₆-inch-wide chamfer in the top outside edges and corners of the base, as shown in the Front and Side Views.

3 Make the glue blocks. I attached the base with special glue blocks that allow the cabinet to expand and contract.

Make eight ³/₄ × 1 ¹/₂ × 1 ¹/₂-inch slotted glue blocks as shown in the Base Detail. To rough out the slots, drill adjacent ³/₁₆-inch holes in the blocks. Center the line of holes on the blocks, positioning the line parallel to the grain on four of the blocks. In the other four blocks, drill the holes perpendicular to the grain. With a chisel or file, connect the holes to form slots. Glue the with-the-grain blocks at the center and at the back edge of each base side. Glue the across-the-grain blocks along the base back, as shown in the Base Detail.

Glue and clamp the base to the cabinet along the front edge, and 3 inches along the front of each side. From beneath, drill through the slotted glue blocks into the bottom of the drawer cabinet for #8 × 1 ¹/₄-inch screws. Attach the blocks to the cabinet with roundhead wood screws and flat washers.

Make the drawers.

1 Mill the drawer parts. Variations in construction may require you to make slight changes in the sizes given in the Materials List. Mill the drawer fronts, sides, and backs to thickness, then trim them to fit your cabinet openings. Leave a maximum of ¹/₈-inch clearance above each drawer, and ¹/₁₆-inch total clearance side to side. Cut plywood drawer bottoms to the dimensions given.

2 Cut the drawer dovetails. Lay out the tails on the drawer sides as shown in the Drawer Detail. Note that the tails at the front of the drawer are half-blind, while those at the rear are through. Spacing is not critical. I like to increase the size of the tails as they move down the drawer side, keeping the pin size constant. Cut along the layout lines and chisel away the waste. Hold or clamp the sides to the drawer faces and backs, and scribe the pins with a sharp knife. Saw and chisel out the waste between the pins. For more on dovetails, see "Cutting Through Dovetails" on page 81 and "Cutting Half-Blind Dovetails" on page 155.

3 Rout the drawer bottom groove. On the router table, rout a 1/4 × 1/4-inch groove in the drawer front and sides for the drawer bottom, as shown in the Drawer Detail.

4 Rout the finger grooves. A V-groove behind each handle provides additional finger clearance when opening and closing the drawers. Rout the groove, shown in the Handle Detail, before assembling the drawer or attaching the handle. Lay out the position of the handle on each drawer front as shown in the Front View. In each drawer face, lay out and cut 1/2-inch-deep × 3-inch-long grooves with a V-groove bit in your router, as shown in the Handle Detail. Angle the rounded ends of the grooves with a chisel to the profile shown. Next, rout a 3-inch-long

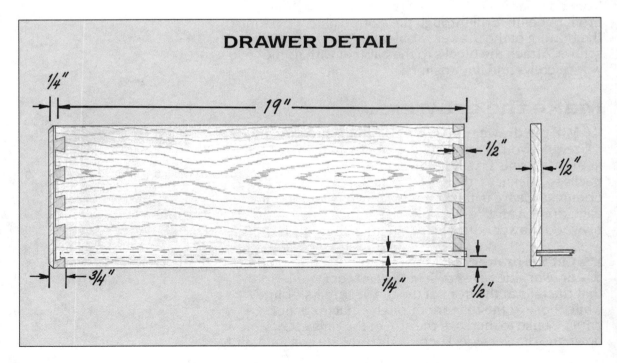

DRAWER DETAIL

chamfer in the back of the drawer handles to match the V-grooves in the drawer fronts.

5 **Glue together the drawers.** Sand the interior of the drawers, but not the dovetails. On a flat surface glue and clamp the drawers together. Square the drawers by measuring diagonally across the corners. If the measurements are equal, the drawer is square. Adjust as necessary. Slide the drawer bottoms into place from the rear. When the glue is dry, countersink and drill through the bottom into the drawer back for three #6 × ¾-inch brass flathead wood screws.

6 **Chamfer the drawer edges.** Rout a chamfer around the face of the drawer to match the chamfer on the cabinet. Fit the drawers to the drawer openings.

Make the door.

1 **Cut the mortise-and-tenon joints.** The door is assembled with through mortise joints, which you can

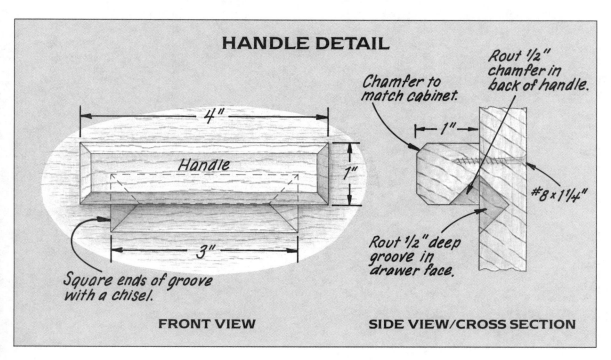

HANDLE DETAIL

Rout ½" chamfer in back of handle.

Chamfer to match cabinet.

4"

Handle

1"

3"

Square ends of groove with a chisel.

1"

#8 × 1¼"

Rout ½" deep groove in drawer face.

FRONT VIEW   **SIDE VIEW/CROSS SECTION**

cut entirely on the table saw. First, lay out and cut the through mortises. Stand the stiles in a tenoning jig and adjust the table saw fence to cut the ¼-inch-wide through mortises. Next, lay out and cut ¼-inch tenons on the rails to fit the mortises. Cut the shoulder first, and then the cheeks. For more on making and using a tenoning jig, see "Tenoning Jig" on page 375.

2 Rout the panel groove. Cut a ⅜-inch-deep groove for the panel in the door parts with a ¼-inch slotting cutter in a table-mounted router. Center the groove in the rail, and run it from mortise to mortise. Extend the groove ½ inch into the tenons to allow clearance for the panel, but do not cut the entire length of the rails.

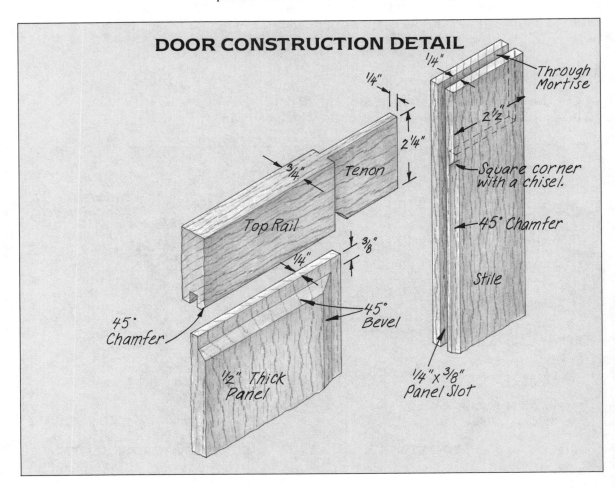

DOOR CONSTRUCTION DETAIL

¼"
2 ¼"
¾"
Tenon
Top Rail
¼"
45° Chamfer
½" Thick Panel
45° Bevel
⅜"
Through Mortise
2 ½"
Square corner with a chisel.
45° Chamfer
Stile
¼" x ⅜" Panel Slot

TENONING JIG

A tenoning jig is a tool that can save you a lot of time and frustration when making tenons or slot mortises. With a tenoning jig, you don't need to set up a dado cutter in your table saw. You can simply use a regular table saw blade. When cutting through mortises and tenons, start by cutting the through mortises in the ends of the stiles, and then cut tenon shoulders and cheeks on the ends of the rails to fit the mortises.

The homemade jig shown here rides along the table saw rip fence. It is simply screwed and glued together, but it must be cut to fit your saw's rip fence. Quick-release clamps like the one shown

can be found at better hardware stores, or are available from The Woodworkers' Store, 21801 Industrial Boulevard, Rogers, MN 55374 (part number 53447).

1 Cut the through mortises. Lay out and cut the through mortises in the ends of the stiles. In ¾-inch-thick stock you will generally cut a ¼-inch-wide mortise to receive a ¼-inch-thick tenon. Cut the mortise in two passes with a standard ⅛-inch-thick table saw blade. Clamp the stile upright in the tenoning jig. Adjust the height of the table saw blade to equal the width of the rails. Adjust the fence so that as the stile

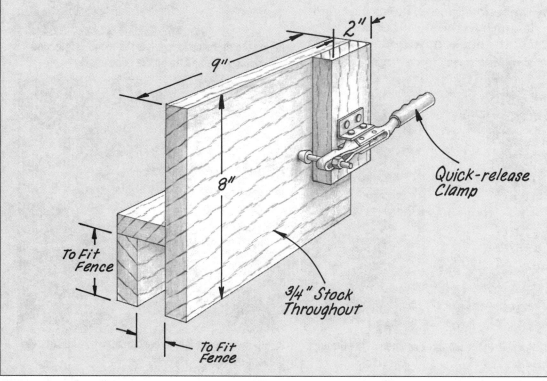

9"

2"

8"

To Fit Fence

To Fit Fence

3/4" Stock Throughout

Quick-release Clamp

(continued)

TENONING JIG—*Continued*

rides in the jig the blade will cut along on the inside of one of the layout lines. When the first half of the through mortise has been cut, adjust the fence to make the second cut.

2 Cut the tenon shoulders. The shoulder cuts define the length of the tenon. When cutting tenons, cut the shoulder first by laying the rail stock flat on the table and crosscutting. Guide the stock with a miter gauge set at 90 degrees, and lower the blade to cut a 1/4-inch-deep kerf.

3 Cut the tenon cheeks. When the shoulders have been cut, clamp the rails upright in the tenoning jig and cut away the tenon cheeks. Raise the blade until it cuts into the shoulder kerf. When both cheeks have been cut away,

you should be left with a 1/4-inch-thick tenon that fits snugly into the through mortise in the stiles.

Adjust the rip fence to regulate the tenon length, and cut the tenon shoulders on the rails.

Clamp the stile in the tenoning jig and cut the through mortises.

Clamp the rails upright in the tenoning jig and cut away the tenon cheeks.

3 **Chamfer the door frame edges.** Put the door together without glue. Rout a chamfer around the inside edge of the door frame, to match the one on the drawers and drawer cabinet.

4 **Cut the tongue and bevel on the panel.** Rout a rabbet in the panel to create a tongue that fits snugly into the panel groove. Rout the rabbet on all four edges of the panel.

Next, cut the 45-degree face bevel. Set the table saw blade at 45 degrees. With the face of the panel flat on the table, adjust the rip fence and blade height to cut a bevel like that shown in the Door Construction Detail. Cut the bevel on all four edges of the panel. Sand the panel, removing the saw marks from the bevel.

5 **Assemble the door.** Glue and clamp the tenons in the mortises, sliding the panel into place before you pull them completely together. Be careful not to get glue in the panel grooves. Make sure the door is square and flat. Once the door has been clamped together, clamp across the joint, bringing the mortises into firm contact with the tenons.

6 **Rout for the finger grip.** Rout a V-groove in the right stile for the finger grip as you did for the drawers.

7 **Make and attach the handles.** Cut the handles to the dimensions given. Rout a ¼-inch chamfer on the front edges. Rout a larger chamfer on the lower back edge of each handle, as shown in the Handle Detail.

Lay out and drill two screw holes for each handle in the drawer faces and door. Attach each handle with glue and two #8 × 1¼-inch brass flathead wood screws.

8 **Hang the door.** Fit the door into its opening. Trim the door to fit, if necessary, with a hand plane or on the jointer. The door should have about 1/16-inch clearance on all four sides. Lay out and cut the mortises for the hinges. Lay out the mortises by tracing around the hinge with a marking knife. The depth of the mortise should equal the thickness of the hinge leaf. You can cut away most of the waste with a straight bit in a router, and then cut the corners square with a chisel. Drill the door

Quick Tip: Make the door panel *long* enough to fit snugly in its grooves, but slightly *narrower* to allow for expansion in humid weather. Measure from the bottom of the groove in one stile to the bottom of the groove in the other stile, and make the panel 3/16 inch narrower. Make the panel tongue as wide as its groove is deep.

Quick Tip: When gluing, avoid getting glue on the corners of the panel, since you want the panel to float. Rather than wax the corners, which can interfere with your finish, prefinish the panel before gluing up the door. The finish will keep any glue from sticking to the panel.

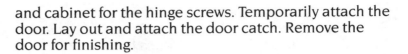
and cabinet for the hinge screws. Temporarily attach the door. Lay out and attach the door catch. Remove the door for finishing.

Make the railing.

1 Notch the corner posts. On the band saw, notch the corner post to fit around the corners of the case as shown in the Front View.

2 Countersink the corner posts for screws. Drill and countersink each brace for two #10 × 1-inch brass flathead wood screws, as shown in the Side View.

3 Mortise the corner post. Rout a mortise in two faces of the left front post, as shown in the Post and Rail Detail.

Rout the mortises with a ⁵⁄₁₆-inch-diameter straight bit in a table-mounted router. Adjust the router table fence to position the mortises, and clamp a stop block to the fence so that each mortise is 1 ½ inches long. Rout the

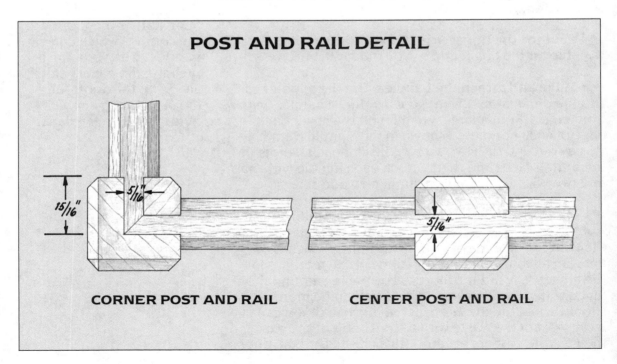

POST AND RAIL DETAIL

CORNER POST AND RAIL

CENTER POST AND RAIL

mortises in several passes, raising the bit about 1/8 inch with each pass. Square the bottoms of the mortises with a 1/4-inch chisel.

4 Mortise the remaining posts. Temporarily screw the posts into place. Clamp sections of rail into place beside the posts. Mark the depth of the mortise on the posts, and at the same time lay out the tenon shoulders on the rails. Cut the mortises on the table saw with a tenoning jig. Clamp the posts at an angle to cut the mortises for the step posts.

5 Cut the rail tenons. Cut the rails to length. Cut the center through tenon on the table saw, with a dado cutter, to the dimensions shown in the Post and Rail Detail. Stand the rails on end in a tenoning jig to cut the remaining tenons. Cut the tenon shoulders for the angled rail with a dovetail saw. Carefully rout away the waste with a hand-held router.

6 Chamfer the edges. Rout a 3/16-inch-wide chamfer in the side and top edges of the posts.

7 Glue the railing together. Screw the posts in position, then glue and clamp the rails into place.

Complete Sarah's lookout.

1 Attach the backs. Fasten the back pieces into their openings with #6 × 5/8-inch brass flathead wood screws.

2 Attach drawer and door stops. For drawer stops, glue and clamp two 1/4 × 3/4 × 1 1/2-inch pieces of wood to the bottom and to each drawer shelf, 3/4 inch from the front edge of the drawer opening. Glue one piece of wood to the underside of the top as a door stop.

3 Apply the finish. Finish sand Sarah's lookout. I finished the cabinet with three coats of clear oil. Do not oil the outside of the drawer sides or the inside of the drawer openings, however, as it might cause the drawers to stick.

MULTIPLE BLIND SPLINES

This joint is strong and faster to make than dovetails. To make it, you need a router and a template guide bushing for the router. These bushings are also sometimes called rub collars. I routed the splines in Sarah's lookout with a bushing that accommodates a ½-inch-diameter straight bit.

1 Make a router template. Cut a 20 × 12-inch template from ½-inch plywood. The template has a series of slots along one edge, as shown in the drawing. The size of the slots is determined by the router bushing, which

must fit into the slot without any play. Set the dado head on the table saw to cut the proper space.

Cut a series of 1-inch-deep dadoes along one long edge, as shown. The exact spacing is not critical, but I like the space between the slots to be about twice the size of the slots.

2 Rout the spline joint. Mark one short edge of the template "Front." Always place the template with its front edge flush with the front edge of the piece to be routed. This automatically aligns the spline slots. Clamp the tem-

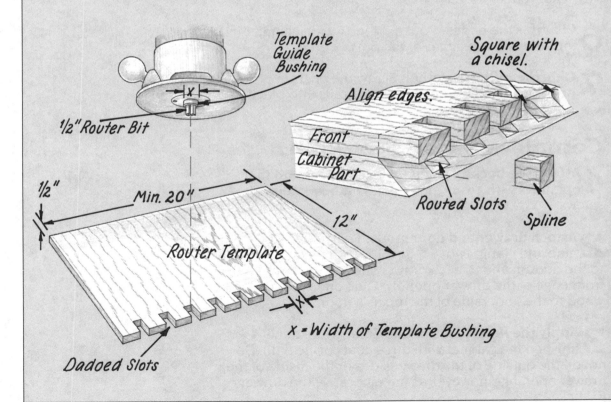

Template Guide Bushing

Square with a chisel.

Align edges.

Front Cabinet Part

½" Router Bit

Routed Slots

Spline

½"

Min. 20"

Router Template

12"

Dadoed Slots

x = Width of Template Bushing

plate to the mitered edge of the stock as shown. The fingers extend over the miter; the base of the slots lines up with the heel of the miter.

Rout the multiple spline slots ½ inch deep. With a ½-inch chisel, square the rounded edge of the slot flush.

3 **Cut splines to match the slots.** Plane several lengths of wood to fit into the spline slots. Rip the required number of splines to width and cross-cut them to length. A stop block clamped to the rip fence determines the length of the splines.

4 **Glue the miters.** Glue the splines into the spline slots in one mitered edge, then glue and clamp the mitered corner together.

Clamp a stop block to the rip fence to regulate the length of the splines.

Clamp the template to the stock as shown and rout the spline slots.

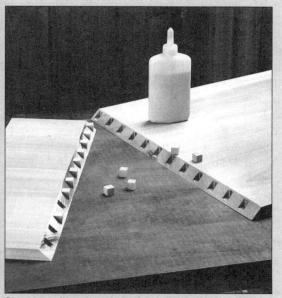

Glue the splines into their slots and clamp the miter.

COUNTRY ARMOIRE
by Randy Pease

This piece is an example of how furniture design can and should evolve with need. I asked my brother what he and his wife would like as a housewarming gift when they moved into an old farmhouse. Like most old farmhouses, theirs has little closet space. So they decided they'd like an armoire for their young daughter.

My mind turned to a dresser I always liked designed by William Draper, a cabinetmaker friend. As I thought about how my young niece would use the piece, it evolved into this armoire. With Draper's permission, I took the moldings and feet directly from his piece.

To make the armoire easier to move, I made it in two pieces. In the top section I installed a rod for hanging clothes; the bottom section contains three deep drawers.

I personalized this piece for my niece with decorative carvings on the doors, drawers, and rails of the chest. These are not difficult to carve, but they are entirely optional.

The chest is built of

pine boards. I used clear #1 pine for the sides and raised panels; the rest is constructed from #2 pine boards with tight knots. This stock is appropriate for an informal country piece such as this. It's relatively inexpensive and is readily available at the lumberyard already planed to ¾ inch thick or 1¼ inches thick

EXPLODED VIEW

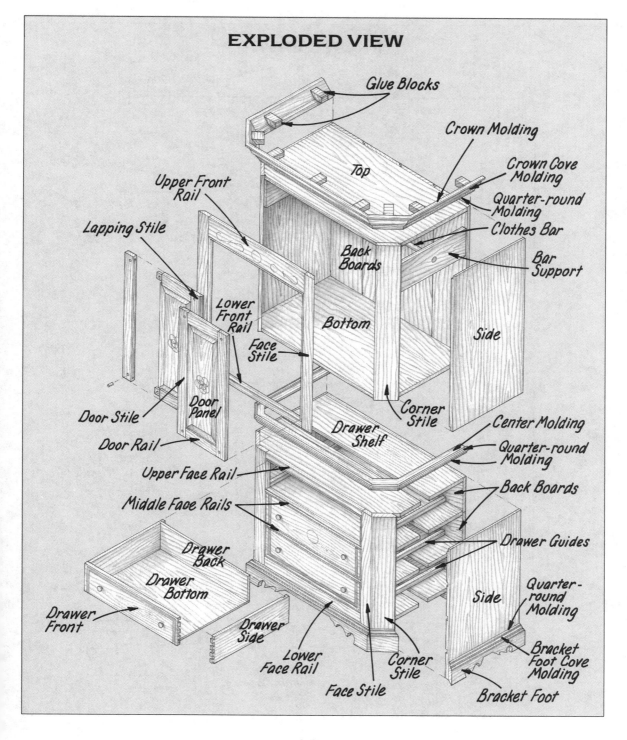

Glue Blocks

Crown Molding

Crown Cove Molding

Quarter-round Molding

Clothes Bar

Bar Support

Top

Upper Front Rail

Lapping Stile

Back Boards

Lower Front Rail

Face Stile

Bottom

Side

Door Stile

Door Panel

Door Rail

Corner Stile

Drawer Shelf

Center Molding

Quarter-round Molding

Upper Face Rail

Back Boards

Middle Face Rails

Drawer Guides

Drawer Back

Drawer Bottom

Drawer Front

Drawer Side

Side

Quarter-round Molding

Lower Face Rail

Corner Stile

Face Stile

Bracket Foot Cove Molding

Bracket Foot

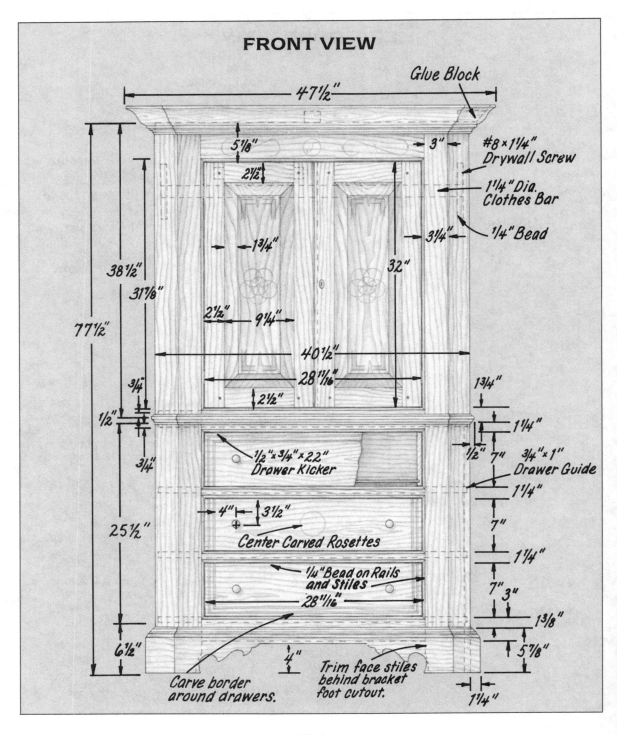

FRONT VIEW

Glue Block

47½"

3"

5⅛"

#8 × 1¼" Drywall Screw

2½"

1¼" Dia. Clothes Bar

¼" Bead

38½"

1¾"

32"

31⅞"

3¼"

2½" 9¼"

40½"

28¹¹⁄₁₆"

77½"

2½"

1¾"

3/4"

1¼"

1/2"

½" 7" 3/4" × 1" Drawer Guide

3/4"

½" × ¾" × 22" Drawer Kicker

1¼"

7"

4" 3½"

Center Carved Rosettes

25½"

1¼"

7"

¼" Bead on Rails and Stiles

28¹¹⁄₁₆"

1¾"

7" 3"

1⅜"

6½"

4"

5⅞"

Carve border around drawers.

Trim face stiles behind bracket foot cutout.

1¼"

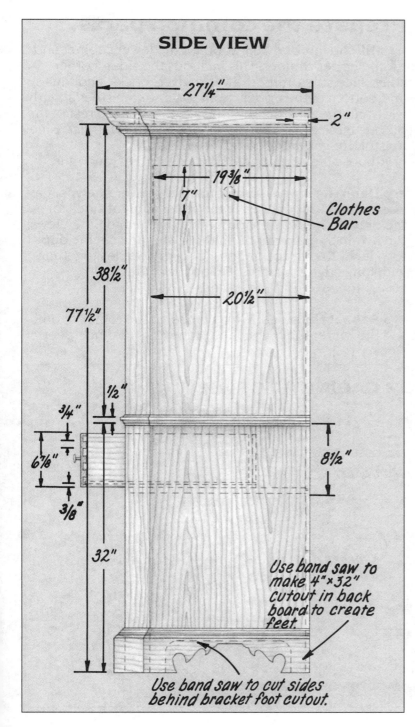

SIDE VIEW

27¼"

2"

19⅜"

7"

Clothes Bar

38½"

77½"

20½"

½"

¾"

6⅞"

8½"

3/8"

32"

Use band saw to make 4"×32" cutout in back board to create feet.

Use band saw to cut sides behind bracket foot cutout.

(5/4, or "five/quarters" stock). You can buy good quality ½-inch-thick stock for the drawers at the lumberyard. Carpenters often order this ½-inch stock as "door stop" because that's what they most commonly use it for. This means you can build the piece without a planer. Pine planes easily so you can cut out a lot of sanding by hand planing the surfaces before assembly. The result is a challenging piece you can build in a basic home workshop.

The lower cabinet and top cabinet are built separately, but because many of the parts require identical table saw setups, it makes sense to prepare them all at one time. Once you've cut the parts, you'll construct the lower cabinet and then the upper cabinet to fit on top.

If you carve the chest, as I did, it is best to carve the designs before attaching the pieces to the chest. For example, carve the top rail on the upper section before nailing and gluing it into place, and carve the drawer fronts before gluing up the drawer. The patterns for the carving are shown near each carved piece. Instructions for this technique are given in "Chip Carving" on page 402.

Prepare the common parts.

1 Mill the lumber. Mill wood for the lower cabinet and the upper cabinet. This includes the sides, corner stiles, face stiles, rails, drawer shelves, backs, and the top and bottom of the upper cabinet. Leave the stiles slightly wide and the rails slightly long for now. Cut the rest of the pieces to the dimensions given in the Materials list. Glue up stock to get wider boards if necessary.

Choose clear lumber for the sides, stiles, and rails.

2 Dado the lower cabinet for the drawer shelves. Lay out and rout dadoes in the lower cabinet sides for the drawer shelves as shown in the Front and Side Views. Put a ³/₄-inch-diameter bit in the router and set the depth to ³/₈ inch. To rout the dadoes, clamp the sides together with long edges touching. Guide the router with a straightedge to rout the dadoes.

3 Rabbet the sides. With a fence on the router or on the router table, rout a ³/₈-inch-wide × ³/₄-inch-deep

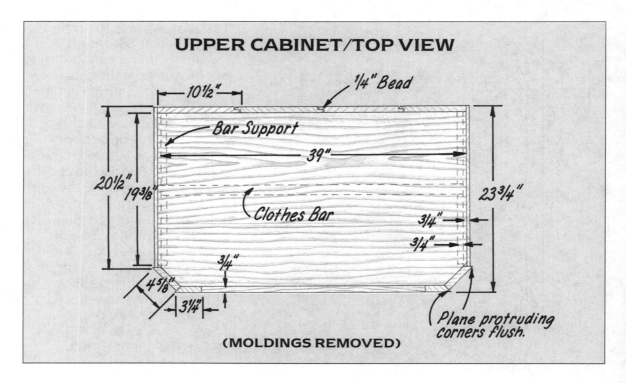

UPPER CABINET/TOP VIEW

¹/₄" Bead

10¹/₂"

Bar Support

39"

20¹/₂"
19³/₈"

Clothes Bar

23³/₄"

³/₄"

³/₄"

³/₄"

4⁵/₈"

3¹/₄"

Plane protruding corners flush.

(MOLDINGS REMOVED)

rabbet along the the sides to house the back. Cut a rabbet in the lower cabinet for its top and another rabbet of the same size in the upper cabinet for its top and bottom.

4 **Bevel the corner and face stiles.** All of the stiles are beveled along one edge, as shown in the Upper

MATERIALS LIST

Part	Dimension	Part	Dimension
Lower Cabinet		Sides (6)	$1/2" \times 6^7/8" \times 22"$
Sides (2)	$3/4" \times 20^1/2" \times 32"$	Backs (3)	$1/2" \times 6^1/4" \times 28^1/8"$
Corner stiles (2)	$3/4" \times 4^5/8" \times 32"$	Bottoms (3)	$1/4" \times 21^3/4" \times 28^1/8"$
Upper face rail	$3/4" \times 1^1/4" \times 29^3/8"$	**Door**	
Lower face rail	$3/4" \times 3" \times 29^3/8"$	Rails (4)	$3/4" \times 2^1/2" \times 11^3/4"$
Middle face rails (2)	$3/4" \times 1^1/4" \times 29^3/16"$	Stiles (3)	$3/4" \times 2^1/2" \times 31^7/8"$
Face stiles (2)	$3/4" \times 3^1/4" \times 32"$	Lapping stile	$3/4" \times 2^7/8" \times 31^7/8"$
Back boards (4)	$3/4" \times 8^1/2" \times 39^3/4"$	Panels (2)	$3/4" \times 10^1/4" \times 27^7/8"$
Drawer shelves (8)	$3/4" \times 10" \times 39^3/4"$		
Drawer guides (6)	$3/4" \times 1" \times 22"$	**HARDWARE**	
Drawer kickers (6)	$1/2" \times 3/4" \times 22"$	#8 × 1¼" drywall screws	
Upper Cabinet		#8 × 1" drywall screws	
Sides (2)	$3/4" \times 20^1/2" \times 38^1/2"$	4 no-mortise hinges. Available from Paxton	
Corner stiles (2)	$3/4" \times 4^5/8" \times 38^1/2"$	Hardware, Ltd., 7818 Bradshaw Rd., Upper	
Face stiles (2)	$3/4" \times 3^1/4" \times 38^1/2"$	Falls, MD 21156. Part #4168.	
Top/bottom (1 each)	$3/4" \times 22^1/4" \times 39^3/4"$	1 surface-mount cabinet lock. Available from	
Upper front rail	$3/4" \times 5^1/8" \times 29^3/16"$	Ball and Ball, 463 W. Lincoln Highway, Exton,	
Lower front rail	$3/4" \times 1^1/4" \times 29^3/16"$	PA 19341. Part #TGI-110.	
Back boards (4)	$3/4" \times 10^1/2" \times 38^1/2"$	8 brass knobs, 1¼" dia. Available from Horton	
Clothes bar	$1^1/4"$ dia. $\times 39^5/8"$	Brasses, Nooks Hill Rd., P.O. Box 95, Cromwell,	
Bar supports (2)	$3/4" \times 7" \times 19^3/8"$	CT 06416. Part #H-30.	
Moldings		As needed, 5d nails	
Crown molding stock	$3/4" \times 3^3/4" \times 9'$	As needed, 4d nails	
Crown cove molding stock	$3/4" \times 1^1/4" \times 8'$	As needed, 6d finishing nails	
Center molding stock	$3/4" \times 2^1/2" \times 8'$	As needed, 4d finishing nails	
Bracket foot cove stock	$5/8" \times 7/8" \times 8'$	As needed, ¾" brads	
Bracket foot stock	$1^1/4" \times 5" \times 8'$	As needed, 6d cut nails. Available from Tremont	
Quarter round stock (4)	$1/4" \times 1/4" \times 8'$	Nail Company, P.O. Box 111, Wareham,	
Drawers		MA 02571.	
Fronts (3)	$3/4" \times 6^7/8" \times 28^5/8"$		

Cabinet/Top View and Lower Cabinet/Top View. Set the table saw blade at 45 degrees and rip the stiles to width. Note that the widths given in the Materials List are for the outside surfaces of the stiles.

5 **Bead the rails, face stiles, and upper back pieces.** Cut ¼-inch-diameter beads on one edge of all four top and bottom rails and on all four face stiles, as shown in the Front View. Also cut beads on both edges of the

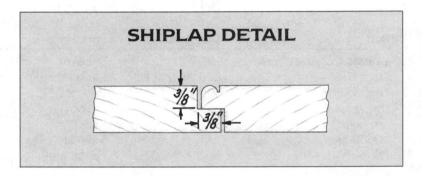

SHIPLAP DETAIL

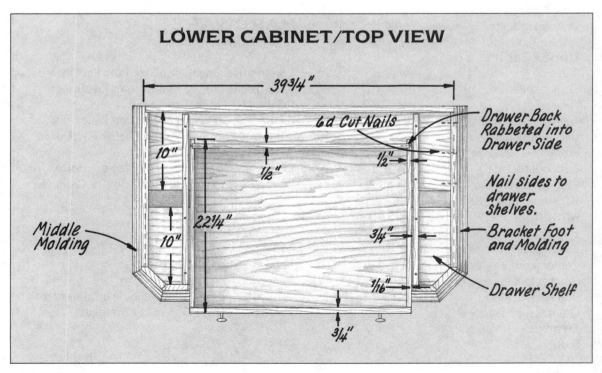

LOWER CABINET/TOP VIEW

two drawer divider rails in the lower cabinet, as shown in Drawer Rail Detail.

The back of the upper cabinet is ship-lapped together, and the seam between the joints is beaded, as shown in the Shiplap Detail. Rout the bead now, while you have the beading bit in the router.

After you have cut the bead, put a 3/8-inch piloted rabbeting bit in the router. Rabbet the back side of the beaded edges, then rabbet the unbeaded edge of the front side.

6 Miter beads on the face stiles. Lay out and miter the face stile bead as shown in the Front View. Cut the miter as explained in "Mitering a Beaded Frame" on

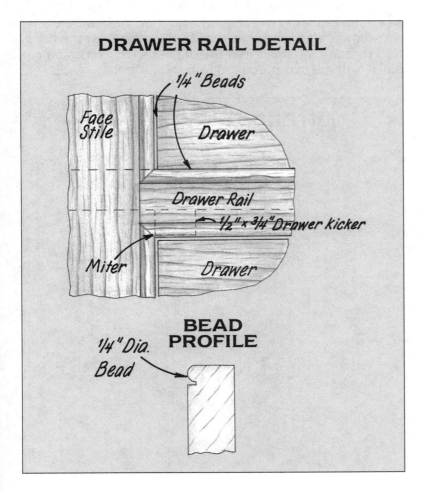

DRAWER RAIL DETAIL

1/4" Beads

Face Stile

Drawer

Drawer Rail

1/2" x 3/4" Drawer Kicker

Miter

Drawer

BEAD PROFILE

1/4" Dia. Bead

page 70. Remove the waste between the miters on the stiles with a router or a sharp chisel.

Assemble the upper and lower cabinets.

1 **Trim the drawer shelves.** Note that each drawer is supported by *two* drawer shelves, one in front and one in back. Cut a 45-degree angle on the front corners of the front shelves and on the upper cabinet top and bottom. Lay out the cuts so that the angled corner is as long as the inside face of the stile.

2 **Assemble the bottom cabinet.** Assemble and temporarily clamp the cabinet together. Make sure the rear drawer shelves are flush with the rabbet for the back. Nail through the sides into the drawer shelves with 6d cut nails. Nail the two-piece top into the rabbets.

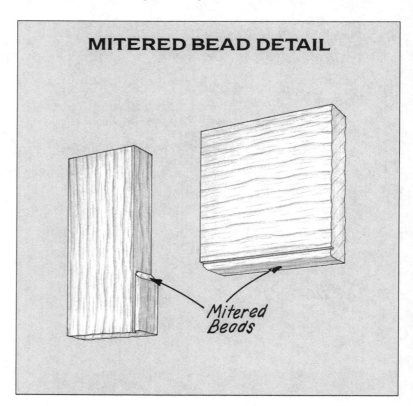

MITERED BEAD DETAIL

Mitered Beads

3 Install the back boards. The back of the lower cabinet is a series of horizontal boards, nailed into the rabbets. Set the cabinet on its face on a flat surface. Make sure the cabinet is square. Nail the back boards into the rabbets, beginning at the top. Drive 4d finishing nails into the rabbets, and 6d finishing nails into the drawer shelves. As you nail, check to make sure the cabinet remains square. Rip the last back board to fit the opening. Before nailing the last back board, cut a curve in it to create feet. The curve is shown as dotted lines at the base of the cabinet in the Front View.

4 Install the corner stiles. Lay the cabinet on its back. Glue the corner stiles to the sides and nail them to the drawer shelves with 6d cut nails. Glue the face stiles to the corner stiles and nail them to the drawer shelves.

At this point, the corners of the beveled stiles extend beyond the neighboring stiles, as shown in the Upper Cabinet/Top View. When the glue dries, trim these corners flush with a hand plane.

Cut the rails to fit between the stiles. Miter the beads to fit the miters you cut earlier on the face stiles, as shown in the Mitered Bead Detail. Glue and nail the face rails to the drawer shelves.

5 Install the drawer guides and kickers. Cut drawer guides and kickers to the dimensions given in the Materials List. Position the guides flush with the face stile, as shown in the Front View. Nail the guides into place with 6d finishing nails.

Nail the kickers to the bottom of the drawer shelves as shown. The kickers prevent the drawer from tilting down when it is opened.

6 Assemble the upper cabinet. At this point you've already milled most of the parts for the upper cabinet. Assembling this cabinet is much like assembling the lower cabinet.

Nail the sides to the top and bottom, as before. Check to make sure the cabinet is square. Lay the cabinet on its face, and nail the backs onto the sides, top, and bottom. Check to make sure the cabinet is square as you work.

Lay the cabinet on its back, and check again to make sure the cabinet is square. Glue the corner stiles to the

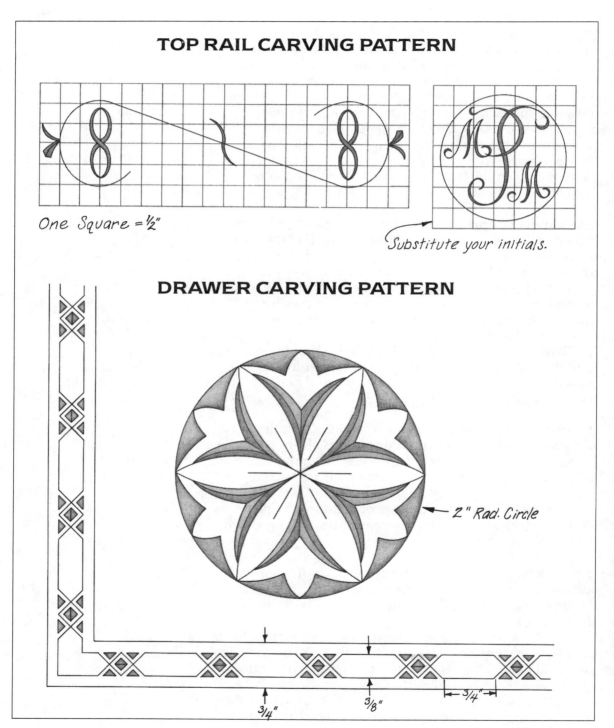

TOP RAIL CARVING PATTERN

One Square = ½"

Substitute your initials.

DRAWER CARVING PATTERN

2" Rad. Circle

3/4"

3/8"

3/4"

DOOR CARVING PATTERN

Remove shaded
areas and pencil
lines only.

3/4"

7/16"

Circles are 1"/16" rad.

sides and nail them to the top and bottom. Glue the face stiles to the corner stiles and nail them to the top and bottom. Trim the overhanging miters, as before. Cut the rails to fit between the stiles, as before.

Make and attach the molding.

There are three sets of moldings that wrap around the front and sides of this armoire. Each molding is built-up from several moldings: The top molding is built-up from four pieces, the center molding consists of three pieces, and the bracket feet are made from three moldings. Purchase the crown molding and the quarter-round molding at the lumberyard.

1 Mill the cove molding. All three sets of molding contain a shop-made ³/₈-inch-radius cove molding. Mill the coved parts to the sizes listed in the Materials List. Rout the cove on the router table with a ³/₈-inch-radius bit.

2 Make the glue blocks. A beveled glue block behind the molding supports the molding and makes it easier to install. Set the saw to rip a 45-degree bevel. Rip the bevel on a piece of stock about 1¹/₈ × 3 × 20 inches and then crosscut it into nine 2-inch-long blocks.

3 Install the upper moldings. Miter the crown cove molding to fit around the cabinet. Glue and nail it into place.

Attach the glue blocks to the top of the cabinet with glue and 5d common nails. Do this by attaching a glue block to support the middle and ends of the front stretch of crown molding and then attaching one block above each stile. Use the remaining blocks to support the ends of the crown molding that fits around the sides.

Miter the crown molding to fit around the front and side stiles and cut it flush with the back. Glue and nail the crown molding to the cove molding and to the glue blocks. For more on mitering crown molding, see "Mitering and Installing Crown Molding" on page 110.

Cut the quarter round to fit under the crown cove

Quick Tip: All of the moldings on the armoire are mitered at 22¹/₂ degrees. Cut the miters on some scrap first, and test the joint on the cabinet. If you are working on a non-adjustable miter box, you can still fine-tune the angle: Apply tape to the vertical surface against which you hold the molding.

MOLDING DETAIL

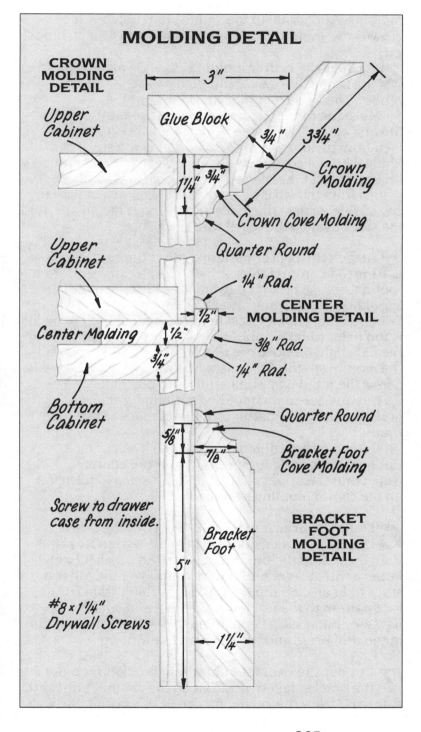

CROWN MOLDING DETAIL

Upper Cabinet

Glue Block

3"

3/4"   3³/₄"

1¹/₄"   3/4"

Crown Molding

Crown Cove Molding

Quarter Round

Upper Cabinet

¼" Rad.

CENTER MOLDING DETAIL

½"

Center Molding

½"

3/8" Rad.

3/4"

¼" Rad.

Bottom Cabinet

Quarter Round

5⅛"

7/8"

Bracket Foot Cove Molding

Screw to drawer case from inside.

Bracket Foot

BRACKET FOOT MOLDING DETAIL

5"

#8 x 1¼" Drywall Screws

1¼"

molding. Apply glue to the surface that touches the crown cove molding. Nail it into place with ³/₄-inch brads.

4 **Rabbet the center molding.** As shown in the Molding Detail, the center molding has a 2 × ¹/₂-inch rabbet. The upper cabinet sits on this rabbet.

Make the rabbet in two passes on the table saw. For the first cut, set the blade ¹/₄ inch high and the fence ¹/₂ inch from the outside of the blade. Run the stock over the blade with the coved edge against the fence. For the second cut, set the blade 2 inches high and set the fence ¹/₂ inch from the *inside* of the blade. Make the cut with the coved side against the fence and the cove facing up. Hold the stock against the fence with push sticks.

5 **Attach the center molding.** Miter the center molding to fit around the cabinet. Use a scrap of quarter round to gauge how far beyond the sides the molding should be. Temporarily attach the molding with #8 × 1-inch drywall screws. Test fit the upper cabinet. If the fit is too tight, trim the rabbet with a rabbeting plane. When the fit is right, remove the upper cabinet. Glue and nail the molding to the drawer shelves with 4d finishing nails. Screw the molding permanently into place.

Cut quarter-round molding to fit under the center molding. Nail the quarter round into place with ³/₄-inch brads.

Put the upper cabinet back on the lower cabinet. Cut quarter-round molding to fit over the center molding. Nail it into the upper cabinet only, pressing it down flat on the center molding as you go.

6 **Make the bracket feet.** Mill wood for the bracket feet to the dimensions given in the Materials List. Rout the feet to the profile shown in the Bracket Foot Pattern with a ¹/₄-inch-diameter roundover bit. Miter the stock to fit around the base of the cabinet. Transfer the foot pattern to the front and side feet and cut it with a jigsaw or band saw. Clean up the cut with a drum sander in the drill press and with files and sandpaper.

7 **Cut out the cabinet behind the bracket feet.** Set the bracket feet in position on the cabinet front and sides and trace their outlines. Cut to this layout line with a jigsaw, so that no wood can be seen behind the bracket foot cutout. At the same time, create feet in the lowest back board by making a 4-inch-high × 32-inch-long cutout centered along its bottom edge.

8 **Attach the bracket feet to the cabinet.** Glue the feet across the front of the cabinet and secure them from the inside with #8 × 1¼-inch drywall screws. From inside, attach the feet to the cabinet sides and to the corner stiles with #8 × 1¼-inch drywall screws.

9 **Cut and attach the bracket foot cove.** Miter, glue, and nail the coved bracket foot molding to the top of the bracket as shown in the Molding Detail. Miter the quarter-round molding that fits on top of the cove molding. Nail it into place with ¾-inch brads.

10 **Fill the nail holes.** Fill the nail holes in the moldings and in the cabinet. Sand the cabinet.

Make the drawers.

1 **Mill the parts.** Select clear wood for the drawer faces, but the wood for the sides and back can have a few

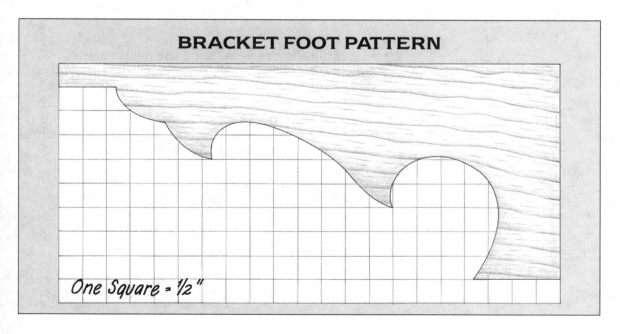

BRACKET FOOT PATTERN

One Square = ½"

small knots. Because of construction variations, dimensions for the drawer and door openings may differ slightly from those given. Measure directly from the cabinet for final dimensions. Cut the drawer parts to leave $1/8$ inch clearance above each drawer, and a total of $1/16$-inch side-to-side clearance.

2 Cut the dovetails. Lay out and cut the half-blind dovetails in the drawer fronts as shown in the Side View. For more on dovetailing, see "Cutting Half-Blind Dovetails" on page 155.

3 Dado the sides for the backs and dividers. The drawer backs are dadoed into the sides. All of the dadoes are $1/2$ inch wide and $1/4$ inch deep and are located $1/2$ inch from the back of the drawer. Rout them with a $1/2$-inch straight bit or cut them with a dado cutter in the table saw.

4 Cut the drawer bottom grooves. With a dado cutter in the table saw, cut a $1/4 \times 1/4$-inch groove in the drawer fronts and sides for the drawer bottoms. If you position the grooves as shown in the Side View, you can cut along the entire length of the drawer side and front. The dovetail will cover the groove when the drawer is assembled.

5 Assemble the drawers. Sand the inside of the drawer pieces. On a flat surface, glue the dovetails together. Attach the sides to the backs with glue and 4d common nails. Make sure the drawer is square. Slide the bottoms into the grooves from the back. When the glue dries, secure the bottoms by nailing through the bottoms into the drawer backs with a couple of 4d common nails.

6 Attach the pulls. Lay out and drill $1/4$-inch-diameter holes for the bolts that attach the wooden drawer pulls. Bolt the wooden pulls to the drawer faces.

Make the doors.

1 Mill the wood. Mill wood for the door stiles, rails, and panels to dimensions given in the Materials List. Pick

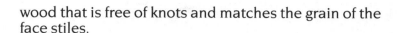

wood that is free of knots and matches the grain of the face stiles.

2 **Mortise the stiles.** Lay out mortises in the doors as shown in the Door Mortise and Tenon Layout. Note that the mortises are ¹/₁₆ inch deeper than the tenon length, to provide room for glue and to ensure a good fit at the shoulders. Rout the mortises with a fence attached to your plunge router. If you do not have a plunge router, drill a series of holes between the layout lines. Clean up to the edge of the layout lines with a chisel.

3 **Cut the tenons in the rails.** Lay out tenons as shown in the Door Mortise and Tenon Layout. Cut the tenons on the table saw. Slide the rails against a stop block to cross-cut the tenon shoulders. Cut the tenon cheeks with a tenoning jig, as explained in "Tenoning Jig" on page 375.

4 **Rout the panel grooves.** With a ¹/₄-inch straight bit in the router table, cut ⁹/₁₆-inch-deep grooves centered in the thickness of the rails and stiles. The grooves run

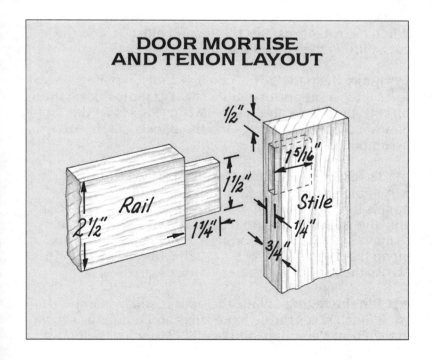

DOOR MORTISE AND TENON LAYOUT

Guide the rails and stiles against a fence as you rout the panel groove.

the entire length of the rails, but stop at the mortises in the stiles.

Begin the cut by lowering the stile over the bit. When the router reaches the second mortise, end the cut by lifting the end off the bit.

5 **Make the panels.** You can make raised panels on a router, a shaper, or a table saw. For more information on cutting raised panels, see "Raising Panels on the Table Saw" on page 200. Finish sand the panels before you assemble the door.

6 **Assemble the doors.** On a flat surface, glue and clamp together the door rails and stiles. Slip the panels into place as you pull the joints together. Do not glue the panels. Measure diagonally across the corners to make sure the door is square. Equal measurements mean the door is square. Make adjustments by clamping across the long measurement if necessary.

7 **Pin the tenons.** While the door is still in clamps, drill ¹/₄-inch holes through the stiles and tenons as shown in the Front View. Glue and tap ¹/₄ × ¹/₄-inch pegs into the holes to pin the tenons. Cut the pegs flush with the stiles.

8 **Rabbet the adjoining door stiles.** A lip on the front of the right door nests in a rabbet on the left door as shown in the Door Detail. This lip is quite common on older cabinets and was intended to keep out dust.

    With a rabbeting bit, rout a $3/8 \times 3/8$-inch rabbet on the front of the left door stile. To create the tongue on the right door, cut a $3/8 \times 3/8$-inch rabbet on the back of the door stile.

9 **Fit and hang the doors.** I always build my doors to the exact dimension of the door opening, and then I trim the assembled door with a hand plane or jointer for a custom fit. So trim the doors for about $1/16$-inch play along each edge.

    Hang the doors on no-mortise hinges. These hinges don't require mortises. Simply position the door and hinge, and screw them into place.

    Drill a hole for the keyhole, and screw the lock to the back of the doors.

10 **Attach the clothes bar.** Closet rods can be purchased at most home supply stores. Cut boards for the clothes bar supports to the dimensions given in the Materials List. Lay out and drill holes for the bar in each support as shown in the Side View. Cut the bar to length, and set it in place when you screw the supports to the sides of the cabinet. Attach the supports with $\#8 \times 1 1/4$-inch drywall screws.

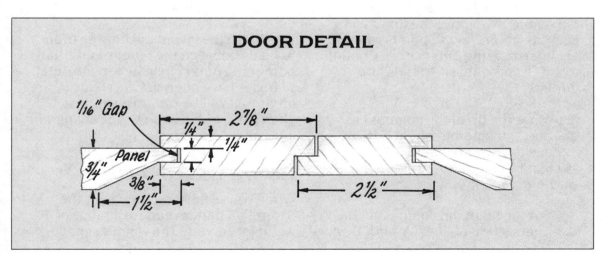

DOOR DETAIL

CHIP CARVING

Chip carving is a simple art that anyone can master. All you need is a compass and pencil, a good knife, and the will to create.

The projects in this book that include chip carving provide the patterns that make layout easy. But you can also design your own pattern. The following steps show you how to lay out a simple rosette. A rosette pattern is made up of three elements: circles, arcs, and triangles. To design your own "custom" rosette, simply add, subtract, or reposition the elements.

Lay out a rosette.

1 Lay out lines "A" and "B" on a piece of graph paper. Put the tip of your compass at the point where "A" and "B" intersect and draw the outer circle of the rosette. The radius is determined by the size of the area that you will carve. When you've drawn the outer circle, move the tip of the compass to one of the points where line "A" intersects the outer circle. Swing an arc from that point, and then move the tip of the compass to one of the points where the arc intersects the outer circle. Continue to swing arcs until six "petals" are formed.

2 Move the tip of the compass to one of the points where line "B" intersects the outer circle, and begin swinging a second set of arcs to create six more petals.

3 Put the tip of the compass at the intersection of lines "A" and "B", and adjust it to draw a circle that passes through the point where the two sets of petals intersect. Then draw another circle creating a "ring".

4 What you have just drawn would make an excellent carving pattern. Just to make things interesting, however, let's go a step further. Erase the small petals in the center of the rosette and the lines within the ring. Draw lines "C" and "D." With the compass set to the radius of the outer circle, redraw the small petals beginning from the points where "C" and "D" meet the outer circle.

5 Next, draw the inner triangles and enlarge the outer petals. Put the tip of the compass at the center point of the rosette, and draw a small circle to define the size of the innermost triangles. Draw these triangles and the triangles within the ring as shown. When the triangles have been drawn, enlarge the outer petals by drawing lines along their edges as shown.

6 Finish the layout by drawing triangles between the outer petals that border the outer circle. When the outer triangles have been drawn, shade in the areas that will be carved away. This gives you an idea of how the carving will appear on the wood.

Carve the rosette.

When you've finished laying out the rosette on paper, prepare a piece of wood for carving. The wood's surface

BASIC ROSETTE LAYOUT

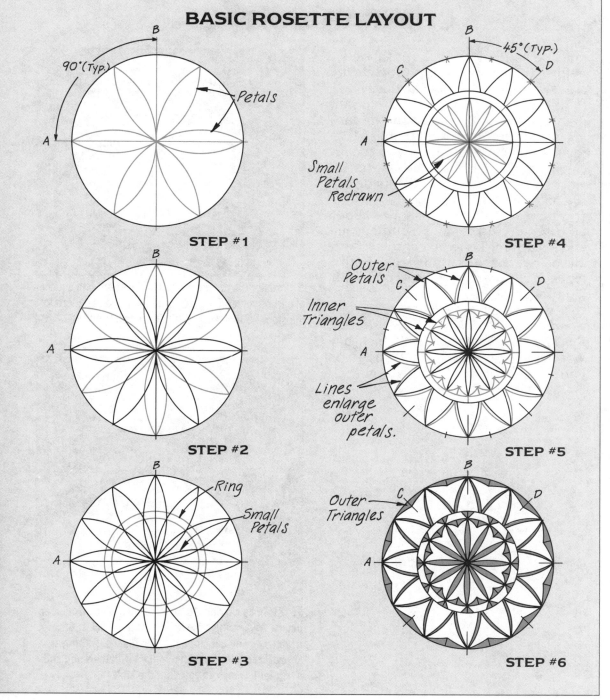

90°(Typ.)

B

A

Petals

STEP #1

B

A

STEP #2

B

Ring

Small
Petals

A

STEP #3

B

45°(Typ.)

C

D

A

Small
Petals
Redrawn

STEP #4

Outer
Petals

C

B

D

Inner
Triangles

A

Lines
enlarge
outer
petals.

STEP #5

Outer
Triangles

C

B

D

A

STEP #6

(continued)

CHIP CARVING—*Continued*

must be hand planed and/or sanded before you do any carving. Chip carving creates little ridges that can easily be broken by sanding. Only touch-up sanding should be attempted after the carving is finished. To prevent damage to the rosette while carving, always begin carving at the middle of the rosette and gradually move toward the outside of the pattern.

There are two types of knives generally used in chip carving: a cutting knife and a stabbing knife. To cut this rosette all you need is the cutting knife. Both types of chip carving knives come with handles and blades in many different styles, and are available from several woodworking catalogs. The Swiss cutting knife shown here is available from Woodcraft, 210 Wood County Industrial Park, P.O. Box 1686, Parkersburg, WV 26102 (Part #05Z11).

1 Transfer the rosette pattern to the stock with a piece of carbon paper. Tape the carbon paper and pattern to the stock so that the pattern doesn't shift during transfer.

2 Begin by carving along one edge of the small inner petals. Always angle the knife at approximately 65 degrees as you cut along the layout lines. As shown, always keep your thumb in contact with the wood and use it for leverage as you draw the knife.

3 Complete a petal by cutting along its opposite edge and popping out the chip. Notice that the knife has to cut deeper as the petal layout gets wider.

5 Finish up the rosette by carving the outer petals and triangles. Carve these shapes with the same techniques you used in carving the little inner petals and triangles.

4 Next, carve out the little triangles along the ring. First jab the knife into the wood along the ridge that separates a pair of triangles. Then cut along the remaining two sides of each triangle and pop out the chip. Always keep the blade angled at approximately 65 degrees.

6 When the carving is finished, give the rosette a light sanding to remove the layout lines. If any part of the carving chips while you are sanding, simply glue the chip back into place.

BEDSIDE CHEST

by Milford Yoder

This little chest was passed on to me by my mother, and I imagine she bought it soon after the turn of the century. Chests like this were common bedroom furniture in the days before running water. I'd get up in the morning and wash up in a basin of water that sat on top of it.

Today, this little chest is still a versatile piece of furniture. Alongside my bed it is just the right height for a reading lamp, while the storage space it offers is perfect for underwear or pajamas. There's even a space for reading matter behind the lower door. We used to have it near the bathroom where the towel rack was a welcome feature, and the drawers served to hold toiletries.

Pieces like this one were commonly made of red oak or chestnut, but they would be attractive in any domestic hardwood. Use a wood that suits the space it will occupy. Although the original is built from solid lumber, 1/4-inch plywood could be used in any of the places where 1/4-inch stock is called for.

The case is a traditional structure composed of a system of frames held together by mortise-and-tenon joints. The sides and back are frame-and-panel, while the web frames which carry the drawers are simple frames. The molding detail supporting the top is another frame, and the little door is also a frame-and-panel. There are three different versions of the mortise-and-tenon joint in the piece.

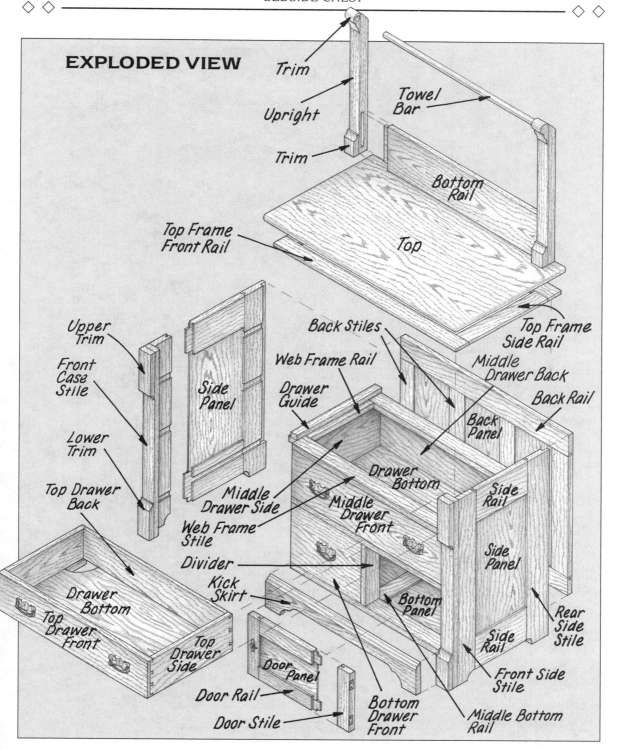

EXPLODED VIEW

Trim

Upright

Trim

Towel Bar

Bottom Rail

Top

Top Frame Front Rail

Top Frame Side Rail

Upper Trim

Front Case Stile

Lower Trim

Top Drawer Back

Side Panel

Back Stiles

Web Frame Rail

Drawer Guide

Middle Drawer Back

Back Rail

Back Panel

Middle Drawer Side

Drawer Bottom

Middle Drawer Front

Web Frame Stile

Side Rail

Side Panel

Divider

Drawer Bottom

Top Drawer Front

Top Drawer Side

Kick Skirt

Bottom Panel

Rear Side Stile

Side Rail

Door Panel

Door Rail

Door Stile

Bottom Drawer Front

Middle Bottom Rail

Front Side Stile

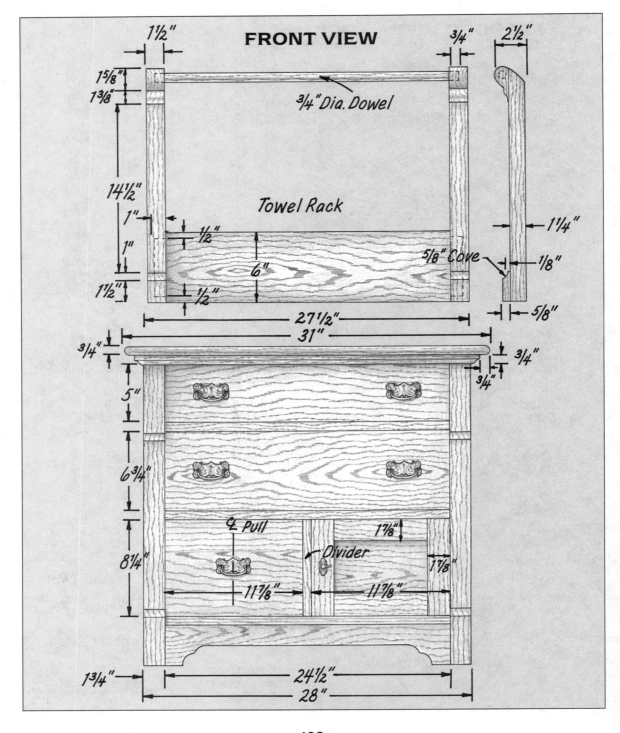

FRONT VIEW

1½"

¾"

2½"

1⅝"

1⅜"

¾"Dia. Dowel

14½"

Towel Rack

1"

½"

6"

1¼"

5/8" Cove

1/8"

1"

1½"

½"

27½"

5/8"

31"

¾"

¾"

¾"

5"

6¾"

1⅞"

⅊ Pull

Divider

1⅞"

8¼"

11⅞"

11⅞"

1¾"

24½"

28"

Make the frames.

As noted, the case is made up of a number of frames. Since all the frames have many steps in common, it is easier to make all of them at once. This saves machine setup time and can increase your accuracy.

1 **Cut the stock to size.** Mill the stock for the sides, back, web frames, and door to the sizes listed in the Materials List. There are a lot of parts, so label them all to help keep things straight. Write the name on each piece as you cut it to size. Always put the mark on the inside or bottom face of each piece. This serves as a guide for some of the following machine operations. It

Quick Tip: Cutting multiple parts to the same length is easy with an extension fence screwed to your table saw's miter gauge. Simply clamp a stop block to the fence at the appropriate distance from the blade and hold the pieces against it as you cut.

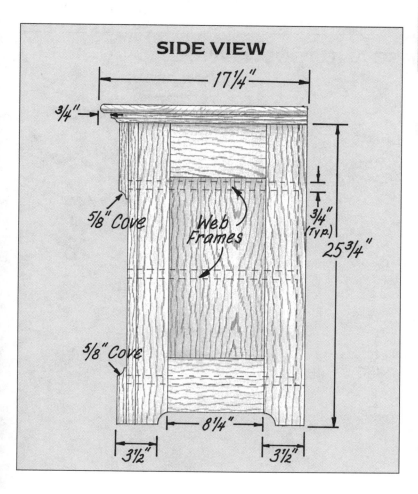

SIDE VIEW

17¼"

¾"

⅝" Cove

Web Frames

¾" (Typ.)

25¾"

⅝" Cove

8¼"

3½"

3½"

also means you won't have to sand the marks off, as they will be hidden inside the cabinet.

2 **Cut the panel grooves.** The panels for the sides, the back, and the door all fit into grooves cut into the rails and stiles. The front and back stiles of the web frames also have full-length grooves for the rail stub tenons. In addition, the bottom web frame rails get grooves cut into them to accommodate the case bottom. Be sure to cut grooves in both edges of the middle rail as shown in the Web Frame Detail.

Set up a dado cutter on the table saw $1/4$ inch wide $\times$ $1/2$ inch high. Set the fence so the groove will be centered on the pieces. Run all the pieces with their marked side against the fence. This will assure that the grooves will be

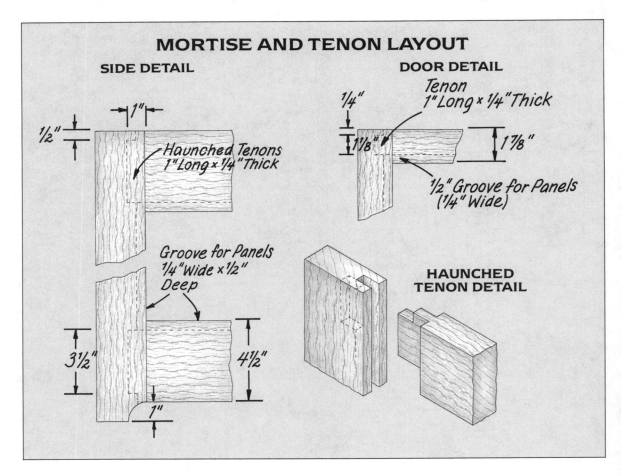

MORTISE AND TENON LAYOUT

SIDE DETAIL

DOOR DETAIL

1"

$1/2$"

Haunched Tenons
1" Long × $1/4$"Thick

$1/4$"

Tenon
1" Long × $1/4$"Thick

$1$$1/8$"

1$7/8$"

$1/2$" Groove for Panels
($1/4$" Wide)

Groove for Panels
$1/4$"Wide × $1/2$" Deep

HAUNCHED
TENON DETAIL

$3$$1/2$"

$4$$1/2$"

1"

aligned on all four sides of the frame even if they are not exactly centered.

3 **Mortise the stiles.** The joints in the sides and the door are made up of haunched tenons and mortises.

MATERIALS LIST

Part	Dimension	Part	Dimension
Side Frames		Middle back	$1/2" \times 5^7/8" \times 24^1/2"$
Side rails (4)	$3/4" \times 4^1/2" \times 10^1/4"$	Drawer bottoms (2)	$1/4" \times 13^1/4" \times 24"$
Front stiles (2)	$3/4" \times 3^1/2" \times 25^3/4"$	Bottom front	$3/4" \times 8^1/8" \times 11^7/8"$
Rear stiles (2)	$3/4" \times 2^3/4" \times 25^3/4"$	Bottom sides (2)	$1/2" \times 8^1/8" \times 13^1/2"$
Side panels (2)	$1/4" \times 9^1/8" \times 17^9/16"$	Bottom back	$1/2" \times 7^3/8" \times 11^7/8"$
Top Frame		Drawer bottom	$1/4" \times 13^1/4" \times 11^3/8"$
Front rail/back rail (1 each)	$3/4" \times 2^1/8" \times 29^1/2"$	**Door**	
Side rails (2)	$3/4" \times 2^1/8" \times 14^1/2"$	Rails (2)	$3/4" \times 1^7/8" \times 10^1/8"$
Back Frame		Stiles (2)	$3/4" \times 1^7/8" \times 8^1/4"$
Back rails (2)	$3/4" \times 2^1/2" \times 27^1/4"$	Panel	$1/4" \times 5^3/8" \times 9"$
Back stiles (4)	$3/4" \times 2^1/2" \times 18^1/4"$	**Towel Rack**	
Back panels (3)	$1/4" \times 6^3/4" \times 18^1/4"$	Uprights (2)	$1^1/4" \times 1^1/2" \times 20"$
Web Frames		Bottom rail	$3/4" \times 6" \times 26^1/2"$
Rails (6)	$3/4" \times 2" \times 11^1/2"$	Towel bar	$3/4"$ dia. $\times 26"$
Stiles (6)	$3/4" \times 2" \times 27"$	Trim (2)	$5/8" \times 1^1/2" \times 2^1/2"$
Middle bottom rail	$3/4" \times 2^1/4" \times 11^1/2"$	Trim (2)	$1^1/4" \times 1^1/2" \times 3"$
Bottom panels (2)	$1/4" \times 11^1/2" \times 11^3/8"$	Mounting brackets (2)	$3/4" \times 1^1/2" \times 12"$
Drawer guides (6)	$3/4" \times 1" \times 13^3/4"$		
Case			
Top	$3/4" \times 17^1/4" \times 31"$		
Front stiles (2)	$3/4" \times 1^3/4" \times 25^3/4"$		
Upper trim (2)	$3/4" \times 1^3/4" \times 6^1/2"$		
Lower trim (2)	$3/4" \times 1^3/4" \times 4^3/4"$		
Divider	$3/4" \times 2" \times 8^1/4"$		
Kick skirt	$3/4" \times 4^1/4" \times 26^1/2"$		
Drawers			
Top front	$3/4" \times 4^7/8" \times 24^1/2"$		
Top sides (2)	$1/2" \times 4^7/8" \times 13^1/2"$		
Top back	$1/2" \times 4^1/8" \times 24^1/2"$		
Middle front	$3/4" \times 6^5/8" \times 24^1/2"$		
Middle sides (2)	$1/2" \times 6^5/8" \times 13^1/2"$		

HARDWARE

3 flathead wood screws, #6 $\times$ 5/8"

As needed, #8 $\times$ 1 1/4" brass flathead wood screws

As needed, #10 $\times$ 5/8" roundhead wood screws

As needed, #8 $\times$ 2" drywall screws

As needed, #8 $\times$ 1 1/2" drywall screws

As needed, #8 $\times$ 1 1/4" drywall screws

5 Victorian drawer pulls. Available from Anglo-American Brass Co., P.O. Drawer 9487, San Jose, CA 95157. Part #P-3.

4 tabletop fasteners. Available from Constantine's, 2050 Eastchester Rd., Bronx, NY 10461. Part #96N4.

This means that one portion of the tenon is smaller, fitting into the groove cut for the panels, while the main portion penetrates deeper into the stile, providing additional strength. The tenons in the back and web frames are short, and fit into simple grooves that you'll cut later.

Lay out the mortises on the side and door stiles as shown in the Mortise and Tenon Layout. Drill a series of adjacent holes between the layout lines. Clean up to the layout lines with a chisel.

4 Cut the tenons. Cut the tenons on the side frame rails, door frame rails, web frame rails, and back stiles with the dado cutter on the table saw. All the tenons run the full width of the stock.

You'll make a number of cuts to create the tenon, and one more to create the haunch.

Cut the tenons for the side frames and door frames first. Put a ³/₈-inch-wide dado cutter in your table saw. Adjust the blade height to remove about ¹/₄ inch. Test the setup on a piece of scrap the same thickness as the rails. Make a cut on each face of the scrap, and fit the resulting

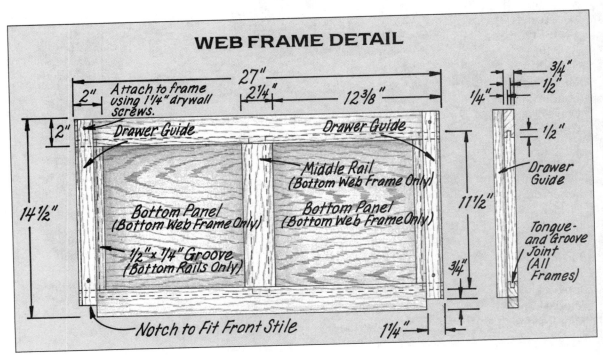

WEB FRAME DETAIL

Attach to frame using 1¼" drywall screws.

27"
2"
2¼"
12³/₈"
3/4"
1/2"
1/4"
1/2"

Drawer Guide   Drawer Guide

2"

Middle Rail
(Bottom Web Frame Only)

14½"

Bottom Panel
(Bottom Web Frame Only)

Bottom Panel
(Bottom Web Frame Only)

11½"

Drawer Guide

½" x ¼" Groove
(Bottom Rails Only)

Tongue-
and Groove
Joint
(All
Frames)

3/4"

Notch to Fit Front Stile

1¼"

tenon into a mortise. Make any necessary adjustments until you have a tenon the proper thickness.

Once you've adjusted the depth of cut, set the rip fence to control the length of the tenon. Position the fence so that it's 1 inch from the outside of the blade. Guide the end of a rail against the fence with the miter gauge to cut away part of the waste. Reposition the rail and make as many cuts as necessary to remove the rest of the waste. Flip the board over and repeat. Cut the door and side frame tenons.

Reset the fence to cut $\frac{1}{2}$-inch-long tenons on the back stiles and web frame rails.

5 Cut the haunches. Only the side and door frame tenons are haunched. Create the haunch by cutting a notch in the existing tenons.

Position the fence $\frac{5}{8}$ inch from the far side of the blade; set the blade height to $\frac{1}{2}$ inch. Stand the rails on edge and cut a notch in the tenons.

6 Sand and finish the panels. Use the Materials List as a guide when cutting the panels. Cut the panels to fit the actual frames, and then trim $\frac{1}{8}$ inch from one edge of each board. This will allow the panel to expand in humid weather.

Finish sand the panels, and apply your favorite wood finish before assembling the frames. Prefinishing keeps glue from sticking to the panel. It also ensures that sections that are exposed when the panel shrinks are finished.

7 Notch the web frame stiles. The front web frame stiles are notched as shown in the Web Frame Detail. When assembled, the notch will wrap around the front stiles. Lay out these notches on the stiles as shown in the Web Frame Detail. Set the blade on your table saw to $\frac{3}{4}$ inch high. Set the rail on edge and use the miter gauge to guide it past the blade to make the shoulder cut. Use the fence as a stop to cut all the stiles the same. Complete the notch by cutting off the waste with a band saw.

8 Test fit the frames. Assemble the frames and panels without glue to check the way the parts go together. Note that because the side stiles are different widths,

Guide the router with the fence attachment to rout the rabbet for the back.

there is a definite right and left side. Be sure to make one of each.

Make any necessary adjustments. Mark all the joints so you can reassemble them properly; then disassemble the frames.

9 **Assemble the frames.** Apply glue to the tenons and mortises. Avoid getting glue in the panel grooves. Clamp the frames together and check to make sure they're square by measuring diagonally from corner to corner. If the measurements are equal, the frames are square. Make sure the frames are flat and that the stiles are not bending from excess clamping pressure.

10 **Make and attach the drawer guides.** Two drawer guides attach to the top of each web frame. The guides are simple strips of wood that keep the drawers from bumping into the front stiles. Mill the guides to the size given in the Materials List. Glue and screw the guides to the frames with #8 × 1 ¼-inch drywall screws. For now, attach a guide to only the left side of the lowest web. You'll add the other guide later.

11 **Dado the sides.** The web frames fit into dadoes cut in the sides. Mount a ³/₄-inch-wide dado cutter

414

on your table saw and set the blade to cut a ¼-inch-deep groove. Note that the dado should not cut into the panel.

Guide the sides against the rip fence to cut the dadoes.

12 **Rabbet for the back.** The back fits into a rabbet joint in the sides. Because it is a stopped rabbet, it's easiest to rout it. Put a ¾-inch-diameter straight bit in your router. Adjust the router to cut ⅜ inch deep, and set the fence attachment so that the router cuts a groove ¾ inch wide. Rout the rear edge of each side. Stop the cut 3½ inches from the bottom of each side.

13 **Cut the feet.** Lay out the curved feet on the sides as shown in the Side View. Either use a compass or find an appropriately sized tin can to draw the curves. Cut out the feet on the band saw.

Make the case.

1 **Make the top.** Mill the wood for the top to the size listed in the Materials List. Glue up narrower boards if necessary. Once the top is cut to its finished size, soften the edges with a hand plane. When planing end grain, a low-angled block plane works best. Finish sand the top surface and edges.

2 **Test fit the case.** Assemble and clamp the case together to check the fit of all the joints. Check to make sure the case is square. Make any adjustments necessary, and mark the joints for reassembly. Disassemble the case to prepare for glue-up.

3 **Glue up the case.** Spread glue on the web frame rails where they will contact the sides. Avoid getting glue on the panels. Place the web frames in their proper places then clamp the case together. Check across the diagonals to make sure it is square. Wipe off any glue drips.

4 **Attach the back.** When the glue dries, remove the clamps from the case and check the fit of the back. If necessary, trim the back with a hand plane until it fits snugly. Glue and clamp it in place.

Quick Tip: When edge-gluing boards, clean up the excess glue before it cures fully. About 15 minutes after you've applied the glue, the excess glue will form a skin and turn rubbery. Slice the excess glue off with a chisel, glue scraper, or putty knife.

Guide the stock against the fence with a square piece of plywood to rout the coves.

5 **Make the front stiles.** Mill wood for the front stiles and trim blocks to the sizes specified in the Materials List. The trim blocks attach to the front stiles as shown in the Front Detail.

Make the curved cutouts on the trim with a ⅝-inch-radius core box bit or roundover bit in your table-mounted router. Guide the cut against both the fence and a piece of plywood, as shown in the photo. Make the cut in several passes. Glue and clamp the trim to the stiles.

6 **Make the kick skirt.** Mill wood for the kick skirt to the size specified in the Materials List. The kick skirt is mortised and tenoned to the front stiles, as shown in the Front Detail. Lay out the joints and cut them as before. Check to be sure the length of the kick skirt from shoulder to shoulder matches the length of the web frame from notch to notch.

7 **Shape the kick skirt.** Make a template for the foot curve from plywood as shown in the Front Detail. Trace the template to lay out the curve on both ends of the skirt. Cut the feet out on the band saw. Cut an ogee along the top of the skirt with a ¼-inch-radius ogee cutter in your table-mounted router.

8 **Assemble the front.** Glue and clamp the front stiles to the kick skirt. When the glue dries, glue and clamp the assembly to the front of the cabinet. Hand plane the top of the front stiles flush with the top of the case if necessary.

9 **Attach the divider.** The divider which separates the door from the lower drawer is simply screwed into place. Position the door/drawer divider in the center of the lower opening. From below the cabinet, drill $^3/_{32}$-inch pilot holes for #8 × 2-inch drywall screws. Screw the divider into place. Repeat from above, drilling the pilot holes at an angle. Attach the remaining drawer guide behind the divider from underneath.

10 **Make the top frame.** Mill wood for the top frame pieces to the sizes in the Materials List. Join the

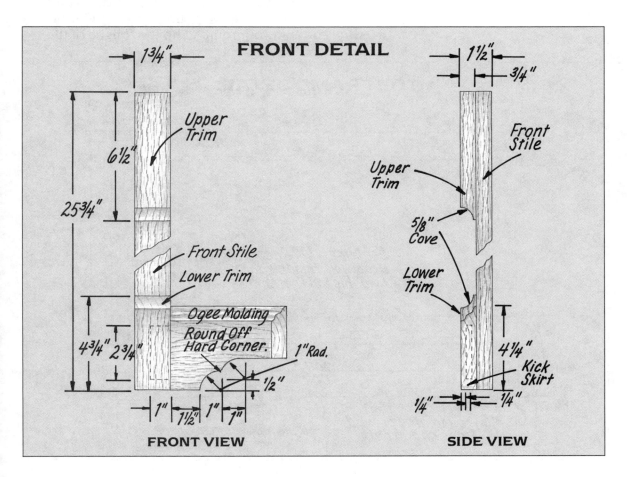

FRONT DETAIL

Upper Trim

Front Stile

Upper Trim

5/8" Cove

Front Stile

Lower Trim

Lower Trim

Ogee Molding
Round Off Hard Corner.

1" Rad.

Kick Skirt

FRONT VIEW

SIDE VIEW

corners with mortise-and-tenon joints, as shown in the Top Frame Detail.

After the frame is assembled, rout a 1/4-inch-radius ogee in the front and side edges.

11 **Attach the top frame.** Set the frame on the case flush with the back. Measure at the sides to get an even overhang. Drill and countersink pilot holes; then mount the top frame to the case with #8 × 1 1/2-inch drywall screws.

12 **Attach the top.** The top needs to be attached in a way that allows the wood to expand and contract with changes in the humidity. Attach the top with commercially available tabletop fasteners, listed in the Materials List. Rout a 1/8-inch-wide × 1/4-inch-deep table-top fastener groove on the inside edge of the top frame with a wing cutter in your router. Slip the tongue of the

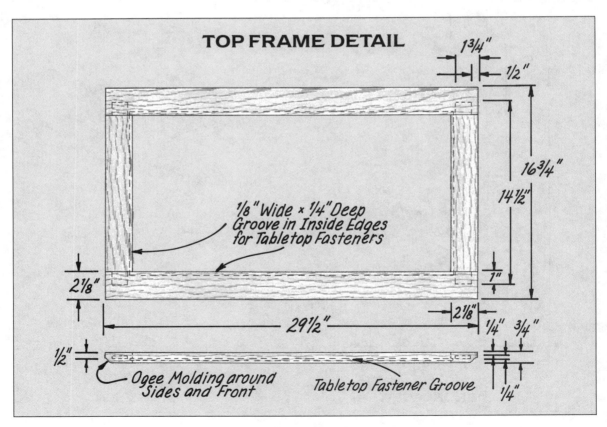

TOP FRAME DETAIL

1/8" Wide × 1/4" Deep Groove in Inside Edges for Tabletop Fasteners

1 3/4"

1/2"

16 3/4"

14 1/2"

1"

2 1/8"

29 1/2"

2 1/8"

1/4" 3/4"

1/2"

1/4"

Ogee Molding around Sides and Front

Tabletop Fastener Groove

fastener into the groove, and screw the body of the fastener underneath the top with #10 × ⅝-inch round-head wood screws.

Make the drawers.

Aside from how good the cabinet looks, the most important thing is how well it works, especially the action of the drawers. For the drawers to work perfectly, they must fit well in the case. Use the dimensions in the Materials List as a guide, but cut the drawer parts to fit their actual openings. Cut the parts to fit snugly, but not tightly, and you can plane or sand them for a perfect fit. Ideally there will be about a 1/16-inch gap above and to both sides of the drawer front.

1 Cut the parts to size. Mill the drawer fronts to the exact size of the openings. Cut the drawer backs to

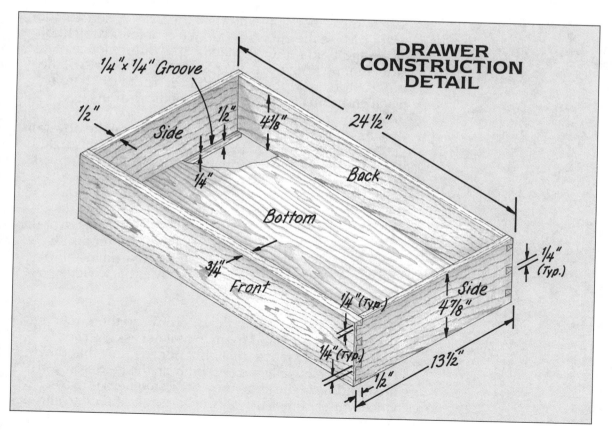

the same length as the front; cut the sides to the same width as the front. The other dimensions should match those in the Materials List.

2 Cut the joints. Lay out the dovetails as shown in the Drawer Construction Detail. The dovetails in the original piece were cut by machine. If you have a router jig to make the dovetails, great! If not, cut the dovetails by hand as shown in "Cutting Through Dovetails" on page 81 and "Cutting Half-Blind Dovetails" on page 155.

The fronts are joined with half-blind dovetails while the backs are joined with through dovetails. Space the dovetails as shown in the Drawer Construction Detail.

Note that the drawer backs are ³/₄ inch narrower than the sides so that the bottoms can slide in after the drawers are assembled. Lay out the back joints so that the top edges of the sides and the back are flush.

3 Rout the bottom grooves. Rout the bottom grooves to the dimensions shown in the Drawer Construction Detail. Make the cut with a ¹/₄-inch-diameter straight bit in a hand-held router, guided by the router's fence attachment. Rout the side grooves the full length of the sides. Stop the groove in the drawer front ¹/₄ inch from each end. Finish sand the inside of the drawers.

4 Assemble the drawers. Spread glue on the dovetails and fit the drawers together. Clamp the joints tight. Measure across the diagonals to check that the drawers are square. Set the drawers aside to allow the glue to dry.

5 Make the drawer bottoms. Cut the bottoms to fit the drawer, using the dimensions in the Materials List as a guide. Finish sand the drawer bottoms and install them. Screw each bottom to the drawer back with a #6 × ⁵/₈-inch flathead wood screw.

6 Fit the drawers. Put the drawers into their openings, and plane or sand them to fit if necessary. The drawers should move freely, but not so freely that they can become misaligned and bind on the guides. If you are building in the summer, a little snugness is okay. Once winter comes the drawers are guaranteed to shrink.

Leave a little more space for expansion if you are building in the winter.

To get a whisper-smooth glide, give a coat of paste wax to the drawer sides and the frame they are running on.

Install the door.

1 Fit and sand the door. Check to see how well the door fits the opening. There should be a $^{1}/_{16}$-inch gap around the entire door. Plane the door, if needed.

2 Hang the door. Lay out the hinges according to the dimensions given in the Front View. Align one leaf of each hinge with its layout line on the door. Trace around the leaf with a sharp knife. Cut away the wood inside the incised lines with a chisel until the hinge leaf is set flush into the door. Repeat on the case. Drill pilot holes for the hinge screws and hang the door.

Make the towel rack.

1 Make the stiles. Mill the wood for the stiles and trim blocks to the sizes given in the Materials List. Cut the cove in the lower trim as before. To make clamping easier, cut the upper trim to shape after you glue it in place. Glue the trim to the stiles.

2 Shape the upper trim. Cut the upper appliqués to shape on the band saw. The profile is shown in the Towel Rack Detail.

3 Cut the joints. Lay out and cut the mortises as shown in the Towel Rack Detail. Drill a $^{3}/_{4}$-inch-diameter hole for the towel bar. Cut matching tenons on the rail.

4 Make the rail, hanger bar, and mounting brackets. Mill wood for the rail and attachment brackets to the sizes listed in the Materials List.

5 Glue up the towel rack. Test fit the towel rack, and make any necessary adjustments. Apply glue to the joints and assemble the rack. Clamp and make sure it's square.

6 **Attach the mounting brackets.** Drill holes in the brackets as specified in the Towel Rack Detail. Attach the brackets to the towel rack with #8 × 1 1/4-inch brass flathead wood screws.

Finish the chest.

1 **Apply finish.** Finish sand the entire piece, and apply your favorite wood finish. Do not finish the inside of the case or the outside of the drawers, as they might stick together. Finish the inside of the drawers with shellac to keep them smelling sweet over the years.

2 **Attach the towel rack.** Center the towel rack on the case. Drill 3/32-inch pilot holes through the lowest holes on the attachment brackets. Screw the rack in place with #8 × 1 1/4-inch brass wood screws as shown in the Back Detail.

3 **Attach the hardware.** Mount the hardware as shown in the Front View. The Materials List gives a source

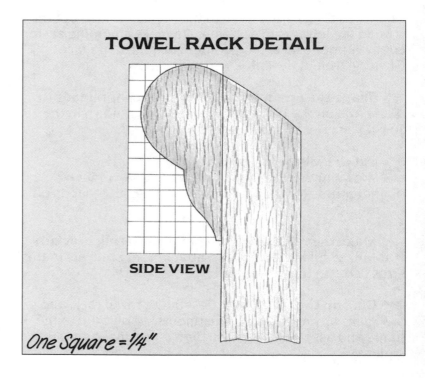

TOWEL RACK DETAIL

SIDE VIEW

One Square = 1/4"

for drawer pulls similar to the ones shown in the photo. I wasn't able to find a reproduction of the door latch shown in the photo. You can substitute a latch of a different style, or look for a similar latch at your local hardware store. Drill holes that conform to the sizes of the pulls you are using. Use a backup block inside the drawer fronts when drilling through, to prevent splintering out the back of the hole.

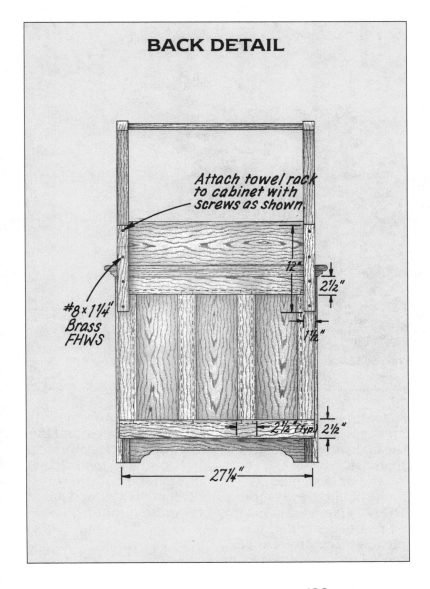

BACK DETAIL

Attach towel rack to cabinet with screws as shown

#8 x 1¼" Brass FHWS

12"

2½"

1½"

2½" (typ) 2½"

27¼"

DRESSING TABLE
by Edward J. Schoen

Using this dressing table will add a certain flavor of elegance to your evening on the town. It may even help when you are just dressing for work. Whatever the occasion, it will be a fine addition to any home. Its three drawers provide space for hair-styling equipment and cosmetics, while the large mirrors aid in their use.

The original piece is made of bird's-eye maple. The fiery grain dramatically enhances the table's simple lines. The project holds several technical challenges.

The four legs are lathe-turned duplicates, and the case involves a fair number of mortise-and-tenon joints. This may be an opportunity for the intermediate to advanced furniture maker to try wood turning.

EXPLODED VIEW

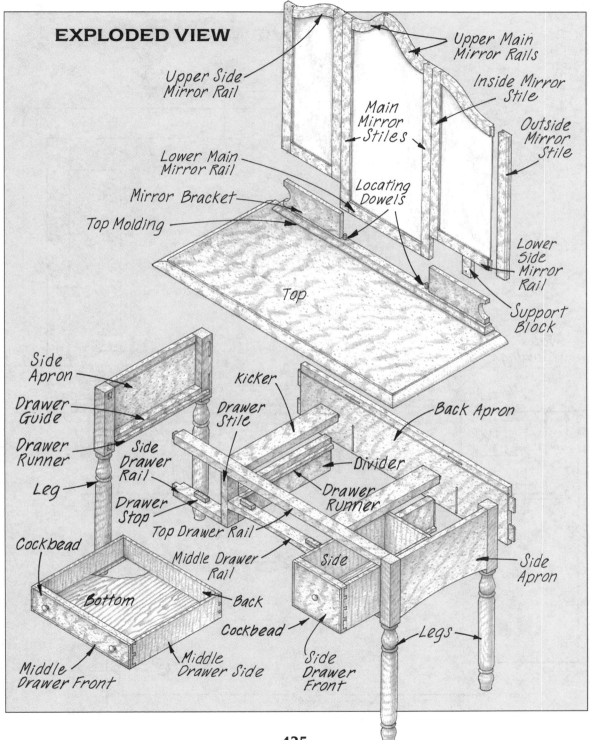

Upper Side Mirror Rail

Upper Main Mirror Rails

Inside Mirror Stile

Main Mirror Stiles

Outside Mirror Stile

Lower Main Mirror Rail

Mirror Bracket

Top Molding

Locating Dowels

Top

Lower Side Mirror Rail

Support Block

Side Apron

Kicker

Drawer Guide

Drawer Stile

Back Apron

Drawer Runner

Divider

Leg

Side Drawer Rail

Drawer Runner

Drawer Stop

Top Drawer Rail

Cockbead

Middle Drawer Rail

Side

Side Apron

Bottom

Back

Cockbead

Middle Drawer Front

Middle Drawer Side

Side Drawer Front

Legs

FRONT VIEW

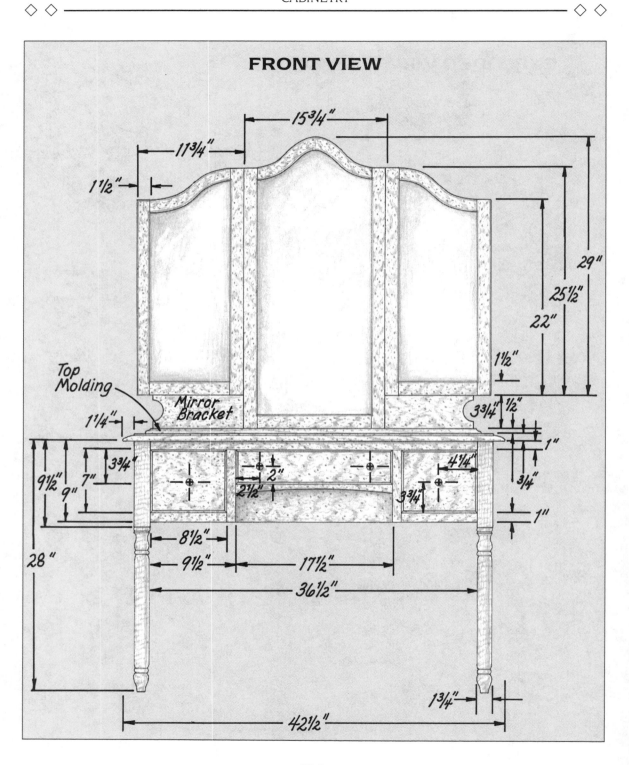

SIDE VIEW

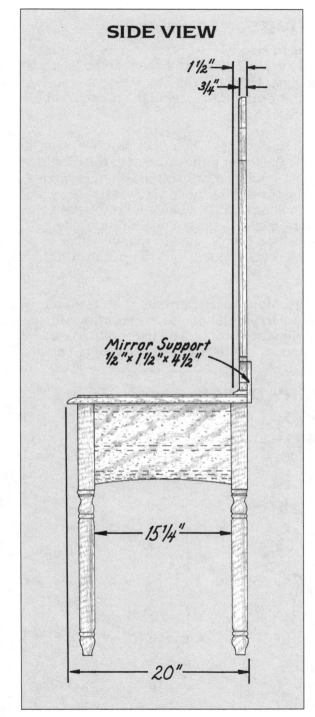

1½"

¾"

Mirror Support
½" × 1½" × 4½"

15¼"

20"

LEG DETAIL

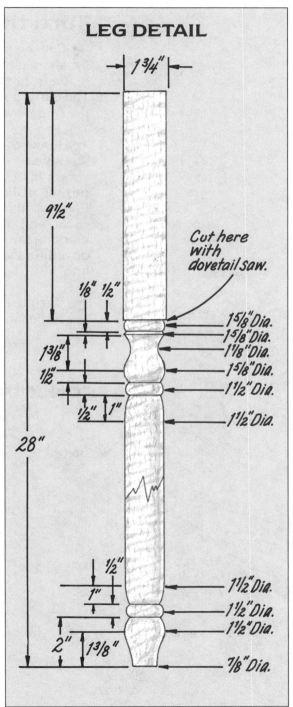

1¾"

9½"

⅛" ½"

Cut here
with
dovetail saw.

1⅝" Dia.
1⅝" Dia.
1⅛" Dia.
1⅜"
1⅝" Dia.
½"
1½" Dia.
½" 1"
1½" Dia.

28"

1½" Dia.
½"
1"
1½" Dia.
1½" Dia.
2" 1⅜"
⅞" Dia.

Turn the legs.

1 **Cut the parts to size.** Mill wood for the legs to the size listed in the Materials List. Note that the legs are made from curly maple, rather than bird's-eye maple. The curly grain pattern works better in the round than the bird's-eye does.

2 **Make the shoulder cuts.** The upper part of the leg is square, while the lower part is turned to the profile shown in the Leg Detail. The grain often splinters when a turning makes the transition from round to square. Prevent this by making a shallow saw cut between the round and square sections. Draw a line on each face marking the transition from square to round. With a dovetail saw, make cuts about 1/8 inch deep along this line.

3 **Turn the legs.** Mount a leg between centers on the lathe, and turn a cylinder on its lower portion. Be careful not to splinter the corners on the square part. Stop the lathe and lay out the details of the leg in pencil.

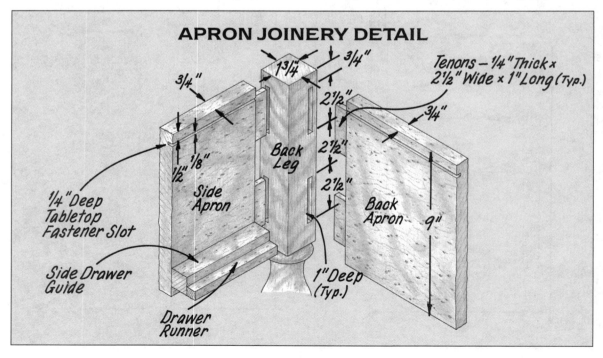

APRON JOINERY DETAIL

3/4"
1 3/4"
3/4"
Tenons – 1/4" Thick x 2 1/2" Wide x 1" Long (Typ.)
3/4"
2 1/2"
1/8"
Back Leg
2 1/2"
1/2"
Side Apron
2 1/2"
1/4" Deep Tabletop Fastener Slot
Back Apron
9"
Side Drawer Guide
1" Deep (Typ.)
Drawer Runner

Turn the leg to the shape shown, and refine and smooth the shapes with sandpaper as you finish the leg. Turn all four legs.

Make the case.

The case is held together with mortise-and-tenon joints. The aprons are joined to the legs with multiple tenons, as shown in the Apron Joinery Detail.

The front stiles and rails are also mortised and

Quick Tip: Once you have finished the first leg, set it up behind the lathe so you can refer to it as you turn the other three.

MATERIALS LIST

Part	Dimension	Part	Dimension
Case		Upper side mirror rails (2)	$3/4" \times 2^{13}/_{16}" \times 14"$
Legs (4)	$1^3/4" \times 1^3/4" \times 28"$	Outside mirror stiles (2)	$3/4" \times 1^1/2" \times 22"$
Side aprons (2)	$3/4" \times 9" \times 16^3/4"$	Inside mirror stiles (2)	$3/4" \times 1^1/2" \times 25^1/2"$
Back apron	$3/4" \times 9" \times 38"$	Main mirror stiles (2)	$3/4" \times 1^1/2" \times 29^1/4"$
Top drawer rail	$1" \times 1^3/4" \times 38"$	Lower side mirror rails (2)	$3/4" \times 1^1/2" \times 9^3/4"$
Middle drawer rail	$1" \times 1^3/4" \times 19"$	Lower main mirror rail	$3/4" \times 1^1/2" \times 13^3/4"$
Side drawer rails (2)	$1" \times 1^3/4" \times 10"$	Mirror brackets (2)	$3/4" \times 3^3/4" \times 10"$
Drawer stiles (2)	$1" \times 1^3/4" \times 9^3/4"$	Top molding	$1/2" \times 1^1/2" \times 37^1/2"$
Dividers (2)	$1" \times 5" \times 17"$	Support blocks (2)	$1/2" \times 1^1/2" \times 4^1/2"$
Kickers (2)	$1" \times 3" \times 17"$	Side pattern	$1/4" \times 10" \times 26"$
Drawer runners (6)	$1/2" \times 1/2" \times 16^1/4"$	Main pattern	$1/4" \times 15" \times 34"$
Drawer guides (2)	$1" \times 1" \times 15^1/4"$		
Drawer stops (4)	$1/2" \times 3/4" \times 2"$	**HARDWARE**	
Top	$3/4" \times 20" \times 42^1/2"$	3 panes mirror glass, $1/8"$ thick, cut to fit	
Locating dowel stock	$3/8"$ dia. $\times 5"$	As needed, #8 $\times$ 1" brass flathead wood screws	
Drawers		As needed, #4 $\times$ $3/4"$ flathead wood screws	
Side drawer fronts (2)	$3/4" \times 7" \times 8^1/2"$	As needed, #8 $\times$ $1^1/2"$ drywall screws	
Side drawer sides (4)	$1/2" \times 7" \times 15^5/8"$	4 cylinder hinges. Available from Woodworker's	
Side drawer backs (2)	$1/2" \times 6^1/4" \times 8^1/2"$	Supply of New Mexico, 5604 Alameda Place,	
Side drawer bottoms (2)	$1/4" \times 15^1/2" \times 8"$	Albuquerque, NM 87113. Part #800-490.	
Middle drawer front	$3/4" \times 3^3/4" \times 17^1/2"$	As needed, tabletop fasteners. Available from	
Middle drawer sides (2)	$1/2" \times 3^3/4" \times 16"$	The Woodworkers' Store, 21801 Industrial	
Middle drawer back	$1/2" \times 3" \times 17^1/2"$	Blvd., Rogers, MN 55374. Part #34215.	
Middle drawer bottom	$1/4" \times 15^1/2" \times 17"$	4 brass knobs, $7/8"$ dia.	
Cockbead stock	$1/4" \times 5/16" \times 10'$	As needed, $1/2"$ brads	
Mirror Frames			
Upper main mirror rails (2)	$3/4" \times 2^5/8" \times 10^5/8"$		

tenoned together. Not all the tenons have shoulders on all sides, as shown in the Drawer Frame Detail. This increases the strength of the joint. It also means you have to be more careful when cutting and fitting the joints so that the mortise does not show. Fortunately, in all the places this could be a problem, the joint is concealed by a drawer.

Quick Tip: To cut multiple parts to the same length, screw an extension fence to your table saw's miter gauge. Clamp a stop block to the fence at the appropriate distance from the blade and hold the pieces against it as you cut.

1 Cut the parts to size. Mill the parts for the case to the sizes listed in the Materials List. If you are using a highly figured wood like bird's-eye maple, use the choice pieces for the most visible parts.

2 Cut the apron mortises. Lay out the mortises on the legs as shown in the Apron Joinery Detail and Drawer Frame Detail. Note that the rear legs are interchangeable but the front legs are not. Be sure to make a right and a left front leg.

Drill a series of adjacent holes in between the layout lines, and clean out the waste with a chisel. Cut these mortises about 1/16 inch longer than is specified in the drawing to allow for the seasonal movement of the aprons.

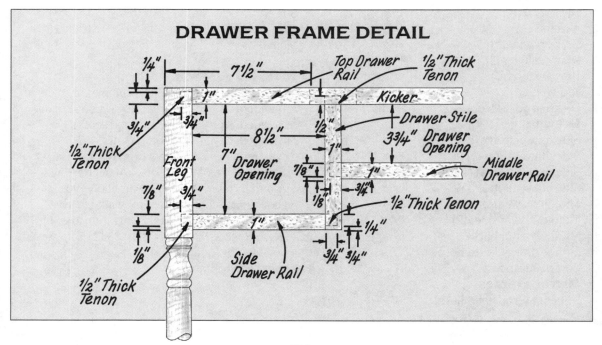

DRAWER FRAME DETAIL

3 Tenon the side and back aprons. Set up a $1/2$-inch dado cutter on the table saw. Set the fence $3/4$ inch from the outside of the blade. Test the setup on a piece of scrap the same thickness as the aprons. Guide the end of the scrap against the fence with the miter gauge. Cut the waste from both faces of the scrap and test fit the resulting tenon in a mortise. Adjust blade height as necessary, and cut the actual tenons.

Readjust the blade height to cut the top and bottom tenon shoulders. Cut the waste from between the two tenons on the band saw. Pare down this area with a chisel to make it flush with the shoulders.

4 Cut the drawer frame mortises. The front of the case is a frame, made from a series of horizontal rails and vertical stiles. Mortise the front legs and drawer stiles as shown in the Drawer Frame Detail. These mortises house the drawer rails. Mortise the top drawer rail for the drawer stile.

All these mortises are $1/2$ inch wide $\times$ $3/4$ inch deep.

5 Tenon the drawer frames. Tenon both ends of the drawer rails and one end of the drawer stiles on the table saw with a dado cutter. Note that these tenons are centered from *edge to edge* rather than from *face to face*, as shown in the Drawer Frame Detail. Readjust the blade to cut the third shoulder.

6 Cut the kicker and divider mortises. Lay out the mortises for the kickers and the dividers on the back apron, the top drawer rail, and the drawer stiles as shown in the Divider and Kicker Detail. These mortises are $5/16$ inch wide and $3/8$ inch deep. The mortises for the divider are 4 inches long, and the mortises for the kicker are $2\,1/2$ inches long.

7 Tenon the kickers and dividers. Tenon the ends of the kickers and dividers to fit in the mortises.

8 Shape the aprons and middle drawer rail. Lay out the curves on the bottom of the side aprons and the middle drawer rail as shown in the Curve Detail. Cut these curves on the band saw. Scrape and sand them smooth.

Some of the mortise-and-tenon joints will have only three shoulders, as shown.

9 **Add the drawer runners and guides.** Glue the drawer runners to the dividers as shown in the Drawer Runner Detail. Be sure the tops of the runners line up with the tops of the drawer rails. To keep the

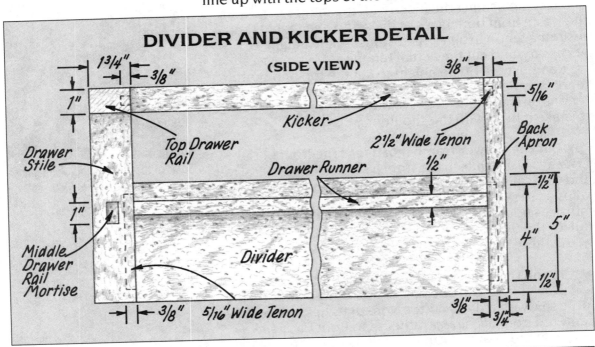

DIVIDER AND KICKER DETAIL

(SIDE VIEW)

Kicker

Top Drawer Rail

2½" Wide Tenon

Back Apron

Drawer Stile

Drawer Runner

Middle Drawer Rail Mortise

Divider

5/16" Wide Tenon

1¾"
3/8"
1"
1"
3/8"
5/16"
1/2"
1½"
5"
4"
1/2"
3/8"
3/4"

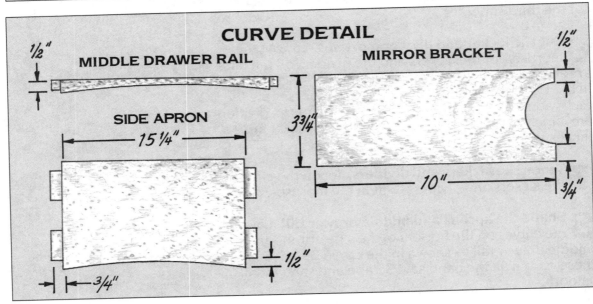

CURVE DETAIL

MIDDLE DRAWER RAIL   **MIRROR BRACKET**

1/2"

SIDE APRON

15 ¼"

3¾"

10"

3/4"

1/2"

3/4"

1/2"

runner from slipping, drive small brads partway into the surface you'll glue into place. Clip off the brads, leaving about ¹/₃₂ inch exposed. The brads will grip the wood and keep the runners from sliding as you clamp them.

Glue the remaining two runners to the drawer guides as shown in the Drawer Runner Detail. When the glue dries, glue the guides to the side aprons as shown.

Assemble the case.

1 **Cut the tabletop fastener slot.** After all of the case parts are ready for assembly, cut the tabletop fastener slot in the aprons and top drawer rail as shown in the Apron Joinery Detail. Cut this ¹/₄-inch-deep slot in one pass on the table saw. Guide the aprons and top drawer rail against the fence as you cut.

2 **Assemble the back legs and back apron.** Before glue-up, assemble all the parts of the case without glue. Check the fit of all the joints, and make any necessary adjustments.

The assembly and glue-up of this piece is somewhat complicated. Because of this, you should glue up the

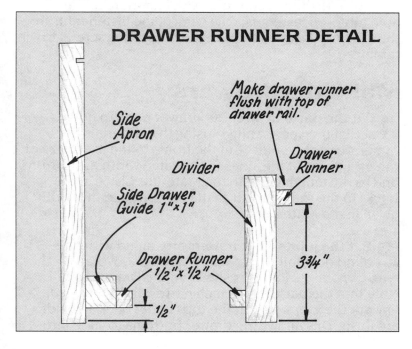

DRAWER RUNNER DETAIL

Side Apron

Make drawer runner flush with top of drawer rail.

Divider

Drawer Runner

Side Drawer Guide 1"×1"

Drawer Runner ½"×½"

3¾"

½"

case in three stages. Glue up the back first. Apply glue to the mortises and tenons. Clamp and check to make sure the assembly is square and that the back legs are parallel.

Next, glue up the drawer frame and front legs. Assemble the drawer frame as a unit. Start by gluing the stiles to the middle rail. Then glue the stiles to the top rail. Finally add the side rails and legs. Clamp all the joints. Check to make sure the drawer openings are square and that the legs are parallel, and allow the glue to dry.

Finally, glue the front and back to the sides. Test fit the front leg and back leg assemblies with the side aprons, dividers, and kickers. Make any necessary adjustments. Apply glue to the joints and clamp the piece together.

3 **Attach the top.** Before attaching the top, rout the edges to the profile shown in the Front View. Make the cut with a 2½-inch-diameter thumbnail bit in a hand-held router. (Thumbnail bit available from MLCS Ltd., P.O. Box 4053AF, Rydal, PA 19046. Part #858.) Rout the front and sides of the top only.

Attach the top to the base with commercially available tabletop fasteners. One wing of the fastener fits in the tabletop fastener groove; the other wing screws to the tabletop.

Make the drawers.

1 **Cut the parts to size.** Cut drawer parts to fit the actual drawer openings, using the Materials List dimensions as a guide. Cut the fronts to the exact size of the opening. Cut the sides to the same width as the front, and to the length given in the Materials List. Cut the backs to the same length as the front, and to the width given in the Materials List.

2 **Cut the joints.** The drawers are joined with half-blind dovetails in front and through dovetails in the rear. Lay out the joints as shown in the Drawer Detail. Note that the backs are ¾ inch narrower than the sides. Lay out the joints so that the tops of the back and sides are flush. This allows the drawer bottoms to slide into their grooves after the drawer is assembled.

Cut the tails first, and lay the pins out directly from the tails. For more on dovetails, see "Cutting Through Dovetails" on page 81 and "Cutting Half-Blind Dovetails" on page 155. Mark each joint so that the pieces do not become mixed up before you assemble the drawers.

3 Cut the bottom grooves. The front and sides of each drawer are grooved for the drawer bottoms. Cut these grooves on the table saw. Mount a ¼-inch dado cutter on the saw and set the fence for ½ inch. Run the fronts and sides through the cutter with their inside surfaces down. The dovetails were designed to allow these cuts to run the full length of each piece.

4 Make the cockbeading. The drawers on this dressing table have a ¼-inch cockbead around their fronts. The beading itself is made from ¼ × 5⁄16-inch strips with a bead profile along one edge. You will need about 10 feet of beading.

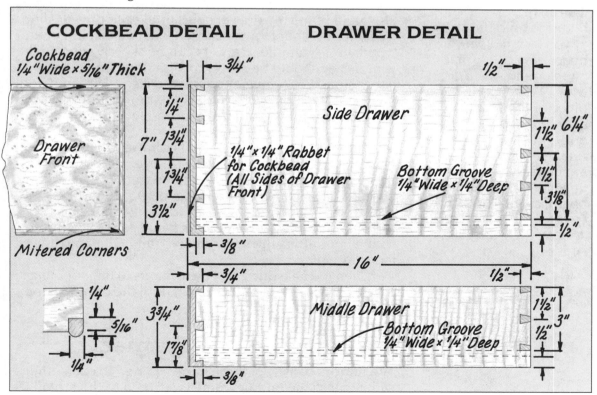

COCKBEAD DETAIL **DRAWER DETAIL**

Cockbead ¼"Wide × 5⁄16"Thick

Drawer Front

Mitered Corners

¼"×¼" Rabbet for Cockbead (All Sides of Drawer Front)

Side Drawer

Bottom Groove ¼"Wide × ¼"Deep

Middle Drawer

Bottom Groove ¼"Wide × ¼"Deep

Feather boards make feeding narrow stock past a cutter much safer. Here, one feather board holds the cockbead down on the table while the other holds the piece tight to the fence.

Quick Tip: Make a feather board to hold the stock as you rout it. Feather boards are easily made on the band saw. Start with a $3/4 \times 2 \times 8$-inch piece of scrap wood. Cut a 30-degree angle on one end, and then make a series of cuts about $1/8$ inch apart to create the fingers. To use a feather board, clamp it into place so the fingers put pressure on the work as it slides by.

Mill the strips to thickness and width. Put a $1/4$-inch-diameter bit in your table-mounted router. Mount a fence on the table to guide the strips past the cutter.

5 Apply the cockbeading. Rout a $1/4 \times 1/4$-inch rabbet around the each drawer front. Miter the cockbead to the lengths required. Glue the bead to the top and bottom of the drawer, clamping it into place with masking tape. Tack the beading to the drawer sides with $1/2$-inch brads.

6 Assemble the drawers. Test fit the drawer joints to make sure everything fits well. Apply glue to the angled surfaces of the dovetails and assemble the joints. Clamp the drawer together and slide the bottom into place. Check to make sure the drawer is square. Attach the bottom to the drawer back with a few $\#4 \times 3/4$-inch flathead wood screws.

7 Fit the drawers. Check the drawers for fit. If necessary, hand plane the drawer sides until each drawer slides freely. Remember to allow for seasonal movement of the wood. In the summer, drawers can be slightly snug. In the winter they should be looser to allow for summertime expansion. When you have achieved a good fit, sand and rub paraffin on the sides and on the runners. This will let the drawers glide in and out effortlessly.

8 Install the drawer stops. The drawer stops are glued to the top of the lower drawer rails as shown in the Exploded View. The side drawers get one stop in the center while the middle drawer gets two stops, one toward each side. Cut the stops to the size specified in the Materials List. Set a marking gauge for $11/16$ inch, and scribe lines along the lower drawer rails. Glue the drawer stops into place.

When the glue dries, test the drawers in their openings. Pare down the stops with a chisel until the drawers stop at just the right spot.

Make the mirror frames.

The mirrors consist of three frames joined to each other with hinges. The middle frame is secured to the table while the outer ones are free to pivot. The frames are joined with mortise-and-tenon joints. The joints are cut before the top rails are shaped.

1 **Cut the parts to size.** Mill the wood for the mirror frames to the sizes listed in the Materials List. Miter the upper mirror rails to the angles shown in the Mirror Detail. Do not cut the lower rails to length until later.

2 **Rout the mortises in the stiles.** Set up a ¼-inch wing cutter with a bearing in your table-mounted router to cut the 1½-inch-long × ½-inch-deep stopped groove mortises. Set the cutter height so that it is centered on the edge of the stiles, and guide the stiles against a fence as you cut. Clamp a stop block to the fence to stop the stiles at the end of the 1½-inch stopped groove mortise.

When the mortises have been cut, square the bottoms of the mortises with a ¼-inch chisel.

Use a wing cutter in conjunction with a fence on the table-mounted router to cut the joints for the mirror. Set the fence so that it is in line with the bit's bearing.

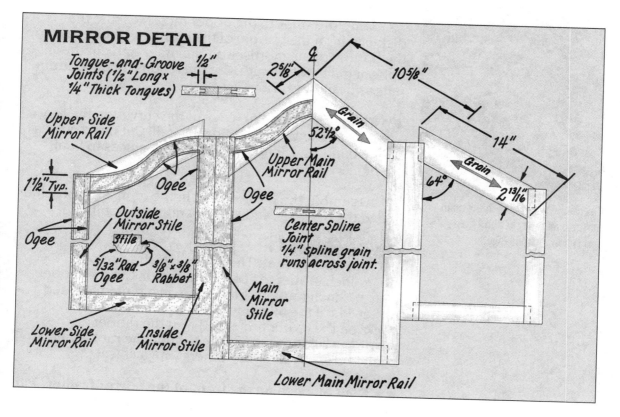

MIRROR DETAIL

Tongue-and-Groove Joints (½" Long x ¼" Thick Tongues) ½"

Upper Side Mirror Rail

1½" Typ.

Ogee

Ogee

Outside Mirror Stile

Stile

⁵⁄₃₂" Rad. Ogee

3/8" x 3/8" Rabbet

Lower Side Mirror Rail

Inside Mirror Stile

2⅝"

Grain

52½°

Upper Main Mirror Rail

Ogee

Center Spline Joint ¼" spline grain runs across joint.

Main Mirror Stile

Lower Main Mirror Rail

10⅝"

14"

Grain

64°

2¹³⁄₁₆"

Clamp the joint in the main mirror's top rail as shown. Lay out the curves on the pieces before cutting the notches, to avoid cutting into an area you want to keep.

Cut clamping notches in the main mirror frame top rails and then glue and clamp the rails together.

3 **Make the joint in the main mirror top rail.** Rout grooves across the upper ends of the main mirror top rails, as shown in the Mirror Detail. Rout the grooves on the same router setting you used for cutting the mortises in the stiles. Guide the cut with the miter gauge, or with a piece of plywood, as shown in the photo. Make a spline to fit snugly in the grooves. The grain of the spline should run perpendicular to the line of the joint. Glue up the rail as shown in the photo. Be sure to lay out the curves on the piece before cutting the notches for the clamp.

4 **Cut the joints.** Cut the tenons on the top rails with your table-mounted router. Readjust the height of the wing cutter to cut the tenons. Start with the cutter partially below the surface of the table, and the fence flush with the guide bearing. Make a pass on both sides of each rail. Repeat, raising the cutter $1/16$ inch per pass until the resulting tenons fit snugly in the mortises. Guide the short pieces past the cutter with a piece of plywood, as before.

Clamp the stiles to the upper rails. Measure the distance from the bottom of the mortises on one stile to the bottom of the mortises on the other, and cut the bottom rail to this length. Cut the tenons on the bottom rails as described above.

5 **Shape the top rails.** Lay out the curves on the top rails as shown in the Mirror Detail. Cut these curves on the band saw. Scrape and sand the pieces to final shape.

6 **Assemble the frames.** Test fit the frames. Apply glue to the mortises and tenons and then clamp the frames together.

7 **Rout the rabbet.** The back of the frame has a $3/8 \times 3/8$-inch rabbet to accept the mirror. Cut the rabbet with a $3/8$-inch rabbeting bit set up in a table-mounted router. Place the mirror frames, one at a time, on their backs on the router table, and rout the rabbet on the inside back edge of the frames. When the rabbets have been routed, square the corners with a chisel.

8 **Rout an ogee on the front of the mirror frames.** Put a $5/32$-inch-radius ogee bit in a table-mounted router.

Adjust the bit to cut the profile shown in the Mirror Detail. Hold the frames face down on the router table, and guide them against the bit's bearing as you rout. First, rout the ogee all around the inside of the mirror frames. Carve the ogee profiles square where they meet at the inside corners.

Next, rout a matching ogee along the outside stiles and top rails of the side mirror frames, and along the top rail of the main mirror frame.

9 **Make the mirror brackets, supports, and top molding.** Mill the wood for the brackets, supports, and top molding to the sizes listed in the Materials List. Rout a ⁵⁄₃₂-inch-radius ogee around the front and sides of the molding on the router table. Hold the molding on edge as you rout.

Cut the brackets to the shape shown in the Curve Detail. Drill and countersink holes in the supports as shown in the Side View.

10 **Mount the main mirror.** Align the top molding on the tabletop. Position it so that it is flush with the back and centered from side to side. Clamp it in place. Drill two ³⁄₈-inch holes through the molding into the tabletop for the locating dowels, as shown in the Mirror

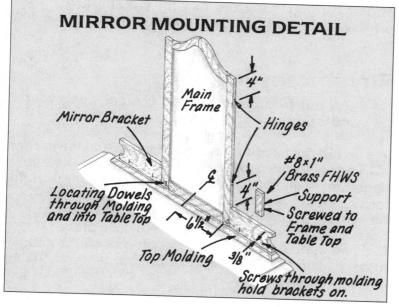

MIRROR MOUNTING DETAIL

Mounting Detail. Place dowel centers in the holes. Center the mirror frame on the molding and press down to mark the hole locations. Drill ³/₈-inch holes into the frame. Cut two locating dowels from ³/₈-inch-diameter dowel stock. The locating dowels must be long enough to go through the molding into the table, and extend above the molding into the mirror. Place the locating dowels in the holes and set the mirror frame down on them. Mark the position of the frame on the molding.

Remove the molding from the table. Put the brackets on top of the molding and align them with the marks you made for the mirror frame. Screw through the molding to attach the brackets with #8 × 1¹/₂-inch drywall screws. Put the molding back on the tabletop using the locating dowels to align it. Glue it in place.

11 **Hinge the frames together.** Hinge the side mirrors with the main mirror as shown in the Mirror Mounting Detail. Use cylinder hinges as specified in the Materials List. Follow the directions that come with the hinges.

12 **Cut the mirrors.** Trace the outline of the rabbets onto a piece of ¹/₄-inch plywood. Cut these patterns out. Check them for fit in the frames. They should be about ¹/₈ inch smaller than the frame to allow for some error in cutting the mirrors. Take the patterns to a professional glass cutter and have mirrors cut to match them.

Finish the piece.

1 **Apply finish.** Sand the entire piece, and apply your favorite finish.

2 **Install the hardware and mirrors.** Install the drawer knobs as shown in the Front View. Set the mirrors in their frames, and back them up with their patterns. Hold the patterns in place with glazing pins set into the frames. Set the main mirror on the locating dowels. Secure it to the table by driving #8 × 1-inch brass flathead wood screws through the support blocks and into the main mirror frame and tabletop, as shown in the Mirror Mounting Detail.